Evidence for
Old English

Evidence for Old English

Material and Theoretical Bases for Reconstruction

Edited by
FRAN COLMAN
Lecturer in English Language
UNIVERSITY OF EDINBURGH

Edinburgh Studies in the English Language 2

JOHN DONALD PUBLISHERS LTD
EDINBURGH

© The Editors and Contributors severally, 1992.

All rights reserved, No part of this publication may be reproduced in any form or by any means without the prior permission of the publishers, John Donald Publishers Ltd., 138 St Stephen Street, Edinburgh.

ISBN 85976 254 8

British Library Cataloguing in Publication Data
A catalogue record for this book is available from the British Library.

Phototypesetting by T.P.S. Ltd, London SE1.
Printed in Great Britain by Hartnolls Limited, Bodmin.

PREFACE

This volume is the second in an occasional series, *Edinburgh Studies in the English Language*, devoted to studies of the English Language, in both its current and earlier varieties. This series is offered as a venue for the publication of research whose primary concern is to reaffirm the vigour of a field distinguished by the descriptive richness of its tradition and by the more general theoretical proposals that have sprung from it. In seeking to fulfil this aim, each volume in the series will be focused, broadly or narrowly, on one particular aspect of the language in a particular period, or over a span of time. But the thematic character projected for individual volumes will not preclude the publication of papers that are important in their own right.

Further details concerning the theme of volume 3, and the arrangements for the submission of contributions, are given in the *Statement by the General Editors*.

Edinburgh, 1992

John Anderson and Norman Macleod

STATEMENT BY THE GENERAL EDITORS

Edinburgh Studies in the English Language is an occasional series of volumes devoted to studies of the English Language. The aim of the series is to add to our understanding of the history and structure of the language in all its contemporary and historical varieties. Volumes are primarily thematic, with individual themes being announced in advance.

The specification of a theme for a particular volume will allow for some contributions to be by invitation, or for the raising of contributions to be assigned to a guest editor. But all interested scholars are encouraged to submit appropriate material for any particular volume. In all cases intended contributions are submitted to two readers for evaluation. One of these will normally be a member of the editorial board, which consists of members of the English Language Department at the University of Edinburgh. In recommending papers for publication the editors will take particular account of the readers' reports, but the decision on final acceptance will rest with the board. It is editorial policy to include in each volume a list of readers consulted.

The announced themes should not be seen as thoroughly exclusive: the editors will consider papers on any aspect of the academic study of the English Language, including Scots. They will particularly welcome the submission of papers concerned with earlier periods of English or its diachronic development. There is no restriction on approach: any appropriate linguistic or philological framework will be acceptable, but in all cases the emphasis should be on the analysis of linguistic material, treated either for what it adds to our understanding of the history and structure of English or in connexion with some significant theoretical issue.

Manuscripts should be submitted to the editorial address in three copies, two of which should bear no indication of authorship or affiliation. Intending contributors are asked to comply with the *ESEL Stylesheet*, which is available upon request from the same address. Return of manuscripts can be guaranteed only if adequate provision for return mailing is also sent. All submissions will be briefly acknowledged on receipt, with an indication of when a decision on acceptability can be expected. This will normally be within two to three months.

The proposed theme for volume 3 is *'Variability' in the history of English;* an outline description is given below. The closing date for submissions to volume 3 will be the end of March 1993. The editors will also welcome suggestions (directed to the same address) concerning possible future thematic areas.

John Anderson and Norman Macleod

Editorial Address:

Department of English Language
University of Edinburgh
David Hume Tower
George Square
Edinburgh EH8 9 JX
Scotland

Proposed Theme for Volume 3:

The proposed theme for volume 3 of ESEL can be summed up in a quotation (from Weinreich, Labov and Herzog's "A theory of language change") that might almost be regarded as a motto for the volume:
> Not all variability and heterogeneity in language structure involves change; but all change involves variability and heterogeneity.

A recognition of the diachronic significance of variability is now a feature of a good deal of work in the history of English — particularly, for example, among those known to us in Edinburgh as "Northern Scholars". The editors of ESEL, seeing such work as fruitfully combining the linguistic and philological traditions, invite contributions from scholars interested in treating variants and variation as evidence for developments in the history of English.

CONTRIBUTORS

Cynthia Allen, Linguistics, The Faculties, The Australian National University, GPO Box 4, Canberra ACT 2601, Australia.

Anne King, Department of English Language, University of Edinburgh, David Hume Tower, George Square, Edinburgh, EH8 9JX, Scotland.

Willem Koopman, Engels Seminarium, Universiteit van Amsterdam, Spuistraat 210, 1012 VT Amsterdam, The Netherlands.

Roger Lass, Department of Linguistics, University of Cape Town, Private Bag, Rondebosch 7700, Cape, South Africa.

C. B. McCully, Department of English Language and Literature, The University of Manchester M13 9PL, England.

Donka Minkova, Department of English, University of California Los Angeles, California 90024, U.S.A.

Matti Rissanen, Department of English Philology, Hallituskatu 11-13, 00100 Helsinki 10, Finland.

Veronica Smart, University of St. Andrews, St. John's House, 69 South Street, St. Andrews, Fife, Scotland.

Robert P. Stockwell, Department of Linguistics, University of California, Los Angeles, California 90024, U.S.A.

Anthony R. Warner, Department of Language and Linguistic Science, University of York, Heslington, York YO1 5DD, England.

Wim van der Wurff, Department of English, University of Leiden, Postbox 9515, 2300 RA Leiden, The Netherlands.

REVIEWERS

John Anderson, University of Edinburgh

Cynthia Allen, Australian National University

Fran Colman, University of Edinburgh

David Denison, University of Manchester

Heinz Giegerich, University of Edinburgh

Richard Hogg, University of Manchester

George Jack, University of St Andrews

Charles Jones, University of Edinburgh

Roger Lass, University of Cape Town

Peter J. Lucas, University College, Edinburgh

Stewart Lyon, affiliated with the British Numismatic Society

Donka Minkova, University of California, Los Angeles

Matti Rissanen, University of Helsinki

Herbert Schendl, University of Vienna

Robert P. Stockwell, University of California, Los Angeles

Anthony R. Warner, University of York

CONTENTS

Preface   v

Editorial Statement   vii

Contributors   ix

Reviewers   x

Introduction   xiii

1. Old English and the Syntactician: Some Remarks and a Syntactician's Guide to Editions of the Works of Ælfric   1
   Cynthia Allen

2. You say [æjðər] and I say [æjhwæðər]? Interpreting Old English Written Data   20
   Anne King

3. Old English Clitic Pronouns. Some Remarks   44
   Willem Koopman

4. Front Rounded Vowels in Old English   88
   Roger Lass

5. The Phonology of Resolution in Old English Word-stress and Metre   117
   C. B. McCully

6. Poetic Influence on Prose Word Order in Old English   142
   Donka Minkova and Robert P. Stockwell

7. Computers are Useful - for *aught* I Know   155
   Matti Rissanen

8. Die-cutting and Diatopic Variation: the Variant <LIOF-> on late Anglo-Saxon Coins   169
   Veronica Smart

9. Elliptical and Impersonal Constructions: Evidence for Auxiliaries in Old English?   178
   Anthony R. Warner

10. Another Old English Impersonal: Some Data   211
    Wim van der Wurff

INTRODUCTION

This volume is the second of an occasional series devoted to studies of the English Language. The concerns of the volume, implicit in its title, might be summed up in the statement that there is no fact independent of theory (or even, as Morris Zapp would have it, 'every decoding is another encoding').[1] The materials which are the primary data for reconstructing Old English, consisting of manuscript orthography and runic and coin epigraphy, do not alone constitute evidence. This comes from interpretations of the available data within a theoretical framework (or frameworks); and the volume reflects an increased awareness of the significance of linguistic theory in interpreting the philological material, with respect to various levels of grammar.

That the same data may be susceptible to different interpretations, depending on one's theory, can be illustrated by a comparison of the approaches to manuscript orthography as potential evidence for reconstructing phonology, adopted in Anne King's 'You say [æjðər] and I say [æjhwæðər]? Interpreting Old English written data' and Roger Lass's 'Front rounded vowels in Old English'. The treatment in the former of the ⟨a⟩ ~ ⟨o⟩ variation for reflexes of Proto-Germanic [a] / – N invokes external historical, palaeographical and onomastic data in an analysis invoking neutralization, rejecting the orthographic variation as direct evidence for 'sound change in progress', and for spread of a feature from one dialect to another. Luick's 'man schrieb wie man sprach', eschewed by King, is embraced by Lass, in a neo-Labovian interpretation of orthographic variation (augmented by crucial evidence from interpretations of English and non-English runic and non-runic data), seen in the light of the 'Pre-Ambrosian Praxis' for whose formulation the reader is referred to its source. Veronica Smart's 'Die-cutting and diatopic variation: the variant ⟨LIOF-⟩ on late Anglo-Saxon coins' provides a reminder which can bear the clichéd modifier 'salutary', of the importance of analysing what can be reconstructed about methods of production of the materials available as data for reconstructing Old English. Illustration is given of the possibility that certain variant spellings may have their origin in numismatic causes, rather than in the concern of the perpetrator of a spelling to preserve for posterity a diatopically significant phonological shape of a personal name. C. B. McCully's 'The phonology of resolution in Old English word-stress and metre' clarifies the close links between phonological structures and the structures of verse-prosody and illustrates the importance of resolution as a structural device in OE metrics. Significantly, different interpretations of resolution are produced by linear and non-linear 'notation' (suggesting to me that the difference is not merely notational, but theoretical); and in a framework of metrical phonology, McCully gives a phonological 'reality' to Sievers's 'types'.

Evidence from verse texts is deduced also with respect to syntax, by Donka Minkova and Robert P. Stockwell, in 'Poetic influence on prose word order in Old

English'. They address the claim that verse had a syntax of its own, and that this syntax directly affected the development of the syntax of prose, in a relation roughly that of exemplar to derivative. Their analysis of aspects of the poetry results in an interpretation of word-order changes which reverses an earlier claim of A. Campbell's: Stockwell and Minkova suggest that Old English main clauses became V-second, and so more like Dutch and German, as a result of poetic influence; and that only much later did English change to become an atypical West Germanic language in this respect. Willem F. Koopman points out how a theoretical interpretation can allow us to see order in apparent chaos: specifically, how the analysis by van Kemenade of Old English personal pronouns as syntactic clitics results in greater regularity in the characterisation of word-order. In 'Old English clitic pronouns. Some remarks', Koopman argues for a different interpretation of one of the clitic positions set up by van Kemenade, and questions whether all pronouns should be regarded as clitics. The claim that not all object pronouns could be clitics, supported by analyses of syntactic patterns and processes, leads to the conclusion that cliticisation may be seen as optional. The focus of W. van der Wurff's 'Another Old English impersonal: some data' is the adjective plus infinitive construction. Here, too, the data, taken from a fresh corpus study, are susceptible to different interpretations: even identifying the construction under discussion poses problems recognised in this investigation of the restrictions to which certain subtypes seem to have been subject in Old English. Cynthia Allen underpins the need for both adequate recourse to appropriate data and recognition of the dependence of 'fact' upon theory, in 'Old English and the syntactician: some remarks and a syntactician's guide to editions of the works of Ælfric', offering as well, invaluable bibliographic information. In 'Elliptical and impersonal constructions: evidence for auxiliaries in Old English?', Anthony Warner revivifies the question as to whether or not Old English had auxiliaries, itself raising the question of defining 'auxiliary'. The argument both illustrates the theory-specificness of any definition thereof and exemplifies what can and cannot be ascertained as evidential in the Old English materials.

All of the papers here are appropriately heavily dependent on data. And one of the great luxuries — indeed, now become a necessity — for researchers in historical English linguistics, is the availability of computerized corpora (although it must be remembered that these represent data already interpreted), the sensible use of which, to quote Matti Rissanen, 'certainly enables the student to diminish the time spent on monotonous drudgery and to focus his energy on more creative aspects of research'. 'Computers are useful — for *aught* I know' provides a detailed introduction to the Helsinki computerized corpus, and illustrates its use by presenting an argument that the high frequency of the negative form which lies between *not* and *nought* supported the survival of *aught*. The debt of the contents of this volume to the Microfiche *Concordance of Old English* and the work of the Toronto team is also manifest, and in this context it is fitting to register the loss we will all suffer, from the death of Professor Ashley Crandell Amos.

I wish on any editor the good luck of working with contributors and reviewers as efficient, painstaking and ineffably tolerant of 'impossible deadlines' as those responsible for this volume. And we all owe a debt to Mr Russell Walker for steering the volume over and around inevitable hurdles. Nice work. If there's ever such a thing as a free lunch, I'll charge one for everyone to the University of Embrough.[2]

Fran Colman

NOTES

1. See Lodge, David. 1985. *Small World*. London: Penguin.
2. See Lodge, David. 1989. *Nice Work*. London: Penguin.

Evidence for Old English

1

OLD ENGLISH AND THE SYNTACTICIAN: SOME REMARKS AND A SYNTACTICIAN'S GUIDE TO EDITIONS OF THE WORKS OF ÆLFRIC

Cynthia Allen

1. Introduction

There has been a recent upsurge in interest in historical syntax among theoretical linguists. Much of this interest has focused on the history of English. Modern syntactic theories make a number of predictions about the ways in which languages can change, and English, with its long literary tradition, as well as its tradition of grammatical comment and analysis, seems like a good proving ground for hypotheses about what sorts of syntactic changes are likely to happen, and when. English can indeed be used as a proving ground for some hypotheses about the nature of syntactic change, but the study of the history of English syntax is fraught with problems.

Because a good deal of work has been done on the history of English syntax, linguists commonly assume that they can get the facts they are looking for to confirm their theories from a descriptive work. But this is nearly always not the case, for reasons which will be outlined below. Since it is normally impossible to get a ready-made collection of facts that suit the syntactician's purpose, anyone working on a topic in the history of English syntax will need not only to look at what other scholars have said about the question, but also to gather some facts for themselves, which will involve working with Old or Middle English texts. It is unfortunate that linguists have frequently made pronouncements on 'facts' which could readily be disproved by looking at a few texts. The reluctance of syntacticians to take the trouble (which is quite considerable) to familiarize themselves with the texts from which examples they use have been garnered (usually by others) is understandable. However, I shall argue here that a first-hand knowledge of the texts is a necessary prerequisite for the study of diachronic English syntax.

The purpose of this paper is twofold: to urge linguists to pay attention to the relevance of philology to historical linguistics, and to make a modest contribution towards helping them to make use of the fruits of philologists' labours. In Section Two I put forward some reasons why syntacticians working on Old English (OE) or the history of English need to read texts from the period they are dealing with, and why they must take the trouble to acquaint themselves with some basic facts about the manuscripts containing these texts. I also point out some difficulties with dealing with the texts, largely stemming from the different aims of the philologist and the theoretical syntactician. This difference in aims means that the excellent guides to Old English works which are readily available are not organised in a way most useful to linguists, and that no one guide gives all the information a linguist working on a particular period would want. A syntactician's guide to the entire output of the Old English period would be highly desirable, but it would also be an enormous task. In Section Four I attempt a much more modest task — a syntactician's guide to editions of the works of Ælfric. My reasons for the choice of Ælfric's works will be set out in that section.

2. Why study the Texts?

2.1 Different theory, different facts

Why is it necessary for syntacticians to look at Old English texts at all? Haven't enough descriptive studies been done so that normally we can just rework someone else's data?

Although careful descriptive studies are frequently very useful, they will hardly ever give all the facts that the syntactician needs. The reason is that any description of a language must be dependent on some linguistic theory, although this may be implicit rather than explicit and vague and ill-defined. It is impossible to talk about the syntax of any language without setting up categories such as noun, nominative, subject, relative clause, etc. But the categories that one uses will necessarily reflect one's notion of how languages are organised.

A simple example will illustrate the point that there is simply no such thing as an atheoretical description, and the problems that can result from this. Most descriptive grammars of English have found it necessary to use the term *subject*, but what the term refers to depends on the grammatical theory of the analyst. In traditional studies, the subject is taken to be that NP which appears in the nominative case (or would, if case were marked) and controls subject-verb agreement. However, linguists have now found strong evidence that non-nominative NPs in some constructions pattern syntactically with nominative subjects in more 'ordinary' constructions in languages as closely related to English as Icelandic (for a review of the evidence, see Zaenen, Maling, and Thráinsson (1985)). This has led to a widespread view that some verbs in Icelandic govern non-nominative subjects, which differ from ordinary subjects only in their case marking. Given this different way of looking at 'impersonal' constructions, a linguist may be interested in the question of whether 'impersonal' constructions in OE such as *him lyst ðaes wifes* could best be analysed as containing a subject, although not a nominative one. But little help will be obtained from grammars which take case to be a defining characteristic of grammatical relations, and therefore do not distinguish between *him* in this example and fronted objects of more ordinary (i.e. 'personal') verbs which govern dative objects. The problems multiply when one considers that studies of word order will also be affected by how one analyses such examples; is this example to be categorized as OV or SV, or perhaps some other way? Whether or not *him* in this example is actually best analysed as a subject or object is beside the point here: facts do not exist except within some sort of framework, i.e. theory. Nor is what we call 'traditional grammar' a monolith; there will be variation in the framework which will be reflected in the selection of things the observer reports as facts, and it is not to be expected that a coherent picture of the history of English syntax can be pieced together entirely from the work of investigators working within different frameworks.

Linguists who ignore the fact that previous investigators were simply not looking for the same things that they were looking for can be led into serious errors. For example, as discussed in Allen (1984), linguists have been misled into thinking that the 'raising' of 'empty' subjects (e.g. *I believe it to be true that he resigned*) is a recent phenomenon in English, when in fact it dates from at least the early fifteenth century. This mistake seems to stem from the fact that Visser (1963-73) gives no examples earlier than 1968 of this construction with a dummy *it* . The lack of examples in Visser is not due to any faulty observations on Visser's part; he surely would have documented the history of empty subjects in this construction if he had realised that the difference between 'empty' and 'full' subjects would be considered crucial by some linguists. But it is impossible to tell how everyone else will categorise constructions, and at any rate a grammar trying to accommodate all known possible systems would be impossible to write. The fault lies rather with linguists who do not realise that if Visser happens to give them an example of a 'type' that he was not looking for, it will be fortuitous.

It is rare that a descriptive work (on OE or any other language) reports all the facts that a theoretical linguist wants to know about. For this reason, not even the publication of Mitchell's (1985) monumental *Old English Syntax* will obviate the need to do one's own data-gathering. As long as linguists conceive of new ways of looking at a language, new descriptions will be necessary, and new facts will be discovered.

2.2 Familiarity with the periods

A second very important reason for working with texts, rather than simply using data gathered by someone else is that one acquires a 'feel' for the language of a period that simply cannot be obtained from any grammar. A linguist not conversant with the texts of the periods being studied is prone to making several mistakes. First, without familiarity with the texts, it is impossible to get an idea of whether an apparently late example of a construction is a genuine retention of an old construction or a deliberate archaism. For example, it is possible to find solitary examples from the nineteenth century of constructions like *me thinks that S* in works like Visser and the *Oxford English Dictionary* (OED), but no-one who has compared the literature of this period to that of the fifteenth century could believe that this construction had a similar sort of grammatical status in the two periods. Nevertheless, it has been claimed on the basis of such dubious evidence that 'impersonal' constructions involving complement sentences remained productive after similar constructions involving two NPs had disappeared, and that this putative fact supports a particular syntactic theory.[1]

A second problem arising from lack of familiarity with texts is that it reduces the tendency to forget that terms like 'Old English', 'Middle English' and early Modern English', while they are convenient labels, do not refer to unified periods. It is easy to telescope together events that took place a long time ago. It is not unheard of for linguists eager to find a cluster of changes that could be seen as the results of one triggering event to treat changes which apparently took place approximately 200 years apart as 'nearly simultaneous'. The dangers inherent in this sort of approach become evident when one considers that this time span encompasses the end of the American Revolution and the beginning of the Vietnam War.

2.3 Translations and interlinear glosses

Finally, it should be noted that not all sentences written in genuine Old English manuscripts are equally good evidence for Old English grammar. A good deal of Old English was translated from Latin originals, and Latin influence is a significant problem. By comparing translations with the Latin originals (when these are available), we can learn much about Old English grammar. If the Old English text consistently replaces a Latin construction with a completely different construction also found in native prose and poetry, we can feel confident that the Latin construction was considered too alien to English grammar to be used, and that the substituted construction was a genuine Old English idiom.

Old English translations from Latin vary a great deal in their literalness; some are quite free, and some are fairly slavish. If texts are not read, but examples are simply plucked from manuals, then the linguist will have little notion of whether a given example is representative of Old English, or an awkward attempt at translation.

One very important distinction which is often[2] not taken into account is the difference between a translation and an interlinear gloss. Interlinear glosses pair up Latin words with English ones:[3]

(1) ðu arð sunu min leaf
    tu es filius mus dilectus

    on ðec ic wel licade
    in te complacui
    MkGl(Li) 1.11

Such glosses cannot be used as evidence for the existence of a construction as part of Old English grammar, although they can be used for comparative purposes; in the above example, for instance, the order of elements within the NP is quite alien to Old English syntax. Unfortunately, linguists[4] have sometimes used such glosses as examples of particular constructions in Old English; for a discussion of a recent instance of using a variant of (1) as illustrating the syntax of the verb *lician,* see Allen (1986).

It should finally be noted that translations of Bible passages sometimes show syntax otherwise found only in word-for-word glosses. Since the Bible was a sacred book, Old English writers were nervous about tampering with the language found there, so the English renderings of the Latin Vulgate are often quite literal; also, an accepted translation tends to become fossilized, as evidenced by the fact that many people still prefer to use the King James version of the Lord's Prayer, which has such phrases alien to Modern English idiom as *Our Father, which art in heaven*. I believe that Old English translations of Bible verses should be used as examples of OE syntax only if such examples also exist in less suspicious texts.

2.4 The importance of learning about the manuscripts

Having put forward reasons for my belief that linguists must deal with texts, I will now point out that it is necessary to go beyond this and to learn something about the nature of the manuscript containing the text being used. The main reason is that there is not infrequently a long gap between the time that a particular text was composed and the date of the extant manuscript(s) containing it. The farther we get from the original author of a text, the less we can be confident that we are dealing with the language of a particular individual or period. A good example of this problem is found in King Alfred's translation of St Augustine's *Soliloquies*. Since King Alfred lived in the late ninth century, it might be supposed that this text would furnish a good example of early West Saxon. However, it turns out that this text is now found in its entirety only in MS Cotton Vitellius A.XV, which belongs to the middle part of the twelfth century (Ker, 1957: item 215, article 1). Such a long gap means that this text cannot be assumed to be representative of the language of any particular period. Such texts are useful for comparative purposes, but any construction found in them and not in earlier manuscripts cannot be used as evidence that the construction existed at all in Old English, much less in an early period of Old English.

Not differentiating between the different types and ages of manuscripts can lead to some mistaken beliefs about Old English syntax. A striking example of this which I have recently discovered has to do with the syntax of the verb *behofian* 'behoove'. This verb has shifted in meaning since Old English; it now (insofar as it is still used at all) conveys a meaning of fittingness, but the central meaning in Old English was one of necessity or obligation. In modern English, the role of the human being, which we can call 'experiencer', is assigned to the grammatical role of object, as in *it behooves us to proceed with caution*. In OE, however, the experiencer role was typically given nominative case marking; the needed thing ('theme'), if it was an NP and not a clause, was marked with a non-nominative case - usually genitive, but occasionally accusative. The Bosworth and Toller dictionary of Anglo-Saxon reports this case marking pattern, but also says that *behofian* could be used 'impersonally' in Old English, and gives a few examples of this verb occurring with an experiencer in a non-nominative case. The OED offers a similar example from *c*.950 (in *behove* 4.C), and Mitchell (1985: 458), in his list of verbal rections, also lists *behofian* as a verb which could have either a nominative or a dative experiencer. Since these three authorities agree that this verb was used 'impersonally' in Old English, it would seem quite reasonable to assume that the modern usage pattern is simply a continuation of an Old English pattern, which won out over another pattern and meaning.

However, it turns out that all the examples of dative experiencers with *behofian* in the OED and Bosworth and Toller (Mitchell offers no examples in his list) fall into one of two categories: they are either from word-for-word glosses, or from manuscripts dating after the beginning of the twelfth century. Therefore, none of these examples is a convincing illustration of Old English usage. An examination of Healey and Venezky's OE *Concordance* reveals a few more examples of this verb with a dative experiencer, but none that do not fall into the categories just mentioned. For instance, consider this example:

(2) we nabbað na mare ðonne us selfum behofað
 we not-have no more than us self-DAT behooves
 'We do not have any more than we ourselves need.'
 HomS 48 (TristrApp3) 18

Although this homily was probably composed earlier, it is extant only in a twelfth century manuscript (CCCC 303). In view of the fact that similar examples are not found (outside of glosses) in tenth or eleventh century manuscripts, it is reasonable to suspect that this example does not reflect the syntax of the original author, but of a later scribe, and that dative case-marking of the experiencer of *behofian* was a fairly late (probably early twelfth century) innovation. At the least, we can say that no convincing evidence for this pattern in the prose or poetry of Old English has been offered.

Finally, it should be noted that assignments of dates and authorship, provenance, etc. are frequently quite tentative. It is easy to get the impression that all examples listed in a historical grammar for a particular period are equally useful, but a look at the philological literature will quickly show that these 'facts' are sometimes hotly disputed. It is therefore important to familiarise oneself with scholarly opinion concerning the texts and manuscripts from which one's examples are drawn, and to remember also that the findings of the philologists, like the findings of the linguists, are based on the assessment of the available evidence, and some of these conclusions carry more weight than others.

3. Pitfalls in the Ælfric Texts

Before moving on to the guide to Ælfric's works, I will point out a few of the pitfalls of working with texts that make such a guide for linguists necessary.

The syntactician gathering Old English data will normally be working not with manuscripts, but with edited texts. A major problem for linguists in working with such texts is that the aims of the editor of the text are almost certainly not going to be the same as the aims of a linguist, and this will effect the presentation of the text. The editor normally will be interested in presenting a coherent text of some particular work, and this may involve piecing together bits from different manuscripts when no one extant manuscript contains the whole. For example, anyone reading Pope's (1967-8) edition of some of Ælfric's homilies without bothering to wade through the introduction might think they were dealing with the language of a single period. But in fact this is a collection intended to round out already existing editions of the different series of Ælfric's works, and as such contains texts found only in some manuscripts copied considerably later than when Ælfric wrote the original. For example, Pope's homily xxiii is found only in

MS Hatton 114, dating from the third quarter of the eleventh century. Similarly, several of these homilies are not found intact in any one manuscript, and although the text will be based mainly on one early manuscript, missing parts will be supplied from other, possibly later, manuscripts. Whether or not this gap between composition and copy is important to the linguist will depend on exactly what is being investigated.

Fortunately, modern editors like Pope give detailed information on the manuscripts upon which they have based their editions. Pope tells us at the beginning of each homily which manuscripts contain it, which has been chosen as the basis of the text, and which, if any, parts are based on other manuscripts. Such editors also scrupulously detail any emendations they have thought it necessary to make and also variant readings from other manuscripts. However, standards and practices were different in the last century. For example, Skeat's (1881-1900) edition of Ælfric's *Lives of Saints*, which is still the standard edition, gives no information about the manuscripts used or about editorial practice. It is also now generally accepted that a few of the pieces in this collection were not actually by Ælfric, a fact which will not matter to someone looking generally at the language of the early eleventh century, but might matter a great deal to someone focusing only on Ælfric's usage.

4. A Syntactician's Guide to Editions of the Works of Ælfric

For the reasons outlined above, guides to Old English texts written with a syntactician's aims in mind would be highly useful. In Section Four I offer a syntactician's guide to the works of Ælfric, who became Abbot of Eynsham in 1005. Ælfric's works are an excellent starting place for anyone interested in Old English syntax. These texts offer the largest corpus of Old English prose by one author, and are mostly preserved in manuscripts written when Ælfric was still alive; some were probably from his own scriptorium. In addition, Ælfric was a master stylist, and his translations from Latin are graceful and idiomatic, in contrast with the awkwardness sometimes found in such works as King Alfred's translation of Gregory's *Pastoral Care*. Finally, reliable editions of Ælfric's works are readily available.

Although lists of Ælfric's texts and the manuscripts containing them, along with a wealth of philological information, now exist, these lists were drawn up by philologists and are therefore organised in a way that reflects the philologist's particular interests. This organisation makes them difficult for the linguist to use, and it is frequently necessary to shuttle back and forth among several sources to compile the needed information.

A classified list of the Ælfric canon is given in Clemoes (1959), and the continuing importance of this work is reflected in the fact that it was reprinted (with some corrections) in 1980 as *Old English Newsletter* Subsidia 5. The lack of information about manuscripts in this list reflects the fact that Clemoes' concern here was to establish the chronology of Ælfric's works — not that of the manuscripts containing them. Ker's (1957) immensely important *Catalogue of Manuscripts Containing Anglo-Saxon* provides a helpful table of the manuscripts containing the homilies of Ælfric's two series of *Catholic Homilies*, along with the dates of the manuscripts, but the fact that this is a catalogue of manuscripts, not editions, results in a lot of to-ing and fro-ing, and the information on editions is at any rate more than 30 years old.

Pope's exhaustive introduction to his edition, covering 191 pages, is extremely useful; its scope includes the entire output of Ælfric, and it is rich in general information, as well as more detailed discussion of the pieçes edited. For my own purposes, I have found it useful to make up a list of the individual homilies edited by Pope, containing the details of dates assigned to the manuscripts from which the texts are edited, and also the numbers assigned to the manuscripts in Ker's *Catalogue*. I hope that this list will prove helpful to others also.

Finally, Cameron (1973) is an exhaustive and invaluable list of all Old English texts. The texts are divided into six different categories — poetry, prose, interlinear glosses, Latin-Old English glossaries, runic inscriptions and vernacular inscriptions in the Latin alphabet — and these are labelled A-F. Within these divisions, each text is assigned a number. The works of Ælfric falling into the category of prose are all assigned the number B1, and individual items are B1.1.1 (first homily of the first series of *Catholic Homilies*), etc. The list gives the location of the text in Ker's *Catalogue* and also information about editions of the text, but it is necessary to use the Cameron list in conjunction with the *Catalogue* in order to determine the date of the different manuscripts, and also usually to determine which manuscript was used as the base text by the editors mentioned.

In composing the following list, the debt I owe to the works just mentioned is enormous. My list is almost completely derived from these earlier lists, except that I have added a few more recent editions. Some of the information is also taken from the introductions to the editions.

The organisation of this list is as follows : the editions are first divided into two categories, A and B. A-editions are editions of texts which are found in manuscripts dating no later than the first half of the eleventh century. B-editions are edited from later manuscripts. I have only included here editions based on manuscripts dated no later than the end of the eleventh century. In the case of eclectic collections, it has sometimes been convenient to draw up separate lists for manuscripts and texts. For example, for Pope's editions I list the manuscripts falling into the A category in Table 1 and refer to the texts edited from those manuscripts as A-texts.

Within the A and B categories, I list first collections of Ælfric's works (by editor), and then individual pieces. The Cameron number is given for each series or individual piece (I have not included the prose prefix *B*), along with information about the manuscript on which the edition is based, including the number of the manuscript in Ker's *Catalogue* and its approximate date. For the most part, I have followed Cameron's order, but the organisation is by edition, rather than text, so that the Cameron numbers are not always in sequence, nor is there any attempt to give the Cameron numbers of individual pieces which are found in an edition based on only one manuscript, although these are given in the case of eclectic collections.

The dates given for the texts are always those given by Ker. Ker uses the following system: s.X/XI = end of the tenth century or beginning of the eleventh, s.XI^1 = first half of the eleventh century (usually 'about the middle of the first half of the eleventh century'), s.XI med = around the middle of the eleventh century and s.XI^2 = second half of the eleventh century. Sometimes it is possible to date manuscripts a bit more precisely: s.X ex. means 'around the very end of the tenth century', s.XI in. means 'within a few years of the beginning of the eleventh century', and s.XI (3rd quarter) means 'in the third quarter of the eleventh century'. In category A I have included manuscripts dating no later than s.XI^1; category B includes XI med. and later eleventh century manuscripts.

It should be noted that no attempt has been made to list every edition of Ælfric's works. I have not listed editions of fragments or of very short pieces, unless they are fairly recent and contain discussions of the language, variants, etc. My purpose has been to acquaint syntacticians with useful editions which are readily available.

4.1 A - Editions
4.1.1. Catholic Homilies: First Series
Cameron 1.1
According to Clemoes, Ælfric wrote his first series of *Catholic Homilies* in 989. This series underwent various changes (dictated by Ælfric) as it was recopied, so slightly different versions are found in the 35 copies containing portions of it. The earliest version is found in MS British Museum Royal 7 C.xii (Ker 257, s.X ex). This manuscript is particularly interesting because it contains marginal notes assumed to have been made by Ælfric himself. It contains only the first series of homilies, and lacks the preface found in MS Cambridge, University Library Gg.3.28, an authoritative manuscript also containing the second series. No edited version of the Royal MS has yet been published, but a facsimile was published by Eliason and Clemoes (1966).

MS Cambridge, University Library Gg.3.28 was edited by Thorpe (1844-6). It is Ker 15, s.X/XI.

A new edition of the first series, to be published by the Early English Text Society, has been proposed by Peter Clemoes.

4.1.2. Catholic Homilies: Second Series
Cameron 1.1.2
MS Cambridge Library, Gg.3.28 (Ker 15), is the only manuscript containing the whole second series. It is dated s.X/XI by Ker. It was edited by Thorpe 1884-6 (volume II), but this edition has been superseded by Godden's 1979 edition. Godden's introduction contains detailed information about all the manuscripts containing this series.

Cameron 1.2.10, 1.2.11 and 1.2.42 (the lives of Saints Gregory, Cuthbert and Martin) have also been edited by Masi in a 1969 dissertation which includes a linguistic analysis of the variants.

4.1.3 The Lives of Saints
Cameron 1.3

Ælfric's third series of homilies, consisting mostly of sermons for feasts of saints, is found in its entirety only in MS London, British Museum, Cotton Julius E.vii (Ker 162). Ker dates it s.XI in. It was edited by Skeat in four volumes spanning 1881-1900. Note: Skeat's numbers XXIII, XXIIIB, XXX and XXXIII are generally agreed not to be by Ælfric, and XXXVII is from a late twelfth-century manuscript.

Skeat's edition of the whole series has not yet been superseded; however, individual items have been edited more recently. Cameron 1.3.12 (Forty Soldiers) was edited by Algeo in a 1960 dissertation which has several readings diverging from Skeat's, along with notes and a glossary.

Cameron 1.3.22, 1.3.26 and 1.3.31 (Lives of St Swithum and St Oswald, and passion of St Edmund) were published by Needham (1966), an edition which contains an introduction giving basic information about Ælfric and his works and also a glossary. This edition was reprinted in 1976, with an expanded bibliography.

4.1.4 Pope's Collection
Cameron 1.4

In 1966-8 John C. Pope edited a two-volume collection of homilies attributable to Ælfric which had not yet been edited. These homilies are drawn from several different manuscripts, some of which date from the second half of the eleventh century or later. It will therefore be necessary to enumerate the manuscripts of our type A, along with the homilies based on them. In Table 1 I list the sigla used by Pope and the manuscripts they refer to, the number of the entry in Ker's *Catalogue* and the date given by Ker. This information is extracted from Pope's introduction.

In Table 2 I list the texts edited from these A-manuscripts using the sigla explained in Table 1, along with the Cameron numbers of the texts.

TABLE 1
A-Manuscripts used by Pope

Pope	MS	Ker	Date
F	CCCC 162	38	XI in.
H	BM Cotton Vitellius C.v	220	X/XI, XI^1
R	CCCC 178	41a	XI^1
Q	CCCC 188	43	XI^1
V	CCCC 419	68	XI^1

Note: CCCC = Cambridge, Corpus Christi College
BM = London, British Museum

TABLE 2
A-Texts in Pope's Volume

Pope	Cameron	MS	Ker
I	1.4.1	H	220, art.4
II	1.4.2	H	220, art.63
III	1.4.3	F	38, art.20
IV	1.4.4	Q	43, art.12
V	1.4.5	F	38, art.22
VI	1.4.6	F	38, art.24
(Lines 1-208, 292-end)			
VI			
(lines 209-291)		H	220, art.66
XI	1.4.11	Q	43, art.23
XIa	1.4.12	H	220, art.1
XVII	1.4.18	H	220, art.45
XVIII	1.4.19	R	41A, art.9
XXI	1.4.22	R	41A, art.18
XXV	1.4.26	R	41A, art.30
XXVI	1.4.27	R	41A, art.10
XXVII	1.4.28	H	220, art.46
(Lines 1-14 are 'probably not by Ælfric')			
XXIX	1.4.30	R	41A, art.8
XXX	1.4.31	V	68, art.15

Note: As indicated in Table 1, MS H has an earlier part, and a later one.
Pope's II and VI (interpolation) are in the earlier part, and the other texts from H are in the later.

4.1.5 Assmann's collection

Assmann (1889) is a collection of Old English homilies and saints' lives, of which the first nine are attributed to Ælfric. The A texts of this eclectic collection are set out in Table 3.

TABLE 3

A-Texts in Assmann's Collection

Piece No	MS	Cameron	Ker
II	Cotton Vitellius C.v	1.8.5	220, art.49

Note: Lines 1-12 and 225 are from a later MS

III	CCCC 188	1.5.8	43, art.35
IV	CCCC 188	1.5.11	43, art.45
V	CCCC 162	1.5.4	38, art.26

Note: MS Cotton Vitellius C.v is dated s.XI^1, CCCC 188 is s.XI^1, and CCCC 162 is s.XI in.

4.1.6 Dedication of a church
Cameron 1.5.12

This piece was edited from MS Paris, Bibliotèque Nationale, Lat. 943 by Brotanek (1913) as homily No 3. It is Ker 364, art.a, s.X/XI.

4.1.7 Interrogationes Sigewulfi in Genesin
Cameron 1.6.1

This piece is found in several manuscripts. MacLean (1884) is an edition based on CCCC 178, Ker 41A, art.3, s.XI^1.

4.1.8 De duodecim abusivis
Cameron 1.6.2

This is printed as appendix II to Morris (1868), pp.296-304. The version found there is of CCCC 178, Ker 41A, art.7, s.XI^1.

4.1.9 Heptateuch
Cameron 8.1.4 and 1.7

The *Heptateuch*, edited by Crawford (1922) is not all attributed to Ælfric by Clemoes and Pope, nor is this edition based only on one manuscript. Table 4 lists those parts attributed to Ælfric which are found in MS Claudius B.iv, Ker 142, s.xi^1.

TABLE 4

Ælfrician A-Texts in the *Heptateuch*

Genesis 1-3

Genesis 6-9

Genesis 12-14

Genesis 22

Numbers 13-31

Joshua 1:16-11

Joshua 21-24

4.1.10 Grammar
Cameron 1.9.1
Ælfric wrote a grammar of Latin in Old English, which was edited by Zupitza (1880) from MS Oxford, St John's College 154, Ker 362 art.1, s.XI in. Caution must be exercised in using any Old English which is a translation of Latin, but the rest of the text can certainly be used, and much can be learned from the way the Latin is translated into English.

4.1.11 Admonitio ad filium spiritualem
Cameron 1.9.3
This piece, found only in Oxford, Bodleian Hatton 76, Ker 328A art.2, s.XI^1, was edited by Norman in 1848. It has been edited more recently by Mueller (1974).

4.1.12 De temporibus anni
Cameron 1.9.4
This work is found in several manuscripts. Henel (1942) is an edition based on MS Cambridge, University Library Gg.3.28, Ker 15, art.93, s.X/XI (this is the same manuscript containing both series of *Catholic Homilies*).

4.2 B - editions
In this section I list editions based on manuscripts later than s.XI^1. It should be remembered that some of the morphological changes which we associate with Early Middle English had already taken place by the later part of the eleventh century; for example, the ending *-e* is frequently extended to the nominative form of feminine nouns. Little is known about how much the syntax of these manuscripts differs from the syntax of earlier manuscripts containing Ælfric's works.

4.2.1 Pope's edition

The earlier texts of the edition by Pope of Ælfric's works have been listed above in Tables 1 and 2. The later eleventh-century manuscripts used in this edition are listed in Table 5, and the texts edited from them are listed in Table 6.

TABLE 5
B-Manuscripts in Pope's Edition

Pope	MS	Ker	Date
M	ULC Ii. 4.6	21	XI med.
P	BL Hatton 115	332	XI^2
T	BL Hatton 114	331	XI (3rd Qtr)
U	TC B.15.34	86	XI med.

ULC = Cambridge, University Library
BL = Oxford, Bodleian Library
TC = Cambridge, Trinity College

TABLE 6
B-Texts in Pope's Edition

Pope	Cameron	MS	Ker
VII (lines 1-93, 162-226)	1.4.7	M	21, art.25
VII lines 94-161	1.4.7	U	86, art.7
VIII	1.4.8	M	21, art.26
IX	1.4.9	M	21, art.32
X	1.4.10	M	21, art.34
XII	1.4.13	M	21, art.35
XIII	1.4.14	U	86, art.22
XIV	1.4.15	U	86, art.23
XV	1.4.16	U	86, art.24
XVI	1.4.17	U	86, art.27
XIX	1.4.20	P	332, art.6
XX	1.4.21	P	332, art.29
XXII	1.4.23	P	332, art.17
XXIII	1.4.24	T	331, art.84
XXIV	1.4.25	P	332, art.7
XXVIII	1.4.29	P	332, art.25

A slightly different version of Pope's number XI (which was included in the A-texts) was edited (as their No 6) by Bazire and Cross (1982) from MS Cambridge, University Library ii.4.6, Ker 21 art.27, s.XI med. Cross and Bazire's lines 1-43 and 248-255 are different from the version used in Pope.

4.2.2 Assman

The A-texts of Assmann's edition have already been listed. The B-texts are listed in Table 7.

TABLE 7

B-Texts in Assmann's Edition

Piece Number	MS	Cameron	Ker	Date
I (lines 7b-end)	BL Hatton 115	1.8.6	332, art.27	s.XI^2
I (lines 1-7a)	Laud Mics. 509		344, art.3	s.XI^2
VI	TC B.15.34	1.5.5	86, art.6	s.XI med.
IX (lines 394-445)	BM Cotton Otho B.X	1.5.15	178, art.1	s.XI med.

BL = Oxford, Bodleian Library.
The Laud MS is also found in the Bodleian Library.
BM = British Museum; TC = Trinity College, Cambridge.
The first 393 lines of No. IX are from a twelfth-century MS, and the lines from 446 to the end are from a transcript made by Wanley of the Otho MS.

4.2.3 Fehr

Fehr (1914) is a collection of Ælfric's letters, both in Latin and English. Table 8 lists the English contents, three letters from late eleventh century manuscripts. Where more than one manuscript is printed, I list the B-manuscripts used.

TABLE 8
Old English Contents of Fehr's Edition

Fehr	Cameron	MS	Ker	Date
I (sects. 1-72, 74-104, 111-161)	1.8.1	CCCC 190	45B, art.17	s.XI^2
II	1.8.2	CCCC 190	44B, art.2	s.XI med.
		CCCC 201	49B, art.17	s.XI med.
III	1.8.3	CCCC 190	45B, art.3	s.XI^2
		BM Cotton Tiberius A.iii 186, art.29		s.XI med.
		Bodleian, Julius 121	338, art.27	s.XI (3rd quarter)

4.2.4 Hexameron
Cameron 1.5.13

Although the *Hexameron* is also found in some earlier manuscripts, the only edition printed so far, Crawford (1921), is based on MS Oxford, Bodleian, Hatton 115, Ker 332, art.1, s.XI^2. However, the variants found in earlier manuscripts are given.

4.2.5 De Septiformi Spiritu
Cameron 1.6.3

This piece is found in MS Cambridge, Trinity College, B.15.34, Ker 86, art.16, s.XI med, which was edited as Nos. VII and VIII by Napier (1883) in a collection of sermons attributed to Wulfstan, a contemporary of Ælfric.

The text is also found in MS London, British Museum Cotton Tiberius C.vi, Ker 199 art.b, s.XI med, which was edited by Logeman (1989).

4.2.6 Heptateuch
Cameron 8.1.7

The Ælfrician A-texts of the *Heptateuch* were listed in Table 4. *Judges* is an Ælfrician B-text, based on MX Oxford, Bodleian, Laud Misc,509, Ker 344 art.2, s.XI^2. The letter to Sigeweard introducing the compilation is also by Ælfric and is also found in this same manuscript, article 4. A version of this letter from a twelfth-century manuscript was also printed by Assmann as Number VII.

4.2.7 Colloquy
Cameron C3

Ælfric wrote a colloquy between different members of society as a tool for teaching Latin. The English is an interlinear gloss, and cannot be regarded as representative of Old English syntax; because of Ælfric's aim, the syntax here is distorted to follow the Latin as closely as possible, and constructions are found here which are not found in Old English not heavily influenced by Latin. This text is classified as an interlinear gloss by its Cameron number. The Colloquy was edited by Garmonsway (1939) on the basis of MS London, British Museum Cotton Tiberius A.iii, Ker 186 art.11, s.XI med.

NOTES

1. See Fischer and Van der Leek (1983), and for a discussion see Allen (1986).
2. The importance of this distinction is reflected in the fact that the Cameron list and Healey and Venezky's concordance separate interlinear glosses from other prose and poetry.
3. The references used in the examples are those found in the guide to Healey and Venezky's *Concordance*.
4. It is hardly surprising that linguists should make such an error when handbooks of Old English such as Quirk and Wrenn (1957) occasionally use such glosses to illustrate a construction. Even if these handbooks limit the use of the glosses to the illustration of genuine Old English constructions also found elsewhere, an impression that such examples are suitable for discussions of Old English syntax is created. I am indebted to Roger Higgins for drawing my attention to the use of glosses in Quirk and Wrenn's discussion of Old English word order.

REFERENCES

Note: EETS = Early English Text Society

Allen, C.L. 1984. On the dating of raised empty subjects in English. *Linguistic Inquiry* 15:3. 461-465.

Allen, C.L. 1986. Reconsidering the history of *like*. *Journal of Linguistics* 22. 375 - 409.

Algeo, J. 1960. *Ælfric's* The forty soldiers; *an edition*. Unpublished University of Florida dissertation.

Assmann, B. ed. 1889. *Angelsächsische Homilien und Heiligenleben*. (= Bibliothek der angelsächsischen Prosa, 3). Reprinted with an introduction by Peter Clemoes, 1964. Darmstadt: Wissenschaftlice Buchgesellschaft.

Bazire, J. and J. Cross 1982. *Eleven Old English rogationtide homilies*. Toronto: University of Toronto Press.

Bosworth, J. and T.N. Toller 1898. *An Anglo-Saxon dictionary*. London: Oxford University Press.

Brotanek, R. 1913. *Texte and Untersuchungen zur alternenglischem Literatur und Kirchengeschichte*. Halle.

Cameron, Angus. 1973. A list of Old English texts. In R. Frank and A. Cameron eds. *A plan for the dictionary of Old English*. Toronto: University of Toronto Press.

Clemoes, P. 1959. The chronology of Ælfric's works. In P. Clemoes (ed) *The Anglo-Saxons. Studies in some aspects of their history and culture presented to Bruce Dickins*. London: Bowes and Bowes. A reprint of this article with corrections appears as *Old English Newsletter* Subsidia 5.

Crawford, S.J. ed. 1921. *Exameron anglice or the Old English Hexameron*. (=Bibliothek der angelsächsische Prosa, 10.) Reprinted in 1968, Darmstadt: Wissenschaftlice Buchgesellschaft.

Crawford, S.J. 1922. *The Old English version of the heptateuch*. (=EETS, 160) London : Oxford

University Press. Reprinted 1969 with additions by N.R. Ker.

Eliason, N. and P. Clemoes eds. 1966. *Ælfric's first series of Catholic Homilies*. (=Early English Manuscripts in Facsimile, 13) Copenhagen.

Fehr, B. ed. 1914. *Die Hirtenbriefe Ælfrics*. (=Bibliothek der angelsächsischen Prosa, 3). Reprinted with a supplement by Peter Clemoes, 1966, Darmstadt: Wissenschaftliche Buchgesellschaft.

Fischer, O.C.M. and van der Leek, F. 1983. The demise of the Old English impersonal construction, *Journal of Linguistics* 19. 337 - 368.

Garmonsway, G. ed 1939. *Ælfric's Colloquy*. London: Methuen and Co.

Godden, M. ed. 1979. *Ælfric's Catholic homilies: the second series* (=EETS Supplementary Series, 5.) London: Oxford University Press.

Healey, A. and R. Venezky 1980. *A microfiche concordance to Old English*. Toronto: Centre for Medieval Studies, University of Toronto.

Henel, H. ed. 1942. *Ælfric's de temporibus anni*, (= EETS, 213) London: Humphrey Milford.

Ker, N.R 1957. *Catalogue of manuscripts containing Anglo-Saxon*. Oxford: Clarendon Press.

Logeman, H. 1889. Anglo-Saxon minora. *Anglia* 11. 107-10.

MacLean, G.E. 1884. *Ælfric's version of Alcuini Interrogationes Sigeuulfi in Genesin*. *Anglia* 7. 1-59.

Masi, M 1969. *Three Homilies by Ælfric: the lives of Saints Gregory, Cuthbert and Martin: an edition*. Unpublished Northwestern University dissertation. [Dissertation Abstracts 1969 4009-A].

Morris, R. ed. 1868. *Old English homilies: Volume 1*. (=EETS, 34.) London: N. Trübner and Co.

Mitchell, B. 1985. *Old English syntax*. Oxford: Clarendon Press.

Mueller, L.E. ed 1974. *Ælfric's translation of St Basil's* admonitio ad filium spritualem: *an edition*. Unpublished University of Washington dissertation [Dissertation Abstracts International 35 4444-A].

Murray, J. *et al* eds. 1933. *Oxford English dictionary*, Oxford: Clarendon Press.

Napier, A. ed. 1883. *Wulfstan*. Reprinted 1967, Berlin: Wiedmann.

Needham, G. ed. 1966. *Ælfric: lives of three English saints*. London: Methuen & Co. Rpt. with additional bibliography, Exeter, 1976.

Norman, H.W. ed 1848. *The Anglo-Saxon version of the hexameron of St Basil... and the Anglo-Saxon remains of St Basil's admonitio ad filium spiritualem*. London.

Pope, J.C. 1967-8. *Homilies of Ælfric: a supplementary collection* (=EETS, 259, 260) London : Oxford University Press.

Quirk, R. and C.L Wrenn, 1957. *An Old English grammar*. 2nd edition. New York: Holt, Rinehart and Winston.

Skeat, W. ed. 1881-1900. *Ælfric's lives of saints*. (=EETS, 76, 82, 94, 114.) Reprinted. London: Oxford University Press, 1966.

Thorpe, B. (1884-6). *The homilies of the Anglo-Saxon church*. Printed for the Ælfric Society. Reprinted 1971 New York: Johnson Reprint Corporation.

Visser, F. Th. 1963-73. *An historical syntax of the English language*. Leiden: Brill.

Zaenen, A., J. Maling and H. Thráinsson 1985. Case and grammatical functions: the Icelandic passive. *Natural language and linguistic theory* 3:4. 441-484.

Zupitza, J. ed. 1880. *Ælfric's Grammatik und Glossar*. Reprint with an introduction by H. Gneuss 1966 Berlin: Max Niehaus Verlag.

2

YOU SAY [æjðər] AND I SAY [æjhwæðər]? - INTERPRETING OLD ENGLISH WRITTEN DATA*

Anne King

1. The Problem
In all dialects of Old English (OE), before the tenth century, the lexemes *man* 'man, one', *hand* 'hand' and others of the same class containing the reflex of Pre Old English /a/ /-Nasal Consonant (N), appear in manuscripts (MSS) spelt alternately with an <a> or an <o> graph in stressed vowel position (see Bosworth and Toller 1898: 507-8, 666, 668-9; Campbell 1959: §130, n 2; Hogg MS: §§ 5.3, 5.5).

1.1 Traditional interpretations
Most commentators on Old English interpret this synchronic orthographic variation as a reflection of some kind of corresponding phonological variation, and there is more or less a consensus among them on what this orthographic alternation means phonologically. Sweet (1888: 415, 412, §§ 1-8), for instance, has this to say about the reflex of Pre Old English /a/ in Old English [he uses Visible Speech symbols, transliterated here according to his own descriptions and the examples he cites to illustrate them]:

> ...*a* before nasals was at first no doubt simply [ã] which was afterwards rounded, the nasality being gradually lost giving [ɔ]... It is possible that the fluctuation between *a* and *o* in the earlier period is purely graphic, [ɔ] lying between [a] and [o], and therefore capable of being expressed by either *a* or *o*.

Sweet seems to see the graphic <a> ~ <o> alternation, then, as scribal confusion arising from the limitations of the Old English orthographic system which, because it contained only <a> and <o> for segments in this general range, was incapable of perfectly indicating the output [ɔ] of a sound change Pre Old English [a] → [ã] → eOE [ɔ] /-N. He makes no statement on the phonological status of any of the segments involved. The position of Campbell (1959: §130, cf. also §§ 40, 48 and n 1) is not significantly different:

> ...before nasal consonants a development of PrGmc *a* to *ã* occurred...which became in Old English a sound distinct from Old English *o* and at first also distinct from OE *a*. It is spelled both with *a* and with *o*.

From the rather vague description he gives in §§32 and 130 of values for his italic symbols, Campbell appears too to be advocating a sound-change like the following, again with no comment on segment status and no reasons given for the spelling variation: PrGmc [a] → Pre Old English [ã] → eOE [ɑ̃] /-N, (or 'slightly rounded' segment - perhaps [ɒ̃]).

Kuhn (1961: §2.17) describes ⟨a⟩ ~ ⟨o⟩ as representing an allophone [ɔ] of /a/ /-N in early Old English, but offers no explanation for the alternation of graphs. Lass and Anderson (1975: 61) say that 'the segment represented in some OE dialects as *o* < pre-OE *a before nasals...seems to be merely a variant of *a* ... that we cannot specify any further' (their *a* is described, p. 206, as 'low, back, unrounded', hence presumably [ɑ]). They do not discuss the spelling variation. Hogg (MS: §5.3) puts forward a sound change more or less identical to Campbell's suggestion, but one expressed notationally-differently, thus:

$$\begin{bmatrix} V \\ + \text{low} \end{bmatrix} > \begin{bmatrix} + \text{nasal} \\ + \text{back} \\ \pm \text{round} \end{bmatrix} \quad / - [+ \text{nasal}],$$

i.e., Gmc [a] → Pre Old English [a] → eOE $\left[\left\{ \begin{array}{c} \tilde{a} \\ \tilde{ɒ} \end{array} \right\} \right]$ /-N.

He accounts for the ⟨a⟩ ~ ⟨o⟩ alternation by saying that 'scribes were attempting to represent a low back unround or round vowel [ɑ] or [ɒ]'.

The usual interpretation of the spelling variation is, broadly, then, that it indicates the previous or synchronic operation of a sound change whereby PreOE [a] develops to (1) a nasalised and/or rounded and/or raised non-high back vowel phone which is awkward to represent in spelling for the reasons already given and, as a consequence, spelling of the output phone fluctuates between ⟨a⟩ and ⟨o⟩, or (2) at least two sub-phonemic variants answering to the description just given, one rounded and/or raised, spelt ⟨o⟩, the other rounded or unrounded, spelt ⟨a⟩.

2. Toon (1983)

2.1 One of the most recent and detailed accounts in print in English of this graphic variation is that of Toon (1983). It differs quite radically in approach and conclusions from traditional interpretations like those just outlined and calls, therefore, for fuller consideration. A fair amount of the remainder of this paper will, then, be taken up with discussion of his interpretation, theoretical approaches and claims and the evidence informing them.

In his book, Toon devotes a chapter (ch. 3, and references *passim*) to putting forward a case for a sound change PrGmc *a → Pre OE [ɒ] → [ɔ]: ⟨o⟩ /-N (cf. pp. 49-50, 207, 209) which occurred in Mercian and passed thence to all areas under its political control, especially Kent, because the eighth and ninth-century Mercian political hegemony over southern Anglo-Saxon England (cf. 2.2 below) involved, according to Toon, a consequent linguistic hegemony. He sees evidence for the sound change he posits in the appearance, alongside ⟨a⟩, of the ⟨o⟩ graph in non-Northumbrian MSS, (principally Mercian and Kentish ones) of this period. He dismisses explanations of the ⟨a⟩ ~ ⟨o⟩ variation which involve 'free variation or scribal uncertainty due to "dialect" mixture' (p. 90). He claims instead that the apparent growth in the use of ⟨o⟩ bears written witness to the sound change beginning 'variably in a small subset of the lexicon' and diffusing 'through the lexicon on a word-by-word basis but sensitive to phonetic environment' (p. 118), i.e., that the increase in the use of ‹o› (where it occurs) provides spelling evidence which charts the progression of his postulated sound change (ɒ) → [ɔ] /-N from its beginning in Mercian through to 'near completion' (p. 110) and finally, between 'AD 812 [and] 845', to a 'completed sound change' (p. 110) in Mercian and Kentish.

Toon's interpretation of the data he discusses (his pp. 42, 66-70) is governed primarily by his determination to see in it 'structured [linguistic] heterogeneity' (p. 60) and, as a corollary of this, by a belief that '...linguistically-significant variation representative of sound change in progress can be found in these texts' (p. 65). These concepts form an integral part of the theoretical framework adopted by Toon for the analysis of these and other early Old English data. His approach is an amalgam of the methods used by Kuhn in his analysis (1939) of the linguistic data of the 'Corpus Glossary' and in his account of the syllabic phonemes of Old English (1961) (see Toon pp. 55-7) and, more especially, those employed by Labov, Yaeger and Steiner in their 1972 sociolinguistic study of contemporary American English sound change in progress, with the theoretical framework employed there and proposed earlier in Weinreich, Labov and Herzog (1968) — see Toon pp. 60-65.

The extent to which Toon's interpretation of the Old English linguistic data is influenced by his interpretation of Labovian theory is indicated by the statements he feels able to make on the linguistic significance and effects of the eighth- and early ninth-century Mercian political hegemony over southern Anglo-Saxon England:

> [all geographical areas under Mercian political control during this period constitute] the Mercian speech community. (pp. 118, 201)....eighth-century literacy...was Mercian literacy. (p. 38).

From the first statement, we can gather that, for the socio-cultural factor which, in the theory of Labov *et al.*, conditions linguistic behaviour and variation and causes linguistic change, Toon substitutes a factor *socio-political*. From the second, it appears that Toon sees the Mercian hegemony over southern England, especially Kent, as not only a political, but a linguistic one too.

Toon's application of this socio-politico-linguistic theory and the Labovian method to the interpretation and presentation of the data which show ‹a› ~ ‹o› variation results in his making two claims. His first is that they represent a record of the gradual progression in speech of the sound change already described above — see, for instance, his comments on the alternation in the 'Corpus Glossary' (p. 106) and those on the Kentish charter data (p. 118). Most of the linguistic data, certainly as far as Kentish is concerned, for this period of Mercian political hegemony, are found in MSS of charters. These contain at first only personal- and place-names (on which cf. 2.4.2 below), the bulk of each text being written in Latin. Toon supposes that '[charters] are more likely to reflect the language of the dominant political force than that of the locale of the grant' (p. 42). Following Kuhn (1943), Toon (p. 67) adduces 'evidence of the influence of Mercian scriptoria' in: *Kentish-Mercian MSS* — almost exclusively charters, as just noted. These are traditionally described as 'Kentish-Mercian' because they concern grants of land in Kent made to Kentish grantees by, or with the permission of, a Mercian King — see Sweet (1885: 421-5); *Kentish MSS* — traditionally designated thus on the grounds that, to paraphrase Sweet (1885 : 421-5): (1) They concern the granting of land in Kent by a King of Kent to a Kentish recipient and/or (2) Palaeographical comparisons among the extant charter MSS reveal similarities of handwriting and thus allow charters of the same place [presumably Sweet means *produced* in the same place] and period to be grouped together as representative of a particular dialect (bracketed qualifications here are not original); (on these questions see also Campbell 1959: §§ 9, 14-15 and further below at Section 2.3).

Toon's second claim is made on the bases of (a) his supposition that the linguistic character of the charter data will, as a matter of course, be determined solely by socio-political factors and (b) the palaeographical (i.e., handwriting) evidence he reproduces (it should be noted that Toon sometimes misrepresents Kuhn's use of the terms *palaeography* and *palaeographical* by using them to mean 'orthography' and 'orthographical'—see, for instance, Toon's p. 71). It is that any occurrence of ‹o›, rather than ‹a›, in the relevant environment in Kentish texts (classified thus by Toon if they are associated in any way with Kentish matters) provides evidence not only for the chronological progression of the [ɒ] — [ɔ] sound change in *Mercian speech*, but also that 'Mercian political domination' *did* 'effect' *this* 'linguistic change in Kent', i.e., *Kentish speech* (cf. his pp. 118 and 212).

2.2 External historical evidence

2.2.1 Toon's attempt to explain the synchronic (and diatopic) ‹a› ~ ‹o› variation and its relation to Old English phonology in a way that is new, in its greater, closer reference to historical and palaeographical information than is found in e.g, Sweet (1885, 1888), Campbell (1959) or Hogg (MS.) (though cf. Hogg 1988), is certainly commendable. As Hogg (1988: 188) points out: 'by now we are all aware that dialectal divisions can correspond rather closely to political...divisions... . But students of Old English language have rarely bothered to investigate...[the] political structure [of Anglo-Saxon England]... . However, knowledge about the history and politics of Anglo-Saxon England is a sticking point — this will become evident below — as Colman (1988: 116) says, 'the term "reconstruction" [is] as applicable to our concepts of Anglo-Saxon society [as it is] to those of Old English language'.

2.2.2 Toon's case for a Mercian linguistic hegemony relies almost totally on the fact of Mercian political hegemony. His interpretation of the latter is that it was one of direct and constant rule and absolute, unopposed power (cf. his pp. 25-43). But, while the *fact* of Mercian political hegemony over southern England from c.725 to c.825 (spanning the reigns of the Mercian kings Æthelbald, Offa, Cenwulf/Cuthred, Ceolwulf and Beornwulf) is not in doubt, its details, as Stenton (1971: 236) points out, 'will always be uncertain' (cf. also his pp. 206 and 230 and Brooks 1984:113). If the historical details of the Mercian hegemony are in doubt to this extent, it follows that any possible social, cultural and linguistic effects attributable to it are even less certain.

Moreover, when the few known historical details of Mercian and Kentish political relations in particular are considered, Toon's interpretation of them can only be described as oversimplified and strained. The impression given by him of constant and direct rule of Kent by Mercia, especially during the reigns of Kings Æthelbald and Offa, is, for instance, contradicted by Æthelbald's apparent policy of minimal interference in the rule of the early-to-mid-eighth-century Kentish kings (cf. Brooks 1984: 111-2); by the seven- or eight-year break in Mercian control of Kent which was occasioned by the murder of Æthelbald in 757 and the consequent civil war in Mercia which allowed Kentish rule of Kent to be (temporarily) re-established (cf. Stenton 1971: 204-7), as well as by the two-year hiatus in Mercian rule in Kent which occurred after Eadberht Præn — a Kentish native — seized the Kentish throne on Offa's death in 796 (cf. Stenton 1971: 225; Brooks 1984: 114, 121).

Toon's notion that Mercian power in Kent was absolute and unopposed also has very little basis in (known) fact. Mercian influence and power were resented and resisted in Kent — not welcomed. This is suggested by events and factors like: the occurrence and outcome of the Battle of Otford in 776; the change in Offa's title in 'Kentish' (see 2.3.1 below) charters and coins minted for him in Kent, after c.785); Archbishop Jænberht's hostility towards Offa which necessitated Offa's establishing a controllable and dependably-loyal southern Archbishopric at Lichfield and, finally, the four-year dispute between Archbishop Wulfred (despite his apparently strong Mercian ties) and Cenwulf and Ceolwulf (cf. Stenton 1971: 207, 215-8, 226, 229-30 and Brooks 1984: 113; 119-20; 114-20; 134-6).

Toon's case for a Mercian political hegemony over Kent, certainly of the absolute kind which any possible corresponding and dependent linguistic hegemony would require, has therefore practically no external historical evidence to support it.

2.3 Palaeographical evidence

2.3.1 Kuhn's (1943) palaeographical evidence (cf. 2.1 above) is taken over and employed by Toon to further support his claim for a Mercian linguistic hegemony over native Kentish speakers in Kent. But the evidence itself, Toon's interpretation of it and the use to which he puts it are highly questionable.

Partly following Keller (1906: 20-21), Kuhn (1943: 464-6, 473, 458) associates three particular written forms of the letters, *g, t* and *ð*, which occur in charter MSS of roughly the first third of the ninth century, particularly those which were written during the reign of the Mercian King Coenwulf (798-823), with 'Mercian' (he does not specify whether 'Mercian' for him is a linguistic, geographical or even political designation). Kuhn's hypothesis that a correlation obtains between these three letter-forms and 'Mercian' rests on an assumption, shared also by Toon, that charters bearing the name of a Mercian King will of necessity be Mercian in linguistic or palaeographical character, or both. The historical evidence just put forward does not bear out this assumption. Nor does the evidence of the charters. The original and contemporary charter B326[1], MS. Cotton Augustus II.98, dated 808, which is not wholly atypical, suggests, in fact, that the circumstances surrounding the production of Old English charters were far from being as simple and straightforward as Kuhn, and Toon, suppose. It records a grant by King Coenwulf of Mercia to Eaduulf, his thegn, of land at Culingas (Cooling), Kent. This estate lay within the diocese of Rochester, rather than Canterbury, yet the wording of the charter follows Canterbury, rather than Rochester formulae (see below 2.3.2). According to Brooks (1984: 169-70) it was 'produced by a Canterbury clerk or...based upon a Canterbury model'. On the charter itself, however, is stated 'actum est in loco...quae a uulgo uocatur tomeþoroig...eodem die pascha', i.e., it was transacted on Easter Day at Tamworth, described by Toon (pp. 37-8) as 'the royal city' where 'Mercian kings held court at Christmas and Easter' (King Coenwulf was at Tamworth in 808 apparently — cf. Hill 1984: 83).

Given that the information obtainable from the charters themselves about the actual production of the charter MSS will often be as inconclusive, with regard to linguistic or geographical origin or political affiliation as this instance shows (cf. also 2.5.1.1 below) and given that the details of the process of recording all such transactions are vague (we do not know, for example, whether the Old English place- and personal-names contained in the MSS, were written down from dictation at the time or copied from previously-written archive documents or from an ad-hoc written source, say, a wax tablet engraved at the time of recording) it is doubtful whether charter MSS can be identified as 'Mercian' with the certitude taken for granted and relied upon by Kuhn (see e.g. p.476 of his 1943 paper) and, following him, Toon.

Underlying Kuhn's correlation of these three letter-forms with 'Mercian' is the further assumption that they are peculiar to 'Mercian' palaeography. The lack of a sufficient number of contemporary, original MSS, from the various different medieval cartularies of the major churches like Worcester, Rochester, Christ Church, Winchester, etc. means that there is too little scope for the kind of broad-ranging and inclusive palaeographical examination necessary before a correlation like Kuhn's can be made. Furthermore, the correlation manifestly cannot hold in the face of the following considerations: (1) The same *ð* letter-shape occurs also in the tenth-century Northumbrian MSS containing the glosses to the 'Lindisfarne Gospels' (Kuhn 1943: 465 acknowledges this and classifies the letter-form as 'Anglian *ð*'); (2) Of the charter MSS cited and used by Toon (pp. 67-70), not all those traditionally classified as 'Mercian' contain these three letter-forms. Indeed, seven out of the nine 'Mercian' charter MSS — B154, B187, B201, B203, B230, B416 and B452 — do not; (3) When these letter-forms *do* occur they are not confined exclusively to 'Mercian' MSS. So, in addition to the Northumbrian MSS just cited as containing 'Anglian *ð*', they appear, for instance, in the following MSS of charters traditionally classified as 'Kentish': B330, B332, B380 and in one — B536 — classified by Sweet (1885) as a 'Surrey' charter (on these charters, see further below).

Aside from the poor quality of Kuhn's palaeographical evidence, its paucity also is remarkable. It consists of only three letter-shapes. It is untypical for all of these to co-occur in the same MS, so when Toon in his charter list (pp. 67-70) places an asterisk before the 'charters in which Kuhn found evidence of the influence of Mercian Scriptoria' (p. 67) this 'influence' in the case of two-thirds of the MSS listed by Kuhn and used by Toon amounts to either only two letter-shapes (e.g. B318 which contains 'clear examples of Mercian *g* and *t*' (Kuhn 1943: 468); one clearly-written letter-shape (e.g. B274 which has 'clear examples of Mercian *g* [but only] doubtful or compromise *t*'s' (Kuhn 1943: 468); or only one letter-shape (e.g. B310 which has 'clear examples of Mercian *t*'(Kuhn 1943:468). Moreover, as Kuhn admits (1943:470) 'some of [the charter manuscripts in his list] contain very few clear examples [of those letter-shapes they do contain and] not one of these documents uses the letter-forms exclusively'. The 'Mercian *g*, *t*' and 'Anglian ð' letter-shapes are in fact only one variant in each case of three possible shapes for each of these letters (cf. Kuhn 1943: 470, 460-8).

There is therefore no persuasive argument to connect in theory or in practice, the limited occurrence of three (or two if 'Anglian ð' is excluded as being not strictly 'Mercian') letter-forms with 'Mercian' as Kuhn does. (See also Brooks 1984: 168 and n. 69).

2.3.2 A close scrutiny of the circumstantial evidence provided by the contents of the charters, together with a detailed, extensive examination of the palaeography of the individual MSS in which they are written, produces a rather different, and convincing, explanation for the appearance of these letter-forms. Brooks (1984: 169), by analysing the formulae of the extant, contemporary ninth-century charters, concludes that, no matter who the grantor of the land being granted was, or in which cartulary a particular charter was lodged after the Old English period, 'the location of the estate that was the subject of the grant was more important'. He found, too, that 'the significant distinctions [of formulae] follow diocesan, rather than political divisions'. Combining these two observations, he suggests that normally the Canterbury (Christ Church) scriptorium seems to have been responsible for the production of charters concerned with land in East Kent; Rochester with those in West Kent; Worcester with those in its diocese, etc. It is surely much more reasonable on the whole to link and attribute the writing of charter MSS with and to religious, rather than political centres and areas and to scribes trained in them. (It was in such religious scriptoria, after all, that literacy in Latin and Old English ultimately had its source and flourished). The evidence of formulae—formal, prescribed and largely standard expressions—and that deducible from the comparison and grouping together of their use in charter documents (the recognition of whose legality would almost certainly depend precisely upon a high degree of standardisation and adherence to precedent) form much more secure bases for inferences about the origin of charter MSS than the tenuous, unsupported hypotheses of Kuhn and Toon. They also provide welcome back-up for the fairly frequent statements in the charters of where a grant was *transacted* because these could refer, literally, to the place of transaction or agreement which need not necessarily accord with the time and place of the recording or writing-up of the grant.

Making use of such circumstantial evidence and informed, detailed palaeographical study of the MSS, Brooks (1984: 170, n. 76) identifies the MSS of the following charters as original and contemporary 'products of the Canterbury writing office': B162, B289, B332, B335, B341, B348, B370, B373, B378, B380, B384 (x2), B400, B536 (cf. Toon's charter MSS list, pp. 67-70). Evidence, in the form of formulae, the diocesan location of the land granted and information given by the charters (e.g., B330 which states that Wulfred, Archbishop of Canterbury 'recited and confirmed' the words and details of the charter, which grants land in East Kent to Christ Church, Canterbury, and is not a royal diploma, etc.) allows a further three charter MSS plausibly to be added to those listed above and identified by Brooks as deriving from the Canterbury scriptorium. These are B321, B318 and B330.

This list of charter MSS accounts for seventeen out of the twenty-one MSS described by Toon (pp. 67-70), after Kuhn, as containing the 'Mercian' letters. They span the period 798 to 835 (only one charter, B536, is later than this — see below). Brooks produces evidence (1984: 168, 170; 191-3) which suggests that the scribe who wrote three of these seventeen 'Mercian'-letter charters was Wulfred, Archdeacon at Christ Church, Canterbury, before becoming (cf. Brooks 1984: 132; 170-1) Archbishop of Canterbury from 805 to 831, *viz.* B162, B370 and B373. All three of these charter MSS contain all three of the distinctive letter-forms of *g, t* and *ð*. Wulfred himself seems to have been responsible for teaching Latin and for establishing the style of handwriting which was characteristic of the Canterbury scriptorium for about 40 years, from *c.*799 to 839. All of the seventeen charters, produced, according to Brooks, in the Canterbury scriptorium, which contain the distinctive letter-shapes were produced during Wulfred's time there. These letter-shapes disappear within four years of Wulfred's death in 831, with the exception of the one charter—B536—mentioned above, which is dated 873; the scribe who wrote this appears, however, to have been trained at Canterbury during Wulfred's terms of office there (cf. Brooks 1984: 168). When all of this evidence is brought together, it can, with justification, be concluded that the introduction and use of the three distinctive letter-forms are attributable to Archbishop Wulfred himself, i.e., that they were a peculiarity of Wulfred's own handwriting which was passed on to those scribes under his tuition and supervision at Canterbury. Kuhn (1943 : 480) believes that Wulfred was 'probably Kentish'. It is equally possible that he was a Middle Saxon; he may well have been Mercian (cf. Brooks 1984: 132; 197). Even if he were Mercian, however, the source of distinctive letter-forms can only rationally be ascribed to Wulfred personally and not to his Mercian origin. The factors enumerated above which count against a 'Mercian' derivation may be invoked again here. To these should be added the consideration that what Kuhn (1943: 480) calls 'the Mercian domination [between 731 and 764 and, with gaps, between 792 and 805]...built up by [the Archbishops of Canterbury] Tatwine, Nothhelm, Cuthberht, Breguwine and Æthelheard [who were Mercian, though there is uncertainty in the cases of the last two — cf. Brooks 1984: 81;120]' at Christ Church (hence presumably also in its scriptorium) signally failed to produce these so-called 'Mercian' letter-forms.

2.3.3 Given, therefore, the poor quality and paucity of Kuhn's palaeographical evidence and the lack of any warrantable correlation between the letter-forms and 'Mercian', Toon's unhesitating and uncritical acceptance as fact of Kuhn's very dubious hypothesis, renders invalid and pointless Toon's attempt (pp. 71, 111) to show that a correspondence between the presence of these letter-forms and ‹o› spellings in charter MSS provides firm evidence to support his claim for a Mercian linguistic hegemony over native Kentish speakers in Kent (cf. also 2.5 and 3.1 - 3.5 below).

As a prerequisite to his claim, Toon takes for granted that at least two three-way correlations hold: (1) 'Mercian letter-forms' ~ ‹o› spellings ~ Mercian; (2) No 'Mercian letter-forms' ~ ‹a› spellings ~ Kentish (cf. his statement (p.110) relating to B254 and B339). Neither of these holds in view of the palaeographical evidence just put forward, but even if that were laid aside for the moment, his correlations still do not hold. His list (pp. 108-9) of twenty-nine charter MSS, with and without the letter-forms, presented along with the [ɑ]/- N(C) data they contain, includes five charters — B154, B187, B230, B201, B416—which have data with only ‹o› spellings and which, on the evidence of Worcester formulae, Worcester diocesan locations for the estates being granted and Worcester archival provenances, can only be regarded as Mercian in origin, but which, despite these Mercian 'credentials' have no 'Mercian letter-forms'. Further he cites (p. 110) two charter MSS in particular — B254 and B339 — which contain only ‹a› spellings (two examples in each), which have no 'Mercian letter-forms' and which, he alleges, are Kentish. The first charter, however, (a grant from King Offa to his thegn Osberht was translated at Chelsea and the second, according to the usual circumstantial evidence and to Campbell (1973: xiii-xxx *passim*; 20) is a Rochester charter (these, as noted above are different in many respects from Canterbury ones—Toon's 'Kentish' label is too all-inclusive). The remainder of the charters, traditionally described as 'Kentish', 'Mercian-Kentish' and 'Mercian', which have no 'Mercian letter-forms'—five of them: B312, B319, B326, B343, B452—use a mix of ‹a› and ‹o› spellings in the relevant data. Finally, the remaining seventeen charters, all of which contain, according to Toon, the 'Mercian letter-forms' also do not agree with his correlations. Only six—B274, B289, B293, B341, B348 and B400—use ‹o› spellings exclusively in what little [ɑ] /-N (C) data they contain; the other eleven use ‹a›, as well as ‹o›.

2.4 Toon's selection and handling of data

2.4.1 Hogg (1988: 190) puts forward two 'rules' concerning the interpretation of data available in eOE MSS 'Firstly, have respect for scribes [of Old English] and the data they present us with; secondly, make sure that the linguistic analyses we reach have some plausibility'. On the latter rule, see 2.5 below; the former, in connection with data and Toon's treatment of them will now be discussed.

2.4.2 Not only are Toon's palaeographical ~ spelling data ~ dialect correlations spurious, but his selection and handling of the [ɑ] /-N(C) data are, in some cases, linguistically inexact and inept. So, for example, from six charters (B330, B332, B348, B378, B384 and B536) he selects the preposition 'on, in', spelt ‹on›, and from one (B330), he selects the adverbial form spelt ⟨hwonne⟩, 'when', to use as evidence for his postulated [ɑ] → [ɔ] /-N(C) development in Mercian, and thence, by Mercian influence, in Kentish. Campbell (1959: §333), however, describes *on* and *hwonne* as two of 'a group of words generally used in low sentence stress [in which the graph] *o* appears'; he continues, 'spellings with *a* are rare'. Indeed they are so rare that Bosworth and Toller (1898: 744-6) list only five instances where *on* appears in MSS spelt with ⟨a⟩ rather than ⟨o⟩. Considering that the examples cited by Toon are spelt exactly as would be expected in all dialects of Old English, it is hard to see how they provide evidence for his theory.

Apart from the fact that Toon uses place-names as linguistic data without taking into account that proper names of a language may function linguistically, certainly phonologically, differently from common words (cf. Colman 1988; Lass 1973), his handling of such data is objectionable in other ways. Take, for instance, the place-name variously spelt — as Toon cites it (p. 109) — ⟨grafonaea⟩ (B335), ⟨grafoneah⟩ (B341 and B348). This corresponds to Present-day English *Graveney* in Kent (see Ekwall 1940: 194). Although Toon does not say explicitly that he is concerned with the reflex of Pre Old English [ɑ] /-N(C) only in stressed syllables, this can only be the case for two reasons: the nasalizing and/or rounding development, where it did occur, was, it seems, confined to stressed syllables (cf. Campbell 1959: §§333; 377, 380 — though further research is needed on the ⟨on⟩/⟨an⟩ variation in inflectional syllables); Toon does not present as data in his lists (pp. 108-9) forms to be found in the MSS of the charters cited by him on these pages which contain the reflex of the Pre Old English vowel in unstressed syllables, e.g ⟨offan⟩, an inflected form of the personal-name *Offa* (B187), or ⟨...to ðære cirican saldon⟩ 'to the church gave' (B330). Yet the ⟨o⟩/-⟨n⟩ spellings in the place-name cited above appear to represent an *un*stressed vowel. This is suggested by (1) The forms as they are actually written in the MSS Toon presents these as compounds, but in the case of the B335 form, another—uncompounded—version of the name—⟨grafon aea⟩—occurs in the same MS; in the case of the B341 and B348 forms, separate words—⟨grafon eah⟩—are written in the MSS and, further, the name is repeated in both MSS as two separate words: ⟨grafon aea⟩ (B341) and ⟨grafon ęa⟩ (B348). The MS representation agrees with and supports Wallenberg's etymology for the place-name: *grafan* 'to dig, cut, carve' (cf. Go, OHG *graban*) + *ēa* 'river' (1931: 117). It can be seen then that ⟨o⟩ in these forms of the name occurs in unstressed vowel position and represents the reflex of an originally unstressed vowel; (2) 1OE/eME (eleventh-century) orthographic renderings of this name, e.g. ⟨gravanea⟩, ⟨grafene(a)⟩ (cf. Wallenberg 1931: 117). The variation in spelling and the use of the graph ⟨e⟩ in particular, point to the confusion and coalescence in an unspecified vowel ([ə]?) of the unstressed back vowels in the eleventh century (cf. Campbell 1959: §§377-8). Again, therefore, these data are disqualified as evidence for Toon's thesis.

Two more place-names cited by Toon—⟨hegeðonhyrs⟩ and ⟨sponleoge⟩ (B343)—whose ⟨o⟩/-⟨n⟩ spellings are supposed to represent the reflex of PreOE [ɑ] /-N in fact do not. Wallenberg (1931: 173 ff) gives the following etymologies for these names, respectively—*hæg* + *ðorn* + *hyrst*, 'haw' + 'thorn' + 'hurst'; *spōn* +

lēah 'chip, shaving' + 'lea'. ⟨o⟩ in the first name therefore represents [o], the reflex of Gmc [o], OHG *dorn*, ON *þorn*, and in the second, [o:], derived from Gmc [æ:] /-N, cf. OHG *spān*, OFr *spōn*, etc. (and see Campbell 1959: §127) — these forms should not therefore be included among Toon's data.

The place-name element spelt ⟨homm(e)⟩ (e.g. ⟨iognes homme⟩ in B384) or ⟨homm⟩ (e.g. ⟨colanhomm⟩ in B400) is linguistically dubious as, according to Ekwall (1940: 203-4), it could derive from either *ham(m)* (with etymological [ɑ] /-N or *hām* (with etymological [ɑ:]). These two forms, then, provide only questionable evidence for Toon's argument. Furthermore, if the element *does* derive from *hām*, ⟨o⟩ is most unlikely.

Other forms containing ⟨o⟩ spellings in Toon's list of data can be satisfactorily explained otherwise. The ⟨o⟩ graph in ⟨noman⟩, for instance, found in B452 and B536, could conceivably have been written due to confusion with the Latin root *nom-*, present in almost every charter using Latin formulae at this period, e.g...*ubi nominatur*...(B274, B162, B199, B370, etc.), or *nomen, nominant, nomen est* (B154). Near-contemporary analogies for this phenomenon exist. Sweet (1885: 187) states, for example, that 'a frequent source of error' on the part of the 'Vespasian Psalter' glossator, who too was working backwards and forwards from Latin to Old English, 'is the repetition of part of the corresponding Latin word in the gloss...sometimes the whole of the Latin word is repeated as in *nomen : nomen*'. Kuhn (1943: 467) also speaks of the possibility of such interference from Latin spelling.

Finally, the ⟨o⟩ spellings (found alongside some ⟨a⟩ spellings) in the words *lond* and *mon(n)*—in their root forms, as here, or as an element in compound nouns like *aldormonn* (B330), *bōclonde* (B384), or place-names, e.g. *babinglond* (B332) and personal-names, e.g. *dudemon* (B321)—make up the largest proportion of Toon's ⟨o⟩-spelling data. These *land* and *man* type words and *and* occur again and again in the charters. It is not outwith the bounds of possibility that the process of standardisation due to the copying of archival exemplars noted above as characterising the appearance of formulae, should extend also to the spelling of these lexical items. The fact that they recur so often and the probable influence of previously-recorded forms of these words, especially as elements in names (cf. earlier in this section), make these words strong contenders for orthographic standardisation. If, then, the use of ⟨o⟩ in the *land, man* etc. forms is attributable to a spelling habit, and the appearance of ⟨o⟩ in *nomen* is ascribable to the influence of Latin spelling, these data give no support to Toon's proposition.

2.5 The Labovian framework, Old English written data and Old English phonology

Old English written data in themselves mean nothing; it is only in the light of a theory (or theories) which inform(s) and guide(s) selection and interpretation of them that they potentially become, and can function as, evidence for Old English phonology (cf. Lass 1980: ch. 2: Appendix; Romaine 1982: 3-4, 274-5; Colman 1988: 113).

2.5.1 Toon's theoretical approach (already described at 2.1 above) to the pre-tenth-century spelling variation in Old English MSS is essentially a Labovian one. Various problems attend the workings and notions of Labovian variationist theory generally (see Romaine 1982: Chs. 8, 9, especially pp. 234-5, 244, 246-7, 262-3, 266-7 and §§9.2 to 9.2.3). Apart from these, however, Toon's approach is surely inapplicable to Old English written data because (a) he conflates socio-linguistic variation and linguistic variation in general (from a non-societal point of view, as in lexical diffusion studies) and (b) as Lass (1976: 225-6) points out:

> The utility of variation theory decreases sharply the further back we go in time [because its] methodology requires two kinds of material: quantifiable low-level data, and a set of parameters (social, stylistic) against which variation can be plotted, and directionalities uncovered, etc.

The requisite set of parameters is not available to us because we are dealing, particularly in the case of Old English written data, with what Lass (1976: 226) describes as 'monostylistic', 'formal' documentary material produced by a 'single class' in a culture with 'minority literacy' (cf. also, e.g., Hogg 1988). Neither is the first type of material available to us — we have no access to spoken Old English. MSS containing written data cannot be considered, as they are by Toon (p. 66) to be 'informants' in the Labovian sense. As our primary means of access (along with other written or epigraphic sources like coin- or rune-spellings) to Old English phonology, the question of how they are interpreted — in particular how the relationship between spelling and phonology is viewed — is crucial (cf. King 1988: 161).

2.5.1.1 Toon attempts (understandably?) to circumvent the obstacle we face in having no access to speakers of Old English by asserting in a virtual re-statement of Luick's 'man schrieb wie man sprach', that scribes wrote practically as they spoke: 'a scribe's habits are motivated by surface phonetic forms' and 'scribes (unconsciously) recorded their phonetic habits' (pp. 210-11). Even if this were true (cf. 3 below), Toon's attempt would founder because (a) The *sine qua non* of his assertion is the possession of precisely that knowledge we lack, viz., information about who the scribes were (in most cases); which diatopic variety/varieties of Old English they spoke, or were familiar with (or even *if* they spoke Old English[3]); whether or not, depending upon the age of the scribe, he was a conservative or advanced speaker of this variety or these varieties; how representative scribes were of the 'speech community' to which they belonged (cf. *2.5.1* above and references therein to Romaine 1982), etc, etc; and (b) The written data in Old English MSS cannot, as Labovian variationist theory requires, (cf., for example, Romaine 1982: 246-7) be located precisely in place or time. Toon himself admits (p. 196) 'we cannot know the exact geographical provenience [*sic*] of most manuscripts'. Even if we did, as Colman (1988: 112) says, 'the provenance of the manuscript is not evidence that the language represented therein reflects the dialect spoken in that particular area...'. The dating of MSS is also often uncertain. Beside texts like either the 'Moore' or 'Leningrad' 'Cædmon's

Hymn' which can be dated fairly precisely to *c.*737 on the external evidence of the genealogical and chronological notes appended to the end of both MSS, are others like the Corpus Christi College, Cambridge MS 144 of the 'Corpus Glossary', whose date has been disputed. Toon, for instance (pp.72 — 7 and p.206) gives the chronology (1) 'Épinal' *c.*700; (2) 'Erfurt' *c.*750; (3) 'Corpus' *c.*800, and bases his argument on this for the progression of his postulated sound change. Hessels (1906: ix) thought 'Corpus' must have been written in the early part of the eighth century (this would place it somewhere between 'Épinal' and 'Erfurt' according to Toon's dating of these two texts) and Campbell (1959: §112) suggests that, although 'Corpus' usually has later forms that 'Épinal' and 'Erfurt', it would appear, nevertheless, to be the oldest MS (this would place it before 'Epinal' and 'Erfurt'). Sweet (1885: 5), on palaeographical grounds, dated 'Corpus' to 'not later than the first half of the eighth century' (this would make it roughly contemporary with 'Erfurt'). Chadwick (1894-99: 249) (circularly) argues that the linguistic forms of 'Corpus' point to a date at the end of the eighth or the beginning of the ninth century. (Of the four suggested datings, this one alone would allow Toon to place 'Corpus' after both 'Épinal' and 'Erfurt' and so allow him to use it as evidence for the chronological progression of the sound change he puts forward.)

2.5.1.2 Toon's interpretation of the relationship between spelling and phonology (cf. *2.5.1* and *2.5.1.1*) in the Old English MSS he examines depends on the naïve and dubious supposition that Old English spelling accurately, directly and always reflected Old English pronunciation, i.e., that Old English spelling was allophonic. Even if we knew how and with what linguistic output the basic inventory of Old English phonemes was transformed in articulation and transmission into actually-realised, or pronounced, sound-segments, the available written evidence suggests strongly that (1) The orthographic and phonological systems of Old English operated partially independently of each other; (2) The orthographic system of Old English operated at a fundamentally phonemic level; (3) Old English spelling variation did not always correspond with, or reflect, Old English phonological change; and (4) Phonological change was not necessarily represented in Old English orthography. Evidence for each of these claims will now be put forward.

3. Old English Spelling and Old English Phonology

3.1

The partially-autonomous nature of the Old English orthographic system is demonstrated by, for instance, written forms like *sēcean* 'to seek' and *gear* 'year' in which, as Colman (1985: §4) suggests, the ‹e› graph following the graph representing a palatal consonant (‹c› : /tʃ/ in the first form and ‹g› : /j/ in the second) in each case most credibly functions as a diacritic to indicate the palatality of the preceding consonant (cf. also Campbell 1959: §45; Penzl 1947: §§1.4, 1.7, 3.3; Lass and Anderson 1975: 280 and references).

3.2

The claim that the Old English orthographic system functioned with regard to the representation of phonological units at an essentially phonemic level is supported by the consideration that:

> ...people possess what...[EDWARD SAPIR]...called 'phonemic intuitions', which come into action as soon as they begin attempting to write their own languages alphabetically...[I]t is natural that in their early attempts at representing their languages by means of an alphabet men should write them phonemically. (Jones 1967: 253).

Recent experimental evidence confirms the linguistic reality for speakers (certainly of Present-day English) of the phoneme as the principal 'overt, conceptual unit [of sound]' (Derwing *et al.* (1986: 63-4)).

The likelihood of this consideration applying in the writing of Old English is strengthened by the following factor: the spelling system used for writing Old English was an adoption and adaptation of the Roman-letter-based one already established and in use for writing Latin. Allen (1965: 9) observes of the latter system that it 'comes very near to being completely phonemic'.

In practice, written data bear out these expectations that Old English spelling will, by and large, represent only the most significant/distinctive phonic segments, i.e., phonemes. So, as a very basic instance of this, the use can be cited of two different graphs ⟨d⟩ and ⟨þ⟩ in the following examples, where the graphs are commutable word-initially, -medially and -finally, and are obviously capable of signalling a difference in meaning, indicating that the use of differing graphs is intended to represent in spelling a phonemic difference - ⟨d⟩ : /d/ ≠ ⟨þ⟩ : /t/ :

⟨dūn⟩ 'hill'	≠	⟨tūn⟩ 'enclosure, farm'
⟨lǣdan⟩ 'to lead'	≠	⟨lǣtan⟩ 'to let'
⟨bād⟩ 'he/she/it waited'	≠	⟨bāþ⟩ 'he/she/it bit'

Moreover, a primarily phonemic basis for Old English spelling seems only reasonable when the practical difficulties attending a fundamentally phonetic spelling system are borne in mind, *viz.*, a much larger inventory of graphs and graphic devices than was available (or employed) for writing Old English would have been necessary in order to represent even major allophonic differences (such as that between [ɑ] and [æ], cf. Colman 1983). A phonetic spelling system like this, apart from being cumbersome and impracticable to use would also nullify the communicative function of MSS, since it would render their contents virtually inaccessible to anyone other than the scribes who wrote them. Furthermore, if Old English spelling did operate at a phonetic level, the MS data we have would, overall, show much less regularity and stability of graphic usage than are to be found.

3.3

The use of two different graphs ⟨ð⟩ and ⟨þ⟩ (though the latter was diachronically and diatopically restricted, cf. Blomfield (1935: 95)) for the most part in free variation where they do co-occur, to represent the dental fricative, or ⟨u(u)⟩ or ⟨ƿ⟩ ('wynn') for [w], cf. Campbell (1959: §§57.6, 60) provide evidence to support the claim made above that Old English spelling variation did not always correspond with, or reflect Old English phonological change. These instances of diachronic spelling variation operate only at the level of orthography, as does that of the replacement of the eOE trigraph ⟨aea⟩ by ⟨ea⟩ (Lass and Anderson 1975: 280; Stockwell and Barritt 1951: 16).

3.4

Absence of diachronic alteration in Old English graphic representation does not necessarily signify absence of Old English phonological change. The graph ⟨c⟩, for instance, remained in use throughout the Old English period, despite the fact that the Pre Old English velar /k/ it originally represented developed various reflexes, i.e. [k]: ⟨c⟩ in ⟨cuman⟩ 'to come', [k']: ⟨c⟩ in ⟨bæc⟩, [tʃ]: ⟨c⟩ in ⟨cirice⟩ 'church', (Campbell 1959: §§426-9; Hogg 1979; Penzl 1947 and references therein).

3.5

From the evidence just presented, it must be concluded that Toon's interpretation of the relationship between Old English spelling and phonology is not acceptable—he ignores the autonomous orthographic aspect and, in effect, denies system to Old English spelling *qua* system. Since Old English orthography does not merely reflect Old English pronunciation, it follows, then, that Toon's reading of the ⟨a⟩ ~ ⟨o⟩ /- ⟨ $\left\{ \begin{array}{c} m \\ n \end{array} \right\}$ (C)⟩ data — the result of an over-literal interpretation of spelling forms — as marking in writing the progress of a contemporary, corresponding sound change is contentious.

4. Old English Spelling and Old English Sound Change

To the remarks made and discussions presented on this question already should be added the logical consideration, expressed succinctly by Colman and Anderson (1983: 169) that 'spelling is always later in representing a sound change than the sound change itself'; if familiar, established spellings are going to be changed to make them correspond to the result(s) of a sound change, there would be no point in changing them until after the sound change had occurred, or was in the process of occurring, at least. The question then arises of how the occurrence of sound changes is indicated synchronically in spelling.

4.1.1 The usual pattern, certainly for Old English, is that after the occurrence of a sound change, a period of synchronic orthographic variation ensues, which is succeeded by a settling-down into use of a different graph (or graphs) to represent the new segment (or segments)—at least if the sound change is a phonemic one and its output is lexicalised, cf. Weinreich *et al.* (1968: 187). This pattern is exemplified by the Old English unstressed front vowels which were, in the early eighth century apparently still distinct, but which, by the end of that century had, with the exception of [i]: ⟨i⟩ in derivational suffixes like those represented by ⟨-ig⟩, ⟨-isc⟩, ⟨-ing⟩, etc. merged in the indistinct vowel [ə]: ⟨e⟩ cf. Campbell (1959: §§369, 371). The originally distinct vowel-graph spellings ⟨æ⟩, ⟨e⟩ and ⟨i⟩ gave way to orthographic free variation as a result of the change occurring, ⟨æ⟩ appearing for original ⟨e⟩, ⟨e⟩ appearing for original ⟨i⟩, etc, and were finally replaced (except for ⟨i⟩ in the suffixes mentioned above) by the different vowel graph ⟨e⟩ when the merger had been phonemicised/lexicalised.

4.1.2. The appearance of back spellings is also a sure indication that a sound change has been completed, whether or not it is a phonemic one: the case of the spellings of the Kentish long and short front stressed vowels in the ninth century may here be cited, cf. Campbell 1959: §§288 - 292; Anderson 1988a): ⟨æ⟩ and ⟨y⟩ appearing where ⟨e⟩ would be expected as in ⟨wær⟩ for expected ⟨wer⟩ 'man', or ⟨byrene⟩ for ⟨berene⟩ 'of a/the she-bear'.

4.2

When Toon's ⟨a⟩ ~ ⟨o⟩ /- ⟨ $\left\{\begin{smallmatrix} m \\ n \end{smallmatrix}\right\}$ (C) ⟩ spelling data are examined (pp. 98-110), especially those from the charters (pp. 108-9), what emerges is a pattern of fluctuation of the ⟨a⟩ ~ ⟨o⟩ spellings, but one which involves temporal and/or locative co-occurrence. Moreover, the use of ⟨a⟩ in the pre-tenth-century period never dies out completely, except in the gloss to the 'Vespasian Psalter', dated by Toon (p. 80) to the 'first part of the ninth century' and in which, according to him (p. 107) only ⟨o⟩ is used in the relevant context. Even in this MS, however, ⟨a⟩ *does* appear in loanwords from Latin, cf. Hogg (MS §5.4) for example, *plant* 'plant' (cf. Latin *planta*), *geplantades* x 2 '(you) planted' (cf. Latin *plantasti*), or *organan* 'musical instrument' (cf. Latin *organum*), etc. The native Old English inflexions on *geplantades* and *organan* — a Verb of Weak Class 2, 2nd Sg Pret Ind and Weak Noun Plu respectively — suggest that these words had been assimilated into at least the Old English grammatical system and therefore, in all probability, into the phonological system too (cf. Fisiak 1968: 42). If Toon's sound change was, as he insists, all-pervasive and 'completed [by] AD...845' (p. 110) by which time the 'Vespasian' gloss, including these lexical items, would have been written, according to Toon's dating, surely [ɑ] in these words (regardless of whether native or loan stress placement is assumed, since Toon includes—cf. 2.4.2 above — unstressed vowel data in his discussion) would automatically, because of the /-N context, have been affected by the sound change producing Toon's [ɔ] and would, therefore, if Toon's correlation [ɔ]: ⟨o⟩ is correct, be expected to be spelt with the

⟨o⟩ graph? Yet the graph ⟨a⟩, rather than ⟨o⟩, appears /- ⟨n(C)⟩ to represent the non-high back vowel. (These ⟨a⟩ spellings could, however, just conceivably be analogical, cf. 5.1).

Middle English (ME) evidence shows that, of the geographical areas subject in the Old English period to Mercian political control, in only one is this ⟨a⟩ ~ ⟨o⟩ variation followed by a complete, constant change of graph to ⟨o⟩, as Toon's claim of a 'completed' sound change requires (cf. Weinreich *et al.*), 1968: 187; Campbell 1959: §130); Hogg MS: § 5.5; Prins 1974 : § 3.7, p 241 and Strang 1970 : §159). The additional fact that in all areas, apart from this West Midlands one, the reflex of eOE [ɑ] /-N merged in ME with /a/ and not /o/—cf. Kuhn (1961: §3.3); Hogg (MS: §5.5)—as would be expected from Toon's suggested sound change output [ɔ], further argues against a phonemic, lexicalised sound change having occurred (this would have involved the [ɔ] output being identified, and merging, with the reflex of Pre Old English /o/, developing thence to /o/ in ME).

Although Toon is inexplicit about the phonological status of the segments involved in his posited sound change, his statements about it being 'completed' are based upon what he interprets as a change to use of the ⟨o⟩ graph and they thus involve lexicalisation. These factors suggest that he believes the sound change [ɒ] → [ɔ] /-N to have been a phonemic one, as Sweet (1888) also seems to do. (it should be noted that Toon's output value seems an unlikely one, as Hogg 1982 shows). Because spelling variation of the kind here being discussed cannot reasonably be interpreted as mirroring the chronological progress of a sound change as it happens and because the notion that this is a phonemic sound change resulting in lexicalisation can be applied to only one area or original Mercian territory, Toon's suggested sound change cannot be accepted (cf. also 5.2 below).

5 Let's Call the Whole Thing Off?

An explanation, if there is one, must therefore be sought in some of the options either rejected by Toon, or not considered by him. Various alternatives are available to account for the ⟨a⟩ ~ ⟨o⟩ spelling fluctuation.

5.1 Analogy

One of these is analogy. 'The operation of analogy can result in variation in [the] spelling of... a particular sound; and it is not always clear whether the analogy is one based on phonology or spelling' (Colman and Anderson 1983: 169). Analogy based on Latin spelling is certainly an acceptable explanation for the ⟨o⟩ spellings which occur among Toon's data from the Latin ~ Old English charters (cf. 2.4.2). Spelling analogy would explain only a few of the forms with ⟨o⟩ graphs, however.

5.2 Non-phonemic sound change

A second, more productive, explanation is that a non-phonemic sound change, Pro

Gmc /a/ → Pre Old English [ã] → eOE $\left[\left\{\begin{array}{c}\tilde{a}\\ \tilde{\textrm{o}}\end{array}\right\}\right]$ /-N, occured. The change would necessarily be phonetic because the conditioning context, a following N [m, n, ŋ], remains, i.e., the newly-developed phone(s) is /are (an) allophone(s) or the original phoneme. But, 'as long as the context for a sound change is maintained, the spelling need not alter' (Colman and Anderson 1983: 169) — consider, e.g., the Pre Old English voicing of the originally voiceless fricatives [f], [θ], [s] in voiced contexts and their orthographic representation, (cf. Campbell 1959: §444; Anderson 1988 (b) especially §2).

The *man*, *hand*, etc. forms, despite the retention of the conditioning environment, are, however, characterised by spelling variation. If a phonetic sound change were involved, the graph ‹a› could reasonably be expected to remain unchanged (cf. also 3.2 above). On the other hand, the opinions held by Campbell, Kuhn and Hogg (cf. 1.1 above) agree with the suggestion here of a phonetic sound change. If what Lass and Anderson say (cf. 1.1) is considered, in conjunction with the implications of Sweet's (cf. 1.1) and Hogg's comments on the ‹a› ~ ‹o› alternation, a reasonable compromise can be reached whereby the idea of a phonetic sound change having operated is acceptable and the spelling variation is explicable in terms of its output. An output of a low, back, rounded allophone (ɒ) of eOE /a/ /-N would, to paraphrase Sweet's words, lie between [ɑ] and [o]; it would combine the [+ back] and [- high] features of both [ɑ] and [o] with the [+ round] feature of [o] and could therefore be identified by scribes with either the sound value [o] — resulting in the use of the relevant graph ‹o› — or with [ɑ] — resulting in the use of <a>. An output which alternated synchronically between, or consisted of (at least) two sub-phonemic variants, say [ɑ] and [ɒ] in free variation (i.e., either could be substituted for the other /-N without producing a difference in meaning) would for the same reasons, and from the consideration that Old English spelling was, on occasion, allophonic (cf. Colman 1983), be liable to be spelt either with ‹a› or ‹o›. Furthermore, uncertainty over how to spell the reflex of Gmc /a/ /-N would perhaps be expected anyway, given the frequent instability of vowels in the low, back area of the vowel space, cf. Anderson and Ewen (1987: ch. 6). As Davidsen-Nielsen (1984: 15-6) points out, in Old English 'before nasals there is never more than a two-way contrast between high and non-high vowels'. So, with the back vowels, if the vowel graph appearing before ‹ $\left\{\begin{array}{c}m\\ n\end{array}\right\}$ (C) › is not ‹u› representing the high vowel, it is in theory unimportant whether ‹a› or ‹o› appears, or even both in the same MS, because the signification of either graph must be a non-high, rather than a high, vowel.

Either ‹a› or ‹o› could predominate depending upon two things: (1) Possibly upon the influence of individual scribes' phonetic realisations in speech (or dictators' if the MS in question were dictated as, for instance, the Old English content of some charters may reasonably be assumed to have been) — though it would be a mistake to suppose, as Toon does, that these are always, or even usually, what is represented by the spelling variation; or (2) More probably, merely scribes' spelling preferences or habits. This is suggested by, for example, the uniform use of ⟨a⟩ in the relevant context in the 'Épinal Glossary'—see Pheifer (1974: §37) and by the post-tenth-century overall stabilisation of the spelling of the reflex(es) of Gmc /a/ /-N. This regularisation was geographically, rather than phonologically, determined, ⟨a⟩ was the usually-favoured graph in the South, ⟨o⟩ in the North, despite the fact that in Nb, in the lOE/eME period, the reflex(es) merged with other instances of lOE [ɑ] and not [o] (as the earlier use of the ⟨o⟩ graph would suggest, cf. Hogg MS: §5.5; Campbell 1959: §130, n.2). Besides this, it is odd that the spelling was regularised when the phonetic variability, or indeterminacy with regard to height and roundedness, can fairly be assumed to have continued because of the retention and influence of the nasal environment. Moreover, the orthographic regularisation involved the diatopic, synchronic use of two graphic constants and not one only: this does not favour the idea of a concomitant phonological regularisation. These factors suggest that the orthographic regularisation was the result of a conscious scribal decision to opt for, and standardise the use of, either ⟨a⟩ or ⟨o⟩ as the graph representing the reflex(es) of Gmc /a/ /-N.

5.3 Neutralisation

A third explanation for the spelling alternation, perhaps the most attractive because it is credible in relation to Old English spelling practice and phonological plausibility (cf. Hogg 1988: 190) and it accommodates both variability and systematicity, is that the spelling variation arises from, and reflects, phonological neutralisation of the contrast between /ɑ/ and /o/ in the environment of a following N (on neutralisation see, for example, Lass 1984: ch. 3), thus:

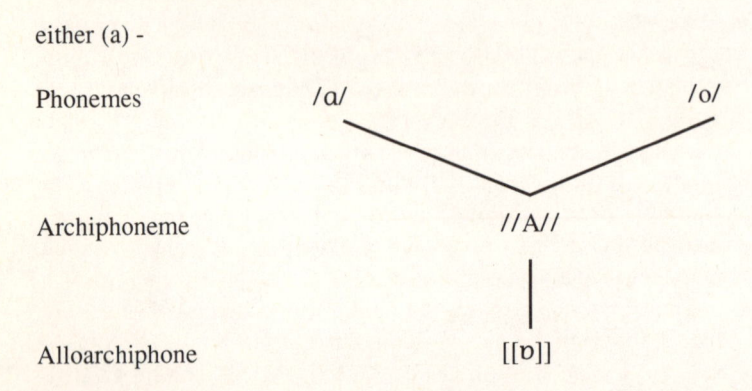

either (a) -

Phonemes   /ɑ/   /o/

Archiphoneme   //A//

Alloarchiphone   [[ɒ]]

or (b) -

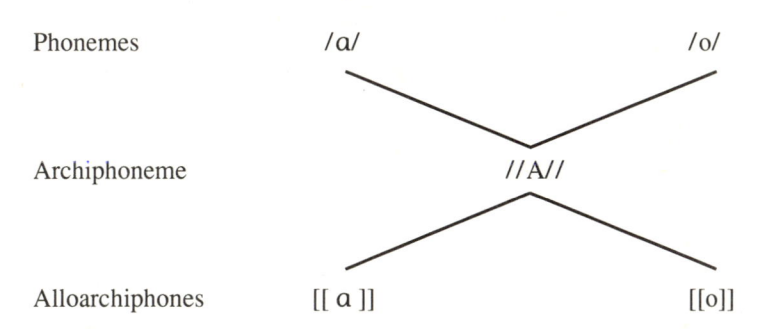

Phonemes	/ɑ/		/o/
Archiphoneme		//A//	
Alloarchiphones	[[ɑ]]		[[o]]

In a neutralisation of type (a)—cf. Lass (1984: 50), neither member of the opposition /ɑ/ ≠ /o/ appears as the alloarchiphone [my own term and notation[4] for the realisation or product of neutralisation], but instead a third, non-phonemic segment [[ɒ]] sharing properties of the others, *viz.*, lowness with /ɑ/, roundness with /o/ and backness with both. The alloarchiphone is, therefore, the product of the neutralisation /-N(C) of the feature contrasts *mid* vs. *low* and *rounded* vs. *unrounded*. Neutralisation in this context is proposed also by Davidsen-Nielson (1984), although he describes it in terms only of suspension of the height contrast. The alloarchiphone could therefore be represented by either of the two graphs available to represent non-high, back vowels in the spelling: ‹o›, capturing specifically the feature [+ round] usually associated in Old English spelling with [+mid] and both ‹a› and ‹o›, the features [- high, + back], ‹a› being especially indicative of [- high].

In a neutralisation of type (b), either member of the phonemic opposition /ɑ/ ≠ /o/ can appear indifferently, without producing a difference in meaning in the neutralising /-N(C) environment. It therefore yields two alloarchiphones [[ɑ]] and [[o]] which vary with each other. The situation of neutralisation envisaged here would perhaps explain why both graphs ‹a› and ‹o› could be used to represent its products. This usage possibly derives from, or at least mirrors, that found elsewhere in Old English to represent two vowels which are contrastive as in, e.g. the minimal pairs (both Weak Class 2 Verb Infinitives): *lafian* 'to lave, bathe' ≠ *lofian* 'to praise' where the contrast /ɑ/:‹ a› ≠ /o/: ‹o› is illustrated. This means that, even though in words of the *man, hand* class where [[ɑ]] and [[o]] do not contrast since both occur /-N(C), because these sound values serve to distinguish meaning elsewhere as in words like *lafian* and *lofian*, they are recognisable and naturally identifiable or able to be correlated with the phonemes /ɑ/ and /o/. The alloarchiphones are accordingly treated orthographically in the same way as the sound values [ɑ] and [o] which are elsewhere phonemic, by being written with either of the two separate, distinct graphs ‹a› and ‹o› depending on the alloarchiphone produced by the neutralisation.

If neutralisation is accepted as the explanation for the pre-tenth-century spelling variation, the orthographic stabilisation which followed could accordingly reasonably be seen as a resolution of the neutralisation in favour of /o/: ‹o› in the

ME West Midlands and Northern areas and /ɑ/: ⟨a⟩ elsewhere.

5.4 Conclusion

Consideration of the synchronic spelling variation manifested in pre-tenth-century forms of *man, hand*-type words has, first of all, shown that it is susceptible of a number of interpretations as to the corresponding synchronic phonological (or non-phonological) variation it reflects. It has, secondly, revealed the kinds of possible phonological (and non-phonological) variation that orthographic variation synchronic with it can indicate. These are:

(a) The output of previous phonemic sound change (cf. 4.2);
(b) Phonological or spelling analogy, or both (cf. 5.1);
(c) The output of non-phonemic sound change (cf. 5.2)—though diachronic (later and any extant earlier) spelling evidence would, strictly, also have to be taken into account before the phonological status of such sound changes could be determined. This consideration might also apply to (a); (cf. 3.4);
(d) Synchronic sub-phonemic variation or synchronic phonological indeterminacy, coupled with inadequate orthographic resources (cf. 5.2);
(e) Contemporary variations in pronunciation arising from politico-/sociolinguistic influence bringing about variable-rule-governed lexical diffusion of the output of a phonemic sound change (Toon's interpretation—cf. above *passim*);
(f) Phonological neutralisation in a given phonetic environment of a contrast phonemic elsewhere.

Of these possibilities, only (b) [applicable in some cases only though], (c), (d) and (f) are acceptable explanations of this particular instance of spelling variation in that the linguistic viewpoints informing them are in keeping with what is reasonably surmisable about Old English phonology, both from the point - of - view of appropriate linguistic theory (or theories) and of what can credibly be deduced about Old English spelling and MS-writing practice from the Old English written data considered here.

NOTES

*For Big Murn and wee Minnie.

1. Charter MSS are here and throughout referred to by their listing number in Birch (1885-89), hence B154, e.g., means the charter so numbered by, and in, Birch; cf. also Toon (1983: 66-70) and cross-references there to Sweet (1885) and Kuhn (1943).
2. It should be noted that Toon prefixes an asterisk in his citation of B416 and B452 (his p.109) to indicate that the MSS they are written in contain 'Mercian letter-forms'; these MSS do not, in fact, have these letter-shapes—cf. Kuhn (1943: 478-9, n. 2). Since they have been included in the discussion just above, they will not be mentioned further here.

3. This is a pertinent question given that we have Old English data in, e.g. the 'Erfurt Glossary' (MS. Amplonianus F.42 in Erfurt Stadtbücherei) which was written by an 'Old High German scribe (who was) himself ignorant of Old English' (Toon p. 73) and who 'consistently makes errors that could not be made by a speaker of Old English' (Toon p.100); on these 'errors' see Sweet (1885: 3-4). Toon, incidentally, uses data from this MS as evidence for his posited Mercian and Kentish sound change and its chronological progression.

4. But see Anderson (1985) and cf. the suggestion—*archiallophone*—put forward by Roger Lass (personal communication). I am very grateful to both him and Fran Colman for comments made on the first draft of this paper.

REFERENCES

Allen, W.S. 1965. *Vox Latina: a guide to the pronunciation of Classical Latin.* Cambridge: Cambridge University Press.

Anderson, J.M. 1985: The status of voiced fricatives in Old English, *Folia Linguistica Historica* 5 215-43.

Anderson, J.M. 1988a. The great KEntish collapse. In Dieter Kastovsky and Gero Bauer (eds.) *Luick Revisited* 97-107. Tübingen: Narr.

Anderson, J.M 1988b. The status of voiced fricatives in Old English. In John M. Anderson and Norman Macleod (eds) *Edinburgh Studies in the English Language.* Edinburgh : John Donald. 90 - 112

Blomfield, J.E. 1935. *The origins of Old English orthography with special reference to the representation of spirants and w.* D Phil thesis, unpublished, Oxford.

Bosworth, J and T.N. Toller 1898. *An Anglo Saxon dictionary.* Oxford: Oxford University Press. *Supplement* by Toller 1921: *Addenda and corrigenda* by A. Campbell 1972, both Oxford: Oxford University Press.

Brooks, N. 1984. *The early history of the church of Canterbury; Christ Church from 597 to 1066.* Leicester: Leicester University Press.

Campbell, A. 1959. *Old English grammar.* Oxford: Clarendon Press.

Campbell, A. ed. 1973. *Charters of Rochester.* London: Oxford University Press for the British Academy.

Chadwick, H. M. 1894-1899. Studies in Old English. *Transactions of the Cambridge Philological Society* 4. 85-265.

Colman, F. 1983. Old English /ɑ/ ≠ /æ/ or [ɑ] ~ [æ]? *Folia Linguistica Historica* IV/2. 265-85.

Colman, F. 1985. Old English *ie:* quid est? *Lingua* 67. 1-23.

Colman, F. 1988. What *is* in a name? In Jacek Fisiak (ed.) *Historical Dialectology: Regional and social,* 74-92. Amsterdam: Mouton de Gruyter.

Colman, F. and J.M. Anderson 1983. Front Umlaut: a celebration of Second Fronting, *i*-Umlaut, life, food and sex. In Michael Davenport, Erik Hansen and Hans Frede Nielsen (eds.) *Current topics in English historical linguistics 4,* 165-90. Odense: Odense University Press.

Davidsen-Nielson, N. 1984. Old English short vowels before nasals. In N.F Blake and C. Jones (eds.) *English historical linguistics: studies in development,* 12-23. Sheffield: CECTAL Conference Papers Series, No. 3.

Derwing, B., T. Nearey and M. Dow 1986. On the phoneme as the unit of the 'second articulation'. *Phonology Year-book* 3. 45-69.

Ekwall, E. 1940. *The concise Oxford dictionary of English place-names* [2]. Oxford: Clarendon Press.

Fisiak, J. 1968. *A short grammar of Middle English*. Warsawa : Pánstwowe Wydawnictwo Naukowe.

Hessels, J. H. 1906. *A late eighth-century Latin-Anglo-Saxon glossary preserved in the library of the Leiden University*. Cambridge: Cambridge University Press.

Hill, D. 1984. *An atlas of Anglo-Saxon England*. Oxford: Basil Blackwell.

Hogg, R. M. 1979. Old English palatalisation. *Transactions of the Philological Society*. 89-113.

Hogg, R. M. 1982. Was there ever an /ɔ/-phoneme in Old English? *Neuphilologische Mitteilungen* 83. 225-9.

Hogg, R. M. 1988. On the impossibility of Old English dialectology. In Dieter Kastovsky and Gero Bauer (eds.). *Luick Revisited*, 183-203. Tübingen: Narr.

Hogg, R. M. Old English grammar notes . MS.

Jones, D. 1967. *The phoneme: its nature and use* [3]. Cambridge: Cambridge University Press.

Keller, W. 1906. *Angelsächsische Palaeographie* (Palaestra xliii), 2 Vols. Berlin.

King. A. 1988. The long and the short of it: Old English spelling and Old English vowels. *Belgian Journal of Linguistics* 3. 157-78.

Kuhn, S. 1939. The dialect of the Corpus Glossary. *Publications of the Modern Language Association*. 54. 1-19.

Kuhn, S. 1943. The *Vespasian Psalter* and the Old English charter hands. *Speculum* 18. 458-83.

Kuhn, S. 1961. The syllabic phonemes of Old English. *Language* 37. 522-38.

Labov, W. M. Yaeger and R. Steiner 1972. A quantitative study of sound changes in progress. Philadelphia: The US Regional Survey.

Lass, R. 1973. Review of P. H. Reaney, *The origin of English surnames. Foundations of Language* 9. 392-402.

Lass, R. 1976. Variation studies and historical linguistics. *Language in Society* 5. 219-29.

Lass, R. 1980. *On explaining language change*. Cambridge: Cambridge University Press.

Lass, R. 1984. *Phonology: an introduction to basic concepts*. Cambridge: Cambridge University Press.

Lass, R. and J.M. Anderson 1975. *Old English phonology*. Cambridge: Cambridge University Press

Penzl, H. 1947. The phonemic split of Germanic *k* in Old English. *Language* 23. 34-42.

Pheifer, J.D. 1974. *Old English glosses in the Epinal-Erfurt Glossary*. Oxford: Clarendon Press.

Prins, A. A. 1974. *A history of English phonemes from Indo-European to present-day English* [2]. Leiden: Leiden University Press.

Romaine, S. 1982. *Socio-historical linguistics*. Cambridge: Cambridge University Press.

Stenton, F. M 1971. *Anglo-Saxon England* [3]. Oxford: Clarendon Press.

Stockwell, R. P. and C. W. Barritt. 1951. Some Old English graphemic correspondences; a, ea, a. *Studies in Linguistics: Occasional Papers 4*. Oklahoma: Battenburg Press.

Strang, B.M.H. 1970. *A history of English*. London: Methuen and Co Ltd.

Sweet, H. ed. 1885. *The Oldest English texts* (Early English Text Society, Vol. 83). London: N. Trübner & Co.

Sweet, H, 1888. *A history of English sounds from the earliest period* [2]. Oxford: Clarendon Press.

Toon, T. E. 1983. *The politics of early Old English sound change.* New York: Academic Press, inc.

Wallenberg, J. K. 1931. *Kentish place-names: a topographical and etymological study of the place-name material in Kentish charters dated before the Conquest.* Uppsala: A.-B Lundequistska Bokhandeln.

Weinreich, U., W. Labov and M.I. Herzog 1968. Empirical foundations for a theory of language change. In Winfred P. Lehmann and Yakov Malkiel (eds.) *Directions for historical linguistics: a symposium*, 95-195. Austin: University of Texas Press.

3

OLD ENGLISH CLITIC PRONOUNS. SOME REMARKS*

Willem F. Koopman

Introduction

It has often been noted that Old English personal pronouns do not show the same syntactic patterning as full NPs. The commonly held view that word order patterns in Old English show a great deal of free variation (Quirk and Wrenn 1955: 92) has now been discarded. Careful analysis has shown that Old English syntax is much more constrained than was originally thought. Bacquet (1962) tried to establish the 'base' or unmarked order for many syntactic patterns. Mitchell (1964: 119) was the first to point out that pronoun objects usually precede the verb in main clauses and that this order should be regarded as a variation of SV order. Van Kemenade (1984) was the first to recognise that Old English personal pronouns could be regarded as clitics (Barrett 1967 had rejected the idea), and the first (1987) to offer a systematic treatment of them as syntactic clitics, which is in many respects an enormous contribution to Old English syntax. The analysis she presents results in even greater regularity in the syntax, but it is not clear whether all pronouns should be regarded as clitics. The purpose of this chapter is to evaluate her analysis and to look in detail at the object pronouns in a number of Old English texts[1].

This chapter is organised as follows: Van Kemenade's analysis is summarised in 1; the occurrence or non-occurrence of full NPs in the positions occupied by (clitic) pronouns in the surface syntactic string is evaluated in 2. This will lead to a critical discussion of some aspects of her analysis; the cases where pronouns are not clitics are given in 3; the cases where pronouns are perhaps not clitics follow in 4; in 5 I shall present the bulk of the textual evidence and provide some statistics to try and measure degrees of (de) cliticization. The possible influence of Latin is evaluated in 6; in 7 the available phonological evidence for clitic status follows, and the conclusion in 8.

1 Van Kemenade's Analysis

The theoretical framework used by Van Kemenade is government-binding theory. She sets out to provide an explanation for a number of synchronic and diachronic facts in the early history of English (Old and Middle English), focusing 'primarily on constructions with preposition stranding, clitics, passivization, transitive adjectives, and on word order' (1987: 1). What they have in common is that 'they are all related to the case properties and thematic properties of verbal and prepositional elements' (1987:1), which in turn are related to the inflectional system of Old English. Changes in these constructions are linked to changes in underlying word order and to the loss of the inflectional system.

Within the theory of government-binding underlying word order determines a lot of syntactic phenomena. It is therefore important to establish what the underlying word order of Old English is. Van Kemenade argues extensively and convincingly that Old English is an SOV language (evidence from Modern Germanic languages plays an important role in her discussion). Any deviation from this underlying order must be accounted for by stylistic rules or by syntactic rules (such as movement rules), on which van Kemenade concentrates. Movement rules necessary to account for surface word order are: Topicalization (by which an S-element is moved to the TOPIC position), Extraposition (by which an S-element is moved to the right of the base position of the verb), and various verb raising rules which determine the position of finite (and non-finite) verb in subordinate clauses (see also Koopman 1990 b).

The position of the finite verb in main clauses in such Modern Germanic languages as Dutch and German can be accounted for by a verb movement rule (a V2 rule)[2] which moves the verb in main clauses from its base end position to INFL in COMP (see H. Koopman 1984 for details). The effect of this rule is that the finite verb regularly appears in the second position in main clauses. Van Kemenade extends this analysis to Old English. Though the finite verb in main clauses in Old English often appears in second position, it does so less regularly than in modern Dutch and German, which led some scholars to claim that Old English is not a V2 language but a V3 language (Bean 1983). As van Kemenade shows, almost all examples of V3 involve pronouns (subject or object), and she claims that pronouns in this position should be regarded as (syntactic) clitics, and therefore do not 'count' for the V2 rule as separate constituents. The clitic analysis enables her to propose more or less the same V2 rule for Old English as has been developed for some modern languages. It also allows her to account for the syntactic distribution of pronouns (which is often different from nouns). She makes a distinction between the two forms of case assignment the theory allows: oblique case (in Old English these are genitive, dative, and in some cases accusative) is assigned at D-structure by various case assigners (mainly verb and preposition), and structural case (nominative and accusative) assigned at surface structure by INFL for nominative case, and by an abstract case assigner in the leftmost position in the VP for accusative case. The distinction between oblique and structural case is reflected in the different behaviour of accusative objects in passivisation (van Kemenade 1987: 86ff.). Personal pronouns are found in clitic positions (A´-positions) on their case assigners (subject on INFL, objects either on the abstract case assigner or on the verb, clitic objects of P to the left of P) and can, under certain conditions, move to another A^1-position. This means that object pronouns can be found on INFL, or that clitic objects of P can be found on COMP. Thus van Kemenade explains why personal pronouns often occupy positions in the syntactic string which are different from the positions in which full NPs are found. She claims that practically all pronouns are clitics in this sense, and that there is therefore a fundamental difference between pronouns and full NPs. The clitic analysis allows her to explain certain aspects of preposition stranding, and forms an important part in her subsequent discussion of changes in the ME period, where she argues for a decliticization process. The loss of clitics is explained as follows: 'Clitics are in a sense case affixes, and thus are dependent on the presence of inflectional morphology. Accordingly, when inflectional morphology was lost, case affixing was lost' (van Kemenade 1987 : 204). In turn this leads to changes in some syntactic constructions. Below I shall investigate in how far it is right to claim that practically all Old English personal pronouns are clitics, starting with a discussion of the clitic positions recognised by van Kemenade (first for subject clitics, then for object clitics of V, and finally for pronominal objects of P). I shall distinguish each position by a letter to make reference easier.

1.1 Subject pronouns as clitics
In *main* clauses with V2 subject clitics can appear in the following positions: Position A (pos. A) is to the left of the finite verb if the TOPIC position is filled:[3]

(1) On ðæm gesuincum *he* sceal hine selfne geðencean
     in the hardship he must him self remember
     (='in hardship he must remember himself') (CP 3.35.8).

Position B (Pos. B) is to the right of the finite verb if the first position is filled by *ne*, a *wh*-word, or þa:

(2) Ne oncneow *heo* weres gemanan
     not knew she man's society
     (=' she didn't know the society of man') (ÆCHom i.2.42.9)

(3) Hwæt hæfst *ðu*
     what have you
     (= 'what do you have') (ÆCHom ii.7.63.84)

(4) þa gewende *he* to rome
     then went he to Rome
     (= 'then he went to Rome') (ÆCHom i.5.80.7)

In *subordinate* clauses the subject clitic appears immediately to the right of the complementizer (Pos. C):

(5) Ic bidde þe, Ælflæd, þæt *ðu* uncre spræce on minum life nanum
     I pray you, Ælfled, that you our discourse during my life no one
     ne ameldige
     not mention
     (= 'I ask of you, Ælfled, that you will not mention our discourse to
     anyone during my life') (ÆCHom ii.10.87.229)

All three positions are located on INFL, the nominative case assigner.

1.2 Clitic objects of V
Within the VP there are two case assigners, V (for oblique case), and an abstract case position for assigning structural accusative case. This is situated at the beginning of the VP in order to meet the requirement that structural case is assigned to the right. The clitic positions are then as follows:

Position D (Pos. D) is on the abstract case assigner (leftmost position in the VP):

(6)   þæt hi *hit* ðam folce dælan scoldon
that they it the people give might
(= 'that they might give it to the people') (ÆCHom ii.29.233.101)

Position E (Pos. E) is to the left of V:

(7)   for ðan þe he ða gastlican lare *him* forgeaf
for he the spiritual teaching them gave
(= 'because he gave them spiritual teaching') (ÆCHom ii.29.233.101)

In addition clitic objects can also occur in the clitic positions open to subject clitics, i.e. in positions A, B, or C:

(8)   Iob *hire* andwyrde (Pos. A)
Job her answered
(= 'Job answered her') (ÆCHom ii.35.264.122)

(9)   þa andwyrde *hire* se halga...(Pos. B)
then answered her the saint...
(= 'the saint answered her then...') (ÆCHom ii.10.87.217)

(10)   gif us deoful drecce mid manigfealdum geþohtum (Pos. C)
if us devil trouble with manifold thoughts
(= 'if the devil trouble us with manifold thoughts') (ÆCHom i.10.156.21)

1.3 Clitic objects of P
With prepositional phrases the preposition can sometimes occur in postposition, practically always with pronouns.[4] The clitic position for these pronouns is to the left of the case assigner (P):

Position F (Pos. F) is to the left of P:

(11)   ða hyrdas ða spræcon *him* betweonan
the shepherds then spoke them among
(= 'the shepherds then spoke among themselves') (ÆCHom i.2.40.1)

In addition, just like pronominal objects of V, clitic objects of P can move to other clitic positions, i.e., to the two positions within the VP, and to the three positions on COMP:

(12) ac hæland crist of heofenum *me* spræc to (Pos. E)[5]
but saviour Christ from heaven me spoke to
(= 'but Christ the Saviour spoke to me from heaven'
(ÆCHom i.26.378.34)

(13) ðætte sio forsewennes *him* ege & ondrysnu on gebringe (Pos. D)
that the contempt them fear & reverence on brings
(= 'that the contempt may instill into them fear and reverence')
(CP 37.265.17)

(14) þat *him* eall middaneard to beah (Pos. C)
that him all world to submitted
(='that all the world submitted to him') (ÆCHom i.2.32.17)

(15) þa sende *him* god to micelne wind (Pos. B)
then sent them God to great wind
(='then God sent them a great wind') (ÆCHom i.18.244.28)

(16) se heahfæder abraham *him* cwæð to (Pos. A)
the patriarch Abraham him said to
(= 'the Patriarch Abraham said to him') (ÆCHom i.23.322.1)[6]

Clitic Pronouns 49

The various clitic positions are shown in the tree diagrams in (17):

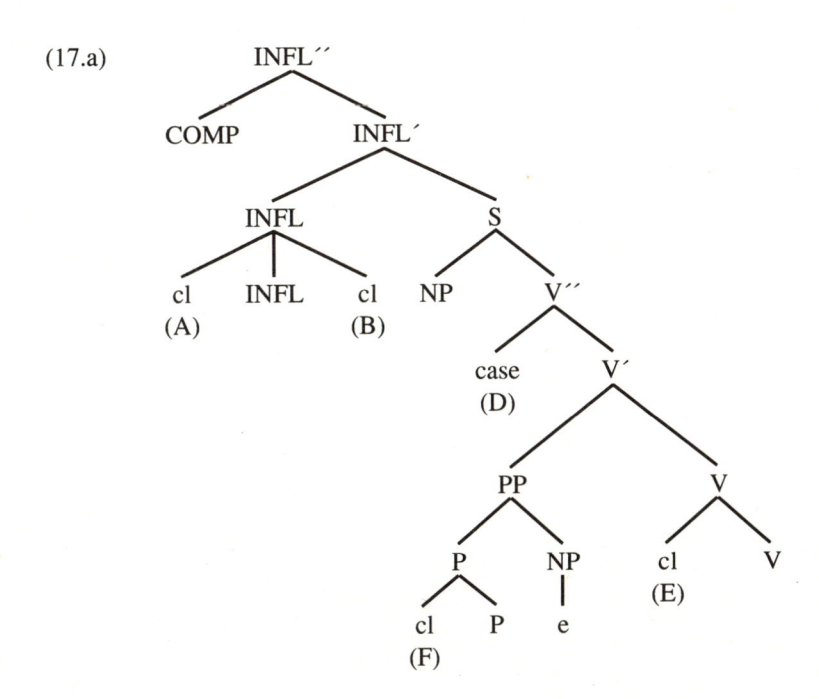

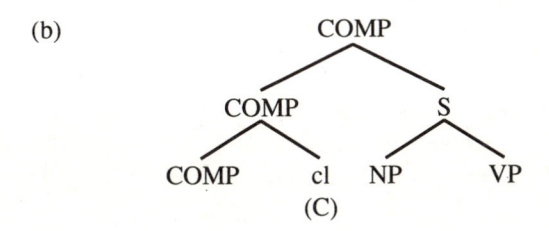

(17.a)
```
              INFL″
         ┌─────┴─────┐
       COMP        INFL′
                ┌────┴────┐
              INFL         S
           ┌───┼───┐   ┌───┼────┐
          cl  INFL cl  NP       V″
          (A)      (B)       ┌──┴──┐
                            case   V′
                            (D)  ┌─┴─┐
                                PP    V
                              ┌─┴─┐ ┌─┴─┐
                              P  NP cl  V
                            ┌─┤  |  (E)
                           cl P  e
                           (F)
```

(b)
```
              COMP
          ┌────┴────┐
        COMP        S
     ┌───┼───┬───┐ ┌┴─┐
   COMP   cl  NP   VP
          (C)
```

According to van Kemenade clitics absorb the case features of their governing head, and are base-generated in A´ positions, co-indexed with an appropriate NP position. They can move to other clitic positions. As is clear from the examples given above, subject clitics cannot move 'down', neither can object clitics move 'down' to position F on P. This is because, when they move, clitics are subject to antecedent-trace relations, in particular c-command. The c-command definition used by van Kemenade (1987: 67) explains why subject clitics cannot go 'down': they would not c-command their source position. Neither can object clitics go 'down'. The only clitic which can go to a lower position in the tree is the one on D. It can move to E, because it stays in the maximum projection and thus does not violate antecedent-trace relations.

1.4 The Positions on COMP

As we have seen, there are three positions on COMP. Schematically (following van Kemenade 1987: 139).

(18.a) [INFL´´   [COMP   TOPIC]   cl-INFL]

                                                    V2

(18.b) [INFL´´   [COMP   wh/ne/þa]   INFL-cl]

                                                  V2

(18.c) [INFL´´   [COMP   INFL-cl]]

                                                  that

The position given in (18.a) should be regarded as unmarked because cliticization is on the left of the case assigner, as with the other case assigners (1987: 139). The other two positions (18.b) and (18.c) should be regarded as in some way marked. Van Kemenade offers the following explanation for cliticization to the right of INFL: she regards *wh/ne/þa* as 'operators', which transmit an index to the head INFL, which has the effect that COMP and INFL behave as one constituent, so that cliticization is on the INFL projection, and on its right. It is not clear why *þa* should be an operator. It seems to be entirely different from *ne* and *wh* elements, which can be said to have a certain scope, something which seems to me not to be the case with *þa*. Furthermore, *þa* is not the only adverb which has this property. Similar effects on word order are shown by other adverbs such as *þonne* and *nu* , though they do so less systematically. The words in question can also function as conjunctions, and almost invariably the word order signals whether there is a main or a subordinate clause. There are very few exceptions (see Mitchell 1985: §3922). *Ne* is a clitic itself, inseparable from the finite verb. In Old English the verb sometimes has first position:

(19) Cwæþ þeah heora an...
said though of them one...
(='One of them said though...') (ÆCHom ii.34.1.292.164)

We could interpret these cases as in a sense clauses with the finite verb in Topic. What is important is that when it has this position (with or without *ne*) the only position for the subject (pronominal or not) is to the right of the verb (see also Mitchell 1985: §3930 ff.).

As to (18.c) van Kemenade remarks that there is a distinction between 'V2 as a lexicalization of INFL' and a complementizer as a lexicalization of INFL. She adds that the complementizer 'is the proper base-generated lexicalization of INFL, whereas V2 must be viewed as a default lexicalizer' (van Kemenade 1987: 140). I do not see how this explains why cliticization should be on the right in this instance and not on the left.[7] This concludes our discussion of van Kemenade's clitic positions.

2 True Clitic Positions or Ambiguous Ones?

In this section I want to look at the distributional facts of pronouns and full NPs in order to establish which clitic positions can be recognised as true clitic positions (only pronouns can appear there), and which positions are ambiguous. A position is ambiguous when pronouns as well as full NPs are found in the same position in the surface syntactic string. They could of course occupy different positions in the tree, but that is often hard to prove. The distributional facts will lead to some critical remarks and discussion.

It is obvious that the language learner can recognize clitic positions as clitic positions if there is *positive* evidence for their existence. Such evidence exists if only clitic pronouns are found in a particular position. Even when it appears that both pronouns and full NPs can occupy the same surface position, it is often the case that different syntactic behaviour can be shown when another pronoun / full NP is present, therefore indicating that full NPs and pronouns do not occupy the same position in the syntactic string.

I shall discuss the clitic positions in the order described above (A to F) using the same examples.

2.1 Pos. A
Left of the finite verb if the Topic position is filled:

(20)   On ðæm gesuincum *he* sceal hine selfne geðencean (=1)
       in the hardship he must him self remember
       (='in hardship he must remember himself') (CP 3.35.8)

As far as the evidence goes full subject NPs also occupy this same position. The difference here is that full NPs can also occur *after* the verb, a position not open to subject pronouns as far as I am aware:

(21)   ðas word crist geclypode to his fæder
        these words Christ cried to his father (ÆCHom ii.1.8.198)

(22)   For þæm slege noldan Romane brengan þæm consule þone triumphan
        For the killing not wanted Romans give the consul the triumph
        (= 'The Romans did not want to grant the consul the triumph on account
        of the killing') (Or 3.6.108.12)

Full object NPs never occupy the position *before* the verb, but pronominal objects of V and pronominal objects of P can occur there (see 8 and 16). Clearly we are here dealing with an unambiguous clitic position.

2.2 Pos. B
To the right of the finite verb if the first constituent is an operator (*ne*, *wh*, or *þa*):

(23)   Ne oncneow *heo* weres gemanan (=2)
        not knew she man's society
        (='she didn't know the society of man') (ÆCHom i.2.42.9)

In this position full subject NPs can also be found:

(24)   þa becom se apostol æt sumum sæle to þære byrig Pergamum
        then came the apostle on certain time to the city Pergamus
        (='then at a certain time the apostle came to the city of Pergamus')
        (ÆCHom i.4.62.24).

However, when we look at what can happen when pronoun objects are present we get a different picture. As far as I am aware the object pronoun cannot come between verb and *pronoun* subject, whereas with full subject NPs this is certainly possible and relatively frequent:

(25)   *þa seah hine he

(26)   þa andwyrde *hire* se halga (=9)
        then answered her the saint
        (='the saint answered her then') (ÆCHom ii.10.87.217)

The available evidence suggests that although this positions seems ambiguous, it can be disambiguated, and it can be shown that pronominal subjects do indeed occupy a position which is different from full subjects NPs.

2.3 Pos. C
In subordinate clauses the subject pronoun appears immediately to the right of the complementizer:

(27)   Ic bidde þe, Ælflæd, þæt ðu uncre spræce on minum life nanum
I pray you, Ælfled, that you our discourse during my life no one
ne ameldige (=5)
not mention
(='I ask of you Ælfled, that you will not mention our discourse to anyone during my life') (ÆCHom ii.10.87.229)

Although both pronoun subjects and full NP subjects can occupy the position to the right of the COMP, only pronoun subjects remain there at all times. Full NP subjects can be separated from COMP by pronoun objects or pronominal objects of P (see 10 and 14).

2.4 Pos. D and Pos. E
On the abstract case assigner in the VP:

(28)   þæt hi *hit* ðam folce dælan scoldon (=6)
that they it the people give might
(='that they might give it to the people') (ÆCHom ii.29.233.101)

To the left of V:

(29)   for ðan þe he ða gastlican lare *him* forgeaf (=7)
for he the spiritual teaching them gave
(='because he gave them spiritual teaching') (ÆCHom ii.29.233.101)

Clitic objects of P can occur in these two positions. In that sense they are clitic positions. It is not so clear whether pronominal objects of V should always be regarded as clitics when they occupy these positions. It can be shown that full NPs apparently can also occupy the first position in the VP or be to the left of V:

(30)   þæt he ðone dead mid his ariste tobræc
that he the death with his resurrection shattered
(='that he shattered death with his resurrection') (ÆCHom i.15.226.15)

(31)   þæt he his modor mid unasecgendlicere arwurðnysse on his rice
that he his mother with unspeakable veneration in his kingdom
gewurþode
honoured
(='that he honoured his mother with unspeakable veneration in his kingdom') (ÆCHom i.30.442.23)

(32)   þæt hi his sawle on þam forðside mid him to hellicum clysungum
gepripon

that they his soul on the departure with them to hell enclosures snatched
(='that they might snatch his soul on its departure with them to the enclosures of hell') (ÆCHom i.28.414.7)

The full NP occupies the leftmost position in the VP in (30), (31) and (32), with one, two, and three PPs respectively between it and the verb. Full NPs are certainly less frequent than pronouns in this position, particularly when the VP contains a lot of material. It seems reasonable therefore that at least a portion of the pronouns in this position are clitics, but some may occupy a normal NP position. Unfortunately, there is no way for us to establish which proportion of pronouns should be regarded as clitics here.

The fact that there are two clitic positions in the VP means that pronominal objects can only be non-clitic in van Kemenade's view if they do not occupy one of these two positions within the VP. The nature of most of the material is such that VPs do not normally have enough material to show such a position. Schematically one possibility is:

(33)   VP [X pronoun Y V]

where X and Y stand for any material. We would have a good case for claiming that object pronouns within the VP are always clitics if it can be shown that they never occur in a non-clitic position. However, this is not the case as the following example shows:

(34)   gif we ealle ðas gatacnunga eow nu ætsomne gereccað
        if we all these signs you now together narrate
        (='if we now narrate to you all these signs together')
        (ÆCHom ii.12.1.115.175)

In such examples, as (34), X and Y are frequently adverbs, but prepositional phrases also sometimes occur there.

2.5 Pos. F
To the left of P:

(35)   ða hyrdas ða spræcon *him* betweonan (=11)
        the shepherds then spoke them among
        (='the shepherds then spoke among themselves') (ÆCHom i.2.40.1)

Postposition of prepositions is rare with full NPs. Wende (1915: 137) found only a few cases with full NPs. In the light of the available evidence the conclusion seems warranted that we are dealing with a genuine clitic position here.

2.6 Discussion
We have seen that some positions are exclusive to pronouns or when ambiguous

can be shown to be exclusive (Pos. A-C, F). Within the VP such disambiguation is not possible, and it is perhaps not surprising that indeed exceptions are found there. Van Kemenade proposes two clitic positions in the VP, both on case assigners. The one left of V seems relatively uncontroversial, but the abstract case assigner posited on the left of VP needs to be discussed in some more detail.

2.6.1 The abstract case position

Van Kemenade, following H. Koopman (1984), assumes that structural case assignment is unidirectional. As INFL assigns its case to the right, structural case in the VP must be assigned to the right as well, to maintain this unidirectionality. The verb is in final position so it cannot assign structural case. The proposal therefore is that there is an abstract case marker at the left of the VP. H Koopman (1984) argues that unidirectionality of structural case assignment is required on theoretical grounds and she offers supporting evidence for an abstract case assigner in the left position of the VP in Dutch, where the verb is also in final position. The evidence she gives, such as the adjacency of the object to this case marker, does not hold for Old English. It remains a fact, however, that pronominal objects of P can be found in this position. But are we dealing with a case marking position or with something else? The system of Chomsky (1986) allows a SPEC-VP position, which is exploited for instance in Larson (1988). Let us assume that such a position is present in the VP and that it can be occupied only by pronouns.

Before we discuss this any further let us explore the reasons for assuming a case position on the left of the VP, as given by van Kemenade. She remarks (1987: 92-93) that the 'opposing directions of structural and oblique case-marking...in the VP predict that in sentences with an accusative and an oblique object in the VP, the linear order will be...ACC NP — OBL NP'. She claims that word order counts of some Old English texts support this assumption. I am not convinced by her argument here. It is extremely difficult to establish what the order of ACC and OBL NPs in the VP is. Pronouns, as she claims herself, cannot be taken into account, precisely because they show different syntactic behaviour as clitics. What remains are full NPs, but these very often show extraposition. It means that there is relatively little clear evidence. Research in progress shows that there is no marked preference for either order (see also Koopman 1990a for more details). Until further information becomes available we must conclude that the order of ACC NP — OBL NP cannot be used to support the existence of an abstract case marker in the VP.

Because the abstract case marker assigns structural case, we must assume that it is only present where such structural case can be assigned (when there is a transitive verb with an accusative object). Surely it is absurd to argue that such a position is always there even if no case assignment takes place. After all, we do not assume an empty P case assigner when there is no PP. It seems to me that support for the abstract case marker can be found if it can be shown that clitics do not occur in this position when there is no structural case. There is no structural case where auxiliaries are concerned (*beon*), with intransitive verbs (such as cuman etc.) (36), with transitive verbs in the passive (37), and with verbs that do not have an accusative object (38). The evidence shows quite clearly that when there is no structural case pronouns occur in the left position of VP:

(36) Geðenc hwelc witu *us* þa becomon for ðisse worulde
Consider what punishments us then came for this world
(='Consider what punishments would come upon us on account of this world') (CPLetWærf 23)

(37) þæt hio *him* sona forgiefen wære swa he geðoht hæfde...
that it him soon forgiven was as he thought had...
(='that it was forgiven him as soon as he had thought...')(CP 53.419.10)

(38) ðæt we *his* to suiðe ne gitseden
that we it too much not coveted
(='that we should not covet it too much') (CP 3.33.16)

We have seen that there is little support for an abstract case assigner, and that it is often not present. If we assume that pronouns in the VP can be in the SPEC-VP position, then there are two logical possibilities to consider:

(39.a) There is no abstract case assigner and clitic pronouns can occur in the SPEC-VP position.
(39.b) There is an abstract case assigner only when structural case is assigned. When there is no structural case clitic pronouns can be in the SPEC-VP position. The only support for the case assigner comes from the behaviour of clitic pronouns.

Before we discuss these two possibilities some further remarks must be made about clitics.

2.6.2. Double clitics?
Clitics are base-generated and co-indexed with an appropriate NP position. Movement from a base-generated position to another clitic position is possible, but is it possible to have two clitics in the same clitic position?[8] Theoretically this could be the case for positions A-E when two object clitics are involved or an object clitic and a clitic object of P (I use hypothetical sentences here for ease of exposition):[9]

(40.a) He hit him geaf
He it him gave
(='he gave it to him')

(40.b) þa geaf hit him se mann
than gave it him the man

(='then the man gave it to him)

(40.c) þæt hit him se mann geaf
that it him the man gave
(='that the man gave it to him')

(40.d) þæt se mann hit him eft geaf
that the man it him again gave
(='that the man gave it again to him')

(40.e) þæt se mann eft hit him geaf
that the man again it him gave
(='that the man gave it again to him')

The textual evidence shows that (40.a) indeed occurs:

(41) he hit us forgylt be hundfealdum on ðam toweardan life
he it us rewards a hundredfold in the future life
(='he will reward us a hundredfold in the life to come')
(ÆCHom ii.7.64.110)

Examples are few and far between and all are open to a different interpretation. In the light of the fact that some main clauses in Old English fail to undergo the V2 rule, we cannot be certain that we are dealing in (41) with a V in INFL; it could also be in the base final position with extraposition of two PP's (in which case it is an example of (40.d). There are therefore no certain cases of (40.a).

No examples were found of (40.b). There are in any case few cases of a clitic object occupying Pos. B (see also section 5.2), so the gap could be accidental. This is not likely to be the case with (40.c) for clitics occur often in Pos. C. The texts examined contained one example:

(42) þeah hit him man secge
though it him one says
(='though people say it to him') (WHom 4.77)

There are numerous examples of (40.d):

(43) gif he hit him ðonne sellan mæge
if he it him then gave can
(='if he can give it to him then') (CP 44.323.24)

As far as I am aware there are no clear cases of (40.e). Two pronoun objects only occur left of V when there is no distinction between Pos. D and Pos. E:

(44) gif he hit him iewe
      if he it him shows
      (='if he shows it to him') (CP 26.185.25)

The material presented above shows that there is little or no evidence that two clitics can occur in one clitic position. The evidence for positions other than D (left position in VP) is very meagre. Until more evidence becomes available I assume that two object pronouns can appear only in Pos. D, and it is significant that it is exactly this position which we were questioning above.

2.6.3 Two pronoun objects
Let us now see whether we should assume (39.a) or (39.b). A consequence of (39.a) is that there is only one case assigner (V) in the VP, which assigns both oblique and structural case. The SPEC-VP position is available for pronouns. When a verb has two pronominal objects the oblique clitic object gets case from the verb at D-structure, but if the verb also assigns structural case where should the accusative object be generated if it is a clitic? It cannot be generated on V as well since that would result in a double clitic position and we have argued that there is no evidence for this. The alternative is that it goes to SPEC-VP (45) or to another clitic position (46):

(45) þæt we hi swutelicor eow onwreon
      that we them more distinctly you explain
      (='that we explain them more distinctly to you') (ÆCHom i.20.278.13)

(46) buton hit mon him secge
      unless it they them say
      (='unless they say it to them') (CP 31.207.1)

Suppose we adopt (39.b). There are then two clitic positions in the VP when two objects (one of which is accusative) are present. When both objects are generated on their case markers we get (45), the order in surface structure being ACC — DAT. With very few exceptions this is the order we find (see Koopman 1990a for details). Theoretically clitics can move to other clitic positions. It is striking in the material at my disposal that ACC clitics can move outside the VP, but that there are no examples of DAT clitics doing so (see also 46):

(47) ðæt hi God him forlæte
      that them God them permits
      (='that God will permit them to them') (CP 54.423.28)

(48) ne hi hit ne magon hym mid nanum þingon forgyldon
      nor they it not can them with no things repay
      (='nor can they repay it to them with anything') (WCan 1.2 (Torkar) 31).

(49)   & God hit geþafað him sume hwile for twam þingum
        and God it allows them some time for two things
        (='and God allows it to them for a while for two things') (WHom 4.15)

(50)   gif hit crist sylf us ne behete
        if it Christ himself us not promised
        (='if Christ himself had not promised it to us') (ÆCHom ii.30.240.148)

When we can distinguish between Pos. D and Pos. E both pronoun objects are found together at the beginning of the VP.

Why do clitic pronouns cluster at the beginning of the VP in the order ACC-DAT and why can the oblique clitic apparently not move outside the VP? With the adoption of (39.b) it seems impossible to suggest an acceptable answer. There is no apparent reason why the pronouns should cluster only on the abstract case marker and not in other clitic positions, and there is no reasonable explanation why the oblique clitic cannot move outside the VP short of saying that the lack of evidence is accidental. Note that the adoption of (39.a) allows us at least a possible explanation. Let us assume that clitic movement takes place through the SPEC position (a kind of 'escape hatch', see van Riemsdijk (1978)). Such movement is blocked when the SPEC position is filled. In (47) — (50) the accusative occupies the SPEC position and the oblique clitic cannot move to a position outside the VP. In the case of a clitic object of P and an accusative pronoun in the SPEC position we expect that movement of the clitic object of P to a position outside the VP is blocked. Thus we would expect that there are no examples of a clitic object of P in a clitic position outside the VP when there is also an accusative pronoun in the VP. As far as I am aware there are indeed no examples in Old English. As van Kemenade observes, a clitic object of P can move to the SPEC-P´ position, but in Old English 'such movement is string-vacuous' (1987: 133). For a clitic object of P to get to a position outside the VP it would have to go through SPEC-P´ and SPEC-VP. Presence of an accusative pronoun in SPEC VP would block this.

My conclusion is that there is more support for the adoption of (39.a) than for (39.b).

2.6.4 Pronouns in TOPIC position

NPs can be topicalized in Old English, and also pronouns. In the topic position they do not end up in a clitic position on a case assigner. Van Kemenade assumes that clitics are base-generated in A´ positions and can move to other A´ positions. It should be noted however that full NPs can also be topicalized, thus showing movement from an A to an A´ position. There does not seem to be any difference between topicalized pronouns and topicalized full NPs, and one could just as easily assume that topicalized pronouns come from an A position, particularly as it can be shown that not all pronouns occupy A´ positions.

2.6.4.1 Subject pronouns

A large number of subject pronouns are topicalized. This is the case when they occur in first position in a sentence. In the standard accounts of V2 the (finite) verb is in INFL. When the subject precedes it cannot be in its normal subject position, but must be in TOPIC position. Evidence for this in Old English is not as clear as for say Dutch where we can very often insert a so-called *d* -word between subject and verb (see H. Koopman 1984: 196):

(51)   Jan die loopt over straat
        John that one walks on the street

As far as I am aware there is no such construction in Old English. However, there are cases where between subject and verb there is an adverb:

(52)   he þa gesamnode ealle ða ealdorbiscopas
        he then gathered all the chief bishops
        (='he gathered all the chief bishops then') (ÆCHom i.5.78.10)

These constructions strongly suggest that the subject is also in Topic position. This is supported by the fact that it is possible to have more than one TOPIC position (see also 52):

(53)   He þa gebealh hine
        he then got angry him
        (='he then got angry with him') (ÆCHom i.26.376.32)

2.6.4.2 Object pronouns

Just as subject pronouns, object pronouns can be topicalized (see also van Kemenade 1987: 117):

(54)   hine geswencte seo wædlung
        him afflicted the poverty
        (='poverty afflicted him') (ÆCHom i.23.332.9)

2.6.4.3 Pronominal objects of P

Pronominal objects of P can also be topicalized:[10]

(55)   him com þa mycel folc to
        him came then many people to
        (='many people came to him then') (ChronE (Plummer) 1087.78)

2.6.5 Passivization

Only accusative objects can be passivized in Old English and become the subject of a passive sentence. Accusative is a structural case, and a passive participle cannot assign structural case to its object. The object moves to the subject position where it can receive case from INFL (van Kemenade 1987: 88). Note that the subject position is an A position. If we assume that all object pronouns are base-generated in A´ positions, we would have movement from an A´ position to an A position, which is not allowed. The alternative is to say that the pronoun subject in the passive originates in an A position, i.e., in a position where full NP objects occur. This strongly suggests that not all pronoun objects are clitics (see also section 3)[11]. Cliticization should then be regarded as an optional process in Old English. Further evidence about the non-clitic nature of some pronouns follows in the next section.

3 Pronouns not Clitics
In 2.4 an example was given where an object pronoun was clearly in a non-clitic position within the VP. There are also object pronouns which simply cannot be clitics, because they should be regarded as in all respects showing identical syntactic behaviour as full NPs. One can easily get the impression from van Kemenade (1987) that all object pronouns should be regarded as clitics. It seems useful to me to summarise in this section when pronouns are not clitics. The following cases can be distinguished:

3.1 Postmodified pronouns
When pronouns are postmodified (most frequently by *an* or *self*, or *bam*) the resulting NP behaves as a full NP, and as such can occupy all positions where full NPs are found, but is never found in the typical clitic positions for subject or object clitics:

(56)   and eall mennisc him anum cynelic gafol ageaf
       and all mankind him alone royal tribute paid
       (='and all mankind paid royal tribute to him alone') (ÆCHom i.2.32.9)

(57)   swilce seo burh him bam to wurðmynte swa genemned wære
       as if the city them both in honour so named was
       (='as if the city was so named in honour of them both')
       (ÆCHom i.26.364.29).

3.2 Pronouns co-ordinated with another pronoun or a full NP

(58)   ði læs ðe hit ne genihtsumige us and eow
       lest it not suffice us and you
       (='lest it is not sufficient for you and us') (ÆCHom ii.44.327.16)

(59)   and þæt he him and his geferan bigleofan ðenian wolde
       and that he him and his companions food serve would
       (='and that he would serve him and his companions food') (ÆCHom ii.9.78.198)

3.3 Pronouns as part of a larger phrase:

(60) ðonne ðæt mod ðenceð gegripan him to upahefenesse ða eaðmodnesse
      when the mind thinks seize for him as pride the humility
      (='when the mind thinks to make humility a pretext for pride')
      (CP 8.55.12).

(61) he sohte hine him to latðeowe on ðæm wege
      he sought him for him as guide on the way
      (='he sought him as a guide on the way') (CP 41.305.4)

3.4 Pronouns as complements of prepositions

(62) ðeah se halga wer ealne middaneard ætforan him gesawe
      though the holy man all world before him saw
      (='though the holy man saw all the world before him')
      (ÆCHom ii.11.107.540)

3.5 Object pronouns in the VP which are not in a clitic position

Object pronouns are not clitics in subordinate clauses or in main clauses without V2 when they do not occupy the first position in the VP (Pos. D) or are left of V (Pos. E). This is the case in the following configuration:

(63) VP [X pronoun Y V]

The VP usually does not contain enough material to determine whether a pronoun is in the position as in (63), and it is to be expected that the total number of examples will be relatively small. Examples can be found when the VP is clearly marked, i.e. the verb remains in its base generated position and there is a subject:

(64) þe fram eastdæle middaneardes hine mid þrimfealdum lacum gesohton
      who from east earth him mid threefold gifts sought
      (='who sought him from the east with threefold gifts')
      (ÆCHom i.7.104.18)

(65) Witoldlice laurentius mid bliþum mode him þæs getiþode
      indeed laurentius with cheerful mind him this granted
      (='indeed, Laurentius granted him this with cheerful mind')
      (ÆCHom i.29.422.22)

(66) and he þa hine on wræcsiðe asende
      and he then him in exile sent
      (='and he then sent him into exile')(ÆCHom i.32.478.16)

3.6 Object pronouns which are extraposed

Object pronouns are not clitics either when it can be proved that they are extraposed. They have then moved to a non-clitic position. Extraposition can be seen in main clauses when there is a finite and a non-finite verb form. The non-finite verb marks the end of the VP in underlying structure. Anything to the right must have been extraposed:

(67)   We willað secgan eow sum byspel
        we want say you a parable
        (='We want to tell you a parable') (ÆCHom i.14.1.212.6)

In subordinate clauses extraposition can be seen most easily when a single verb is involved. Because the verb does not move in subordinate clauses and therefore indicates the end of the VP, anything to the right must have been extraposed:

(68)   þæt hi ne onhofon hi
        that they not exalted themselves
        (='that they should not exalt themselves') (ÆCHom i.26.378.18)

(69)   for þon þe hit mon ne sæde him æror
        because it people not said them earlier
        (='because people had not told it to them earlier') (Or 6.2.254.25)

Things are slightly more complex with subordinate clauses with a finite and a non-finite verb. The finite verb marks the base position of V, but the non-finite verb and part of the VP may have been moved through Verb Projection Raising (see Haegeman and van Riemdsijk (1986), van Kemenade (1987: 55ff.), and Koopman 1990b). In (70) the VP has been raised leaving the finite verb in the base position of V with a VP immediately behind it. Thus the pronoun is in a clitic position (Pos. D):

(70)   þæt we ne magon us swa geornlice gebiddan
        that we not can us so fervently pray
        (='so that we cannot pray so fervently') (ÆCHom i.10.156.11)

Extraposition sometimes is over the non-finite verb:

(71)   se wolde geagnian him þa læssan Asiam
        who wanted acquire him the lesser Asia
        (='who wanted to acquire Asia Minor')(Or 5.4.224.1)

Of all the above cases (except 70) we can be certain that they do not represent clitics, as they can easily be recognized. There are no great problems in establishing what the position of the verb is, where the VP begins, and when a verb has been moved through V2 or raising in subclauses. Not all of the material

4 Object Pronouns Perhaps Not Clitics

4.1 Introduction
In section 2 I have discussed Pos. D and Pos. E. One very practical problem is how to know that we are dealing with a *clitic* and not with a pronoun in a NP position (a non-clitic). We cannot simply assume that every pronoun that is found in the surface string at the beginning of the VP (Pos. D) or left of V (Pos. E) is a clitic. The evidence from passivization and the examples in 3.5 and 3.6 clearly show that non-clitic object pronouns exist. The problem is that full NPs can occupy these positions equally well. It is, however, realistic to say that the more material there is in a VP the more likely it is that a pronoun at the beginning of the VP is a clitic. They are far more frequent in that position than full NPs. With two object pronouns it seems reasonable to assume that they represent clitics when they cluster at the beginning of the VP on the basis of the evidence from other Germanic languages. As the examples in section 3 make clear, at least some object pronouns are not clitics, and it is very likely that there are many more of them than we can be sure of.

4.2 Main or subordinate clauses?
More complex and less easy to deal with are sentences of which it is not certain whether they are main or subordinate. Consider (72):

(72)   for ðan þe he tæhte him þa gastlican lare
         for he taught them the spiritual learning
         (='for he taught them spiritual learning') (ÆCHom. i.12.186.22)

In the context it could be interpreted as a subordinate clause, but if it is, then both objects have been extraposed and *him* cannot be a clitic. On the other hand if we take it as a main clause we could argue that it is ambiguous whether *him* is a clitic or not. With V2 *him* could be on the trace of V, with *þa gastilican lare* extraposed, or *him* could be in the clitic position on the left of VP. We cannot be sure which position we are dealing with. A third possibility is that *him* is not a clitic at all, as explained above.

4.3 Ambiguous cases
With a V2 rule, Verb Raising in subordinate clauses, and Extraposition we are often confronted with clauses where some kind of movement has taken place, or could have taken place. The movement rules all have the effect of obscuring boundaries, especially of the VP, and of obscuring the underlying verb position. Thus in an ordinary main clause with V2 the verb has moved from its base position, and extraposition may have taken place. Consider (73):

(73)   ða bead se apostol him syfon nihta fæsten

then entreated the apostle them seven days fast
(='then the apostle entreated them to a fast for seven days')
(ÆCHom i.4.74.7)

In (73) *bead* is in INFL, but where it comes from is not obvious. Combined with Extraposition we have the following possibilities (square brackets mark the original VP):

(74.a) þa bead$_i$ se apostol [him seofon nihta fæsten t_i]
(74.b) þa bead$_i$ se apostol [him t_j t_i] seofon nihta fæsten$_j$]
(74.c) þa bead$_i$ se apostol [t_k t_j t_i] him$_k$ seofon nihta fæsten$_j$

Both in (74.a) and (74.b) *him* is in what is potentially a clitic position, but in (74.c) it is extraposed and cannot be a clitic. Sentences such as (74) with a noun subject are not nearly as frequent as sentences with a pronoun subject, where essentially the same problem arises.

4.4 V2 or not?
In sentences with V2 there can be more than one constituent in the Topic position (see (60)). It is not clear whether prepositional phrases occur in Topic position following the subject. Thus in (75) there could be no V2 and the pronoun could be extraposed:

(75)   se fæder ðurh hine gesceop us
       the father through him created us
       (='the father created us through him') (ÆCHom ii.1.3.11)

On the evidence of the Modern Germanic languages the object cannot occupy the Topic position after the subject. Thus in (76) there is no V2 and *ðe* is in Pos. D:

(76)   Ic ðe geþyldelice gehyre
       I you patiently hear
       (='I will hear you patiently') (ÆCHom i.38.590.2)

Though the Topic can be filled by more than one constituent, it becomes less easy to analyse sentences the more constituents appear to be in the Topic:

(77)   He þa eft syððan hine beþohte
       He then again afterwards himself bethought
       (='He then bethought himself again afterwards') (ÆCHom i.30.448.16)

Should we take this as a main clause with V2 or not? It does not make much difference for the clitic status of *hine*.

Consider (78) and (79):

(78)   Symon me mid his englum geþiwde
        Simon me with his angels threatened
        (='Simon threatened me with his angels') (ÆCHom i.26.378.1)

(79)   Se Godes wiþersaca hine ða gehathyrte
        Then God's adversary himself then became angry
        (='God's adversary then became angry') (ÆCHom i.30.450.9)

Both examples show that the pronouns involved (*me* and *hine*) cannot occupy a position on the verb. In fact the verb appears to be in clause final position, with the clause having SOV order. We would be entitled to say that both pronouns occupy a position at the beginning of the VP, which seems a reasonable analysis. It is also possible perhaps (but less likely) that the verb is in INFL and everything preceding it in Topic. A problem of a different kind is encountered in (80):

(80)   ða se engel gelæhte hine be þam feaxe
        'then the angel seized him by the hair' (ÆCHom i.37.572.3)

There is no doubt that (80) is a main clause, but the subject does not come after the verb as is almost always the case when *þa* is in first position. We could say that (80) is a main clause without V2, in which case *hine* has been extraposed and cannot be a clitic, but this seems rather far-fetched.[12]

It is only rarely that the trace can be located when there is only a finite verb form moved away from its base position through the V2 rule. Consider (81):

(81)   þa sæde se Hælend eft syððan him þus to
        then said the Saviour again afterwards them thus to
        (='then the Saviour spoke afterwards again to them as follows')
        (ÆCHom 17.35)

Him is the object of the preposition *to*. Because it is not found in the complement position of P it must be a clitic. Because it is separated from P it must have moved to another position, either on SPEC-VP or on V. It cannot be in SPEC-VP (*him* is not the first item in the VP), so the only remaining possibility is the position on V (the original VP is marked with square brackets):

(82)   þa sæde$_i$, se Hælend [eft syððan him t_i] þus to

Pronominal objects after V in V2 sentences can be divided into two groups:

(83.a) Depending on where the verbal trace is, the object occupies one of the positions (D and E) where clitics can occur.

(83.b) Depending on where the verbal trace is, the object occupies a *non-clitic* position.

4.5 Co-ordinated clauses

Co-ordinated clauses are notoriously difficult to treat consistently. Mitchell (1985) and others feel justified in setting up a separate category for these clauses. (See also the discussion in Stockwell and Minkova 1990. There are co-ordinated main clauses (84) and coordinated sub-clauses (85), and there are co-ordinated clauses with a subject (86) and without a subject (85):

(84) and adam him eallum naman gesceop
and Adam them all names made
(='and Adam made names for them all') (ÆCHom i.1.14.13)

(85) þæt se hælend æteowde hine sylfne his apostolum and cidde him
that the Saviour showed himself his apostles and reproached them
(='that the Saviour showed himself to his apostles and reproached them')
(ÆCHom i.21.300.20)

(86.a) and God him sette naman adam
and God him gave name Adam
(='and God gave him the name Adam')(ÆCHom i.1.12.28)

(86.b) ðylæs...oððe eft ænig durre on eaðmodnesse hiwe hit
lest...or again anyone dare in humility pretext it
ofermodlice forcweðan
haughtily refuse
(='lest...or again anyone dare refuse it haughtily under the pretext
of humility') (CP 7.49.23).

Following Stockwell and Minkova (1990), it seems sensible to make a distinction between co-ordinated clauses with a subject and those without a subject. The reason in the case of clitic pronouns is that with a subject the full range of clitic positions is visible, and without a subject it is not. As remarked by Mitchell (1985: §1719 ff), Stockwell and Minkova (1990) and others it is a peculiar feature of Old English that co-ordinated main clauses frequently do not show V2. They often have the word order of subordinate clauses. However, any attempts to treat the co-ordinator (*and, ac oððe,* etc) as in a sense on a par with complementizers are doomed to failure. One reason is that it is clear that co-ordinated clauses (unlike subordinate clauses) can have a TOPIC position (87) and that unlike in subordinate clauses the pronominal subject can be separated from the co-ordinator (88):

(87) 7 him cierde eall þæt folc to[13]
and him submitted all the people to
(='and all the people submitted to him') (ChronA (Plummer) 922.14)

(88) and þurh his willan he hi ealle geliffæste
and through his will he them all endowed with life
(='and through his will endowed them all with life') (ÆCHom i.1.10.5)

The problem with co-ordinated main clauses is that we cannot be sure in many instances that we are dealing with a co-ordinated clause with or without V2. When there is a subject it seems reasonable to treat all coordinated clauses of the following type as instances of V2:

(89)   co-ordinator-subject-verb-X

In practice this means that some clitic positions are clear under this assumption. Consider (90):

(90)   and we hit magon eow secgan...
         and we it can you say...
         (='and we can tell it to you...') (ÆCHom i.17 (App) 177.11)

In (90) *hit* can be treated as a clitic on INFL (Pos. A).

When there is no subject in a co-ordinated main clause it becomes almost impossible to recognize clitic positions, particularly when there is only one verb. The combined effect of the absence of a subject (where should it go given the possibility of having the TOPIC positions filled?), potential V2, and potential Extraposition is to increase the possible structures enormously. This is illustrated in (91), where (91.a) can have the underlying orders (91.b-h):

(91.a)   ac forgeaf him agenne cyre
         but gave them own choice
         (='but gave them their own choice') (ÆCHom i.7.112.3)

    b)   ac [forgeaf$_i$ [him agenne cyre t_i]]

    c)   ac [forgeaf$_i$ [him t_j t_i]   agenne cyre$_j$]

    d)   ac[forgeaf$_i$ [t_j him t_i]   agenne cyre$_j$]

    e)   ac [forgeaf$_i$ [t_k t_j t_i]   him$_k$ agenne cyre$_j$]

    f)   ac [forgeaf$_i$ [t_j t_k t_i]   him$_k$ agenne cyre$_j$]

    g)   ac [[t_k t_j forgeaf]   him$_k$ agenne cyre$_j$]

    h)   ac [[t_j t_k forgeaf]   him$_k$ agenne cyre$_j$]

In (91.b) the verb moves to INFL through the V2 rule. The pronoun occupies the leftmost position in the VP, which can be a clitic position. In (91.c) *agenne cyre* is extraposed, and the verb is moved to INFL, leaving *him* in its base position, and in a clitic position, similarly in (91.d) but in a different clitic position. In (91.e) the verb has moved to INFL and both objects have been extraposed, as in

(91.f) but from different positions. In (91.g) the verb remains in its base position with both objects extraposed, as in (91.h) again from different positions. In (91. e-h) *him* cannot be a clitic because it is extraposed. There are many sentences like (91).

4.6 Constructions with *uton*
Imperative verb forms always occupy first sentence position, at least they precede the subject. Similar to imperatives are *uton* constructions. They have an infinitival complement. With an object pronoun the most frequent word order is as in (92):

(92) uton him offrian stor
 let us him offer incense
 (='let us offer him incense') (ÆCHom i.7.116.23)

Here the object pronoun is to the left of V (Pos. E). There is the occasional example with the verb in final position (93), and with the pronoun after the infinitive (94):

(93) and utan word 7 weorc rihtlice fadian
 and let us word and work correctly arrange
 (='and let us arrange word and work correctly') (WHom 20.3.189)

(94) Uton on ælce wisan gearwian us
 Let us in every way prepare ourselves
 (='Let us prepare ourselves in every way')(WPol3 (Jost)51)

It seems reasonable to assume that *us* is in a non-clitic position in (94).

4.7 Summary
In this section I have illustrated a number of problems that crop up when one tries to determine clitic positions. The combined effect of some of the rules necessary for Old English (V2, Extraposition, Topicalization, Verb Raising) makes it frequently impossible to decide with any certainty whether an object pronoun is a clitic, and if so which clitic position it occupies. It is particularly hard in co-ordinate clauses.

5 Textual Evidence

5.1 Introduction
Van Kemenade (1987: 188ff) in discussing diachronic developments makes some remarks about the Peterborough Chronicle (Chron E). She notes that the Old English part of this text (certainly from 1070 onwards) already shows a number of cases where pronouns are used in positions which they do not normally occupy in Old English. 'Personal pronouns in the entries up to 1122 follow the patterns

described for Old English, albeit with an increasing number of exceptions' (1987: 189), and '...we find a remarkable number of personal pronouns in post-verbal position, i.e. to the right of the base-generated position for the verb. This is a position where they rarely occurred in Old English, and that indicates a step towards the loss of clitic status' (1987: 191). The purpose of this section is to evaluate these claims. Is the Peterborough Chronicle on the road to decliticization and different from other Old English texts? Other Old English texts also show exceptions to the clitic positions (see (64-9)), but are they less frequent? In order to find out I have looked at a number of texts, and have counted all the non-subject pronoun forms. The following texts were examined, chosen in such a way that they are representative of various periods of Old English:

(95)   Early Old English: *Cura Pastoralis*
                                   Orosius
                                   Bede

        Late Old English: Ælfric's *Catholic Homilies* vol. 1 and 2
                                   Wulfstan (homilies, and WCan and WPol)

        Chronicles   Parker Chronicle (ChronA)
                                   Peterborough Chronicle (ChronE)

To evaluate van Kemenade's claims about the Peterborough Chronicle I intend to look at the total percentages of recognizable clitics (5.2). If she is right this should be lower in the Peterborough Chronicle (more exceptions). Next, the exceptions themselves will be looked at (5.3). They should be more frequent in the Peterborough Chronicle. Clitic objects of P follow in 5.4, and in 5.5 I shall try to isolate in which way the Peterborough Chronicle is different.

5.2 Clitic pronouns
In Table 1 the total number of non-subject pronouns is set out. Not included are postmodified pronouns (3.1), pronouns which are part of a larger phrase (3.3), pronominal objects of P (3.4), and topicalized pronouns (2.6.4):[14]

TABLE 1

CP	1681
Orosius	1089
Bede	1194
ÆCHom i	1871
ÆCHom ii	1842
Wulfstan	662
ChronA	186
ChronE	700

The total number of pronouns is of course largely determined by the length of the text involved, and also to some extent by the nature of the text. ChronA is considerably shorter than ChronE. Both volumes of ÆCHom are of about equal length, and show almost the same number of pronouns. These texts can be compared quite well in that the nature of the texts is the same. Any individual preference might come out by comparing the works of Ælfric and Wulfstan.

How can we measure degrees of (de)cliticization? One approach is to count the number of clear clitic pronouns as a percentage of the total number of pronouns. This can be done with a fair amount of exactness for Pos. B (to the right of the finite verb if the first constituent is an operator), and Pos. C (immediately to the right of the complementizer in subordinate clauses). It stands to reason that there will not be all that many examples of Pos. B, for with an object pronoun this is only clear if the subject is not a pronoun. Cases of Pos. A (left of V in INFL) can be counted as well, but it is often difficult to interpret specific clauses (see Section 4). The figures for Pos. E (left of V) include all those cases where there is no formal difference between Pos. D (left in the VP) and Pos. E (left of V). Here, the problem of interpretation crops up as well. It should also be kept in mind that it is by no means certain that all pronouns in Pos. D and Pos. E can be regarded as clitics. I have tried to be consistent in my treatment of the material, but obviously cannot claim that the figures are completely reliable. Calculations were done for the following texts: CP, ÆCHom i, ChronA, and ChronE.

TABLE 2

Positions	A	B	C	D	E	Totals
CP (N=1681)	99 (6%)	15 (0.9%)	140 (8%)	402 (24%)	483 (29%)	1139 (68%)
ÆCHom i (N=1875)	174 (9%)	13 (0.7%)	50 (3%)	234 (13%)	607 (32%)	1078 (57%)
ChronA (N=186)	12 (6%)	4 (2%)	8 (4%)	39 (21%)	21 (11%)	84 (45%)
ChronE (N=700)	60 (9%)	4 (0.5%)	24 (3%)	96 (14%)	118 (17%)	302 (43%)

Table 2 shows a reduction in the total percentage of clitic pronouns from CP to ÆCHom i, but this is largely accounted for, I suspect, by the increasing number of co-ordinate clauses which are difficult to analyse. Both ChronA and ChronE show fewer clitic pronouns than the other texts, but again this is almost totally due to the nature of the texts involved (many co-ordinate clauses). There is no great difference between ChronA and ChronE. Even when we break down ChronE into sections, there is no appreciable difference between the sections and ChronA.[15]

Clitic Pronouns

TABLE 3

Positions	A	B	C	D	E	Totals
ChronA (N=186)	12 (7%)	4 (2%)	8 (4%)	39 (21%)	21 (11%)	84 (45%)
ChronE (to 1070) (N=384)	34 (9%)	2 (0.5%)	16 (4%)	48 (29%)	69 (18%)	169 (44%)
ChronE (1070-1121) (N=174)	13 (7%)	1 (0.5%)	6 (3%)	31 (18%)	34 (20%)	54 (49%)
ChronE (1121-end) (N=142)	13 (9%)	1 (0.5%)	2 (1%)	17 (12%)	15 (11%)	48 (34%)

The combined percentages of A, B and C, stay fairly constant in the three sections. The differences are slight given the relatively low numbers involved. The total percentage of pronouns recognizable as clitics is lowest in the last section of ChronE. It is difficult, however, to see in this positive corroboration of van Kemenade's view that ChronE is on the way to decliticization. ChronE has many co-ordinate clauses with the pronoun object following the verb. It cannot be established whether they are in a clitic position or not (see Section 4.5). For further discussion see Section 5.5.

On the basis of the figures presented above we cannot conclude that ChronE has appreciably more exceptions to the clitic positions. Let us therefore look at the exceptions themselves.

5.3 Non-clitic pronouns

In Section 3 various classes of non-clitic pronouns were discussed, and many have already been excluded from the count in Table 1. Two classes of non-clitic pronouns stand out, for they can be said to be genuine exceptions. They are object pronouns not occupying any of the two clitic positions in the VP (3.5) and extraposed pronouns (3.6). In both cases it would have been possible for the pronoun to have occupied a clitic position. Table 4 gives numbers for these two categories, and percentages of the total number of pronouns.

TABLE 4

	non-clitic in VP (3.5)	extraposition (3.6)	Tot		N
CP	8	1	9	(0.5%)	1681
Orosius	4	4	8	(0.7%)	1089
Bede	11	2	13	(1.1%)	1194
ÆCHom i	17	28	45	(2.4%)	1871
ÆCHom ii	22	7	29	(1.6%)	1842
Wulfstan	3	14	17	(2.6%)	662
ChronA	1	2	3	(1.6%)	186
ChronE	2	21	23	(3.2%)	700

From Table 4 we can see that there is a gradual increase in the percentage of exceptions, but the percentages involved are low in all texts. It is also clear that ChronE is not startlingly different from other late Old English texts. In the Middle English section of ChronE there are as far as I have been able to establish no instances of those discussed in 3.5, and only 8 of those discussed in 3.6 (=5.6%). The percentage is somewhat higher in the latter part of ChronE, but on the whole the material hardly warrants the conclusion that ChronE is very different from other Old English texts, and on the road to decliticization. With equal justification it could be maintained that the other texts show decliticization as well.

5.4 Pronominal objects of P

Pronominal objects of P are often clitics. Decliticization would show up when we compare the number of pronominal clitics of P with the total number of pronouns with P. If ChronE is indeed different it should show a lower percentage here. In Table 5[16] the number of clitics are given, and in Table 6 the clitic positions are shown for a few texts:

TABLE 5

	clitics	after P	Totals (=N)
CP	56 (19%)	235	291
Orosius	130 (34%)	253	383
Bede	61 (14%)	388	449
ÆCHom i	158 (28%)	407	565
ÆCHom ii	180 (34%)	347	527
Wulfstan	33 (33%)	68	101
ChronA	41 (52%)	38	79
ChronE	30 (13%)	206	236

TABLE 6

Clitic Positions	A	B	C	D	E	F[17]		Totals
CP	3	-	14	6	-	33	(59%)	56
ÆCHom i	8	1	4	-	3	142	(90%)	158
ChronA	1	-	3	3	-	34	(83%)	41
ChronE	5	1	6	2	1	15	(50%)	30

Table 5 does indeed reveal a low percentage for ChronE, but the percentage in Bede is also fairly low. The Middle English part of ChronE only has instances of F, a position favoured by all the texts examined. It seems reasonable to draw the conclusion that the Peterborough Chronicle in its Middle English part shows a reduction in clitic objects of P.

5.5 Peterborough Chronicle

There is one construction in which ChronE clearly shows a difference with the other texts. It occurs in co-ordinated clauses without subject:

(96)   7 brohte him þider mid micel ferd
        'and brought him thither with great levies' (ChronE(Plummer)1140.14)

As indicated in section 4.5 there are a number of possible analyses for (96), some of which involve non-clitic pronouns. We cannot be certain however. There is an alternative construction with the pronoun object before the verb:

(97)   7 hiene gefliemde
        and it put to flight
        (='and put it to flight') (ChronA (Plummer) 876.16)

Of all the texts ChronE shows the greatest number of constructions as in (96), with relatively few of (97). All the other texts have about equal numbers. This explains the low percentage of recognizable clitics in Table 3. There is a strong tendency in ChronE to put the object after the verb in co-ordinate clauses.

5.6 Conclusion

The evidence presented in this section shows that there is no appreciable difference in usage between Ælfric and Wulfstan. It also reveals quite clearly that ChronE is not really different from the other texts investigated, with the possible exception of clitic objects of P. Van Kemenade's claims about ChronE are not supported by my evidence. ChronE shows a marked difference only in the number of coordinate clauses with the object after the verb, but it is not clear that all of them (or even which of them) are in a non-clitic position.

6 Latin Influence?

6.1 Introduction

It is relatively unusual for personal pronouns to occur in absolute final position in a clause. Some pronouns occur in clause final position because there is no choice:

(98)   soðlice ne finde ge hine
        indeed not find you him
        (='indeed you will not find him') (ÆCHom i.31.456.28)

The subject is in a clitic position and there is no alternative for the object pronoun but to have end position. Notice, though, that we can argue that it is on the trace of the verb. It is different for clauses with final pronouns if another position is available:

(99) ne fæste ge ðæs nawuht me
      not fasted you of-this not me-DAT
      (='you did not fast for me') (CP 43.315.24)

(100) ac ge ne oncneowon hine
      but you not knew him
      (='but you did not know him') (ÆCHom ii.13.128.32)

Clauses of this kind are very rare in the early prose and in the Chronicles, but occur sporadically in ÆCHom i and ii. In the early prose they are almost exclusively in quotations from the Bible. In Ælfric quite a few occur in Bible quotations where contrast is often a factor:

(101) Ne gecure ge me, ac ic geceas eow
      not chose you me but I chose you
      (='You did not choose me, but I chose you') (ÆCHom ii.40.301.63)

However, there are also instances in Ælfric of pronouns in clause final position which are not quotations of the Bible, and where contrast is not explicit:

(102) se ælmihtiga god cyð his godnysse us
      the almighty God manifests his goodness us
      (='Almighty God manifests his goodness to us')(ÆCHom ii.21.188.262)

Could it be possible that Latin influence (more particularly the influence of the sacred text that the Bible is) is at work here, and could it be possible that this may account for the fact that Ælfric occasionally puts pronouns in clause final position, where they would not naturally or often occur? A possible answer lies in an analysis of pronoun usage in Bible translations.

6.2 A native pattern

I want to begin the discussion with a quotation from Æflric's preface to the translation of Genesis, in which he talks about translating the Bible from Latin:

> Nu is seo foresæde boc on manegum stowum swyðe nearolice gesett, & ðeah swyðe deoplice on ðam gastlican andgyte; 7 heo is swa geendebyrd, swa swa God sylf hi gedihte ðam writere Moyse, 7 we ne durron na mare awritan on Englisc þonne ðæt Leden hæfð, ne ða endebyrdnysse awendan, buton ðam anum, ðæt ðæt Leden 7 ðæt Englisc nabbað na ane wisan on ðære spræce fandunge: æfre se ðe awent oððe se ðe tæcð of Ledene on Englisc, æfre he sceal gefadian hit swa ðæt ðæt Englisc hæbbe his agene wisan, elles hit bið swyðe gedwolsum to rædenne ðam ðe ðæs Ledenes wise ne can (Crawford 1922: 79-80).

> Now the forementioned book is in many places very densely composed and yet profound in its spiritual meaning and it is arranged just as God directed to the writer Moses, and we dare not write more in English than the Latin has, nor change the order except for one reason, namely that Latin and English do not have one manner in the disposition of language. Anyone who translates or teaches from Latin into English must always phrase it in such a way that English has its own order, else it will be very misleading to read for those who do not know the Latin order.

This quotation illustrates, I think quite clearly, that Ælfric was aware of differences in idiom and syntax between Latin and Old English, and we can assume that what he wrote himself and the translations he made are written within the possible patterns of Old English. We should therefore regard the object pronoun in end position as a possible, though perhaps unusual pattern in Old English.

6.3 Object pronouns in Bible translation

In the Bible object pronouns occur frequently after the verb and therefore in end position. A survey of Chapters 1-10 of the Gospel of St. Mark in the West Saxon Gospels[18] shows that there is often a one-to-one correspondence between the Latin pronouns and the Old English translation:

(103)   7 he sæde him
        et dicebat eis
        'and he said to them' (Mk (WSCp) 4.11)

(104)   hi onfengon hine swa he on scipe wæs
        adsumunt eum ita ut erat in navi
        'they took him even as he was in the ship' (Mk (WSCp) 4.36)

(105)   7 hi awehton hine
        et excitant eum
        'and they awoke him' (Mk (WSCp) 4.38)

Note that in all three quotations the Old English object pronoun could have been put before the verb. The author of the Gospels chose not to do so. In Mark 1-10 pronouns appear in clause final position some 30 times, which is far more often that in the texts that I have examined. That the Gospels are not simply an adapted interlinear gloss is shown by the fact that the translation does not stick mechanically to the position in Latin for the object pronoun. In Mark 1-10 the position of the pronoun corresponds with the position in Latin in 76 instances, but in 128 cases the Old English text puts a pronoun in a different position from what it has in Latin. Most of these have a pronoun before the verb:

(106)   7 him englas þenodon
        et angeli ministrabant illi
        'and the angels ministered to him' (Mk(WSCp)1.13)

(107)   7 hi him be hyre sædon
        et statim dicunt ei de illa
        'and they told him about her' (Mk(WSCp)1.30)

(108)   7 he hi lærde
        et docebat eos
        'and he taught them' (Mk(WSCp)2.13)

Of particular interest are pronouns in Old English in end position where they do not occupy such a position in Latin (109-110) or where there is no pronoun at all (111):

(109)   gif þu wylt ðu miht geclænsian me
        si vis potes me mundare
        'if you want to you can make me clean' (Mk((WSCp)1.40)

(110)   swa þæt hi æthrinon his
        ut illum tangerent
        'so that they touched him' (Mk(WSCp)3.10)

(111)   aþene þine hand 7 he aþenede hi
        extende manum tuam et extendit
        'hold out your hand and he held it out' (MkWSCp)3.5)

In (109-110) the Old English pronoun is extraposed, as well as in final position. Extraposition cannot be proved for (111). These cases seem to me to be very significant. It shows I think quite conclusively that in Old English end position is a possible position for personal pronouns. That they occur only relatively infrequently in this position in prose could be because it is a position in which 'light' elements are usually not found. In Æflric's Homilies the Gospel text plays a central role, and the fact that object pronouns occur regularly in the Gospel transaction in final position may have made it more acceptable to him to use pronouns in this way in his writings, something which was already possible, but rarely done.

7 Phonological Evidence for Clitic Pronouns

7.1 Introduction

So far we have looked at syntactic evidence for clitic pronouns. Van Kemenade stresses that 'cliticization in Old English is a syntactic form of cliticization, for which we only have syntactic evidence in the form of specific positioning of clitics'. (1987:140). In her view this type of cliticization is quite different from phonological cliticization which shows up in reduced forms. Is there any evidence that personal pronouns had such forms? Van Kemenade does not believe so (1987: 140): 'Phonological evidence for clitic status of personal pronouns...is lacking. It is unclear whether such evidence may have been available to the learner of Old English'. Cliticization in Old English as discussed above involves both procliticization and encliticization. As far as I know there is no evidence for phonological procliticization. Indeed, the fact that the negative clitic *ne* quite clearly cliticizes onto the verb (see such forms as *næfde, næs* etc.) and (when present) prevents the pronoun from doing so suggests that there was probably no form of phonological procliticization in Old English. Is there any phonological evidence for encliticization? I will argue that such evidence for the clitic status of personal pronouns exists, though it is only convincing for the pronoun *þu* and to a lesser extent *hit*. Other personal pronouns do not show up in reduced form in the orthography, but there may be glimpses of evidence.

7.2 Evidence for *þu*

Only one pronoun shows extensive phonological reduction in Old English. That is the personal pronoun *þu* when it occupies a position to the right of the verb. In other positions there is as far as I am aware no orthographic evidence to suggest that reduced forms were used. Assimilation of the ending of the verb (usually-*st*) with the initial consonant of the pronoun is shown in various stages. Such a phonological reduction had apparently taken place at least once before in the history of the English language. Campbell (1957: §731) explains the final *t* of the Old English second person present indicative ending by this process. The Old English orthographic conventions are such that assimilation in this position can only rarely be observed. The available evidence, however, suggests that the process was probably far more widespread than the orthography indicates.

Phonological reduction of *þu* shown in spelling is not very frequent, but not rare either. I have counted well over a hundred instances, using the microfiche concordance as a basis. The following forms can be distinguished:

7.2.1   -*stþu*   (< -st þu)

If the spellings here are at all reliable we could take instances of these as the first step towards reduction. The pronoun in this position cliticizes onto the verb and writing verb and clitic as one word may indicate this. It must be emphasised, however, that as it is common practice in Old English to separate words which we would regard as one (compound words), not too much should be made of the presence or absence of a word division. The examples are all from glosses:[19]

(112)   God deme rihtwis strang & langmodi *cwistþu* eorseð þurh sendrie dagas [Deus iudex iustus fortis et longanimis numquid irascetur per singulos dies] (PsG1E (Harsley) 7.12)

In all instances the word in question is *cwistþu* (which is also sometimes spelt *cwistu, cwisþu, cwystðu, cwystþu, cwysþu, cwysðstþu, quysðu* , and *qysþu* (also *cwedestu* in the Lindisfarne Glossses). We are here dealing with the translation of Latin *num* (*quid*) in questions with an expected negative answer. They are in a sense special cases, but nevertheless show a close cohesion, both linguistically (as some of the assimilated forms show), semantically (as the Latin equivalent shows), and syntactically (they serve as a sort of interjection).

7.2.2   -sttu (< -stþu)
The fricative of the pronoun has been assimilated to the plosive of the ending.

Examples:

(113)   ...& ne *gemesttu* ænig of ðon vel ðæm (MkGl (Ru)(12.14)

(114)   ...cwæð him eftersona simon iohannis *lufasttu* mec (JnGL(Ru) 21.16)

7.3.3   -ttu (< -tþu)
Some verbs do not have a second person ending in *-st*, but in *-t*. They are *scealt*, *þearft*, *meaht*, *eart*, and *wilt*. They show a different assimilation result:

(115)   ...Nu *earttu* sceaðana sum (Sat 57)

(116)   ...hwæt *wylttu* ðæt ic ðe gidoe...(MkGl (Ru) 10.51)

(117)   ...þa cwæð he, hwæt *wylttu* (Mt (WsCp)20.21)

7.2.4   -sþu (< -stþu)
The plosive of the verb ending has disappeared. Examples:

(118)   Hwig *flitsðu* wið þinne nehstan? (Exod 2.13)

(119)   *Agyltsðu* Drihtne ðas ðincg, stunt folc & unwis (Deut 32.6)

(120)   & þu sy tomergen/þon iglande þonne *gesitsþu* hine god/her/cgan (LS 13 (Machutus) 9.v.8)

(121)   ...telsþu oððe demsþu...(BoGl (Hale) P.9.39)

(122)   And hio þonne get cweð, sio sawl, *gehersðu* , min se leofesta lichoma? (HomM 14.2 (Healey) 61)

(123)   Hwi *læddesðu* us ut of Egypta lande...? (Exod.17.2)

(124)   ...ne *oferfærsðu* Iordane (Deut. 31.2)

(125)   Forhwon, earma lichoma, *lufodesðu* þone feond, ðæt wæs se diofol? (HomM 14.1 (Healey)8)

There are a few more examples in glosses.[20]

7.2.5 -tu (< -tþu)

As with the examples under 7.2.3 there are only a few verbs involved. The examples are quite numerous, and are from various texts. Some examples:

(126)   ne *mihtu* mid þæm eallum sauwle þine ut alysan (Exhort 22)

(127)   Hu *mihtu* for sceame æniges þinges æt gode biddan (ÆCHom i.18.256.5)

(128)   *Scealtu* æninga mid ærdæge, emne to morgenne, æt meres ende ceol gestigan (And 220)

(129)   ...huer *wiltu* þæt we gearuiga ðe til eottanne eastro (MtGl (Li)26.17)[21]

7.2.6 -stu (< -stþu)

Over 50 cases have been found. Here is a selection:

(130)   & eft he cuæð to Petre ðæm apostole: Petrus *lufastu* me? (CP 5.43.3)

(131)   þa cwæð se ercebiscop to ðam æðelan læce, *nastu* hwæt þu sægst (ÆLS (Basil) 581)

(132)   Hwi *noldestu* gelyfan þinum drihtene þe wæs ahangen for us (HomS 6 (Ass 14) 80)

(133)   Hweder *siþastu* buton þinum bearne (ÆCHom i.29.416.33)

7.2.7 Some special forms:

(134)   cwæþ to heom fereþ secgaþ arþu...(MtGl (Ru)11.3)

Further *earþu* forms in PsGlJ (Oess) 30.15; (PsGLA (Kuhn) 41.5, 41.12, 42.5, 113.5.

(135)   þa cwæð he, *cwystuþu* magon þæs brydguman bearn fæstan swa lange swa se brydguma myd him ys (Lk(WSCp) 5.34).

The form itself is interesting. It seems to be a blend between *cwystu* and *cwystþu* or *cwyst þu* as the other manuscripts have.

7.2.8. The examples given above will have shown that the spelling sometimes does show evidence of assimilation of *þu* in various degrees. The existence of a reduced form of *þu* is undisputed on the basis of this evidence. The texts in which such forms are found come from the whole of the Old English period, from the CP text at the end of the 9th century to Ælfric and beyond. We can therefore safely conclude that the phenomenon was present during most (if not the whole) of the Old English period. The spellings are not very frequent, most probably due to the influence of a strong orthographic tradition, and the habit of correcting texts before they were actually copied. Such 'sloppy' forms were almost certain to be corrected, just as it is unusual today to use phonologically reduced forms in serious prose. The fact nevertheless that quite a few forms 'slipped through' is revealing. It is also not surprising in this view that the majority of recorded cases occur in glossed texts, where we can assume that the pressure to conform to orthographic practice was not so strong.[22]

7.3 Other pronouns

The evidence for reduced forms for other Old English personal pronouns is almost totally lacking. *Hit* is occasionally spelled *it*, particularly in later texts, ChronE, and charters:

(136)   ac we *it* reccað on Englisc (ÆLS (Maur) 362)

(137)   7 clependen *it* tenserie (ChronE (Plummer) 1137.39)

(138)   buten ic *it* self do (Ch 1521 (Whitelock 29) 32)

All the cases of *it* (subject or object) are in potential clitic positions. There is just one instance of *it* in a non-clitic position and that is in a late text (ChronE (Plummer) 1140.41). This suggests that *hit* lost the *h* first in clitic position.

Though *h* is unstable (see Scragg 1970), it is remarkable that there is no evidence for its loss in other *h* pronouns, with the possible exception of *him* in an inscription:

(139)   Garmvnd mec ah im (Inscr. 6(Ok 13) 1)[23]

8 Conclusion

In this chapter various aspects of Old English personal pronouns were discussed. It was argued that one of the clitic positions set up by van Kemenade should be interpreted differently. The evidence for the existence of an abstract case assigner at the left end of the VP is slight, and it was claimed that the position at the beginning of the VP is the SPEC position, open to pronouns only. The SPEC position acts as an escape hatch, illustrated by the behaviour of double object clitics. Many pronouns cannot be clitics, because they are modified, co-ordinated, or the complement of P. It was also argued that not all object pronouns could be clitics. Distributional facts, passivization, and the occurrence of clear non-clitic object pronouns support this. Cliticization should then be seen as optional. The available material is often difficult to interpret, which makes it hard to determine exactly how many clitic pronouns a text actually has. There is very little evidence that later texts show a greater degree of decliticization than earlier texts. The Peterborough Chronicle proved to be very similar both in type and percentage of exceptions to other Old English texts investigated, with the possible exception of clitic objects of P. It did, however, show many more co-ordinated clauses with pronoun objects after the verb. Clause final position of object pronouns occurs very rarely in the earlier texts, almost always in quotations from Latin. Ælfric occasionally has pronouns in clause final positions in his own prose, thus showing that this was a possible, though rare, pattern. The position of the pronoun in Latin could have helped in making end position of object pronouns more acceptable to Ælfric. Spelling evidence shows that some pronouns had reduced forms in Old English, *þu* probably during the whole period, *hit* towards the end of the period. It cannot be shown that other personal pronouns had reduced forms.

NOTES

* I am grateful to Olga Fischer, Ans Van Kemenade, Frederike van der Leek, Andries Vos, and Wim van der Wurff for comments on an earlier draft of this paper.

1. The texts examined were *Cura Pastoralis* (CP), *Orosius* (Or), Bede, Ælfric's *Catholic Homilies* , vols I and II (ÆCHom i and ii), from Wulfstan the *Homilies* (WHom), *Canons of Edgar* (WCan) and *Institutes of Polity* (WPol), the Parker Chronicle (ChronA), and the Peterborough Chronicle (ChronE). The microfiche concordances were used (Healey and Venezky 1980, and Venezky and Butler 1985). They use the following editions: CP (Sweet 1871), Or (Sweet 1883), Bede (Miller 1890-8), ÆCHom i (line references are to Thorpe 1844-6, but his text is not used), ÆCHom ii (Godden 1979), WHom (Bethurum 1957), WCan (Fowler 1972), WPol (Jost 1959), ChronA and ChronE (Plummer 1892-9).
2. For an extensive discussion of V2 in the Germanic languages see Weerman (1989).
3. I have not used van Kemenade's examples, mainly because she is also concerned with *þær* examples and often does not give an example where I needed one. She is not always clear in her treatment of co-oridinate clauses. Line references are to the concordance quotation in which the text cited is found.
4. See Wende (1915).
5. It could be argued that this is a V2 clause with *hælend crist* and *of heofenum* both in TOPIC position, and that therefore the clitic object of P occupies Pos A: [т [hælend crist] т [of heofendum] INFL [me spræci] VP[PP[to e] t]. I regard such an analysis as unlikely. There is little evidence that PPs occupy Topic positions *after* the subject. It should be said, however, that there are no examples of subordinate clauses with the clitic object of P clearly in Pos. E in my material, neither does Wende record any (1915: 101). In the few examples that exist Pos. D and Pos. E cannot be distinguished (ÆCHom ii.1.7.146), the subject is extraposed (e.g. ÆCHom i.27.386.5), or we are dealing with a co-ordinate clause where the position of the verb is not clear.
6. Some of the examples given by van Kemenade are of co-ordinated clauses. I would analyse her (11.b) (and him com þæt leoht to þurh paules lare syððan) and (11.c) (ac him com fyr to færlice ehsynes) (1987: 116) as having a pronoun in the TOPIC position, rather than on the left of the finite V.
7. Van Kemenade (personal communication) suggests that a clitic left of COMP would

disturb operator positions. She thinks that complementizers do not allow another A¹ position in COMP, possibly for reasons of transparency.

8. I leave out *ne*, because its status is clearly different. The presence of *ne* does not prevent a pronoun from occupying the clitic position left of the verb: Hie his ne geliefað (CP 31.207.1).

9. The distribution of pronominal subjects is such that we cannot prove that a clitic subject and a clitic object occupy the same clitic position.

10. Prepositional phrases can of course be topicalized, as happens frequently. It is unusual for the prepositional phrase to have the prepositon in postposition. I have found one possible instance:

Him to genealæhton his discipuli
him to approached his disciples
(='his disciples approached him') (ÆCHom i.36.548.25)

11. There is a further problem here. If subject pronouns in passive sentences are not clitics, we would expect them to show the same syntactic behaviour as full NP subjects. However, there is no difference between subject pronouns in passive and non-passive sentences. They occupy the typical clitic positions, and do not occur, as far as I am aware, in non-clitic positions: they are not found separated from the complementizer for instance. I am not certain how this should be explained.

12. See on the word order after *þa* Mitchell (1985: §§2518-36; 2543-54, 3922).

13. The word order VS sometimes occurs in subordinate clauses (Mitchell 1985: §3934), but is of course frequent in main clauses.

14. The figures are as exact as possible, but I have refrained from double checking because of the work involved. Even if they are not absolutely correct they still give a good idea of the distribution in the various texts.

15. I have rather arbitrarily divided ChronE in three sections. In many respects a more logical division would be to separate the Middle English portion (1122-end) from the rest. The section up to 1122 was copied in one block from another manuscript (Clark 1970: xviii ff).

16. Wende (1915: 82) found 482 instances of prepositions in postposition in ChronA, ÆCHom i and ii, Bede, and CP. My count is 496. The difference, apart from possible counting errors, lies in the fact that Wende investigated only a portion of ChronA.

17. Included under F are also cases where the exact clitic position could not be established.

18. Text quoted from Skeat (1871-87). For the Vulgate version I have used the Latin of the Lindisfarne Gospels.

19. I have given no translations, but have emphasised the relevant forms.

20. BoGl (Hale) P.8.14; P.4.15; P.5.29; P.5.31.

21. Further instances in Lk (WSCp)9.54; MTGl (Li)5.36; JnGl(Li)5.6; MtGl(Ru)20.21 and 13.28 and 14.22; LkGl(Ru)9.54 and 22.9; and JnGl(Ru)5.6.

22. About half occur in glosses.

23. Okasha (1971: 13) says: 'The significance of IM is uncertain; it could be decorative, to fill up space, an unrecorded abbreviation (e.g. for IHS), or an error due to a misreading of an exemplum as HIM'.

REFERENCES

Bacquet, Paul 1982. *La structure de la phrase verbale à lépoque alfrédienne.* (Publ. de la Faculté de Lettres de l'Université de Strasbourg, 145). Paris: Les Belles Lettres.

Barrett, Charles R. 1967. Aspects of the placing of the accusative object in Ælfric. *Journal of the Australasian Universities Language and Literature Association* 28, 178-202.

Bean, Marian, C. 1983. *The development of word order patterns in Old English.* London and Canberra: Croom Helm.

Bethurum, Dorothy 1957. *The homilies of Wulfstan.* Oxford: Oxford University Press.

Campbell, Alistair 1957. *Old English grammar.* Oxford: Oxford University Press.

Chomsky, Noam 1986. *Barriers.* Cambridge, Massachusetts: the MIT Press.

Clark, Cecily 1970. *The Peterborough Chronicle 1070-1154.* 2nd Edn. Oxford: Clarendon Press.

Crawford, Samuel, J. 1922. *The Old English version of the Heptateuch.* EETS 160. Oxford: Oxford University Press.

Fowler, Roger 1972. *Wulfstan's Canons of Edgar.* EETS 266. London: Oxford University Press.

Godden, Malcolm 1979. *Ælfric's Catholic Homilies: The second series, text.* EETS ss.5, London: Oxford University Press.

Haegeman, Liliane and Henk van Riemsdijk 1986. Verb projection raising, scope and the typology of rules affecting verbs. *Linguistic Inquiry* 17, 417-67.

Healey, Antonette DiPaolo and Richard L. Venezky 1980. *A microfiche concordance to Old English.* (Publications of the Dictionary of Old English 1). Toronto: Pontifical Institute of Medieval Studies.

Jost, Karlt 1959. *Die 'institutes of polity, civil and ecclesiastical'.* Swiss Studies in English 47. Bern: Francke.

Kemenade, Ans van 1984. Verb Second and Clitics in Old English. In Hans Bennis and W.U.S. van Lesen Kloeke (eds.). *Linguistics in the Netherlands 1984*, 101-09. Dordrecht: Foris.

Kemenade, Ans van 1987. *Syntactic case and morphological case in the history of English.* Dordrecht: Foris.

Koopman, Hilda 1984. *The syntax of verbs.* Dordrecht: Foris.

Koopman, Willem F. 1990a. The double object construction in Old English. In S. Adamson, V. Law, N. Vincent and S. Wright (eds.). *Papers from the 5th International Conference on English Historical Linguistic,* 225-43. Amsterdam: Benjamins.

Koopman, Willem F. 1990b. Old English constructions with three verbs. *Folia Linguistica Historica* IX/1, 271-300.

Larson, Richard K. 1988. On the double object construction. *Linguistic Inquiry* 19, 335-91.

Miller, Thomas 1890-98. *The Old English version of Bede's ecclesiastical history of the English People.* EETS 95, 96, 110, 111. London: Trübner.

Mitchell, Bruce 1964. Syntax and word-order in *The Peterborough Chronicle* 1122-54. *Neuphilologische Mitteilungen* 65, 113-44.

Mitchell, Bruce 1985. *Old English syntax.* Oxford: Clarendon Press.

Okasha, Elizabeth 1971. *Hand-list of Anglo-Saxon non-runic inscriptions.* Cambridge: The University Press.

Plummer, Charles 1892-99. *Two versions of the Saxon Chronicle Parallel.* 2 vols. Oxford: Oxford University Press.

Quirk, Randolph and Charles L. Wrenn 1955. *An Old English grammar.* London:

Methuen.

Riemsdijk, Henk van 1978. *A case study in syntactic markedness: The binding nature of prepositional phrases.* Dordrecht: Foris.

Scragg, Donald G 1970. Initital *h* in Old English. *Anglia* **88,** 165-96.

Skeat, Walter W. 1871-87. *The four gospels in Anglo-Saxon, Northumbrian and Old Mercian versions.* Cambridge: Cambridge University Press.

Stockwell, Robert P and Donka Minkova. 1990. Verb phrase conjunction in Old English. In H. Anderson (ed.) *Historical Linguistics 1987. Papers from the 8th international conference on historical linguistics,* 499-515. Amsterdam: Benjamins.

Sweet, Henry 1871. *King Alfred's West-Saxon version of Gregory's Pastoral Care.* EETS 45, 50. London: Oxford University Press

Sweet, Henry 1883. *King Alfred's Orosius.* EETS 79. London: Oxford University Press.

Thorpe, Benjamin 1844-46. *The Sermones Catholici or Homilies of Ælfric.* London: Ælfric Society.

Venezky, Richard L. and Sharon Butler 1985. *A microfiche concordance to Old English: the high frequency words.* (Publications of the Dictionary of Old English 2). Toronto: Pontifical Institute of Medieval Studies.

Weerman, Fred 1989. *The V2 conspiracy.* Dordrecht: Foris.

Wende, Fritz 1915. *Über die nachgestellten Präpositionen im Angelsächsischen. Palaestra* 70. Berlin: Mayer und Müller.

4

FRONT ROUNDED VOWELS IN OLD ENGLISH*

Roger Lass

Trying to see something solid in the mist is the whole fun of life, and most of its poetry.

Hu seo þrag gewat/genap under nihthelm ..

John Buchan, *The Gap in the Curtain*

- *The Wanderer*

1. Preliminaries

Germanic is one of the few language families where front rounded vowels (henceforth FRVs) are common. In a recent survey (Maddieson 1984), only 26 out of a 317-member sample of the world's languages (about 8%) have them; and within this group Indo-European and 'Ural-Altaic' (=Uralic, Turkic, Tungus and a few others) account for 74% of the total. The only other large attestation is in Sino-Tibetan (16%); the rest are thinly scattered through Kwa, Austro-Tai, and Uto-Aztecan. (This is a slightly larger figure than in some earlier surveys: see Lass 1975 for discussion.)

Within Indo-European, most of the FRV languages are Germanic (though there are examples in Western Romance, Breton and Albanian). Looking not at a sample but at modern Germanic as a whole, only Yiddish and English among the literary standards appear to lack them entirely. Restriction to the southern British standard types, however, grossly under-represents English: FRVs or FRV-like vowels (centralised [ø], [ʏ], advanced [ʉ] are widespread in other varieties. To take one example (and see §3 below), qualities in advance of [ʉ] occur for ME /o:/ isolative (GOOSE) in areas as far apart as the West Midlands, Scotland, the southern U.S., South Africa and New Zealand. There is no doubt that FRVs are highly characteristic of Germanic, and—if we avoid excessively restrictive definitions—of English as well.

They are not, however, an original IE category, and in a 'geological time' perspective may not be very old within Germanic itself (but see below). Of the ancient IE dialects, only Greek has any (/y (:)/ ‹ */u (:)/ in Attic and Ionic: Buck 1933: §76, Krahe 1962: §§16ff). It is widely accepted that they are late innovations in Germanic; a fair statement of the Germanist consensus, as I extract it from the handbooks, would be that:

(i) FRVs (phonetically) did not occur in Proto-Germanic, nor in the early post-unity dialects (East, Northwest Germanic: but see §2 below for dissident voices);

(ii) When they did arise, their first source was *i*-umlaut of the back rounded vowels */u(:), o(:)/;

(iii) By the time the major non-runic textual traditions of West Germanic appear, at least some of the dialects (for a while anyhow) have two FRV qualities, high and mid, both short and long;[1]

(iv) These (originally allophonic) qualities are phonemic in the written 'classical' stages of the literary dialects—though when they are phonologised may be debatable (as we will see).

My guess is that these four points are in general well taken; but (i) in particular is arguable, and the evidence curiously ambiguous. I think it's worthwhile exploring why we believe any of these things at all, and I will devote the following section to an exploration of the arguments for and against point (i). I will deal with (iii) and (iv) later; there seems, as far as I can tell, to be no problem with (ii).

2 When did FRV's First Appear in Germanic?

The claim that early Germanic did not have (phonetic) FRVs seems usually to be assumed rather than explicitly argued for. Its source is most likely an *argumentum ex silentio*, built on two facts about early Germanic orthography:

(i) Neither of the earliest graphic traditions, i.e the Older Futhark or Gothic orthography, has distinct symbols for FRVs (but see below on Gothic);

(ii) In those environments where in later times we expect primary FRVs (from umlaut rather than later processes), the categories in question are spelled with the same symbols that represent them in non-umlaut environments.

The directness of the argument from these two points is specious; the situation is considerably more complex. In the light of well-known properties of Germanic (and other) spelling traditions, we could in fact say that (i) either permits or at the very least is neutral with respect to the existence of (phonetic) FRVs in NWGmc and Gothic. In addition, there is a subsidiary argument from Gothic that suggests at first quite different grounds for believing that it didn't have FRVs, but which can be turned on its head to point in two directions, or in none clearly. I am not at this point aiming to take up any firm position at all; just looking in a fairly objective way at the empirical and argumentative foundations for a common faith.

Let's begin, however, with what looks clear: the absence of special FRV graphs and the use of 'neutral' symbols in umlaut environments. In early runic texts, e.g. what are now generally identified as NWGmc inscriptions of the earlier 5th century (not 'Urnordisch' as earlier: cf. Antonsen 1975, whom I follow here), the *u*-rune ᚾ and the *o*-rune ᛟ occur for PGmc */u/ and */o/ respectively in both umlaut and non-umlaut environments. So *-kuni* 'kin' (Turkjö bracteate, Antonsen

No.109: cf. OE *cynn*) vs. *wulafz* [2] 'wolf' (Istaby stone, Antonsen No.177: Old English *wulf*); *dohtriz* 'daughters' (Tune stone, Antonsen No.27: early Old English *doehter*) vs. *horna* 'horn' (acc sg) (Gallehus horn 2, Antonsen No.23: Old English *horn*).

The Gothic material is richer: examples are *ubila* 'evil' (Old English *yfel*), *hugjan* 'think' (Old English *hycgan*) vs. *dumbs* 'mute' (Old English *dumb*), *fugls* 'bird' (Old English *fugol*); *fodjan* 'foster' (early Old English *foedan* , *sokjan* 'seek' (early Old English *soecan*) vs. *goþs* 'good' (Old English *god*), *dauhtar* 'daughter' (Old English *dohtor*).[3] On such evidence it would indeed seem that there was no *i*-umlaut in the early dialects; for non-FRV environments this can be supported further by unfronted/unraised reflexes of PGmc */ɑ/ before /i j/, e.g. *harja* 'warrior' (Vimose comb, Antonsen No. 8: Old English *here*), Gothic *agis* 'fear' (Old English *egesa*).

But how good is this argument? *I*-umlaut is a 'natural' (phonetically motivated, very common) type of metaphony; and processes of this kind so often escape orthographic representation (scribes 'write phonemes, not allophones') that we have grounds for at least initial reservations. The early Germanic traditions are in fact full of cases of the non-representation of quite natural allophonies that we think on good grounds must have been there.

For instance, Old English foot-medial and marginal /f/ (*ofer* 'over' vs. *faran* 'fare', *ceaff* 'chaff') were spelled ‹ f ›; but history tells us that voicing occurred foot medially (*over* vs. *fare*, *chaff*). Even if the historical outcome allowed us to postpone the voicing until it was uniformly represented in spelling (which it doesn't)[4] there are occasional spellings from Old English times that show the voicing. So *hliuade* 'it towered' at *Beowulf* 1799 vs. expected *hlifade* at 81, 1898. And, we might add, even the later phonemicised voicing of medial /s/ (*houses* vs. *house's*) has rarely been spelled, and that of /θ/ never has (*oaths* vs. *clothes* : though this is a rather marginal contrast).

This holds for other well-attested allophonic processes throughout Germanic; aspiration of syllable-initial voiceless stops has never been written, though there are reasonable historical grounds for its being quite early (Lass 1981: 536 and note 14); it is first described only in the 16th century (Hart 1569: 49a). Even when an allophonic rule has major morphophonemic consequences, i.e. produces merger with a segment elsewhere distinct, there may be no graphic reflex. So terminal devoicing of voiced stops is generally not indicated in continental WGmc spellings (German *Tag* / *Tage* with surface /k/ vs. /g/), and so on. Contrariwise of course a process may be indicated at an early stage, and the spelling later shifted to a more 'abstract' mode, as in German: MHG had *tac* /*tage*, and the spelling was later made 'morphophonemic'.

Early Germanic orthographic principles are unfortunately a mixed bag; there seem to be no general laws about what can or can't or must be represented. Not only can allophonic or morphophonemic distinctions remain unspelled; even major phonemic oppositions may be: none of the Older Germanic traditions consistently marks vowel length, which was certainly distinctive. On the other hand, even some low-level allophonies were doggedly noted: the older Futhark and Gothic both have special representations for the velar nasal, which must have been an allophone of /n/ before velars — along with symbols for the nasals /m n/ and the velar stops /k g/.

Such a range of possibilities makes certain kinds of spellings very difficult to interpret. A sequence involving a general symbol for a phoneme and one for an environment that (at some point) triggers an alternation will in principle probably be equivocal. To return to our subject, the symbol-sequence ‹ kuni › in NWGmc or Gothic suggests at least these interpretations:

(i) Umlaut is not operative: ‹kuni› = /kuni/ = [kuni].

(ii) Umlaut is operative : ‹kuni› = /kuni/ = [kyni]

This is actually underdifferentiated: given a more sophisticated view of phonological change, (ii) should probably be resolved into two options:

(iia) Umlaut is variably operative, so that its implementation is token-specific: any ‹kuni› will = /kuni/, but may represent phonetic [kuni] or [kyni].

(iib) Umlaut is categorically operative, so that every token ‹kuni› represents /kuni/, [kyni].

The picture could be even more complicated. If umlaut is at an early and variable stage, it may also be in process of lexical diffusion; the whole range of options might be different for any given lexical item, so that some might be at stage (i), others at (iia), still others at (iib). And for (iia) each word might have its own quantitative profile. I take it that changes are 'neogrammarian' only on completion, but variable and diffusing in the early stages, and that spelling traditions like the Old Germanic ones may under these conditions fail to represent some changes at all, even if they do later, when they become categorical. And conversely—though this is not in question here—that in a variable / diffusional stage, any ambiguous token may represent any value of a variable. I will return to this in §4 below.

So in a case like this, what's to stop us from claiming that a given 'natural' change—regardless of spelling—was operative *ab origine* ? With respect to FRVs, this might licence us to take *all* back-vowel spellings in umlaut environments as reflecting phonetic implementation—no matter how early. Is there any way out of this for the early dialects? For NWGmc there doesn't seem to be (see below on the claim for FRVs there); for Gothic however, we just might have some data allowing us to argue against the possibility.

Overall the Gothic situation is simple, and like that of runic NWGmc: spellings like *kuni*, *sunjus* 'son', *sokjan* could have been used, it would seem, to represent at least fronted allophones, for /u/ conservatively [ü] or [ʉ], radically [y], etc. No effort however is made by the scribes to distinguish these from 'ordinary' /u/, and given the argumentation above, we could project umlaut back to Gothic —if with no strong support, at least without fear of contradiction.

But at least in the case of /u/ there is some indication that Gothic could not have had a FRV in the umlaut environments. Not on the basis of anything quite as vague as some general claim about Germanic spelling, but something positive that Gothic scribes actually did—if not with the category in question. In Greek loanwords the letter upsilon ‹ υ ›, which at this point still represented /y(:)/ is generally rendered not by the Gothic *u*-graph ‹ Π ›, but by what is usually tansliterated ‹w›, actually ‹ y ›. Thus *Swmaion* for Συμείον, *swnagoge* for συναγωγή, *martwr* for μάρτυρ, and so on. This spelling is also used for monophthongised /oi/, as in *fwnikiska* 'Phoenician' ‹ φοινικισσα (cf. Braune-Ebbinghaus 1966: §39 Anm 1).

Now this graph is otherwise reserved in general for Germanic */w/ or nonsyllabic /-u-/ in diphthongs (on the latter see below). Thus its employment for Greek /y(:)/ can be seen as a kind of default option. That is, <w> is not elsewhere used to represent an accented vowel, and hence could not be confused with a writing for /u/. This tactic could have been suggested by the visual similarity between the Gothic graph and an uncial upsilon ‹Y›.[5] Since most of the Gothic corpus is in fact translated from Greek, this choice on the part of scribes literate in both alphabets and bilingual or close to it in both languages is unsurprising (cf. Braune-Ebbinghaus §39). If indeed this graph represents a FRV in Greek forms, it seems reasonable to assume that it would have been used for similar vowel qualities in Germanic words—if they existed. Therefore the non-appearance of ‹w› in any case of potential *i* -umlaut of /u/ is an indirect sign that there was no reason not to use ‹u›, hence no salient difference in vowel quality.

There is one interesting exception to the use of ‹w› for Greek ‹υ› or Germanic /w/. In a few forms, especially neuter *wa*-stem nouns like *waurstw* 'work', *þiadw* 'bondage', ‹w› seems to indicate an unstressed thematic /u/ in alternation with /w/ (cf. nom/acc pl *waurstwa* and derivatives like *waurstweigs* 'effective'). This usage is unproblematical: (a) there are no stems in final */-Cw/; (b) even if Gothic had [y] ‹ /u/, it would not appear in this position, so a final graphic sequence (-Cw) could only be interpreted as /-Cu/. Hence ‹w› is used here as a kind of marker of morphophonemic alternation, a declension-sign, not as a representation of whatever it indicates in Greek. (In any case, nobody would suggest that initial ‹ swn- › in *swnagoge* meant /swn-/!).

Neat as this argument is, it too runs into trouble. First of all, though it's not clear exactly what ‹w› represented in consonantal positions ([w] or [β], etc), it is most unlikely that it could have been palatal (e.g [ɥ]). If it was weakened or vocalised post-vocalically, it must surely have been ([u̯] in such positions, as its connection with the *wa* -stems suggests, as well as its occasional use for Latin [u] in diphthongs (*kawtsjo* ‹ *cautio*). Therefore its use for Greek /y(:)/ would be a gross deviation from its usual nonpalatal denotation, given the rest of the usages. We could then argue from its likeness to upsilon for a totally nonphonetic interpretation even of its use in Greek loans: it simply capitalises on the (adventitious?) visual similarity to give a purely symbolic or graphic expression to perceived 'Greekness'. It is then a learned Hellenism, an elegance, rather than an attempt at rendering a phonetic value. (Given the prestige of Greek in the Byzantine world whose fringes Gothic occupied, this would be unsurprising: a similar use of ‹y› occurs in Late Latin, even where Greek etymology is not in question: Allen 1965: 52f. ‹y› also occurs as a 'foreignism'—not necessarily a Hellenism—in OHG, e.g. *Babylonia, Syri, Moyses, martyra*: Braune-Mitzka 1967: §22).

So we're left with a somewhat ambiguous, if not entirely contemptible argument to the effect that Gothic really did not have FRVs, which added to the general (if weak) argumentum from lack of distinct representation lends some support to the view that they are a late development. This would be less problematic if it weren't for a mildly reprehensible but understandable habit among historians: the free employment of *argumentum ex silentio* where one doesn't want certain things to be the case, but its disregard or deprecation where one does. That is, the manifest lack of FRV spellings can be taken as 'evidence' against them, where other non-differentiated spellings somehow count *for* the existence of alternations. So in a textbook treatment of Gothic, W. H. Bennett (1965: §1.2) simply says that '[y] ... was foreign to Gothic', and was 'probably pronounced... as a native Gothic *u*-sound' in *martwr*, and as 'the vowel-glide [w]' in *kawtsjo, waurstwa*. But on the other hand he claims that <b> and <d> represented 'two positional variants' : stops initially and finally, and fricatives medially (§§1.6ff). In neither case does he give any justification (though there are some interesting arguments from the morphophonemic behaviour of <b, d>: on their import see Anderson 1987); but there are parallels. Similar (unstated) grounds apparently allow Antonsen (1975: §4.9), who would like FRVs to be early, to have them in NWGmc. (More or less the same claim is made by Penzl 1988: 263, since this supposedly 'explains' the absence of FRV spellings in Gothic and their later 'Entfaltung' in the NWGmc daughter-languages.)

Antonsen goes further than deriving them from *i*-umlaut: in addition to [y] in *wulafiz* 'shewolf' (Istaby stone, No. 117: cf. Old English *wylf*), he allows them as reflexes of PGmc */eu/ ([y:] in *bAriutiþ* 'breaks'), Stentoften stone, No. 119: cf. OIc *brýtr*). He provides no arguments: he simply says that *i* -umlaut of nonfront vowels (not to mention *u*-umlaut!) is phonemicised in East and West Norse 'after the loss of conditioning */i/ and */u/'—which is true enough, but doesn't support the early date for the phonetic occurrence.

Antonsen's claim is speculative, and should not have been made so baldly. But is it really that much worse, given the evidence we've looked at, than claiming that FRVs did *not* exist this early? If we make such a (not untenable, but weakish) assumption, then the *terminus a quo* for FRVs vanishes into the mists of Germanic antiquity. We can only say that they are not original IE, and could have arisen at any point in the 'Pre-Germanic' or Proto-Germanic murk, or in the early stages of the separated dialects. The only point at which we (virtually) *know* that they've appeared is when we begin to find special representations for them. So the *terminus a quo* is either open, or can be assigned to the first occurrences of funny new runes or graphs in the appropriate places. (More realistically, if vaguely, to 'some time before' such appearances, given the time needed to invent and propagate new symbols. The historiographic convention of course is that first appearances are a kind of *de facto* birthday). Even given this pussyfooting caution and ambiguity, however, we will see that the early Old English evidence is still in some ways hard to interpret.

3 Excursus: Why FRVs at all?

The state of play at the moment is this: we can't rule out (phonetic) FRVs from very ancient times indeed, but neither can we assert them except on rather feeble grounds. The best we can do on the date-of-origin question is to establish when and where they become salient enough to merit their own symbols, which is easy enough to do. Given the characteristics of these first appearances, we can also investigate the complex questions of their phonologisation; I will have something to say about this in the next section.

At this point though I want to turn to a different question, in keeping with the general concerns of this volume. Why should we imagine that certain spellings in Old English represented FRVs at all, and not something quite different? As far as I know, nobody has recently canvassed all the converging arguments (many of them implicit), and put them together in one place; and it seems worth doing. It's healthy for workers in a field—and even healthier for the students they attempt to teach (or brainwash)—to re-examine occasionally the bases for their most cherished and firmly held beliefs, and see what, if any, support they have. The danger of coming late in a long tradition is that we forget the difference between what we believe on the grounds of rational conviction, and what are simply bits of tradecraft our masters taught us ages ago. I think in this case our masters were on the right track, but that's no reason not to ask.

The standard assumption is that throughout Old English ‹y›, and in the earlier stages ‹œ›, represented FRVs, respectively high and mid (so e.g. Wright and Wright 325: §5, Wyld 1927: § 81, Campbell 1959: §36, Pilch 1970: §6, and so on). Some of these authorities characterise the vowels only roughly (Wyld 'high' vs. 'mid', Pilch 'hoch' vs. 'mittel'); others, on what grounds it's not easy to see, assign a specific 'mid' height to ‹œ›. So Campbell (*loc. cit.*) says that 'it is clear that ȳ was close and œ̄ half open'. The latter must be based (given his aetiology for FRVs in the first place) on the dubious assumption that the PGmc mid back vowel was */ɔ/, which is difficult indeed to support (nobody worries about ‹y›, which must indeed have been high—at least its long version: see below; the corners of dead vowel systems are easy to establish, the middles more of a problem). A number of writers giving 'pronunciations' do not mention ‹œ› at all, but discuss only ‹y› (Sweet-Davis 1957: §2, Mossé 1945: §11, Moore and Marckwardt 1964: §24).

Campbell appears to assume that longs and shorts at both heights were the same in quality; this is also the view of Quirk and Wrenn (1955: §15) judging from their examples *reçu / lune* for short and long ‹y›, and *peu / schön* for ‹œ›: so [y (:)], [ø (:)]; likewise Mossé with *reçu / grün* for ‹y› (probably ultimately from Sweet). The Wrights on the other hand claim a difference like that between long and short German ‹ü, ö›, i.e. closer and more peripheral for longs than shorts (so also Moore and Marckwardt for ‹y› only). So there are at least three possible layouts for early Old English FRV systems:

Quirk and Wrenn		Campbell		Wrights	
y:	y	y:	y	y:	y
ø:	ø			ø:	
		œ:	œ		œ

I would argue for the Quirk and Wrenn interpretation, on historical grounds: there is no good evidence for a split in the qualities of long/short vowel pairs in English before the 17th century (Lass, forthcoming a, b, 1989). Older systems seem to have been of the 'pure length' type, like modern standard Finnish. But this is not really important here; I will use the symbols [y, ø] for both long and short vowels, leaving detailed interpretation to the reader's discretion.

The idea itself that ⟨y, œ⟩ represent FRVs is not the result of any straight-line argument targeted on a conclusion, but grows out of the 'reticulate' convergence of a number of bits of evidence, lines of argument, many of them implicit. Before looking at what might be called the 'traditional' backing, i.e. those items that were probably strongest in building what has been the consensus at least since the time of A.J. Ellis (1867), I want to explore a less conventional pathway. This is a set of possible justifying arguments of a more recent type, which never the less serve (or could serve) as support for the tradition. The strategy here is argument from 'family naturalness' and 'historical naturalness' or 'centres of gravity' (Lass 1977)—the claim that reconstruction of a particular type of object in the early stages of a language is bolstered (a) generally by the occurrence — characteristically — of that object-type in the (sub-)family in question, and (b) more specifically by its characteristic or frequent occurrence in later stages of the language in question. Point (a) is unproblematic (see §1 above); (b) may need some expansion.

Limiting ourselves to those FRV attestations that result from (relatively) modern research, i.e. starting from phoneticians using a metalanguage reasonably interpretable in modern terms, we find the following main sources of FRVs in modern varieties of English (*c.* ninth-century to the present):

(i) ME /o:/ ‹ Old English /o:/ (*goose*). Some attestations are discussed in §1 above; others include Border Scots (Murray 1873: 113, Vaiana 1972), Central Scots (Grant and Dixon 1921: §§148 ff), other varieties of Scots (Lass 1987a: §5.7.1). Qualities here cover the range [ø~œ~Y~y]. In England, the West Country and WML have [œu], [ø:], [y:], [Yu], [Y] (Wright 1905: §§164, 169); [Y:] is widely attested in these areas in the SED materials (Orton and Wakelin 1967, Orton and Barry 1969 s.v. *moon* VIII.6.3). Such values are also typical for ME /ɛu/ (*dew*), /iu/ (*due*): see Wright §§186, 193, and cf. Wells (1982: §4.3.7). Early East Anglian reports (Wright, *loc. cit.*) also have FRVs here.

(ii) ME /u:/ ‹ Old English /u:/ (*house*). Diphthongs of the types [əY] [œY] are reported from Devon by Wright (§§170, 173), and [œ ɤ̃] is reported by the SED for Devon (*out* V8.10a). Wells (§4.3.7) also mentions the type [ɐY~ʌY] in

Lancashire.

(iii) ME /ir er ur/ (*fir, fern, fur*). Values as front as [ø:] for the merged nucleus occur in the WML (Stockport, Cheshire: Lodge 1984), and centralized [ɵ] is the norm in South Africa and New Zealand (Lass 1987a: §§5.8. 3-4).

(iv) ME /ɔ:/ ‹ Old English /ɑ:/ (*home*), Old English /o/ lengthened in open syllables (*nose*). In 'advanced' RP varieties the first mora may be around [œ]; this is characteristic also for (local) standard South African varieties. Cape Town typically has values around [œ̈ɣ-œ̈ʊ], with frequent monophthongization to [œ̈:], leading to minimal contrast with category (iii), e.g. [bø̈:t] *Burt* vs. (bœ̈: t] *boat*, etc.

(v) ME /o/ ‹ Old English /o/, ME / ɔ:/ ‹ Old English /o/ in open syllables, NME /a:/ ‹ Old English /ɑ:/. In Northumberland and Durham especially, conservative rural varieties in the 1950s showed some items in all these categories with a mid FRV: see Orton and Halliday 1962 s.v. *fox* IV5.11, *foal* III.4.1, *toad* IV 9.7).

One could go on almost at will. This of course ignores the more 'reconstructed' cases, e.g. the 14th-century fronting of ME /o:/ in the North, leading to merger with Old French /y(:)/, attestations of FRVs in Scots mentioned by early writers (Hart 1569: 32b on the Scottish 'abuse' of *u*), the developments of Old English /y/ and the /eo/ diphthongs in ME in the SW and WML, and so on. The only point I want to make here is that even though none of the categories spelled ‹y, œ› in Old English have themselves yielded modern FRVs, many others have, in a wide geographical range of English dialect types. FRVs, even leaving aside the conjectural ME cases, are a good English type of segment, and there is no reason not to posit them for any period in which other evidence seems to support them.

But what about the Old English ones themselves? Our support for the likelihood of FRVs here comes from different classes of essentially historical argument: internal (including history and structure), and external (comparative evidence, Germanic orthographic traditions, etc.).

The main internal arguments seem to be as follows. Clearly ‹y, œ› represent categories distinct from ‹i, e› on the one hand and ‹u, o› on the other. We can show this with pairs like *cinn* 'chin' vs *cynn* 'kin', *wulf* 'wolf' vs. *wylf* 'she-wolf' for ‹y› vs. ‹i,u›. Arguments for ‹œ› vs. ‹e, o› are harder, since there are fewer minimal or near-minimal pairs: still, we could instance *dohtor / doehter* 'daughter(s)' for ‹œ› vs. ‹o›, and *oele* 'oil' vs. *el* 'foreign' for ‹œ› vs. ‹e›, and so on.

Assuming (on independent, but I think solid grounds, which I won't go into here) that the vowel symbols ‹i, e, æ, u, o, a› (as usually transliterated) represent values in the vicinity of [i, e, æ, u, o, ɑ], we have a skeleton monophthongal quality system for early Old English of this kind :

    i   u
    e   o
    æ   ɑ

Assuming that ‹y› is high and ‹œ› mid, and that they are something other than these six, there are two obvious systematic gaps they might fill: /y o/ and /ɯɤ/. We have then to decide between front round and back unround.

Take the high vowels as an example (stipulating that whatever holds for them will hold for the mids as well). If ‹i, u› are around /i, u/, then the most parsimonious account giving the outcome [y] from *i*-umlaut suggests [y] ‹ [u], since English does not seem ever to have had non-contiguous unrounding harmony, and this makes [ɯ] rather a non-starter. Another possibility of course is that the umlaut results were not front at all, but central, say [ʉ, θ]. Indeed, given the system and what we know about the units in which sound change generally proceeds (see Lass 1978) they must have been at some stage. But later developments show merger with vowels that were pretty clearly front: merger of ‹y› with ‹i› in the EML and N, and with ‹e› in Kent (and see further the arguments in Anderson 1988, which support this). There is also, in late Old English, a good deal of 'confusion' of the graphs ‹i› and ‹y› (which indeed become close to interchangeable in ME for /i(:)/), but none of ‹y› and ‹u›, which further supports a front value.

With this much established, the distinguishers for ‹i, e› vs. ‹y, œ› could in principle be almost anything, peripherality, height, tongue-root advancement...the list is endless. But not the sensible list. We know that FRVs are a 'good' English type (as well as a good Germanic one); and there is also internal evidence, such as ‹œ› for ‹e› after ‹w› (which we think was rounded), as in 10th-century Northumbrian *woesa* 'to be' = WS *wesan*, etc. There is also a tendency for ‹y› to appear in later WS in place of ‹i e› from various sources, especially in the vicinity of labials and ‹r› (which we have reason to believe may have been rounded: Lass 1983): *hwyrfan* 'turn', *wyrsa* 'worse', earlier *hwierfan, wiersa*, etc. The language-internal evidence then converges on both frontness and roundness.

External (comparative) evidence gives further support, if in some cases indirectly. Still, there are numerous clear cases, in which cognates in other Germanic languages show FRVs, if not always at the same height or of the same length. Thus early ‹œ› typically corresponds (long) to modern German /y:/, as in *coene* 'keen', *groene* 'green' = *kühne*, *grün*. (The height difference here is due to pre-umlaut raising and diphthongisation in OHG, as in *kühne* ‹ *kuoni*, etc, where this raised */o:/ later umlauted to /ye/ and monophthongised to /y:/.) For short ‹œ› the German correspondences are usually direct, e.g *doehter* : *Töchter*, etc.

The long ‹y› correspondences are less direct as well, due to later German developments: putative Old English /y:/ most often = G /ɔY/ as in *fyr* 'fire' = *Feuer*, *hyrian* 'hire' = *heuern*. Short /y/ corresponds generally to G /Y/, as in *brycg* 'bridge' = *Brücke*, *byrden* 'burden' = *Bürde*. Where Old English /y:/ results from compensatory lengthening after Ingvaeonic nasal-loss, it may also correspond to German /Y/, e.g *cyþan* 'make known' = *künden*.

Similar correspondences may be found outside of West Germanic, e.g. Old English *cynd* 'nature, type' = Swedish *kynne* 'natural disposition', *boec* 'books' = *böcker*, *mys* 'mice' = *möss* (Swedish shows various shortenings and lowerings, but the FRV quality is intact). Overall, there is enough left of the older Germanic FRV categories, despite later changes, to justify a claim for such qualities in Old

English.

A final line of argument concerns the FRV graphs themselves. These would appear to instantiate an old Germanic tradition (at least as old as the development of FRV runes) of 'diacritic' spelling, in which parts of a complex letter or digraph may represent different (simultaneous) features of a segment. The diacritic principle is apparent in Germanic spellings as early as the 8th Century (see below and §4); it is interestingly supported by an explicit discussion in the later but still relevant work of the 12th-century Icelandic First Grammarian.

In the course of a pitch for reforming Icelandic orthography, the First Grammarian recommends the adoption of four new complex vowel graphs (among other things): these are ⟨ę, ǫ, ø, y⟩. His remarks on the two relevant for us, ⟨ø⟩ and ⟨y⟩, are as follows:

> (a) The vowel represented by ⟨ø⟩ is made up of the sounds of ⟨e⟩ and ⟨o⟩ categories blended together: 'hann er af hljóði *es* ok *os* feldr saman' (Haugen 1950: 14). The graph ⟨ø⟩ represents this iconically: it is written with the 'stroke' or 'branch' (*kvistr*) of (upper-case) ⟨ E ⟩ and the circle of ⟨o⟩ ('*osins* hring').

> (b) The vowel represented by ⟨y⟩ consists of the sounds of the ⟨i⟩ and ⟨u⟩ categories merged into one sound ('gǫrr at einni rǫddu'). Therefore it has 'the first branch of the upper-case *u*' ('fyrri kvísl af hǫfudstafs-*ue*').

The MS is defective at this point; there is no description of the 'second branch' of ⟨y⟩. Haugen and earlier editors (Haugen, §4.10) are of the (undoubtedly correct) opinion that this missing piece would have referred to the upper-case ⟨I⟩, which would make the analysis parallel to that of ⟨ø⟩. It is further supported by the motivation for the new letters ⟨ę⟩ and ⟨ǫ⟩, which are described (14f) as representing sounds opener than ordinary ⟨e⟩ and ⟨o⟩, and therefore having the 'loop of *a*' ('lykkju *ae*') attached to the regular letters as a modifier.

The principle is explicitly set out; while the First Grammarian's explicitness may be idiosyncratic, there is no doubt the principle is an ancient one, still alive in his time and indeed later. The much older Old English y-rune (attested from the 8th century) consists of the basic shape of the *u* -rune ᚢ, with a copy of the *i*-rune ᛁ inside: thus: ᛦ Some forms of the later Scandinavian *y*-rune also show a similar principle; the 13th century type ᛦ is at least a modified *u* -rune, and the alternant ᛣ may be a full-sized *i* -rune with a small *u* -rune as crosspiece (cf. Elliott 1963: 25).

The diacritic principle is expressed in other ways in early Germanic spelling systems, e.g. by sequential writings that clearly have the same intention. Thus the sequence ⟨ui⟩ occurs in a few items in Old Low Franconian (Kyes 1967) to represent the *i* -umlaut of */u(:)/: duiri* 'doors', *fuir* 'fire'. In late OHG we find the same category occasionally represented by ⟨iu, yu, ui⟩, as in *liuzil*, *lyuzil* 'little' (OE *lytel*), *muillen* 'mill' (Old English *mylen*), alongside the more usual unmodified spellings of the type *luzzil*, *mulina* (Braune-Mitzka §32, Anm 5). It would seem obvious that the import of these spellings is precisely the same as that of the First Grammarian's ⟨ø⟩ and ⟨y⟩: the ⟨u⟩ represents lip-rounding, and the ⟨i⟩

frontness. The fact that both orders ⟨ui⟩, ⟨iu⟩ occur lends this view further plausibility: if the digraph is supposed to represent a single 'compound' articulation, it doesn't matter a great deal which order the components come in. (In fact ⟨iu⟩ is less common than ⟨ui⟩, since it is the canonical spelling for a Germanic diphthong as well, e.g *liuti* 'people', Old English *leod*).

Spellings of this kind, not only ⟨ui⟩ but also the familar ⟨œ⟩ and variants like ⟨oi⟩, appear in the earliest Old English materials as well (see next section). They have been rather perversely interpreted by Campbell (1959: §192) as showing 'epenthesis' (in the form of a 'palatal glide') of the umlaut trigger into the nucleus of the affected syllable; but this is dubious in the light of lack of positive evidence, and supererogatory given the testimony of the First Grammarian, the widespread use of diacritic spellings anyhow, and the early Old English spellings of ⟨œ⟩ for the *i*-umlaut of */o(:)/. All of these would seem to support the diacritic interpretation.[6]

4 FRV Developments in Old English

The story of the eventual phonemicisation of the FRVs is clear in outline: they arose as positional variants of the back rounded vowels before */i(:), j/ and became distinctive when the triggering environments either disappeared or were neutralised to some non-high value (e.g. *doeman* 'judge' ‹ */do:m-j-an/, *cyre* 'choice' ‹ */kur-i/). This much has been clear since Twaddell's elegant account of the OGH scenario half a century ago (Twaddell 1938). What is not so clear is when the phonologization occurred, and what the status of FRVs really was in the earliest Old English materials.

The earliest sources (7th century on) are runic; these are sparse but they do tell us that the symbols for FRVs were available and used. But words and name-elements with potential FRV environments occur in three types of spellings: Type A, back vowel symbols followed by an intact umlaut environment; Type B, FRV symbols followed by an intact umlaut environment; and Type C, FRV symbols followed by a neutralized umlaut environment.

Some examples (after Sweet 1885: 124 ff):[7]

Type A

    rodi 'rood' (loc sg): Ruthwell Cross, 7th c.[8]

Type B

    kyniq, kyninges 'king('s)': Bewcastle Column, 7th c.
    kyniqc 'king': Ruthwell Cross
    limwoerignae 'limb-weary' (acc sg): Ruthwell Cross
    Cynibalþ (proper name), probably ‹ */kuni-/: Lancaster Slab, 7th c.

`Type C`

>*kyng* 'king': Bewcastle Column
>*Kynnburg* (proper name) ‹ */kunj-/: Bewcastle Column
>*foeddae* 'she fostered' ‹ */foːd-i-dæ /: Franks Casket, 8th c.

The form *wylif* 'she-wolf' (Franks Casket) is probably not, as it first appears, an example of Type B: the ‹i› most likely is epenthetic (cf. NWGmc-*wulafz* , *bAriutiþ* cited in §2); the expected Type B would be *wylfi (Old English *wylf*). On the other hand, this could just be a transposition, in which case it would be a failed Type B. (For discussion of this and other cases of early svarabhakti, see Ponelis 1986).

The runic materials suggest that FRVs are salient by say the 7th century, and firmly in place as potential allophones of back vowels in umlaut environments; their status though is ambiguous. Neutralization and loss of umlaut-triggers still seem to be in progress and variable (Bewcastle *kyniq* ~ *kyng*). The later written texts up to about the 9th century show the same kind of picture, but perhaps more clearly (aside from anything else, there's a lot more data).

The early post-runic material consists of two major bodies of data: the early Latin/English glossaries ((Epinal, Erfurt, Corpus, Leiden), and a wealth of onomastic items in early Bede MSS, the *Liber vitae*, and other places. Names of course are always a bit suspicious, since onomastic sound changes often run on tracks somewhat tangential to those of normal lexical items (Lass 1973, Colman 1984), but they are suggestive. I will concentrate here on the glosses, using the names mainly for corroboration.

The glossaries show the three spelling-types listed above, but with more extensive representation of Type A. I give below some characteristic examples from Corpus, the longest of the 8th century glossaries (see below for some material from the related Epinal and Erfurt) :

Type A

>*unsmoþi* (aspera) 'rough' (cf. OS *smoði*)
>*hurnitu* (crabro) 'hornet' [9]
>*ontudri* (effetum) 'barren' (cf. later Old English *tydran* 'bring forth', *tudor* 'fruit').

Type B

>*cyri* (electio) 'choice' (cf. OGH, OS *kuri*)
>*hymlice* (cicuta) 'hemlock' [10]
>*mynit* (nomisma) 'coin' (‹ VL */munit-/ ‹ *monēta*)
>*unsmoeþi* (scabro) 'rough, scurfy' (see Type A)
>*graesgroeni aar* (auricalcum) 'green copper-ore' (cf. OS *groni*)
>*coecil* (torta) 'small cake' (cf. MGH *küechel*)

Type C

ynnelaec (ascalonium) 'shallot' (< L *unio* 'onion' + 'leek')
mygg (culix) 'midge, gnat' (cf. OS *muggia*)
brycg (pons) 'bridge' (cf. OS *bruggia*)
suoeg (fragor) 'noise' (cf. Go *ga-swogjan* 'groan')
boece (fagus/aesculus) 'beech' (cf. OHG *buohha*) [11]
suoetnis (ambrosia) 'sweetness' (cf. OS *suoti*)

Aside from variation within Corpus itself (e.g -smoþi ~ smoeþi), a comparison with the closely related Epinal and Erfurt glosses shows a number of cases where the two latter have more conservative spellings, mostly Type B, but one Type A. I give the Corpus form first, followed by either Epinal or Erfurt or both:

gycenis (prorigo) 'itching': Ep/Erf *gycinis* (cf. OS *juckian*)
cynedom (respuplica) 'kingdom': Ep/Erf *cyni* - (cf. OS *kuning*)
ryge (sicalia) 'rye': EP/Erf *rygi* (cf. OCS *rŭžĭ*)
rysel (axungia) 'axle-grease': Ep *rysil* (cf. OS *rusli*)
ynnelaec (see above): Erf *ynnilaec*
smyglas (cuniculos) 'hiding-places': Erf *smygilas* (cf. Later Old English *smygels* , root *smugan* 'creep')
unbryce (incommodum) 'unfit': Ep/Erf *unbryc(c)i* (cf. OHG *bruhhi* 'useful').
riscðyfel (juncetum) 'rush-thicket': Ep *riscþyfil* ('rush' + *þyfel* 'thicket, bush' < */ θu:f-il-/, cf. OIc *þufa* 'hill', L *tuber* 'excrescence').
mynit 'coin (see above Type B): Erf *munit*

There seems then to be no doubt that in the 8th century the orthographic tradition shows a few apparently unmutated forms (Type A), a good number of 'transparent' FRV spellings with intact triggers (Type B), and lots of 'opaque' ones with the triggers lost or neutralized (Type C). Overall A is rare, B common but not overwhelmingly so, and C the commonest. Rough figures for Corpus, Epinal and Erfurt are as follows (counting frequent and invariant items like *ymb* -'around', -*u(u)yrt* 'plant' once only, but including all genuine occurrences of FRV environments):

	Type A		Type B		Type C	
	N	%	N	%	N	%
Corpus	4	2.2	36	19.8	142	78.0
Ep	1	1.3	25	32.9	50	65.8
Erf	1	1.3	28	36.4	48	62.3
TOTAL	6	1.8	89	26.6	240	71.6

In these glosses, that is, Type C is something over 2.7 times as common as Type B, and Type B is about 15 times as common as Type A. The trend is obvious, but the situation is clearly not 'stable'—though whether this is an orthographic or a phonological matter is open to debate. (I will make clear here what I think it is, but see Appendix I for the other side).

The names from early Bede MSS show a somewhat similar pattern (though I have found no clear cases of archaic Type A, even in the early 8th-century Moore MS). This MS (Sweet 1885: 132 ff) has in books I-III the following types.

Type B

> cynibercti, cynigilso, cyniburgum, cynibill, oediluald

Type C

> badugyð, eaðryð, eðilgyð, osgyð, heregyð, hygbald, cuoenburg, cuoenryð, hroeðburg, hroeðgeofu.

We can see here elements of a general pattern that becomes clearer a century or so later in the *Liber vitae* (Sweet, 152 ff). This text also lacks Type A, but has many examples of B, C with considerable phonological (and in some cases apparently lexical) conditioning. Type B is commonest with light-stemmed themes, like *cyni-* (*cynimund, cyniuulf, cynibald, cynigils*), and Type B with heavy-stemmed themes like *coen* - ‹ */ko:ni-/, *-ðryð* ‹ */θru:θi-* (*coenred*, *aldðryð*). The main exception seems to be *oedil-* (*oedilburg, oediluald*)—if this indeed represents */o:θil-/ 'native land' and not a writing for 'noble' ‹*/αθil-/, (cf. Colman 1988). Retention of *-i* is in any case common after light syllables, as one might expect considering early deletion of high vowels after heavy stems, e.g. in light *i*-stem themes like *-uini* 'friend' ‹ */win-i-z/ (later *wine*). These spellings, being onomastic, may be conservative and somewhat idiosyncratic; but they do suggest something about the neutralization of the umlaut environments: in all probability the phonologization of FRVs is later for short than for long vowels (hence in names consistent *cyni-* vs. *cuoen-* 'queen').

By the mid-to-late 8th century the FRV story appears to have come out as follows:

> (i) Primary FRVs (from i-umlaut) occur in at least some tokens (most likely the majority) of all appropriate lexical items.

> (ii) A reasonably large subset of the forms show phonologization (at this point on token-level anyhow, if not systemically), especially if the vowel in question is long (Type C spelling).

(iii) But in a substantial number of cases the umlaut triggers remain intact, so that (for these) the FRVs are still allophones of back vowels (Type B spellings): i.e. there is partial merger with the phonemicised FRVs.

(iv) In a handful of items (or tokens of items) the old back quality still probably survives as a minority variant (Type A spellings).

Diagrammatically, the situation at this point is one of 'partial overlap', as follows:

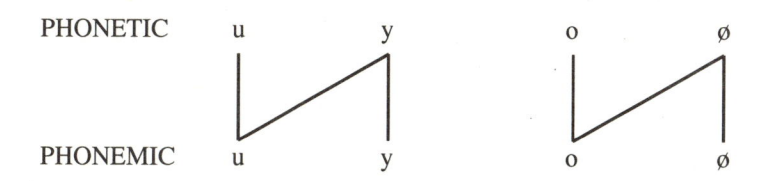

```
PHONETIC    u         y           o         ø
            |\       /|           |\       /|
            | \     / |           | \     / |
            |  \   /  |           |  \   /  |
PHONEMIC    u         y           o         ø
```

This is obviously a late stage in the implementation of a change; the best overall characterization would be that (a) umlaut 'has occurred', and FRVs 'exist' (*sensu lato*); (b) FRVs are (largely) phonemic, at least at token level, but not completely so.

By the 9th century all this has pretty much changed; about the last text to show any Type B spellings is the Cotton Vespasian B6 genealogies (after 814: Sweet 167ff). Otherwise the 9th century texts, of whatever regional provenance, show only Type C: this goes for the 'Northumbrian fragments' (Bede's Death Song, the early Caedmon's Hymn texts and the Leiden riddle), the Kentish Lorica glosses and prayer, the WS genealogies, the Mercian Vespasian Psalter. We can pretty confidently give the mid 9th century as a *terminus ad quem* for the phonologisation of FRVs in all dialects of Old English.[12]

5 The Pre-Ambrosian Praxis: or What *did* Old English scribes write?

In a famous passage in the *Confessiones* (VI, 3), St Augustine comments on the reading habits of his mentor St Ambrose (the book was written in 397, but the events described date back over a decade). When Ambrose was reading, Augustine tells us:

> ...oculi ducebantur per paginas, et cor intellectum rimabatur, vox autem et lingua quiescebant. Saepe cum adessemus...sic eum legentem vidimus tacite, et aliter numquam.[13]

For the thirty-year-old Augustine, trained in rhetoric in Carthage, and already a man of learning and cultivation, this act of silent reading seemed extraordinary; he even speculates that Ambrose may have done it to save his voice ('causa servandae vocis, quae illi facillime obtudebatur'). The point is that this kind of reading ('grapheme-to-mind', as it were) was apparently novel to an educated Roman provincial of the late 4th century. (In fairness, the 'Pre-Ambrosian Praxis', as I've christened it, is a bit of an alliterative conceit; Augustine's surprise would probably not have been shared by Metropolitan Romans. Silent reading was in fact practised in Rome itself, as is clear from the material adduced in Knox 1968. The argument (or speculation) here is designed to apply to 'the Provinces', in which case I would argue that the relevance to 8th-century Germania is not strained).

So what was the norm for a 4th-century Carthaginian might, without too much exaggeration, be suggested as possibly the norm also three centuries later among the inhabitants of the dark Germanic North. Indeed, I want to suggest here that the best way to interpret the kinds of spellings we find in Old English (and in ME and later texts) is in terms of just such a 'Pre-Ambrosian' approach to reading. Such an approach may have as its obverse an account of writing that may be illuminating for historians. Such an assumption, in fact, may be the only principled and reasonable account of the kind of spellings that actually appear in our monuments. (It is indeed assumed—though not in the kind of explicit way I propose here—by just about any historian who places real value on 'occasional' spellings).

That is, it isn't a huge step from an essentially 'oral' reading praxis to an oral *writing* praxis; it may be difficult to make a case for the former without invoking the latter as well. The Ambrose episode, if not a piece of real 'evidence', is provocative, and may offer us a useful framework for considering the rather alien outputs of pre-modern writers. Questions about the import of spellings are often asked in a rather abstract way, quite separated from basic questions about the (possible, imagined, arguable) intentions and behaviours of spellers. For the linguistic historian spellings tend to be things rather than acts, and this may prevent us from understanding the kind of things they actually are. (Some diseases fail to make sense except in terms of their aetiologies).

From our perspective as adult writers of codified standard languages, the act of writing is in principle rather simple and unreflective; though the systems we employ are alphabetic and (quasi-) phonemic, our behaviour as spellers, I would claim, is essentially logographic. Unless a word we want to write is totally unfamiliar, we do not 'spell it phonetically' or 'spell it phonemically': we just write it, without spelling it. (School-kids spell, adults write). Thus the act of spelling the word *three* is no more 'alphabetic' than that of writing the numeral '3'. An adult speller is we might say 'automatised', i.e. the bulk of his orthographic competence is sub-cortically processed; he does not spell *three* by mapping (consciously or unconsciously) a phoneme sequence / θ / + / r / + / i: / onto a grapheme sequence ‹ th › + ‹ r › + ‹ ee ›; his processing is, to be fashionable, analog rather than digital; he invokes a *Schriftbild* rather than a *Lautbild*, and does so holistically. (At least this is what I recover from my own introspection, which I suspect is not atypical).

Further—and perhaps most indicative—if some phonological aspect of the language has changed (nonstandardly) from that which underwrites the orthographic norms, the competent speller doesn't register this. For instance, there are many Americans for whom, due to pre-nasal raising, *pin* and *pen* are phonetically [pʰɪn]; but a decision to write the lexical item *pen* entails the choice of a vowel-grapheme appropriate to *pet, peck* etc.—even though the speaker either realizes or can be made to realize that phonetically the word has the vowel-phone of the set *pit, pick*.¹⁴ This is an important type-case, because the mechanism for a phonetically/phonemically 'correct' spelling exists: one *could* write ⟨pin⟩, not ⟨pen⟩.

And indeed this kind of behaviour does occur among the less well-educated and well-practiced, e.g. among people whose initial education was not of very high quality, and who were not rigorously drilled in the norms of conventional orthography. I found for instance that my first-year students at Indiana University in the 1960s, in an /ɛ/-raising area, often did precisely what one would expect from 'digital', phone-by-phone spellers: the word *sense*, for instance, often occurred in their essays and examinations as ⟨sinse⟩, or ⟨since⟩, *friend* as ⟨frind⟩, and so on. I presume that the level on which they were accessing these items for spelling was—given their backgrounds—phonological/phonetic, not 'automatically' orthographical. In other words they were writing what they (ideally) heard: not producing a holistic *Schriftbild* associated with a particular lexical item.

This is from writers raised (if poorly) in a long-established normative spelling tradition. One can assume in general that the less writers are drilled in purely visual and conventional norms, the likelier they are when writing to use their ears. And one important consequence of this is that, especially if the reading mode they are trained in is at least partly oral (as seems most likely for Old English times), spelling represents not 'system' or 'sentence' level but 'utterance' level phenomena.

With this as background, what follows is partly speculation, and partly a somewhat self-consciously naïve restatement of the obvious which in a sense is what I've been doing all along in this paper. I am suggesting now that given a reading/writing praxis that is essentially or at least significantly oral, the locus of representation becomes the segment rather than the word. Writing in this mode can become, not the simple 'registration' of *Schriftbilder* (as it generally is for us), but a kind of *transcription*. Indeed, on a little reflection, this is the only context in which notions like 'naïve spelling' or 'phonetic spelling' make any sense. And it is this assumption that in one way or another brings us down to utterance-level phenomena, and indeed makes plausible precisely those sorts of spellings that we as historians are used to finding in our texts, and often making history out of. And such an assumption is the only real justification for a 'variationist' approach to older texts at the phonological level, a technique that I would maintain has produced much analysis of interest (e.g. Toon 1983). The study of variation is, by definition, if you think about it, necessarily based on an utterance-level input.

If we look at (much) early writing as 'utterance transcription' of a sort, the variation begins to make sense; quite simply, whatever variant is 'due to surface' at a particular point does so, more or less (or even exactly) as it would in speech. This could even hold, I'd suggest, for one-word utterances like glosses. Consider:

if you speak a language in which some category C has the variants c_i, c_j (say as the result of an ongoing but incompletely diffused change $c_i > c_j$), it is impossible to predict for any given utterance of a C-form (isolated or in context) whether c_i or c_j will occur. What is predictable is that—given a certain quantitative relation between c_i and c_j—both will, in a sufficiently large corpus, occur in that quantitative relation.

To set up a possible model then for the genesis of the forms we've been looking at: let's say that for the Corpus scribe, the word 'smooth' is one of the items potentially (variably) affected by *i*-umlaut, which is for him in progress (if nearing the end of the process). This word then exists *in posse* in two forms, [smo:ði] and [smø:ði], with the second commoner than the first. When our scribe begins his glossing, he comes to the lemma *aspera* and 'says' (to himself or aloud, it doesn't really matter) [unsmo:ði], which he then writes down with the proper graphs, including ⟨o⟩ for the accented vowel. The next time, quite a bit later in the alphabetic sequence, when he comes to the partial synonym *scabro*, he 'says' [unsmø:ði], and associating the graph ⟨oe⟩ with the quality [ø], he writes that. In effect he doesn't know which value of the variable will come up until it does (a familiar situation for anyone who has ever lived with a linguistic variable); but once it has emerged, he writes—unlike us—whichever one it happens to be. (For a possible alternative scenario, see Appendix I.)

My tentative conclusion from all this is that the spelling of these early glosses and the like is not 'irregular' or full of 'mistakes' (though there are plenty of those, of course, which can usually be spotted because of their lack of principle). Rather it is the real thing, properly to be taken as a variation-sample at (imagined) utterance level, more or less as if it were speech. (The medium happens to be graphic here, but we have an 'utterance inscription' all the same). Therefore, these early materials furnish us with an interesting, reasonably dependable and not at all surprising picture, illustrating the genesis of FRVs out of a characteristic situation of variation and diffusion, and they should be taken as pretty much just that. The moral, with apologies to Gertrude Stein, is A corpus is A corpus is A corpus.[15]

APPENDIX I

A Non-Variationist Interpretation of FRV Spellings

In history nothing is unequivocal. All but the most methodologically naïve know that historical remains are not 'facts' until they have been incorporated in a framework that so defines them, and have been assigned some legitimate facthood in that framework. The interpretation of historical spellings is an excellent case in point, as has been eloquently argued by Fran Colman (1988). She shows, with respect to Old English onomastic materials, that what a particular spelling counts as evidence *for* is a theoretical matter, and one which is sensitive to the level of analysis one operates on (phonological, orthographic, etc.) as well as the particular assumptions one brings to the analysis of that level.

In this paper I have pushed one particular interpretation of the vagaries of the early Old English (putative) FRV spellings, at the expense of all other possible ones. I find the one I've chosen intuitively attractive (which is why I push it), but this is neither here nor there: more to the point, one can argue for it in a reasonably coherent way, and it appears to be consistent with a lot that we (think we) know about linguistic variation and change. There is nothing in our current battery of assumptions that would make it empirically impossible, or even unlikely.

There is however at least one other respectable interpretation, which deserves an airing; though I will try to show that it's not quite as good as my Pre-Ambrosian/neo-Labovian one. This is based not on a presumed and admittedly somewhat speculative psychology of writing, but on a well known kind of phonic/graphic interfacing which can lead to conclusions diametrically opposite to those I reached above. I am concerned with an interpretation under which spelling variation is a sign, not of phonetic variation, but of categorical establishment of an allophonic alternation. Graphic alternants may be, paradoxically, a result not of the representation of variant categories, but of a total lack of (phonetic) alternation or variation.

To illustrate, consider the two Corpus examples *unsmoþi* and *unsmoeþi*, discussed above. My claim was that these represented as it were 'utterance tokens'; the glossator's (or as I suggested in note 16, just possibly the dictating monk's) productions varied between older and newer forms, and which one surfaced in a given utterance was a matter of the structure of his particular variant-universe. But there is another possibility: say that on the phonological level the change [o:] > [ø:] had been completed, and that this word was now categorically [smø:ði]. The writer that is has an exceptionless synchronic *i* -umlaut rule, by which [o:] and [ø:] are allophones of /o:/ in complementary distribution. Given such a synchronic 'representation', and an orthography that hasn't caught up with it, it is clear that—for such a speaker—the writings ‹-smoþi› and ‹-smoeþi› are fully equivalent, and could only represent /smo:θi/ = [smø:ði]. If [o:] cannot appear before heterosyllabic /i/, then either graph will educe—for a speaker whose 'internalised system' is as specified—the same interpretation. In such a case the lag that produces the variant spellings is orthographic, not phonological..

In such a situation, then, writing of ‹o› rather than ‹oe› is not a sign of archaism in the form, but precisely the reverse : it is a back-spelling based on the impossibility of [o:] before /i/, and the consequent systematic identity of the graphs ‹o› and ‹oe› in this position.

The trouble is that apparently we can't tell which of the two interpretations is the right one. So the equivocal situation, which we saw at one end, where in the absence of FRV graphs a form like Gothic ‹kuni› could either have them or not, is repeated on the other end, if at a different level. A form like *unsmoþi* could either have an FRV or not, and if it does have one this spelling could be evidence for categorical (if as yet unphonologized) FRVs.

Is it time to give up then? Is this another of those classical stonewalling indeterminacies, where the evidence simply refuses to give us precise instructions under any theoretical interpretation? I suggest we don't, really; that it is possible to construct an argument which, while not conclusive, nevertheless shows the case for categorical FRVs as somewhat weaker than that for variable ones. This involves a conjunction of arguments from methodological isotropy (=uniformitarianism) and ontological parsimony, and goes like this:

(i) The development of FRVs in Old English is an endogenous ('evolutive') change. Penzl's recent nod toward exhumation of the old 'Celtic substratum', which wasn't even very good for French, is not convincing : 1988 : 265 .f).

(ii) It is probably as close as makes no difference to universal that evolution phonetic change *in process* is never a 'quantum' phenomenon: 'jumps' from one categorical state to another do not occur. (*Natura non facit saltum* is true at least here). The mode of linguistic change is cumulatively weighted variation over time. (This isn't of course 'proven', simply a matter of inductive generalisation from just about every study of change in progress and piece of related evidence I know of.) In its temporal aspect, a change is an unfolding, an 'epigenetic landscape' (Waddington 1977 : ch. 7), not a 'catastrophe'.

(iii) On uniformitarian grounds, all past change must then have proceeded by variation as well. In its fundamentals, the linguistic universe, like the natural, is isotropic in time and space.

(iv) Reconstructing (i-iii) syllogistically, it follows by *modus ponens* that *i*-umlaut was implemented by variation over time (the 'Socrates is mortal' principle, if you will).

This is the uniformitarian half of the argument, which stops short of orthography. It is also apparently non-binding on orthographic interpretation, as suggested above : the variation in spelling — even if very *like* what one would get in phonological variation — is a secondary appearance. It is in fact causally the inverse of the (putativley earlier) phonological variation whose categorical output produces by inversion a pseudo-variation of a quite different import.

It is now reasonably clear where the backspelling argument gets us; into a state of undesirable non-parsimony, and an arbitrary (and in general not well motivated) division between variation and completion on two closely interfacing levels of representation. We now argue from parsimony: the non-variationist argument I have tried to reconstruct unpacks as follows:

(i) Under universalist constraint, the epigenesis of *i*-umlaut was achieved by variation, cumulatively weighted in the direction of increasing categoricalness of FRVs.

(ii) The orthographic praxis of Old English (or by extension, any Germanic language) paid no attention to the variable properties of the epigenetic landscape, but (presumably) represented things categorically 'old style' while the process was going on (this would be the position Antonsen or Penzl would have to adopt if they allowed for variation).

(iii) Only when the variation had become fossilized into a categorical alternation did the orthography represent it at all.

(iv) When it finally did, it managed, via quite frequent back-spelling, to produce a pseudo-variation that *looks exactly like* genuine variation of a type that had to exist at some time anyhow (as guaranteed by (i)). But this was adventitious; spelling is only categorically representational, so that orthography is in essence something quite different from phonology, and is not constrained, in change, by its phonological substrate or the normal properties of linguistic variation over time. Only phonological variation is what it really looks like.

I submit that this is even more Byzantine than the complex of arguments used to support the variationist account; Occam's Razor ought to slice it off at the roots.

APPENDIX II

False Type B Spellings in Later Old English

As I remarked in note 15, there are cases (quite numerous, actually) in later Old English where, apparently, the /i/-containing suffixes causing umlaut have not had their vowels neutralised to /e/. These could—at first glance—be taken as survivals of Type B spellings (like *unsmoeþi*, *mynit*, etc), and hence as non-phonologised instances of FRVs. A clear case is *cyning*, which might suggest 'underlying' /kuning/, with a 'persisting' umlaut rule yielding surface [*kyning*] (indeed, in Lass and Anderson 1975 : ch. IV we used this as a subsidiary argument for a synchronic umlaut rule). Similar forms include *gesyndig* 'sound', *þyrniht* 'thorny', *clysing* 'closing, clause'.

That this would be an erroneous interpretation is shown by the existence of forms with these same suffixes, but back vowel spellings (actually in appearance Type A!), whose subsequent developments make it clear that they did not undergo umlaut : *hungrig* 'hungry', *hunig* 'honey' etc. In fact the /i/ in *-ing* (and as we'll see a number of other suffixes) is in later Old English only equivocally involved with umlaut. After the 9th century the FRVs (and other umlaut outputs, like /æ:/ < /a:/) were phonemicized, and once this happened umlaut was completely morphologized.

We note further that all the post-radical elements containing /i/ (which is surely what ‹ i › indicates) are of a particular type: they are all derivational suffixes of one kind or another, whether clearly and motivatedly so (as in *hungr-ig*) or perhaps more opaque (*cyn-ing*). All inflectional /i/, including not only endings but theme vowels, had been lost or neutralized by the 9th century. We further note that none of the suffixes in question consist of naked /i/ (unlike some inflections) : they minimally have /-VC /rhymes).

If we look at a range of Old English derivational suffixes containing /i/, we see by the behaviour of the bases they are attached to that with one exception they are neither uniformly umlauting nor non-umlauting. The list below (based partly on Kastovsky, Forthcoming) contains a variety of umlaut outputs (not just FRVs) to illustrate the main point:

(i) *-ig* (various types)
UMLAUT: *-hydig* '-minded', *untrymig* 'infirm', *þystrig* 'obscure', *gesyndig* 'sound', *gefyndig* 'capable'
NO UMLAUT: *bodig* 'body', *modig* 'brave', *blodig* 'bloody', *hungrig* 'hungry', *andig* 'envious', *cwalmig* 'sad'

(ii) *-iht*

VARIABLE: *stæniht ~ staniht* ' stony', *þyrniht ~ þorniht* 'thorny'
NO UMLAUT: *bogiht* 'full of bends', *croppiht* ' bushy', *sandiht* 'sandy', *wudiht* 'woody', *hreodiht* 'reedy'

(iii) *-isc*

UMLAUT: *mennisc* 'human', *scyttisc* 'Scottish', *wielisc* 'Welsh, foreign', *denisc* 'Scandinavian', *englisc* 'English'
NO UMLAUT: *domisc* 'of the day of judgement', *folcisc* 'popular', *heofonisc* 'heavenly', *eotenisc* 'gigantic', *elþeodisc* 'foreign'

(iv) *-lic*

UMLAUT: *cieplic* 'for sale'
NO UMLAUT: *rummodlic* 'ample', *eadiglic* 'prosperous'

(v) *-incel*

NO UMLAUT: *bogincel* 'small bough', *husincel* 'little house', *stanincel* 'little stone'

(vi) *-ing* (several types)

UMLAUT: *ierming* 'wretch', *cyning* 'king', *clysing* 'closing', *fering* 'vehicle'
NO UMLAUT: *Nathaning* 'son of Nathan', *fostring* 'fosterchild', *beorning* 'incense', *earding* 'dwelling'

(vii) *-ling*

UMLAUT: *ierþling* 'farmer', *niedling* 'bondman'
NO UMLAUT: *deorling* 'darling', *geongling* 'youth', *hæftling* 'prisoner'

Note that none of these is categorically umlauting (indeed - *incel* appears to be categorically NON-umlauting). This suggests that by post-9th-century times, umlaut was losing its position as a central morphophonemic process (in derivation if not in inflection), as English was in the early stages of a typological shift from a variable-stem to an invariable-stem type of morphology (so Kastovsky 1988, with interesting argumentative support). In essence, these derivational suffixes have no more predictable an affect on the shape of a preceding stem than the second element of a compound would: indeed, it seems likely that those which were heavy syllables (*-iht, -lic, -(l)ing*) would have carried secondary stress, and been treated as (relatively) independent items, with a strong boundary of some sort to their left.

NOTES

* I am grateful (I think) to Fran Colman for getting me to write this paper instead of the quite different one I'd already written and was sort of pleased with. I know I'm grateful to her for detailed comments on the first draft of this one. I am also grateful to an anonymous referee (as we have to call them these days) for useful remarks; and on another level to Kate Coleman for putting at my disposal her inexhaustible knowledge of things Latinate and classical, which got me out of some holes. I take full credit however for overall naïveté and eccentricity, as well as for mistakes and infelicities.

1. Not all later dialects are assumed to have a 'unitary' *i*-umlaut. The traditional view for German for instance (cf. Braune-Mitzka 1963: §51) is that there was at least a two-stage development, with low vowels umlauting in OHG (e.g. in *i*-stems like *gast* 'guest', nom/acc pl *gest-i*, <*/ɣɑst-i/), but the higher ones not affected till MHG (OHG *sconi* 'beautiful' > MHG *schoene*, etc. See Sapir 1921: ch. VIII for extended discussion.) As I will show below, the apparently clear spelling evidence is somewhat equivocal; it could be that *i*-umlaut affected all vowels at (about) the same time, but was at first spelled only where the orthographic system already had a reasonably appropriate graph. E.g. <e> was a natural spelling for whatever the umlaut of */ɑ/ was—say [ɛ] or [æ] — since the new value was close enough to that of original /e/. But new symbols had to be developed, eventually, for the quite radically new FRV types: e.g. OHG <ui>, runic ᛙ, OE <y> and <oe> etc. In any case, there is nothing improbable about spelling two (even quite) different vowels with the same symbol: cf. the ME use of <e(e)> for /e:/ and /ɛ:/, and <o(o)> for /o:/ and /ɔ:/.

2. Following Antonsen (1975) and Telemann (1980), I assume that the rune conventionally transliterated as <R> did not represent some special 'palatal *r*', but was simply 'Vernerized' */s/, i.e. [z].

3. The <au> in Gothic *dauhtar* (conventionally <aú>) represents the 'breaking' (lowering) of PGmc */o/ in certain environments. I cite Gothic in standard transliteration, except where specific letter-shapes are in question.

4. The alternation of <bb> and <f> in class III weak verbs (*habban* 'have', pres ind 3 sg *hafað*, etc.) makes it clear that medial <f> represented /f/=[v]—unless there was a most improbable foot-medial devoicing. For the history (where a value [f] is ruled out by etymology as well) see Lass and Anderson 1975: ch.V.

5. Actually the Gothic <w> -graph itself is more likely derived from runic wynn ᚹ, which is why it is used for /w/ in the first place. It has also been suggested, incidentally, that the OE use of <y> for /y(:)/ is a Hellenism, based upsilon as well: Brunner (1965: §4.2) says this was inspired by the practice of early Greek-speaking clerics in England (like Theodore of Tarsus, who came to Canterbury in 669). But there is a (probably better) native and thoroughly Germanic origin for <y>: see §3.

6. OE was in any case prone to sequential diacritics: e.g. <ge>:(s) ce-> spellings representing an unexpected palatal before a back vowel supposed to record a sound change called 'palatal diphthongization'. The arguments for this being not a sound change but a simple diacritic use of <e> are I think compelling (see Lass and Anderson 1975: Appendix III).

7. I have not distinguished velar and palatal variants by using Sweet's system of italic vs. roman type (124); only the vocalisms are at issue here.

8. Ruthwell Cross *rodi* has been seen by some authorities as a problem: Campbell 1959 §§369, 588) considers this and a couple of other early 'datives' in *-i* 'difficult to explain'. (E.g. Franks casket *in romæ cæstri* 'in the (city of) Rome', Epinal *gitiungi* glossing *apparatione* 'in preparation'.) Others more or less accept it for what it looks like, an $\bar{o}$-stem noun with an ending that goes back to an IE locative (so Brunner 1965: §251, Dickins & Ross 1954:11). This ending 'belongs to' the *a*-stems, but has been 'transferred'. Such an interpretation seems, given the frequent fuzziness and analogical remodelling of declensions in OE, to be quite straightforward (see Lass 1986); and the syncretic origin of the Germanic 'dative', containing in various noun-classes survivals of dative, locative and instrumental (cf. Prokosch 1938: §§234ff, Krahe 19654: §§3-30, passim), supports this. I think it is safe to retain *rodi* as a Type A, parallel morphologically to 'genuine' $\bar{o}$-stem

occurrences like the others cited above. (For further arguments Lass forthcoming c).

9. The /i/ in *hurnitu* is etymologically opaque: cf. OS *hornut*, Lith *širšuõ* 'wasp', OCS *šŭšeni*. But later OE *hyrnet(u)* suggests a genuine umlaut context. The modern vocalism clearly does not descend from the normal OE type, but probably represents a development of the original nucleus, with lowering of /u/ before /rC/, as suggested elsewhere in WGmc by the OS form above and OHG *hornaz*.

It might be noted by the way that some scholars consider Type A spellings erroneous: Campbell (1959: §199) thinks the <u> in *hurnitu, ontudri*, etc. are 'errors for *ui*'. This is unlikely, considering the relative rarity of the (continental) <Vi> spelling type outside of onomastic material anyhow: while e.g. the Moore MS of Bede has forms like *oidilualdo, coinualch, coinred*, the only (nearly) certain case in the glosses is Corpus *woidiberge* glossing *helleborus*. At least this is a genuine <oi> representing the *i*-umlaut of */o:/ if *woidi* - is based on */wo:d-/ 'mad' (cf. OE *wod, wedan* 'become mad' < */wo:d-j-an/). This is not unlikely, considering the mystique surrounding hellebores; there is a herbalist tradition that *H. niger* is a cure for madness. The traditional view of hellebore as a cure for madness is at least as old as the Hippocratic writings, and is mentioned in Pliny (*NH* xxv. 47ff.) and in Horace (Ars Poetica 300ff.) See the discussion in Brink (1971: 331ff.). I am grateful to Kate Coleman for calling these sources to my attention.

10. The etymology is difficult (see Holthausen 1963, s.v. *hymlic*), but the FRV is genuine enough, judging from later forms and modern /ɛ/ in *hemlock*, which is a proper Kenticism assuming earlier /y/.

11. Probably a transfer to *i*-stem, hence < */bo:k-i-z/; the modern vocalism in *beech* is consonant with this (cf. the unmutated stem in *book*). The use of this word to gloss *aesculus* (properly 'horse-chestnut') is probably a simple botanical ineptitude on the glossator's part.

12. Full phonologization at the 'surface' (=classical/taxonomic phonemic level) of course; phonologization can be postponed on theoretical grounds in an abstract generative account (see Lass and Anderson 1975: ch. IV, and the 'retraction' in Ch. VI) There are of course cases in later OE where <i> representing /i/ remains, e.g. in *cyning* and the like; but there is contrast with back vowels before /i/ as in *hunig* 'honey', so the distinction is phonemic: see Appendix II for discussion.

13. Text from von Raumer (1876): '(his) eyes were led over the pages, and his heart gleaned the sense, but his voice and tongue were still. Often when we had come to him... we saw him reading silently, and never any other way' (my translation).

14 Some speakers are aware of the homophony: I have encountered disambiguation strategies based on this, such as an incorrect response to a request to fetch a [pʰɪn] (intended *pen*) corrected by 'No, a writing [pʰɪn], not a safety [pʰɪn]' (contrastive stress on *writing, safety*.

15. For comments on a 19th-century 'naïve' text in this light, see Lass (1987b). If the scenario here is too speculative, there is, for certain cases at least, a much less contentious one: there are OE texts that are virtually beyond doubt the product of

dictation to a group of scribes, rather than silent copying of exemplars (Bately 1966, and the detailed discussion in Bierbaumer 1988). If a text were being dictated, there would be no more problem in assuming this to be the basis for variation than a modern informant's treatment of a reading passage or word list, where we know that certain variation patterns will surface. But of course there is no way that one could argue that all (or even a majority) of OE and ME texts could have been dictated. Still, here's a documented oral praxis available for at least some cases.

There is of course an argument that OE scribes really did very little other than devoting most of their efforts to the accurate copying of exemplars, and did not (ever?) 'transcribe';

for a fairly extreme version (ending with an ironic paraphrase of Luick in the form 'man schrieb *nie* wie man sprach') see Stanley (1988), and the corrective to this view in Hogg (1988: 193-8). Stanley does of course provide a good corrective for over-enthusiastic reliance on the phonological import of spellings; there are warnings about this which are well known (Wrenn 1943, sophisticatedly in McIntosh 1956). But there are *some* well-formed babies left in the tub after the bathwater has gone; Stanley and others of his persuasion let rather too much go down the plughole. The spellings I've been concerned with here seem to me good babies, if sometimes a shade equivocal.

REFERENCES

Allen, W. Sidney 1965. *Vox Latina. A guide to the pronunciation of classical Latin.* Cambridge: Cambridge University Press.

Anderson, John M. 1987 Gothic obstruents. In Ramat *et al.* (1987: 1-12).

Anderson, John M. 1988. The great Kentish collapse. In Kastovsky & Bauer (1988: 97-108).

Antonsen, Elmer A. 1975. *A concise grammar of the older runic inscriptions.* Tübingen: Max Niemeyer Verlag.

Bately, Janet 1966. The Old English Orosius: the question of dictation. *Anglia* **84**.255-304.

Bierbaumer, Peter 1988. Slips of the ear in Old English texts. In Kastovsky & Bauer (1988: 127-38).

Brink, C.O. 1971. *Horace on poetry. The 'Ars Poetica'.* Cambridge: Cambridge University Press.

Buck, Carl Darling 1933. *A comparative grammar of Greek and Latin.* Chicago: University of Chicago Press.

Bennett, William H. 1965. *An introduction to the Gothic language*, I.[2] Ann Arbor: Ulrich's Books Inc.

Braune, Wilhelm 1966. *Gotische Grammatik.*[17] Rev. E.A. Ebbinghaus. Tübingen: Max Niemeyer Verlag.

Braune, Wilhelm 1967. *Althochdeutsche Grammatik.*[12] Rev. W. Mitzka. Tübingen: Max Niemeyer Verlag.

Brunner, Karl 1965. *Altenglische Grammatik, nach der Anglesächsische Grammatik von Eduard Sievers.*[3] Tübingen: Max Niemeyer Verlag.

Campbell, Alistair 1959. *Old English grammar.* Oxford: Clarendon Press.

Colman, Fran 1984. Anglo-Saxon pennies and Old English phonology. *Folia Linguistica Historica* **5**.91-144.

Colman, Fran 1988. What *is* in a name? In Jacek Fisiak (ed.), *Historical dialectology*, 111-37. Berlin: Mouton de Gruyter.

Dickins, Bruce & Ross, A.S.C. 1954. *The dream of the rood.* London: Methuen.

Elliott, R.W.V. 1963. *Runes. An introduction.* Manchester: Manchester University Press.

Ellis, A. J. 1867. *On early English pronunciation.* Part I. EETS OS 2.

Grant, William & Dixon, J. 1921. *Manual of modern Scots.* Cambridge: Cambridge University Press.

Hart, John 1569. *An orthographie.* London: Anon. Facsimile edition 1969. Menston: The Scolar Press.

Haugen, Einar 1950. *First grammatical treatise. The earliest Germanic phonology.* Supplement to *Language* 26.4.

Holthausen, Ferdinand 1963. *Altenglisches etymologisches Wörterbuch.*² Heidelberg: Carl Winter.

Hogg, Richard 1988. On the impossibility of Old English dialectology. In Kastovsky & Bauer (1988: 183-204).

Kastovsky, Dieter 1988. Morphophonemic alternation and the history of English: examples from Old English. In Manfred Markus (ed.), *Historical English: on the occasion of Karl Brunner's 100th birthday*, 112-23. Innsbrucker Beiträge zur Kulturwissenschaft, Anglistische Reihe, I.

Kastovsky, Dieter Forthcoming. Semantics and vocabulary. In Richard Hogg (ed.), *The Cambridge History of the English language*. I, *The Beginnings to 1066*. Cambridge: Cambridge University Press.

Kastovsky, Dieter & Bauer, Gero 1988. *Luick revisited. Papers read at the Luick-Symposium at Schloß Liechtenstein, 15.- 18.9.1985*. Tübingen: Gunter Narr Verlag.

Knox, Bernard M.W. 1968. Silent reading in antiquity. *Greek, Roman and Byzantine Studies* **9**.421-35.

Krahe, Hans 1962. *Indogermanische Sprachwissenschaft. I, Lautlehre*. Berlin: De Gruyter.

Krahe, Hans 1965. *Germanische Sprachwissenschaft. II, Formenlehre*. Berlin: De Gruyter.

Kyes, Robert 1967. The evidence for *i*-umlaut in Old Low Franconian. *Language* **43**. 666-73.

Lass, Roger 1973. Review of P.H. Reaney, *The origin of English surnames*. *Foundations of Language* 9.393-402.

Lass, Roger 1975. How intrinsic is content? Markedness, sound change, and 'family universals'. In Didier Goyvaerts & Geoffrey K. Pullum (eds.), *Essays on the sound pattern of English*, 475-504. Ghent: E. Story-Scientia.

Lass, Roger 1977. 'Centres of gravity' in linguistic evolution. *Die Sprache* **23**. 11-19.

Lass, Roger 1978. Mapping constraints in phonological reconstruction: on climbing down trees without falling out of them. In Jacek Fisiak (ed.), *Recent developments in historical phonology*, 245-86. The Hague: Mouton.

Lass, Roger 1981. Undigested history and synchronic 'structure'. In Didier Goyvaerts (ed.), *Phonology in the 1980s*, 525-44. Ghent: E. Story.

Lass, Roger 1983. Velar /r/ and the history of English. In Michael Davenport, Erik Hansen, Hans Frede Nielsen, *Current topics in English historical linguistics*, 67-94. Odense: Odense University Press.

Lass, Roger 1986. Words without etyma: Germanic 'tooth'. In Dieter Kastovsky & Alexander Szwedek (eds.), *Linguistics across historical and geographical boundaries. In honour of Jacek Fisiak on the occasion of his fiftieth birthday*, I, 473-82. Berlin: Mouton de Gruyter.

Lass, Roger 1987a. *The shape of English: structure and history*. London: J.M. Dent.

Lass, Roger 1987b. How reliable is Goldswain? On the credibility of an early South African English source. *African Studies* **46**. 155-62.

Lass, Roger 1989. How does early English get modern? Or, what happens when you listen to orthoepists and not to historians. *Diachromica* b. 75-110.

Lass, Roger Forthcoming a. Phonology and morphology. In Norman F. Blake (ed.), *The Cambridge History of the English Language*. II, *1066-1476*. Cambridge: Cambridge University Press.

Lass, Roger Forthcoming b. Phonology and morphology. In Roger Lass (ed.), *The Cambridge History of the English Language*. III, *1476-1776*. Cambridge: Cambridge

University Press.

Lass, Roger Forthcoming c. On data and 'datives' Ruthwell cross *rodi* again. To appear in *Neuphilologische Mitteilungen*.

Lass, Roger & John M. Anderson 1975. *Old English phonology*. Cambridge: Cambridge University Press.

Lodge, Kenneth R. 1984. *Studies in the phonology of colloquial English*. London: Croom Helm.

McIntosh, Angus 1956 The analysis of written Middle English. *Transactions of the Philological Society*, 1955, 26-55.

Maddieson, Ian 1984. *Patterns of sounds*. Cambridge: Cambridge University Press.

Moore, Samuel & Marckwardt, Albert 1964. *Historical outlines of English sounds and inflections*. Ann Arbor: George Wahr.

Mossé, Fernand 1945. *Manuel de l'anglais du moyen âge*. I, *vieil-anglais*. Paris: Aubier.

Murray, J. A. H. 1873. *The dialect of the southern counties of Scotland*. London: Asher.

Orton, Harold & Barry, M. V. 1969. *Survey of English dialects. B, Basic material: the West Midland counties*. Leeds: Arnold.

Orton, Harold & Halliday, Wilfred 1962. *Survey of English dialects. B*, Basic Material: the Northern Counties and the Isle of Man. Leeds: Arnold.

Orton, Harold & Wakelin, Martyn 1967. *Survey of English dialects. B, Basic Material: the East Midland counties and East Anglia*. Leeds: Arnold.

Penzl, Herbert 1988. Der *i*-Umlaut der Velarvokale im Altenglischen. In Kastovsky & Bauer (1988: 259-68).

Pilch, Herbert 1970. *Altenglische Grammatik*. 2 vols. München: Hueber.

Ponelis, F.A. 1986. Heterorganiese svarabhakti. *Tydskrif vir Geesteswetenskappe* (Pretoria) **26**. 81-94.

Prokosch, Frederick 1938. *A comparative Germanic grammar*. Baltimore: Linguistic Society of America.

Quirk, Randolph & Wrenn, C. L. 1955. *Old English grammar*. London: Methuen.

Ramat, Anna Giacolone, Carruba, Onofrio, Bernini, Giuliano 1987. *Papers from the 7th international conference on historical linguistics*. Amsterdam: John Benjamins.

Sapir, Edward 1921. *Language*. New York: Harcourt Brace.

Stanley, Eric Gerald 1988. Karl Luick's 'man schrieb wie man sprach' and English historical philology. In Kastovsky & Bauer (1988: 311-34).

Sweet, Henry 1885. *The oldest English texts*. EETS OS 83.

Sweet, Henry 1957. *Anglo-Saxon primer*. [9] Rev. Norman Davis. Oxford: Clarendon Press.

Telemann, Ulf 1980. Occam's Razor and the rise and fall of a Germanic phoneme. In Jens Allwood & Magnus Ljung (eds.), *Alvar. A linguistically varied assortment of readings. Studies presented to Alvar Ellegård on the occasion of his 60th birthday* (= *Stockholm Papers in English Language and Literature*, 1), 207- 18. Stockholm: Department of English, University of Stockholm.

Toon, Thomas 1983. *The politics of early Old English sound change*. New York: Academic Press.

Twaddell, W. Freeman 1938. A note on Old High German umlaut. *Monatshefte für deutschen Unterricht* **30**.177-81.

Vaiana, Mary 1972. A study in the dialect of the southern counties of Scotland, Unpublished PhD Thesis. Bloomington: Department of Linguistics, Indiana University.

von Raumer, Karl 1876. *Sancti Autustini confessionum libri tredecim*. Gütersloh: C. Bertelsmann.

Waddington, C.H. 1977. *Tools for Thought.* London: Jonathan Cape.

Wells, J.C. 1982. *Accents of English.* 3 vols. Cambridge: Cambridge University Press.

Wrenn, C.L. 1943. The value of spelling as evidence. *Transactions of the Philological Society*, 14-39.

Wright, Joseph 1905. *The English dialect grammar.* Oxford: Frowde.

Wright, Joseph & Wright, Elizabeth Mary 1925, *Old English grammar.*[3] Oxford: Clarendon Press.

Wyld, Henry Cecil 1927. *A short history of English.*[2] London: John Murray.

5

THE PHONOLOGY OF RESOLUTION IN OE WORD-STRESS AND METRE*

C.B. McCully

1 Introduction: Views of Resolution

Resolution is traditionally held to be a metre-specific phenomenon of equivalence (Sievers 1885; 1893), whereby a bisyllabic metrical lift, the first syllable of which is stressed and short, is interpreted as equivalent to a long, monosyllabic metrical lift. Resolution is thus an important structural device in OE metrics, and one without which the classic metrical typology of half-lines could not be maintained. First, however, as both Strang (1970) and others (Suphi 1985) have pointed out, it is necessary to distinguish clearly between the terms 'stress' and 'lift'. Stress, for example, is assigned by rule (see below) to particular syllables, and there is thus a one-to-one correspondence between stress in syllable x, and (the boundaries of) that constituent x. A lift, on the other hand, may be realised by just one stressed syllable, where that syllable is normally heavy (cf. Strang 1970: 325), but it may also—and this is where the distinction in terminology is needed—comprise a stressed, light syllable followed by another unstressed syllable. In other words, stress in OE is a simplex, a one-to-one relationship; a lift is a complex, a multivalent entity. (This is not to suggest, however, the simple proposition 'all lifts are stresses, therefore all stresses are lifts'. While the former statement is in all probability true, the second is not necessarily so — witness, for example, Campbell's rather odd claim (1959: 35) that there is secondary stress on the penult of *þēodcyningas* but not on that of *cyningas*). In addition, it is necessary to refine on the traditional notions of 'long' and 'short': in this paper I shall assume that a long syllable is a heavy syllable, that is, a syllable with a branching Rhyme constituent, and that a short, stressed syllable (e.g. first syllables of *bi.scop, cy. ning* etc., where ' . ' marks the syllable-division) is a syllable with a non-branching Rhyme, where such non-branchingness depends on a theory of underlying initial-maximal syllabification (Suphi 1985; 1988; and see §2. below). The following examples illustrate these points:

(1a) /   x   /   x   (1b) ◡   x   x   ◡ x   x
    gom ban gyl dan   gu mum æt gæ de re
     1   2   3   4   1   2   3   4

*A preliminary version of this paper was given at the meeting of the LAGB, Exeter 1988. Any mistakes that remain after that provisional excursus are, unhappily, my own responsibility. I am also grateful for the comments of the two anonymous reviewers who read the present work for ESEL; they pointed out several shortcomings, and suggested many improvements.

In (1a), the metrical lifts are formed by heavy (closed) syllables, which are aligned one-to-one with the strong metrical positions (lifts) 1 and 3. In (1b), though, the relationship between syllable and stress is less straightforward: the two syllables of *gumum* provide the environment for resolution, and it is that bisyllabic structure which is aligned with the strong metrical position 1. Exactly the same thing happens with *-gæder-* , where the resolved sequence fills the metrical lift in position 3: (1a) and (1b) are thus interpreted as equivalent. Both are, in traditional terms, varieties of Sievers's type A (Sievers 1885; 1893).

If we turn to a nonlinear notation, however, the issue seems to become clouded. OE, it is sensible to suppose, shares with Present-day English (PDE) the property of being a stress-based language. That being so, it is reasonable to assume that whatever stress rules we propose for OE, they, like their PDE analogues, will function to align certain syllables with the heads of metrical feet (Hogg and McCully 1987: Ch.3; McCully and Hogg 1988). If we concentrate on the stress-equivalence between *gomban* and *gumum*, for example, again it seems reasonable to assume that both items will have identical S W trees assigned to them, as in (2):

(2a)   S   W   (2b)   S   W
             gom ban   gu   mum

If, however, the stress-structure of the two words is identical, and if resolution is correlated solely with stress, then it is difficult to see why, in terms of stress and the poetic metre, *gumum* should be analysed any differently to *gomban* . It will be argued in Section 4. below that, owing to the conceptual difficulties that surround viewing resolution wholly as a phenomenon of linguistic stress, a time-based analysis must also be adopted in order to account for the equivalences involved (and see below).

Commentators have been vexed by these equivalences and differences. Many argue that resolution involves some 'sharing' of stress between two syllables. Bliss (1962: 9) can be taken as representative. 'Two syllables', he writes, 'of which the first is short are counted as equivalent to a single long syllable, and may as it were share the stress'. This claim is echoed elsewhere. Creed, for example, writes that in a resolved structure 'the first and second syllables...appear to *share* the primary stress' (1966: 24; his emphasis), and in a recent study, Russom, while correctly stating that 'in Old English...stress normally implies a phonological domain of one long syllable or two short syllables', relates resolution to 'articulative energy' (1987:11) — a concept which is nowhere defined in his 1987 work — as well as to syllable length (1987:11-12).

I shall argue that these accounts are at least in part mistaken, since it is absurd to claim that the two syllables of *gumum* 'share' stress — especially given the fact that OE stress rules assign stress (foot-headedness) iteratively to just one syllable, not to two syllables simultaneously. It seems perfectly clear that the second syllable of *gumum* is only weakly-stressed (it is after all an inflection, and as such prone to obscuration and/or loss, which typically occur in weak syllables), and it seems equally clear that the first syllable is strong — just as (2b) claims.

Instead of persisting in this error of shared stress, I shall argue for a more principled phonological analysis, one in which resolution has two correlates set in two discrete planes of phonological structure, respectively a stress-plane, and a time-plane. Both planes are anchored in CV- and syllable-structure (cf. Archangeli 1984; 1985). Before looking at these planes, however, and because resolution is usually held to have something to do with syllable configuration, we should briefly examine the theory of syllable-structure on which the following sections of this paper are based.

2 Syllable Structure in OE

The status of the syllable as a metrical constituent is, surely, no longer in doubt: Fudge (1969), Selkirk (1982; 1984 a and b) and Giegerich (1985; 1986)—among others — have argued convincingly not only that the syllable has a particular universal composition, but also that it must be incorporated into the phonological grammar as the smallest metrical unit. This last argument is supported by the fact that English stress rules, in whatever guise they are cast ('tree-only' (Hayes 1982; Giegerich 1985) or 'grid-only' (Selkirk 1984b)), assign foot-headedness to certain syllables according to their composition and/or position in a given domain. The relationship between syllable composition and stress is found crucially at the right edges of words in PDE, where the English Stress Rule (ESR)—ignoring certain specified segments or syllabic Rhymes as extrametrical (Hayes 1982)—aligns the rightmost heavy syllable it finds with the head of a foot (Hogg and McCully 1987: Ch. 3.)

Nevertheless, although the relationship between syllable-structure and stress is clear, the issue of syllabification itself is more problematic. I noted above that the analysis of resolution depended on syllabification in OE being (underlyingly) initial-maximal, but this cannot be merely assumed in view of arguments by e.g. Anderson and Jones (1977) and Lass (1983; 1984) who, albeit in different ways, assume that segments such as the medial /d/ in *fæder* are underlyingly ambisyllabic, and thus not unambiguously syllable-initial. As Suphi (1985) and Suzuki (1985) point out, however, there are several arguments against Lass's point of view.

In order to handle resolved strings, Lass (1983: 170ff.) sets up a separate moric tier of syllable structure whereby medial consonants such as the /d/ of *fæder*, the /n/ of *sunu* and so on are represented on the relevant tier not as -VCV- but as – VCCV-, where the medial segment is interpreted as belonging to both the Coda of a preceding syllable, and to the Onset of the following one (Lass 1983: 171). In this way, Lass argues, 'a VCV sequence counts as heavy because it *is* heavy' (1983:171; his emphasis) — that is, at some abstract level of representation, -VCV- is equivalent to -VCC-. Clearly, in terms of mere moric enumeration this may well be the case; but it is far from desirable, as Suzuki (1985:106) points out, to set up a separate tier of description solely to demonstrate this equivalence. Suphi (1985: 47) goes so far as to call Lass's solution a 'notational trick' and —

given the lack of other motivation for 'pseudo-geminates' (Suphi 1985) in syllable structure representations—that charge seems well-founded. Another substantial argument against Lass's approach focuses on the very equivalence that his moric tier was set up to demonstrate: if -VCV- and -VCC/-VC#C - are indeed formally identical, then Lass's analysis fails to capture the fact that in the latter cases it is these heavy syllables (including, as it turns out, -VC#, see here Suphi 1985: Ch.2.) which can fill metrical lifts on their own, whereas -VCV- as a *whole* can occupy a lift (Suzuki 1985: 107).

These two arguments compromise Lass's analysis, but there are a further two points that should be considered. The first relates to Lass's treatment of u-deletion (Lass 1984: 250ff.). Lass (1984:254) again assumes that -VC# syllables (as in e.g. *scip#u* in his analysis) are 'light' insofar as their Rhymes contain no branching constituent (Peak or Coda). As Suphi (1985) conclusively proves, however, Lass's treatment of -VC# as light is unreliable because his evidence depends largely on how such strings are analysed in terms of the poetic metre. He claims in his 1983 paper, for instance, that -VC# structures may only fill metrical lifts when they are followed by other words whose initial segment is a consonant. Given the abundant evidence to the contrary, however, (well-summarised in Suphi 1985: 47-48; Suzuki 1985:99) this claim is rash, and a later alternative proposal — that strings such as *mon on mōde* (Beo. 2281a) be scanned as containing a verse-initial resolved foot—is unattractive since scansions like this yield verse patterns which cannot be aligned with one of the traditional Types because they lack the required number of metrical positions (Suphi 1985: 48-9). The conclusion must be—admittedly despite the suspicion that arguments or counter-arguments from OE metre may be merely circular—that Lass's arguments for -VC# as light in OE are incorrect, and this still further compromises his analysis of u-deletion: it can no longer be claimed that -u is retained after 'light' (-VC#) syllables, and deleted after heavy ones, because the arguments compel us to treat -VC# as heavy (cf. Bliss 1962:9, who writes that 'a syllable is...long in OE if it contains a vowel followed by a single final consonant'). In fact a more explanatory analysis of u-deletion is available, which stems from the 'bi-planar' work of Keyser and O'Neil (1985), and we shall examine these arguments in Section 4 below.

There is one final point to be considered. Hogg and McCully (1987, Ch.3.) treat ambisyllabicity in PDE as a stress-sensitive phenomenon, that is, as the product of a late adjustment rule by which consonants *become* ambisyllabic (thus preserving the trading relation between syllabic heaviness and stressedness). If we are to propose a congruence between the stress rules of OE and PDE (and this is a proposal we are bound to entertain, since both are 'stress-based' languages in the sense of Dauer (1983)), then it would be unwise to dismiss the argument that ambisyllabicity in OE is likewise stress-dependent—if, indeed, we need to assume that ambisyllabicity is necessary at all in analysis of the metrical phenomena of OE (cf. Suphi 1985: 44ff.).

To summarise, then, I shall here assume that syllabification in OE follows the unmarked, initial-maximal mode, where light syllables are Rhyme-monomoric (first syllables of *sci. pu*, *cy.ning* , *bi. scop* , where '.' symbolises the syllable boundary) and where heavy syllables are minimally Rhyme-bimoric (first syllables of *gom.ban*, *tim.bro.de* etc.). This is not only the simplest assumption to make in terms of resolution, but also, strikingly, the assumption of underlying initial-maximal syllabification is crucial to the working of the Old English Stress Rule, and it is to this issue we now turn.

3 Resolution: The Stress Plane

Is there anything in the working of the Old English Stress Rule (OESR) which hints at a solution to the problems posed by resolution?

As McCully and Hogg (1988) show, the OESR is a rule which applies left-to-right, assigning the property of foot-headedness to certain syllables. Their approach differs from that of Suphi (1985; 1988), who assumes that the OESR is morphologically, rather than phonologically, sensitive, and that the rule applies simultaneously to bracketed items in a level-ordered fashion. There seem to be several difficulties associated with Suphi's model, which are as follows: (i) Bracketing. Suphi assumes bracketings such as [[and][saca]] 'apostate' since 'the stress assignment rule makes reference to the initial boundary of all morphemes' (1988: 178, fn.1). Yet it is clearly the case that, say, compounds such as *andsaca* are headed, where the unmarked case for such (morphosyntactic) headedness falls under Allen's (1980) 'IS A' Condition (see also Marchand 1969), where, crudely, AB=B. In other words, an alternative form of bracketing, such as [and[saca]], is at least a possibility. (ii) The stress behaviour of prefixes. Suphi (1988: 176), following Siegel (1974), assumes that the OE lexicon is ordered into levels at which specific processes take place. In her model, nominal and adjectival prefixation takes place at level 1 (so these affixes undergo the OESR), and verbal and adverbial prefixation takes place at level 2 (so these affixes do not undergo the OESR). Again, however, an alternative (and conceptually simpler) analysis is available, one which assumes that the stress behaviour of prefixes is not a matter of morphological level, but a matter of what constraints (primarily cyclicity) and other devices (extrametricality), bear on the relevant rule(s) handling these items (see McCully and Hogg 1988 for a full account). In addition, it is an unattractive feature of Suphi's (1985) model that it entails a loop device to handle inflection on compounds (Suphi 1985:154). Loop devices, which stem from work on lexical phonology by Mohanan (1982; 1986), have been heavily criticised (Halle 1987; Gussmann 1988). (iii) Simultaneous vs. sequential application. Suphi assumes that the OESR applies simultaneously rather than iteratively. As McCully and Hogg (1988) point out, however, simultaneous application of a stress rule yields a significantly less powerful explanandum for 'stress in language X' than an analysis which assumes that stress rules are directional, i.e. iterate right-to-left (apparently, following Hayes 1981 (1985) the unmarked option) or left-to-right. Where a stress rule migrates right-to-left, as in Latin and PDE, the notion of 'right edge' is crucial to the derivation (in PDE, for example, it is at this edge that extrametrical constituents are found), and as we shall see, where stress rules apply left-to-right, the notion of 'left-edge' is equally crucial. (iv) Zero syllables. Suphi's (1985; 1988) model employs those zero syllables familiar from work by Giegerich

(1985), and, while it is true that zero syllables can be phonetically motivated as Suphi (1988: 181) claims, their employment leads to considerable complication in word-stress derivations, as is evidenced by Suphi's Word Rule (1988: 182), which deletes zero syllables when they occur word-internally. This rule is problematic insofar as it is structure changing; it is unclear whether what is essentially a rule of node labelling should have this power (cf. McCully and Hogg 1988).

Given these problems, it seems preferable to pursue a phonological approach to OE stress, one where all affixes are present when the OESR applies, and where the OESR iterates left-to-right. A provisional version of the rule can be found in (3):

(3) OESR (provisional version)

Assign maximally binary S W feet from left to right

Under (3), monosyllables will be assigned a unary foot, and bisyllables such as *æþel*, *biscop*, *cyning* will unproblematically be assigned one S W foot. Trisyllables with derivational or inflectional endings are, however, a little more complicated. Consider forms such as *æþeling* 'prince', *biscopes* 'of-the-bishop' (g.sg.) Let us assume that, following usual cyclic procedure where stress rules work on innermost brackets first, metrical structure has been assigned on a first cycle, and innermost brackets removed; we then have the forms seen in (4):

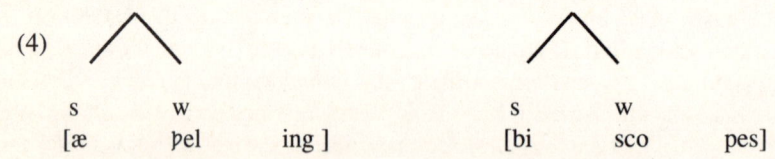

(4)

```
       S     W                    S     W
     [æ    þel   ing ]           [bi   sco   pes]
```

Now let us make the further assumption that the OESR, like the ESR for PDE, iterates strictly cyclically (Kiparsky 1979; 1982). In effect, this means that throughout each iteration the rule must respect the heads of feet which have been created on earlier cycles. (The ESR for PDE operates identically, except it works right-to-left, not left-to-right). This parenthesis aside, it is worth noting that, as far as OE is concerned, nothing in the principle of strict cyclicity would be contravened if the OESR iterated on the examples in (4) by erecting maximally binary feet on *-þeling* and *-scopes*, as in (5):

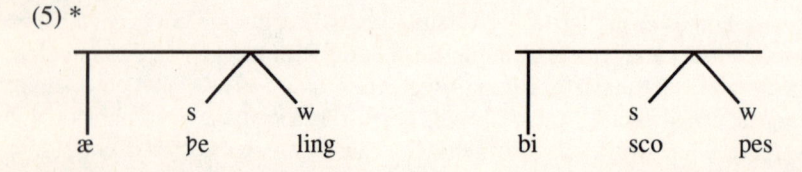

(5) *

```
            S     W                    S     W
     æ     þe    ling             bi   sco   pes
```

In (5), the heads of feet have been respected, but it seems wrong to claim that *æþeling* and *biscopes* are bi-pedal, and will subsequently exhibit secondary stress on their medial syllables. What seems to be happening with these forms is that a subsequent iteration of the OESR must respect the metrical structure that has been erected on *both* syllables of *æpel-* and *biscop-* ; in other words, two syllables, the first of which is light and stressed, here (at the left edge of a derivation) count, as far as the OESR is concerned, as if they were just one heavy, stressed syllable. Therefore, given the factors that seem to bear on reapplication of the OESR where strict cyclicity is the *modus operandi* of the rule, we may propose a revision to the OESR as follows:

(6) OESR (final version)

Assign maximally binary S W feet from left-to-right, where S must contain branching, or in env [__ X be dominated by a branching foot.

This version of OESR claims that the rule is sensitive to syllable weight, and/or branchingness at the left edge of the environment (cf. Suphi 1985, who suggests that the OESR is purely morphologically-sensitive). If S, both at the left edge and elsewhere, contains (Rhyme) branching, then all is well: a subsequent iteration of the OESR may assign S to an immediately following syllable provided that conditions on heaviness are met there as well (cf. the analysis of *timbrode*, 'he built', below). If, however, a leftmost S dominates a light syllable, then the entire S W structure erected on a first iteration at the left edge must be respected. Notice that in terms of (5), the final version of the OESR cannot now operate to align the medial syllables with foot-heads, since to do so would be to deprive the word-initial light syllables of the branching which dominates them; in addition, of course, the root-medial syllable of *biscopes* is light under initial-maximal syllabification, and thus not susceptible to (6), which claims that S must contain branching. (6) means, in effect, that the S W structure previously erected on both syllables of *æpel-* and *biscop-* must be respected, as desired. All the OESR can now do is erect a unary foot on *-ing* and *-es*, as in (7):

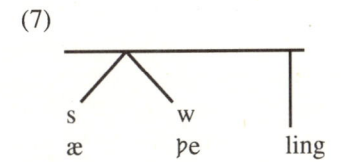

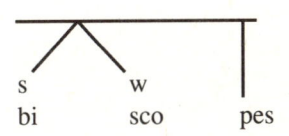

(7)

```
    S   W      |           S    W     |
    æ   þe   ling          bi   sco   pes
```

This is still not quite what we want, since in each case there is an overgeneration of the OESR at the right edge (note the mirror-image with PDE here, since the ESR overgenerates at the left edge, creating unary feet in words such as *balloon* which will subsequently undergo Initial Destressing). In the present context, since neither Destressing rules nor higher-level rules are of direct relevance to the phenomenon of resolution, it is sufficient to note that the structures in (7) undergo a Word Rule, which makes their leftmost foot-nodes strong, and thereafter a postcyclic rule of Final Destressing, which converts word-final unary weak feet into merely W right daughters of a preceding foot (McCully and Hogg 1988). The outputs are those seen in (8):

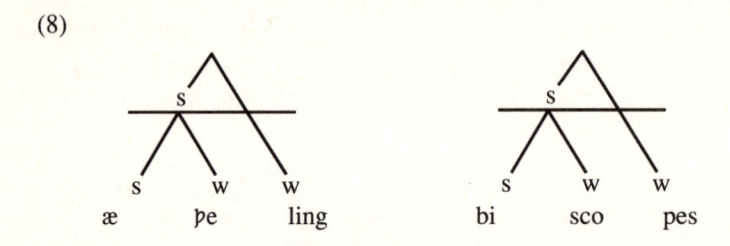

(8)

```
         S                              S
       / | \                          / | \
      S  W  W                        S  W  W
      æ  þe ling                     bi sco pes
```

The really important point, however, and something which should be emphasised, is that the version of the OESR given in (6) encodes the stress-correlate of resolution, since the rule is sensitive to both syllable-weight (at the left edge and elsewhere) and branchingness (at the left edge). To illustrate this further, consider the minimal contrast between e.g *timbrode* and *bifode*. The first example, or so it is traditionally claimed (Campbell 1959: 34-5), bears secondary stress on its medial syllable; the second example does not, because medial -od- of Class 2 weak verbs may only become (secondarily) stressed if it follows another long (heavy) syllable (Campbell 1959: §90). This is puzzling since both strings have the same morphological make-up (and, it should be noted, if Old English stress is purely morphologically-determined then we should expect both strings to have an identical stress composition). The OESR (6), however, solves the puzzle (note that the puzzle is formed not so much by 'resolution' as by what overall principles determine secondary stress in Old English). Assume the first cycle(s) of the OESR erect the following trees, where the morphological bracketing is assumed to be e.g. [[timbrod]e]:

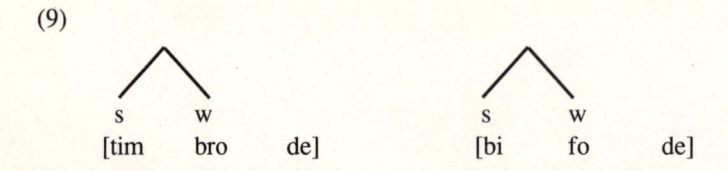

(9)

```
        /\                              /\
       S  W                            S  W
      [tim bro de]                    [bi fo de]
```

Now notice how the OESR obliges us to proceed. In *timbrode* there is little problem as far as syllable composition at the left edge is concerned. The OESR can erect its maximally binary S W foot over *-ode* since the initial foot of the word contains the required syllable-branching. Secondly, the medial *-ō-* is—at least historically—long. This is rather more problematic, because in order to obtain the correct derivation, where terminal S dominates syllable branching, it is necessary to postulate the underlying form *timbrōde* (and *bifōde*). Campbell

(1959: 332), however, notes that this verb conjugation is one where 'endings were added to Gmc. -ō- ‹ I-E -ā-...In the past system and the pass. part. the dental formative elements...were added to -ō-'. It could of course be objected that this analysis employs non-synchronic material criteria to gloss what is essentially a synchronic problem, but if we turn to the poetic metre of *Beowulf*, it seems evident that there, too, the poet feels free to use non-synchronic metrical values, as in the contracted forms stemming from h-loss (relevant verses include e.g. *hêan hūses*, 'of the noble hall'. *Beo*, 116a, *on flet têon* 'to draw to the floor', *Beo* 1036b, and *fæderæþelum onfōn*, 'to inherit paternal rank'. *Beo.* 911a, see Russom 1987: 40-1). Russom's conclusion is that '[G]enerative phonology assumes that a native speaker's grammar contained some underlying forms corresponding to earlier stages of the language...[And it] seems clear that the [*Beowulf*] poet composed during the period after h-loss, but retained the right to employ metrical values of an earlier age' (1987; 40-1). If Russom is correct, then the charge of non-sychronicity is made easier to rebut.

We shall assume, therefore, that for these structural reasons the next iteration of the OESR on *timbrōde* yields (9a):

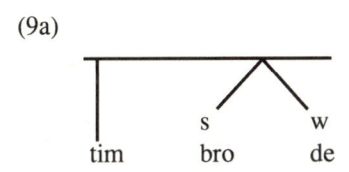

(9a)

```
    |      /\
    |     S  W
   tim  bro  de
```

In *bifōde*, however, the OESR is not free to reassign S to the medial syllable—whatever its syllabic heaviness might be—because to do so would be to deprive the initial syllable of branching. In other words, the OESR respects the existing SW structure of *bifōd-* just as it did the S W leftmost feet of *æþeling* and *biscopes*, and reapplies vacuously. Thereafter the final light *-e* is incorporated into the tree by a rule of Stray Morpheme Adjunction (McCully and Hogg 1988), giving the structure (9b):

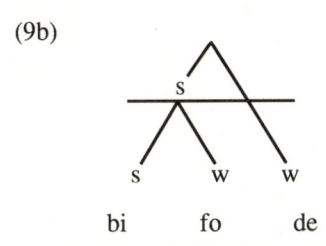

(9b)

```
       /\
      S
     /\  \
    S  W  W
   bi  fo  de
```

This mode of application provides a striking explanation of the minimal stress contrast between *timbrōde* and *bifōde* (as well as yielding some significant generalisations about secondary stress elsewhere, see McCully 1988c), and furnishes additional evidence that, as far as the OESR is concerned, one heavy, stressed syllable at the left edge of the domain (*tim-*) is equivalent to two syllables, the first of which is stressed and light (*bifod-*). It is precisely with strings such as *æþel-*, *biscop-*, and *bifod-* that resolution is an issue, and in fact the form of the OESR seen in (6) suggests that resolution is in fact not a sharing of stress but an analogue of a metrical condition of the phonological grammar. In this sense, therefore, it seems that poets employed resolution out of linguistic necessity and not, primarily, because of stylistic choice: the 'resolved foot' is a part of Old English phonology, and the fact that it has a function in the poetic metre follows from this, rather than from the specific role that foot may play in the poetry. Obviously enough, however, we must look elsewhere in order to justify the claim that the resolved foot is part of Old English phonology (rather than a metre-specific constituent).

One prime candidate that might provide this last kind of evidence is Middle English Open Syllable Lengthening (MEOSL). There, as e.g. Minkova (1982) shows, it is necessary to postulate the (segmental) environment /—-C: e# (Minkova 1982: 42—discounting the consonant clusters, *sp, st, sk* which, given their role in Old English alliterative poetry as well as in PDE phonotactics, qualify here as single intervocalic obstruents) as input to the change (as Minkova puts it (42), MEOSL 'is a much more context-sensitive change than has hitherto been admitted'). It cannot be coincidental that the environment for MEOSL is almost identical to the environment for resolution; the only discrepancy that exists between the two potentially-shared environments is the status of word-final consonants (MEOSL is apparently inhibited if the second syllable of the input string is heavy, see Minkova 1982: 48). This discrepancy does, however, throw up another intriguing idea: notwithstanding the claim made above that Old English showed left-edge extrametricality (on certain morphemes), would it not also be consistent to claim, particularly in view of the assumption that Old English had underlying initial-maximal syllabification; that word-final consonants in Old English were also extrametrical? For reasons of space, however, I shall leave this question there, merely wishing to emphasise the fact that MEOSL would seem to provide persuasive evidence that the kind of syllable (and stress) configurations we have adduced for resolution also appear to operate as inputs to an historically discrete phonological phenomenon.

In sum, if we are to find evidence for Old English verse-prosody, then it seems we must proceed by looking at Old English phonology first, because the structures of that phonology, and the rules that govern them, both underpin and enable a particular metre. The stress-correlate of resolution affords a striking example of such an inter-relationship.

4 Resolution: The Time Plane

The conditions governing stress-assignment, however, provide only a partial explanation of the phenomenon, and I claimed above that resolution has two correlates. What of the correlate embodied in the time-plane? Here we shall make an apparent digression, and return to the problems posed by u-deletion (cf. §.2) by invoking Keyser and O'Neil (1985), who reinterpret u-deletion *(wordu > word,* cf. *scipu*) by relating it in a specific and original way to syllabic Rhyme structure.

Phonology of Resolution

Keyser and O'Neil suppose that there is a separate, rule-governed plane of phonological structure which gathers syllabic Rhymes into what they call, ambiguously, 'feet', but what I shall here, for reasons which will become clear, call 'rhythmemes'. It is important to note that the rhythmemic algorithm is conceptually distinct from the rule which constructs stress feet (to take but one issue, different parameters for headedness are set by (6)). Their rule for doing this runs as follows (cf. Keyser and O'Neil 1985: 6):

(10) Rhythmeme construction:
Gather Rhymes from left to right into maximally binary, quantity-sensitive, right-headed trees.

To see how (10) works, consider the examples in (11), where stress trees are indicated above, rhythmemic trees below, where ' $\downarrow$ ' signifies rhythmemic headedness:

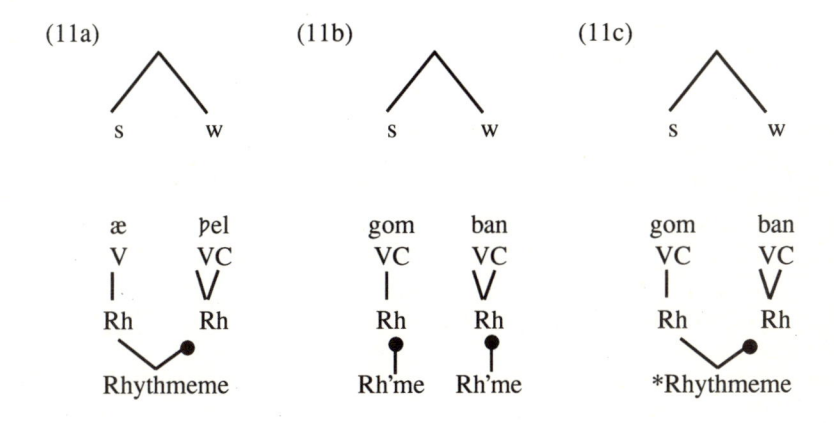

(11a)   (11b)   (11c)

```
    /\                  /\                  /\
   /  \                /  \                /  \
  S    W              S    W              S    W

  æ    þel            gom   ban           gom   ban
  V    VC             VC    VC            VC    VC
  |    V              |     V             |     V
  Rh   Rh             Rh    Rh            Rh    Rh
   \__/               •     •              \__/
     •                ↑     ↑                •
 Rhythmeme          Rh'me  Rh'me         *Rhythmeme
```

The trees of (11a-b) are well-formed. In (11a), the rightmost Rhyme is a branching Rhyme, and rhythmemes are right-headed. In addition, because the parameter for headedness has been set by (10), the leftmost branch may here dominate a non-branching Rhyme (cf. Keyser and O'Neil 1985: 7). In (11b), the bisyllable is parsed into two rhythmemes, since it is impermissible for leftmost binary branches to dominate branching Rhymes (cf. (11a)), as this would violate the headedness constraint (and recall that rhythmemes are quantity-sensitive). Such violation is seen in (11c). In other words, every CV-string is parsable into rhythmemes, working from left-to-right, and if binary construction is impossible, then unary rhythmemes are assigned (11b) which do not violate the parameters set up in (10).

In terms of the job this 'rhythmemic' structure was set up to do — to account for high vowel deletion in e.g *wordu* > *word* as against *scipu* — it works well: it is only those high vowels which immediately follow a rhythmeme that delete, and these abstract representations capture the process more elegantly than e.g Lass's

(1983: 1984) analysis outlined above (Section 2). As Keyser and O'Neil note, '[i]t is noteworthy that it is only at that very abstract level that it is possible to find the property which the deleting environments share' (1985: 10).

Given the fact, then, that (10) sets up structures distinct from those created by word-stress rules, it seems justifiable to follow Keyser and O'Neil (1985: 2) in assuming that Old English actually has two tree construction algorithms, one for vowel deletion and one for stress assignment. Both types of representation are anchored in syllabic Rhyme structure, but differ minimally in the way parameters for headedness are set (feet are left-headed, rhythmemes right-headed). The overall picture of such a set of co-existent representations is reminiscent of current work in non-linear theory (Archangeli 1984; 1985), which claims that certain metrical phenomena may be captured by positing a phonological model that is three-dimensional (or n-dimensional). In McCarthy's analysis of Semitic (1979; 1981), for example (cited in Archangeli 1985: 337), a three-dimensional model captures the fact that consonants, vowels and the CV pattern each constitute a separate morpheme. The CV pattern forms the skeleton or core of the representation; the consonant melody and vowel melody form respectively different 'planes' built up from, and associated with, the core skeleton, and syllable structure is likewise built up from the core skeleton on a still further plane. As Archangeli (1985: 337) puts it, 'the core skeleton may be likened to the axle of a paddle wheel and each melody or structure to a paddle attached to the axle. Each "paddle" is a *plane*, defined along one edge by the line of the core skeleton and along the other edge by the melody or structure of that plane' (her italics). Given that the stress and rhythmemic analyses for Old English developed here form separate, but co-existent, sets of representation, the question now arises as to whether the two representations are actually set in two planes of constituency anchored in the 'axle' of CV (specifically, Rhyme) structure.

The answer, surely, is that we are indeed looking at a multiplanar representation. This is so because we know independently (Section 3) that stress in Old English is quantity-sensitive, and the key for that sensitivity is Rhyme structure. Syllables, let us suppose, are constructed 'upwards' out of CV strings; thereafter, feet are created upon those syllables, again upwards. In Archangeli's (1985) terms, on this vertical axis we are looking at two sets of sequential structure set in one hierarchical plane, where the stress-creating algorithm spreads itself over the sequential structure already built at a lower level. Now let us suppose that rhythmemes are built 'outwards'; this is trivially entailed by the fact that rhythmemes, too, are constructed from CV structure to Rhymes, but any further upwards building on the first plane is already inhibited by the fact that stress trees occupy that plane. Further, we have already seen that the OESR migrates along strings of syllables, not along strings of rhythmemes: feet and rhythmemes are conceptually distinct; and consequently, because of this distinctness (feet and rhythmemes are not, for example, tiers of structure existing together on just one axis), we are not looking at a 'coplanar' representation (Archangeli 1985: 336), but a multiplanar one. Therefore we seem justified in allowing rhythmemic structure to occupy a separate plane. Note that this presupposes that rhythmemes are created after feet; such a mode of application ((6) ordered before (10)) is by no means a mere ad hoc stipulation, but follows from the fact that the rhythmemic plane is not only necessary to account for vowel deletion, but co-operates with the stress plane, as we shall see, in order to allow one characterisation of resolution (and, see below, of rhythm itself). In other words, Keyser and O'Neil's rhythmemes may be put to a use different to the one for which they were originally envisaged, and (10) has therefore a more general utility.

In what follows, then, we shall use the term 'plane' in the specific sense developed by Archangeli (1985); a structure plane is an axis built from a CV core on which, and along which, a sum of a set of representations may be found. A multiplanar representation for a word such as *gomban* 'tribute' (acc. sg.), given informally in (11) above, may be found more fully articulated in (12) (where, for reasons for clarity, association lines linking the CV core to segments have been omitted):

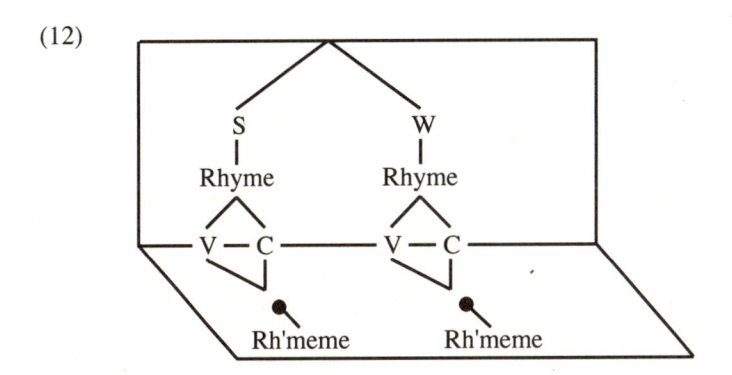

(12)

```
              S           W
              |           |
            Rhyme       Rhyme
             /\          /\
          —V—C——————V—C——
             \_/         \_/
              •           •
           Rh'meme    Rh'meme
```

I noted above that a rhythmemic analysis could also be used to provide a representation of resolved strings. It should immediately be apparent, for instance, that lexical bisyllables such as *æpel*, *biscop*, and *cyning* are monorhythmemic, whereas bisyllables with two intervocalic consonants separated by a syllable-boundary—*gomban, ende* ('end'), *entisc* ('made by giants') and so forth—are birythmemic (consist of two rhythmemes of equal proportion). Clearly, resolution is a phenomenon which implies a domain of two syllables, where those syllables are mapped into a unary rhythmeme on one plane of an abstract representation.

Before pursuing this brand of analysis into its specific applications, however, we should enquire first, what sort of 'headedness' the algorithm of (10) entails, and second, whether we are justified in postulating that rhythmemic structure occupies a 'time plane', where 'time' is the operative modifier.

The heads set up by (10) seem to be purely abstract entities. Possibly, they are simply notional-heads set up in order to account for certain phonological phenomena (u-deletion). On the other hand, we are justified in asking whether the headedness entailed by (10) can be related to any more general set of assumptions concerning the stress or time-structure of Old English.

One possible, albeit very tentative, answer to this enquiry might claim that the heads set up by (10) are in fact not stress-heads, or syntactic heads (since both kinds of headedness have already been assigned) but time-heads. It is particularly intriguing, for example, that the rhythmemic plane encodes structures which correspond strikingly with the range of foot-internal, phonological time-proportions suggested for CV-strings in (Modern) English by Abercrombie (1965). Take the paradigm stress foot, S W. Segmentally, such a foot may embody the following strings:

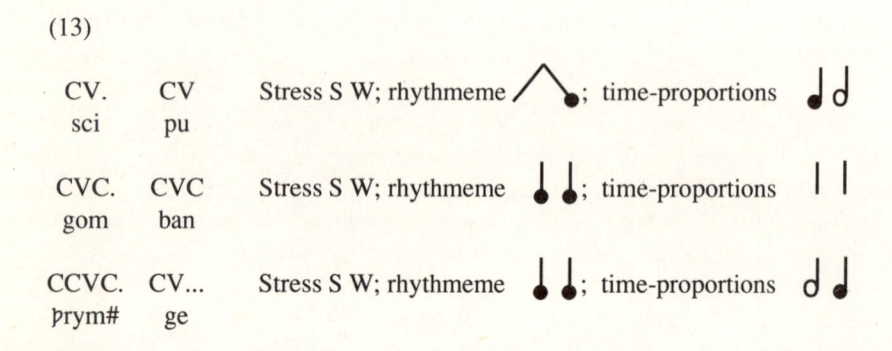

(13)

| CV. | CV | Stress S W; rhythmeme ◠; time-proportions ♩♩ |
| sci | pu | |

| CVC. | CVC | Stress S W; rhythmeme ↓↓; time-proportions | | |
| gom | ban | |

| CCVC. | CV... | Stress S W; rhythmeme ↓↓; time-proportions ♩♩ |
| þrym# | ge | |

scipu patterns with PDE *bitter* in terms of time-proportions, to which Abercrombie would give the value 'short-long' symbolised in a 'temporal' notation | ♩ ♩ |. (For justification of the triple nature of foot-internal structure see Abercrombie (1965) and especially Thomson (1923)). These short-long proportions are, it turns out, congruent with rhythmemic structure, where a left-branch dominates a non-branching Rhyme, and where the right-branch dominates a branching Rhyme and is a rhythmemic head.

gomban patterns with PDE *hunger*; Abercrombie gives the time-proportions of these strings, with two intervocalic consonants separated by a syllable-boundary, as 'equal-equal'. Again, notice the congruence with rhythmemes. Just as the time-proportions are equal-equal, so *gomban* is scanned as one S W foot embodying two rhythmemes. *þrym#ge* (cf. Beo, 2b, *þrym gefrūnon*) is, however, more complicated, since a nonphonological parameter (juncture) is involved. I will assume here that *ge-* attaches under enclisis to the preceding syllable, and that the S W foot thereby produced is then rhythmemically scanned (a clear example of how the rules governing stress-plane and time-plane are ordered). Of course, this is a large assumption to make, given what little evidence there is for enclisis in Old English, see here Suphi (1988: 181). But although the evidence is small (Suphi mentions e.g. *þætte* ‹ *þæt te*), it seems on general grounds to be suggestive. Old English, after all, was a stress-based language, where the tendency to rhythmic regularity is maintained, as in PDE, by left-headed feet. Further, enclisis has an analogue in the fact that stray syllables and morphemes are, in the course of word-stress derivations, drawn into left-headed trees automatically—thus providing evidence for a foot-template, where S W and S W W structures are paradigmatic. And finally, the analysis of Old English verse using half-line templates (see here McCully 1988b,c; and Section 5 below) is made much simpler if it can be assumed that certain weak syllables attach to leftmost heads.

To return to the problems posed by *þrym#ge*: even if it is assumed that *ge-* attaches to *þrym*, the neat correspondences so far exhibited between Abercrombie's time-proportions, and rhythmemic structure, break down. *þrym#ge* would, for example, be analysed as |𝅗𝅥 ♩| in Abercrombie's notation, a 'long-short' foot where the presence of the boundary would seem to be determinate for time-relations. Rhythmemically, however, we would be obliged to scan the foot as duple, as two rhythmemes of equal proportion (cf. *gomban*). This hiatus, however, is once again intriguing. First, feet containing an internal boundary are metrically (temporally) ambiguous. In a specimen line from PDE, *Jack and Jill went up the hill*, it is certainly possible, perhaps preferable, to take the time-proportions as triple |𝅗𝅥 ♩||𝅗𝅥 ♩|...In a similar four-beat line, however, where the feet again contain boundaries, the temporal proportions are preferably duple: *Sing a song of sixpence* appears thus proportionally as |♩ ♩||♩ ♩|...These examples indicate that the time-proportions for the word-boundary foot are not hard and fast, and that the hiatus which exists in these instances between rhythmemic structure and a time-based transcription actually supports the perception of metrical (temporal) ambiguity. Taking examples from PDE, though, and applying the same principles to Old English, may be found suspect; but in Section 5 I shall argue that we are allowed to do this for a time-plane because whereas the stress-structure of English has been in flux, the rhythmemic structure has been historically stable.

There is one final point to make concerning the proposed rhythmemic analysis, before discussing the applications of the bi-planar model. It is interesting to consider it in terms of prosodic historiography. Consider the fact that for many years there was an ongoing debate among metrical theorists about whether the Old English half-line was four-beat (Lachmann 1831 (1833), 1876; and see the summary in Kaluza 1911: 16ff) or two-beat (Bartsch 1858; Rieger 1864; Sievers 1885; 1893). Indeed, echoes of the controversy persist into modern scholarship, where the work of Heusler (1889, 1894) and Leonard (1918) both looks back to that of the four-beat theorist Möller (1888) and anticipates Pope (1942), and where Sievers's *Typentheorie* looks back to Bartsch (1858) and anticipates Bliss (1958; 1962); for a full discussion see McCully (1988b: 294ff.). In terms of the bi-planar analysis adopted here, it is possible to suggest that the two-beat / four-beat debate has been persistent because theorists in each camp have been scanning different planes. The simple specimen half-line *gomban gyldan*, for instance, has two chief stresses (=foot-initial syllables) and, on a discrete plane, four rhythmemes. A two-beat reading scans patterns of intensity; a four-beat reading scans patterns of time-

and-intensity. In short, if we require an answer as to why influential scholars have maintained that a simple half-line A-type should be scanned as four-beat—crudely, / \ / \ as against the two-beat / x / x —then we could do worse than consider the answer in terms of periodicity, plane and a three-dimensional phonological model.

5 Applications

The biplanar analysis has two important applications, the first to phonological history and verseform(s), the second specifically to Old English metrics. To conclude, I shall look briefly at these respective issues.

I noted above that taking examples from PDE, and using their phonological structure to provide evidence for Old English, was a suspect procedure, but that it could be considered more legitimate if it could be shown that the rhythmemic plane is historically stable. As a way of attacking this issue, let us ask why it is that we are able to perceive Old English rhythm at all. This is not perhaps, the straightforward question it seems. As Strang (1970: 325) noted,

> The effect of OE metre is that of rhythmically stylised speech. That it has a rhythmical effect as read by speakers of modern English is of considerable importance, for what we have described [i.e the patterns /x, / \, and so on: McC] are not rhythmical patterns, but stress patterns, patterns of intensity rather than patterns in time. The rhythm is there because *the temporal patterning we impose from our experience of (PDE) corresponds to the temporal patterning of Old English* [my italics: McC].

That is, to interpret a string of sound as rhythmical, we must not only interpret its stress-patterning, but also its time-patterning. For Old English, the distinction is crucial, especially where resolution is concerned. The OESR, for instance, shows up important differences between its operation and the operation of the ESR for PDE (not least in the treatment of secondary stress, see McCully 1988c; McCully and Hogg 1988). In addition, that rule is directionally unlike its PDE analogue. If stress-patterning is the sole correlate of rhythmicity, how can we therefore interpret Old English rhythm? The answer must lie in the fact that in interpreting Old English verse, indeed rhythmical language in general, we are interpreting two co-occurrent planes of phonological structure.

If Strang is correct, this implies that temporal (rhythmemic) structure is historically persistent, and we should therefore expect to find that resolution is a feature not just of Old English verse, but of all English verse of every period—since metrical salience will imply not just one heavy, stressed syllable, but also two syllables, the first of which is stressed and light. Unsurprisingly, this is just what we do find. Danielsson (1948: 459) for instance writes:

> An extra syllable variation not considered by most recent writers on English prosody is what Young [1923: McC] denominates *'resolution of the stressed syllable'* and defines in the following way.... 'the place of any stressed syllable may be taken by two, whereof the first retains the stress, but is short in quantity [i.e 'having a light

vowel, followed by not more than a single consonantal sound'; see Danielsson *loc. cit.*, fn. 27]; while the second is unstressed'. The following lines from Chaucer's Prologue to the Canterbury Tales are quoted by Young as instances of resolution:

A. Prol.   22 To Caunter*bury* with full devout corage
A. Prol. 296 Than robes riche, or *fithele* , or gay sautrye
A. Prol. 321 Nowher so *bisy* a man as he ther was

According to Young §114 'this variation has secured the approval of all first-rate metrists. It abounds in Shakespeare, is further developed by Milton, and has been studiously cultivated by Tennyson.' Cf. also Risberg [1936: McC] §165, who, as an instance of extra syllable variation by resolution, gives the following line from Tennyson: *In cataract after cataract to the sea* (his italics: McC.).

Contemporary writers have had little to say about the matter, although one exception is Kiparsky (1977: 236 ff.), who adduces the following examples from Shakespeare:

And spends his *prodi*gal wits in bootless rhyme   (L.L.L. 5.2.64)
Come to one mark, as *many* ways meet in one town (H5 1.2.208)
Followed my *bani*shment, and this twenty years   (Cym. 3.3.69)
In the affliction of these *terri*ble dreams   (Mac. 3.2.19).

Of these, all seem to be plausibly analysed by positing resolution of the italicised syllables, with the exception, perhaps, of the second example, which Kiparsky handles by positing both resolution (on *many*) and the existence of a rule which disregards monosyllabic clitics (*in one town*). The rule for resolution given by Kiparsky (1977: 236) is, however, suspect, since in effect it is an unordered transformational rule which deletes certain specified syllables in a certain environment. It is unclear whether resolution should be handled by positing deletion (which leaves behind just one stressed, light syllable, e.g *pro-* in the first example above), since this denies the trading relation there is between metrical lifting and syllabic environment. Moreover, stress is nowhere invoked in Kiparsky's resolution rule (R1; see Kiparsky, *loc. cit.*), and it should by now be clear that resolution crucially involves a stress plane. It seems more sensible to adopt a bi-planar analysis, where certain S W strings are optionally monorhythmemic. (Optional status is necessary in view of examples such as *What's Hecuba to him, or he to Hecuba* (Ham. 4.5. 103), where the same word appears to be treated rhythmemically in two distinct ways according to the demands of the Verse Design and the minimal number of positions it entails).

In one sense, however, the fact that later Englishes display resolution is but a commonplace consequence of the fact that the ESR, fully established in the language by 1550 (McCully 1988b: Ch.5), has a Latinate pedigree. In Latin, as Allen (1973) shows, the trading relation between syllabic weight (environment) and stress may be expressed through what Allen calls an 'accentual matrix consisting of either 1 heavy syllable or 2 light syllables'... (1973: 163). But if this uncontroversial statement is true, the interesting fact emerges that historically, despite directional and other changes, the environment for such an 'accentual matrix' has remained stable from Old English, and while one might not wish to go so far as e.g. Sonnenschein (1925: 119), who claimed that 'The substitution of two short syllables for one long is rooted in the rhythmic sense of man', a rhythmemic analysis does imply an abstract set of relations through which that 'rhythmic sense' may be expressed.

The second pertinent application of the analysis has to do specifically with Old English metrics. McCully (1988b, c) develops an analysis of Old English metrical types by utilising metrical templates, which express Verse Design(s) co-extensive with half-line patterns (and recall that in Section 1 I noted that resolution played a crucial role in maintaining the classic typology of metrically discriminated verses, a typology which, because of its powerful and uniquely descriptive nature, may not be abandoned lightly). In what follows I shall give a brief résumé of the kind of template sufficient and necessary to analyse Sievers's D and E type verses (in *Beowulf*), and show how conditions on rhythmemic structure in turn provide conditions on the metrical lifts within the template (for a full analysis and justification of the two templates necessary to generate and constrain the 'Types', see McCully 1988b; Chs. 6-9).

In traditional notation, D and E verses might be represented as follows (notice that there are two sub-types of Type D):

(14)

| wéard Scýldinga | (Beo. 1229b) | Type D1: | / / \ x |
| éal ínnewèard | (Beo. 998a) | Type D2: | / / x \ |

| níhtlòngne fýrst | (Beo. 528a) | Type E: | / \ x / |

This is not to deny that there are other sub-types which might possibly occur, but the forms seen in (14) are the basic structures. There is, in fact, another reason for taking these Types together beyond the fact that secondary stress is a feature of their composition, and that is historical: in the development of English metre(s), it is the D and E Types which are lost post-1066—not lost as speech patterns, but lost as possible representations of the underlying metrical system—as is attested by late Old English or early ME poems apparently composed in the alliterative form such as *The death of Edward* (1066) and *A description of Durham* (c. early 12th century), see here Cable (1981: 78). And there is a final reason for collapsing these Types into one analysis, particularly if one accepts the hypothesis that when clashing or adjacent stresses occur in the half-line, the first is always stronger than the second (Cable 1974; Hollowell 1982; Hoover 1985: 33). Consider Types D2 and E; there, as Cable (1974: 73) claims, the first stress is stronger than the next stress, which is adjacent to it; this is in turn stronger than the next syllable (weak or 'x' in both cases), which in turn is weaker than the line-final secondary stress. In other words, if one assumes the existence of a 'falling' stress contour—as the alliterative evidence seems to suggest—then Types D2 and E may be collapsed into one.

Phonology of Resolution

One thing that is immediately apparent in all these verses is that they are built around a compound kernel, that is, a minimally trisyllabic form which exhibits primary, secondary, and weak stress or primary, weak and secondary. Consider the half-line *weard Scyldinga*, 'guardian of the Scyldings'. As it stands, it is a D Type; yet remove the verse-initial noun from its position, and place it verse-finally. The result is *Scyldinga weard*—grammatically and metrically a perfectly acceptable E Type. What we seem to be looking at, therefore, is a distinction between Types which depends very largely on the placement of elements within the verse. In setting up a template for these verses, therefore, we should take particular account of placement, and its nonlinear corollary, constituency.

Drawing these remarks together, let us suppose that a crude template for these D and E verses might be set up as in (15), where a compound-kernel is preceded, or followed, by a metrical foot:

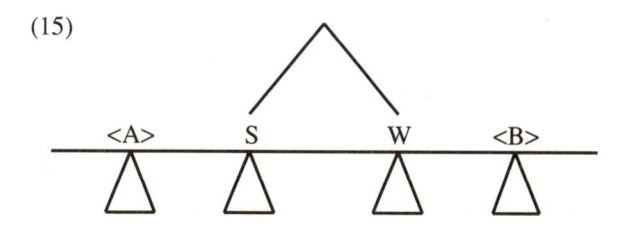

(15)

⟨A⟩   S   W   ⟨B⟩

Clearly, however, we must do more than this, because as it stands, (15) would allow binary or ternary feet to occur under each and every foot-level node, and this does not happen: Old English poets were apparently working with a more constrained set of patterns.

Take D Type verses first, and ignore the ⟨B⟩ expansion which will generate E Types. One problem which we must tackle immediately is what structures may occur under ⟨A⟩. Typically, these will be lexical monosyllables, but resolved bisyllables also crop up, as in the verse *atol āngengea*, 'terrible solitary-walker', (Beo. 165a), as do, occasionally, trisyllabic words where the first two syllables are resolved, as in *æþeling ānhȳdig*, 'resolute prince' (Beo. 2667a), along with, finally, an odd group of D verses (the so-called D∗ subtype) where the ⟨A⟩ expansion is realised by a bisyllable whose first element is heavy, consider here Beo. 223a, *sīde sǣnessas*, 'extensive sea-headlands'. There are, then, four kinds of element which can occur under ⟨A⟩. We can handle their occurrence by setting up a condition on the basic template (fragment), and here is where arguments from rhythmemic structure bear on the overall pattern of constraint upon a Verse Design:

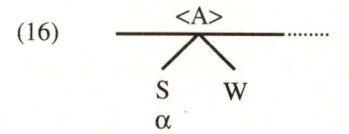

(16)   ⟨A⟩
        S   W
        α

Conditions: ⟨A⟩ may be non-branching; ⟨A⟩ may branch S W where that string is monorhythmemic; exceptionally, α may dominate a heavy, or resolved S W, string.

Notice that if ⟨A⟩ is non-branching, then automatically this means it will dominate a (heavy) lexical monosyllable; if it branches S W then it permits structures such as *atol* (cf. above) to occur provided that string is monorhythmemic (cf. Sievers 1893: 299, who noted that 'auflösung der ersten hebung ... ist häufig'); and if α branches S W then this enables structures such as *æþeling*...to occur in the first position of the verse. The only apparent complication stems from the fact that α may be allowed to dominate a heavy syllable (the D* subtypes), which, given the restricted status and limited occurrence of these verses, is to be expected. Further, if α may dominate a monorhythmemic S W string, then the parity between such a string and a heavy, stressed syllable is demonstrable and allowable: in each case, the foot dominated by ⟨A⟩ will be bi-rhythmemic, as against the monorhythmemic norm. Putting matters another way in order to recapitulate, we may observe that the condition constructed above falls into two parts: first, if ⟨A⟩ is non-branching, it is necessarily monorhythmemic; similarly, and by definition, a resolved S W string is monorhythmemic. These correlations help to explain why it is that ⟨A⟩ most frequently dominates such strings (i.e. they are the simplest strings that can be dominated by a foot). Less frequently, and second, ⟨A⟩ dominates bi-rhythmemic strings—a trisyllable whose first two syllables are resolved, or a bisyllable whose first syllable is heavy. The parity noted above between these last two metrical shapes is entirely expressible through and in a rhythmemic (although not, notably, a stress) notation, and ultimately helps to explain why 'D*' verses occur in the corpus at all (given their apparent dissimilarity and lack of relation to the standard D1 or D2 verse).

Once we have set up this condition, we then have to look elsewhere in the basic template in order to constrain what structures may occur after the first foot of the verse. This means that we have to examine what structures may occur under the foot-level S of (15). Once again, the normative structure that fills this position is a non-branching foot or lexical monosyllable, consider such D type verses as *lēof landfruma* (Beo. 31a), 'dear prince-of-the-land', but it is also the case that S W strings occur in this position too, as in *mǣg Higelāces* (Beo. 758b), a D1 verse, or in D2 verses such as *eal inneweard* (Beo. 998a). Once again, just as under ⟨A⟩, we may bring rhythmemic structure into play, by extending the fragmentary template seen in (16), and revising it as (17):

(17)

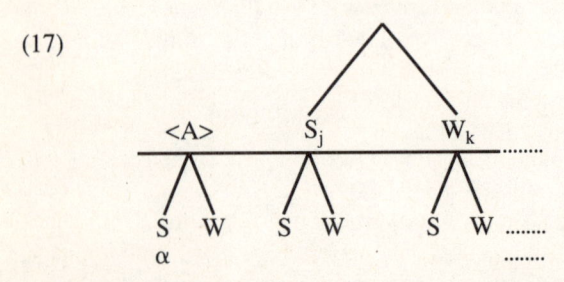

Conditions : a. ⟨A⟩ may be non-branching; ⟨A⟩ may branch S W where that string is monorhythmemic, exceptionally, α may dominate a heavy, or resolved S W string.
b. S_j may be non-branching, or branch S W where that string is monorhythmemic, but if so, W_k must also branch. Where conditions on resolution are not met when S_j branches, W_k, must be non-branching.

This looks like a periphrastic way of putting things, but the template and conditions seen in (17) will in fact generate the most common examples of D1 and D2 verses, as well as most subtypes of these patterns. Consider again the normal D1 verse, say, *weard Scyldinga*. Here, ⟨A⟩ is non-branching, as allowed under condition a. Then the next foot along, the foot dominated by S_j, is also non-branching (*Scyl (d)-* is a heavy syllable), as allowed under condition b. Where the foot under S_j, is non-branching, however, then W_k has to branch. *weard Scyldinga* meets all these constraints. Now consider a D2 verse, say *eal inneweard* or *Heort innanweard* (Beo. 991b), 'interior-of Heorot'. Here, ⟨A⟩ is non-branching, as allowed under a., but the foot under S_j branches S W, and is non-resolved (*inn-* displays a medial geminate, and thus cannot be equivalent to a light syllable); where this is so, then W_k may not branch, as specified by the condition b. of (17). It is perhaps important to emphasise that rhythmemic structure actually seems to work not only as a condition on the heaviness and structure of individual feet, but also as a conditioning process across an entire verse—in this sense, perhaps the first clause of condition 'b.' may be more simply stated as 'if S_j is monorhythmemic, W_k must branch'.

Verses showing resolution in one or both feet are equally simply handled by (17). In fact, D Types showing resolution of the first foot in the embedded dipody are rare, according to Sievers's statistics, involving in the first half-line examples of the word *Wedera*, 'of-the-Weders', see Sievers (1885: 307), with just one example, in a D2 verse, in the second half-line (*cyning æþelum gōd*, Beo. 1870b). A condition on their occurrence, however, is necessary since we shall employ an extended version of the template to handle E Type verses, where the first foot of the embedded dipody may branch S W (*Scedelandum in*, 'in the Danish realm', Beo. 19b).

With that note, and the observation that although the above template-analysis of D Type verses is far from complete, its simplicity is suggestive, let us now turn to E verses. Recall that for these Types, the <A> expansion is ignored, and the <B> activated.

We should examine the <B> expansion first, and defer, for the moment, further discussion of what happens in the embedded dipody. Recall that D and E Types are, in a sense, reversals of one another: both consist of a kernel structure preceded by a foot (D Types) or followed by one (E Types). This being so, we might expect the structures that fall under ⟨B⟩ to be more or less the same as those that fall under ⟨A⟩; and this is just what happens. The commonest E Type verses are those where ⟨B⟩ dominates a lexical monosyllable; consider here verses such as *weorðmyndum þāh* (Beo. 8b), 'thrived in honour' or *glēdegesa grim* (Beo. 2650a), 'grim fire-terror'. But, just as the ⟨A⟩ expansion could dominate feet branching S W, where that foot was resolved (=monorhythmemic), so may the ⟨B⟩ expansion dominate monorhythmemic S W feet, consider here verses such as *uncūþes fela* (Beo. 876b), 'many-of-the-unknown', or *healðegnes hete* (Beo. 142a), 'hostility of the hall-thanes'. Also, recall that the ‹A› expansion could—if somewhat problematically—dominate unresolved S W feet (*mǣre maððumsweord*, 'renowned treasure-sword', Beo. 1023a). As we might by now expect, the reverse happens in E Types, consider e.g. *wælfāgne winter* (Beo. 1023a), 'slaughter-stained winter', or *sincmāððum sēlra* (Beo. 2193a). These verses, however, just like their D Type analogues, are awkward for any theory, since they are of limited, and apparently, strictly constrained, distribution: they are, for example, entirely absent from any b-verse (2nd half-line) in *Beowulf*. I have no explanation for this, and can only point to the work of other scholars (such as Russom 1987), who suggest that complex sub-types occur less frequently in b-verses. Whether the notion of 'complexity' is a valid one in this context, however, remains to be determined (and see McCully 1988b: Ch. 8).

This wrinkle aside, let me give a revised version of the template, one which can accommodate some E Type verses:

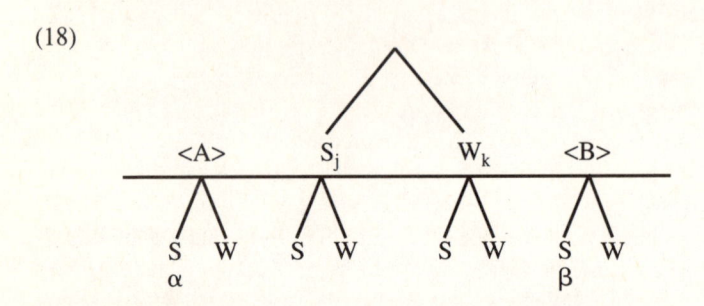

(18)

‹A› S_j W_k ‹B›

S W   S W   S W   S W
α   β

Conditions : a.‹A›, ‹B› may be non-branching; ‹A›, ‹B› may branch S W where that string is monorhythmemic; exceptionally, α or ß may dominate a heavy, or resolved S W string.
b. S_j may be non-branching, or branch S W where conditions on resolution are met, but if so, W_k must also branch (i.e. if S_j, is monorhythmemic, W_k must branch). Where conditions on resolution are not met when S_j branches (i.e if S_j is bi-rhythmemic), W_k must be non-branching.

(18) in fact generates many E Type verses—without any further revision. This is because of what I claimed at the outset; basically, the structure of the embedded kernel remains the same, and the cardinal difference between D and E Types is simply that one has a kernel preceded by a foot, while the other has a kernel followed by a foot. There are, though, two further problems which must be considered. First; there are many E Type verses whose second foot—the foot under the W_k node—is trisyllabic, such as the already-cited *glēdegesa grim* or *wīgheafolan bǣr* (Beo. 2661b), 'he bore the helmet'. Where that foot is trisyllabic, and the first two syllables are resolved, however, then the foot under S_j either must not branch, or only branch S W where resolution applies (e.g. *fæderæþelum onfōn*, Beo. 911a). The frequency of these verses entails another revision to the template; all that seems necessary is to include a symbol, say χ, under the appropriate node

(the S dominated by W_k), and then include a note on branchingness in the conditions ('χ may branch S W where that string is monorhythmemic, but where χ branches, S_j must be maximally monorhythmemic'), see McCully (1988b: 526). Notice that here, as elsewhere, the invocation of rhythmemic structure is crucial; it is insufficient to cast this condition on the template simply in terms of mere branchingness, and further, notice once again that the constraints provided by rhythmemic structure act as a conditioning factor on what elements may occur in other positions of the verse.

A second problem involves prefixation. A few (11 examples in the whole corpus of *Beowulf*) D Type verses have a prefixed foot under ‹A›; consider *befongen frēawrāsnum* (Beo. 1451a, 'encompassed by the splendid chains'; similarly—and as we might expect on our reversal analogy—a very few E Type verses involve prefixation under ‹B›, such as *fǣrnīða gefremed* (Beo. 476a), 'accomplished the hostile attack' or *fæsttrǣdne geþoht* (Beo. 610b), 'firmly-resolved thought'. Apparently, all we need to do for these subtypes is to include a further condition 'c' on (18) such that 'c. exceptionally, ‹A› or ‹B› may be prefixed'. Matters are complicated, however, in that one also finds prefixation under the W_k node. I do not intend to attack this issue here, however, because I believe enough has been said to demonstrate that a template analysis of Old English half-line patterns is both intuitively plausible and attractively simple. A great deal depends on first principles—how secondary stress is derived, metrical weight, the environment for resolution—but once these principles are stated, and the environment for what constitutes a metrical left is established (see the discussion under (16) above), it becomes possible to see the close links there are between phonological structures and the structures of verse-prosody. Ultimately, this brand of analysis seems to confirm not only Sievers's (1885: 1893) theoretical standpoint (in that it gives a phonological reality to the 'Types'), but also the view of Daunt (1946: 64), who wrote that '[O]ld English verse is really the spoken language...tidied up'.

REFERENCES

Abercrombie, D, 1965. Syllable quantity and enclitics in English. In *Studies in phonetics and linguistics*. London: O.U.P.

Allen, C.L. 1980. Movement and deletion in Old English. *Linguistic Inquiry* **11**. 261-323.

Allen, W.S 1973. *Accent and rhythm* . Cambridge: C.U.P

Anderson, J. and C. Jones 1977. *Phonological structure and the history of English* . New York and Oxford: North-Holland Publishing.

Archangeli, D. 1984. *Underspecification in Yawelmani phonology and morphology* . Doctoral dissertation, M.I.T.

Archangeli, D. 1985. Yokuts harmony: evidence for coplanar representation in nonlinear phonology. *Linguistic Inquiry* **16**. 335-72.

Aronoff, M. and R.T. Oehrle eds. 1984. *Language sound structure* . Cambridge, Mass: M.I.T. Press.

Bartsch, K. 1858. Zum Muspilli. *Germania* **3**. 7-21.

Bliss, A.J. 1958. *The metre of* Beowulf. Oxford: Blackwell.
Bliss, A.J. 1962. *An introduction to Old English metre.* Oxford: Blackwell
Cable, T. 1974. *The meter and melody of* Beowulf. Illinois Studies in Language and Literature **64**. University of Illinois Press.
Cable. T. 1981. Metrical style as evidence for the date of Beowulf. In ed. C. Chase. *The dating of* Beowulf, 78-82.
Campbell, A. 1959. *Old English grammar*. Oxford: The Clarendon Press.
Chase, C. ed. 1981. *The dating of* Beowulf. Toronto Old English Series No. 6 : University of Toronto Press.
Creed, R.P. 1966. A new approach to the rhythm of Beowulf. *PMLA* **81**. 23-33.
Danielsson, B. 1948. *Studies on the accentuation of polysyllabic Latin, Greek, and Romance loan-words in English*. Stockholm: Almqvist and Wiksell.
Dauer, R. M. 1983. Stress-timing and syllable-timing reanalyzed. *Journal of Phonetics* **11**. 51-62.
Daunt, M. 1946. Old English verse and English speech rhythm. *Transactions of the Philological Society* 56-72.
Fudge, E. 1969. Syllables. *J. Linguistics* **5**. 253-86.
Giegerich, H. J. 1985. *Metrical phonology and phonological structure: German and English*. Cambridge: C.U.P.
Giegerich, H. J. 1986. *A relational model of German syllable structure.* Duisburg: L.A.U.D.T.
Gussmann, E. 1988. Review of Mohanan 1986. *J. Linguistics* **24**. 232-9.
Halle, M. 1987. Why phonological strata should not include affixation. Unpublished MS, M.I.T. (cited in Gussmann 1988).
Hayes, B. 1981. *A metrical theory of stress rules.* Doctoral dissertation, M.I.T. published New York and London, 1985: Garland Press.
Hayes, B. 1982. Extrametricality and English stress. *Linguistic Inquiry* **13**. 227-76).
Heusler, A. 1889. Der Ljóþháttr: ein metrische untersuchung. *Acta Germanica* **1**. 91-169.
Heusler, A. 1894. *Über germanischen Versbau.* Berlin.
Hogg, R.M. and C.B. McCully, 1987. *Metrical phonology: a coursebook.* Cambridge: C.U.P.
Hollowell, I.M. On Old English verse rhythm. *English Studies* **63**. 385-93.
Hoover, D.L. 1985. *A new theory of Old English meter.* New York: Peter Lang.
Hulst, H. van der and N. Smith eds. 1982. *The structure of phonological representations.* Parts 1 and 2, Dordrecht: Foris.
Kaluza, M. 1911. trans. A.C. Dunstan. *A short history of English versification.* London: George Allen.
Keyser, S.J. and W. O'Neil. 1985. *Rule generalization and optionality in language change.* Dordrecht: Foris.
Kiparsky, P. 1977. The rhythmic structure of English verse. *Linguistic Inquiry* **8**. 189-247.
Kiparsky, P. 1979. Metrical structure assignment is cyclic. *Linguistic Inquiry* **10**. 421-41.
Kiparsky, P. 1982. From cyclic phonology to lexical phonology. In H. van der Hulst and N. Smith (eds.). *The structure of phonological representations*, Part 1, 131-75.
Lachmann, K. 1876. Über althochdeutsche betonung and verskunst. (First presented 1831). *Kleine Schriften* **1**. 358-406.
Lachmann, K. 1876. Über des Hilderbrandslied. (First presented 1833). *Kleine*

Schriften **1**. 407-48.

Lass, R. 1983. Quantity, resolution and syllable geometry. In *Folia Linguistica Historica* **IV**. 151-80. Societas Linguistica Europaea.

Lass, R. 1984. *Phonology*. Cambridge C.U.P.

Leonard, W.E 1918. Beowulf and the Niebelungen couplet. *University of Wisconsin Studies in Language and Literature* **1**. 99-152.

McCarthy, J. 1979. *Formal problems in Semitic phonology and morphology*. Doctoral dissertation, M.I.T.

McCarthy, J. 1981. A prosodic theory of noncatenative phonology. *Linguistic Inquiry* **12**. 373-418.

McCully, C.B and R.M Hogg, 1988. An account of Old English stress. MS, Department of English, University of Manchester. Paper first presented (1987) to the Linguistic Seminar, University of Manchester, and to the English Society, University of Durham.

McCully, C. B. 1988a. The phonology of Old English resolution. Paper presented to the LAGB, Exeter.

McCully, C. B. 1988b. *The phonology of English rhythm and metre, with special reference to Old English*. Doctoral dissertation, University of Manchester.

McCully, C. B. 1988c. Metrical templates and Old English versecraft. Paper presented to the Old and Middle English Conference. University of Manchester.

Marchand, H. 1969. *Categories and types of Present-day English word-formation*. München : C. H. Beck'sche Verlagsbuchhandlung.

Minkova, D. 1982. The environment for Open Syllable Lengthening in Middle English. In *Folia Linguistica Historica* III/I. 29-58. Societas Linguistica Europaea.

Mohanan, K.P. 1982. *Lexical phonology*. Bloomington: Indiana University Linguistics Club.

Mohanan, K.P. 1986. *The theory of lexical phonology*. Dordrecht: Reidel.

Möller, H. 1888. *Zur althochdeutschen alliterationspoesie*. Kiel.

Pope, J. C. 1942. *The rhythm of* Beowulf. New Haven: Yale University Press.

Rieger, M. 1864. Bemerkung zum Hildebrandslied. *Germania* **9**. 295-320.

Risberg, B. 1936. *Den svenska versens teori*, Vol. II: *Rytmik och metrik*. Stockholm.

Russom, G. 1987. *Old English metre and linguistic theory*. Cambridge: C.U.P

Selkirk, E. O. 1982. The syllable. In H. van der Hulst and N. Smith (eds.). *The structure of phonological representations*, Part 2, 337-83.

Selkirk, E. O. 1984a. *Phonology and syntax: the relation between sound and syntax*. Cambridge, Mass: M.I.T. press

Selkirk, E. O. 1984b. On the major class features and syllable theory. In Aronoff, M and R.T. Oehrle (eds.) *Language sound structure*, 107-36.

Siegel, D. 1974. *Topics in English morphology* . Doctoral dissertation, M.I.T. Published New York and London, 1979. Garland.

Sievers, E. 1885. Zur rhythmik des germanischen alliterationsverses. *Beiträge der geschichte der deutschen sprache und literatur* **10**. 209 - 314; 451-545.

Sievers, E. 1893. *Altgermanische metrik*. Halle: Max Niemeyer

Strang. B.M.H 1970. *A history of English* . London: Methuen.

Suphi, M 1985. *Non-linear analyses in English historical phonology*. Doctoral dissertation, University of Edinburgh.

Suphi, M. 1988. Old English stress assignment. *Lingua* **75**. 171-202.

Suzuki, S, 1985. Syllable structure in Old English poetry. *Lingua* **67**. 97-119.

Thomson, W. 1923. *The rhythm of speech*. Glasgow : Maclehose.

Young, Sir G. 1923. *An English prosody on inductive lines*. Cambridge C.U.P.

6

POETIC INFLUENCE ON PROSE WORD ORDER IN OLD ENGLISH [1]

Donka Minkova and Robert Stockwell

Taking speech, prose and verse as three types of instantiation of a single syntax, we can imagine several ways of explaining the differences between them. Since our corpus is Old English, we leave aside speech and concentrate on prose and verse. Existing theories about the differences are summarised below in five[2] somewhat artificially polarised forms, as a basis for discussion; the truth probably lies in some mixture, and certainly the scholars who hold each position are aware of that. We seek to take an expository, not an adversarial stance toward these positions, though we believe there is more validity in some than in others.

1. Verse had a syntax of its own, and this syntax directly affected the development of the syntax of prose. The relation between them was roughly that of exemplar to derivative. (Campbell 1970).

2. There is nothing more than time and normal change between earlier verse and later prose. Pintzuk (1988b: fn. 6) asserts that 'most of the qualitative and quantitative differences between poetry and prose...can be explained by positing processes of syntactic change rather than by genre differences'. (See also Pintzuk 1989, Hock 1985).

3. There is, in general, no relevance in verse examples, for the study of Old English syntax. This is Kemenade's view (1987: 4): 'Old English poetry had a language of its own, going back to Old Germanic traditions...(and) cannot be considered a reliable source of information on the standard of Old English'.

4. Verse was 'made up of a selection of ordinary prose patterns'. (Mitchell 1985: §3959). Presumably this entails that there should exist no syntactic patterns in poetry which do not also exist in prose, but not conversely. The word 'selection' suggests something very close to (5).

5. There is a syntax common to verse and prose, with special conventions for verse, rhythmical or otherwise, which introduce apparent violations of the syntax found in the prose. This position differs from (4) primarily in that it entails the existence of verse patterns which do not exist, or only rarely exist, in prose. This is our position.

In this paper we wish to address only one of these positions in detail, the first one. We return to the others in more detail, in a forthcoming paper devoted to the verse constraints, if such they are, documented in Kuhn 1933.

To discuss the general question of possible relations between verse and prose, we begin with two familiar observations which clarify our assumptions about the written material we are dealing with, i.e. verse and prose together, on the one hand, and speech, on the other:

(i) Written prose that accurately (as distinct from 'artistically') mirrors actual speech is rare and difficult to create even in languages with long literary traditions.

(ii) Nevertheless, in the effort to construct prose, deliberate deviations from one's internal grammar are rare: it requires effort, sophistication, and ingenuity to construct ungrammatical sentences which violate one or more rules of the core grammar.

From (i) and (ii), we infer (iii) and (iv):

(iii) Old English prose is not a reliable or direct reflection of everyday Old English speech: i.e. Old English prose is *not* spoken language.

(iv) Old English prose does not grossly or consistently violate grammatical regularities of the spoken language.

(iii) and (iv) constitute the logical background against which the early scribes put pen to parchment. *Their* only experience in prose was through their training in Latin, and their only experience of a stylized form of their own native language was in the poetic tradition. Of these two, Latin did violence to their grammatical intuitions. The only models they had for developing a coherent prose style that were compatible with their grammatical intuitions were the products of the continental poetic traditions found in *Beowulf*.

1 Word Order in Old English Prose and Verse

The aspects of word order that we want to examine here are all related to the rule of verb-fronting:

(i) Verse commonly had verb-first order in main clauses, which occurs but rarely in prose.

(ii) Verse allows syntactic ambiguity in clauses introduced by *þa, þonne, þær, ær, nu*. In prose, such clauses are rarely ambiguous because of verb-second position.

(iii) In verse, when the finite verb was not at the end of the clause, it was within the first dip but not guaranteed to be either first or second. In prose, there was a regular, near-absolute, verb-second constraint in main clauses, given that clitics do not count as constituents.

The rules which generated these effects were a verb-fronting rule in main clauses and a verb-raising rule in subordinate clauses,[3] which placed a finite verbal constituent in first or second position regularly in main clauses and sometimes in subordinate clauses. *In verse*, this position was reinterpreted to allow a broader constituency in the required clause-initial 'first dip' described by Kuhn, which manifests itself in (i), (ii) and (iii) above. *In prose*, on the other hand, the constituency was never broadened. Moreover, the verb-fronting rule co-occurred so regularly with initial orientational adverbs and other topical elements that the result was a constraint (verb-second) that was essentially exceptionless—provided, again, that we discount preverbal pronouns on the grounds that they were syntactically cliticised.

2 The Relevant Poetic Conventions: Kuhn's Laws

The background for Campbell's position (the first in the list above) is the set of principles governing verse composition advanced in Kuhn 1933. Briefly, Kuhn's laws assert that sentence particles [4] — mainly sentence adverbs, subject and object personal pronouns, and finite verbs (especially auxiliary-like ones) — must either appear unstressed in the first metrical dip of a clause, or (appearing elsewhere) they will be stressed; and that a clause-initial dip must contain sentence particles. These principles are specific to verse, since they are defined in terms of metrical constituents.[5] The two peculiarities of clause-initial constituents in verse, as defined by Kuhn, are (1) the licensing of multiple adverbials in the first dip; and (2) the disallowing of demonstratives, the first constituent of definite NPs, in the first dip (and therefore the extreme rarity of definite NP subjects — those consisting of DEMONSTRATIVE + NOUN [6] — in first position of a verse clause).

In prose, the position corresponding to an initial dip contains conjunctions, orientational adverbs, and pronominals; or a full definite NP may appear first, in which case the clause begins with a metrical dip disallowed in verse, and another dip follows after the noun in the form of a finite verb in second position. The two striking differences from the point of view of the prose, then, are (1) the absence in verse of full NPs in clause-initial position, and (2) the absence in verse of fixed relative order between adverbs and finite verbs in initial position.

3 Campbell's Hypothesis

Ignoring for now the possibility of influence from Latin, we examine the proposition explicitly advanced in Campbell (1970). To what extent can properties of prose word order be attributed to verse conventions, as compared with the extent to which these properties were shaped by the grammatical intuitions of ordinary speech? Campbell argues that the prose writers' familiarity with the conventions of poetic composition might have prompted them to favour rules or patterns which were archaic in the spoken language. The result of this favouring, according to Campbell, was to *obscure* word order regularities which otherwise should have proceeded along the lines familiar in other West Germanic languages.

The three respects in which Campbell believed Old English prose word order to be 'much obscured', of which he attributes the first two to verse influence, are these:

1. Verb-initial order in principal clauses
2. Ambiguity of clausal status after initial adverbs
3. Failure of the verb-second constraint to become well-established in Old English main clauses.

3.1 Verb-initial principal clauses

Such clauses are much more frequent in the poetry than in the later prose. Bean (1983:66) counts less than 4% verb-initial main clauses in the entire Anglo-Saxon Chronicle. In our own count of *St Edmund*, the verb-first figure is significantly less than in the Chronicle, less than 2%. Compare this with *Beowulf*. Of the principal clauses in *Beowulf*, according to Todt 1894:259, approximately 25% are absolute verb-initial. Donoghue's count (1987b:42) of clause-initial auxiliaries yields a compatible figure of 24%, which is also the percentage he cites of clause-initial auxiliaries for 19 of the longer poems (about two-thirds of the extant poetry).

It is almost true to say that verb-first sentences in the prose are anomalous. They must be allowed by the syntax, but usage does not favour them. The anomalous instances may indeed be well-explained as 'leakages' [7] of poetic preference.

Campbell explicitly attributes verb-initial configurations in the poetry to the influence of Kuhn's law, in the following way. If a clause is SV (say, in the scop's head) and the subject is a pronoun, it will conform to Kuhn's law; but if the subject is a full noun phrase (not just a single noun, which will place the dip *after* the first stressed word), then Kuhn's law will require that the scop *invert* the order. Thus a sequence like *þas wundor gewurdon* must be inverted in verse to the order *gewurdon þas wundor*.[8]

Thus we would be led to believe, for example, that an Anglo-Saxon Chronicle declarative sentence like *Hæfde se cyning his fierd on tu tonumen* 'Had the King his army in two parts divided' (ASC 893.46) resembles typical instances from Beowulf, like:

Hæfde Kyningwuldor
'Had the-glorious-king'

Grendle togeanes swa guman gefrungon
'Grendel against as men learned'

seleweard aseted
'hall-guardian appointed'
(Beo. 665-7)

Com þa to recede rinc siþian
'Came then to the hall, warrior traveling'
(Beo 720).

in ways that suggest influence of the latter types on the former.

The effect of the Kuhnian constraints is encapsulated in the metrical rendering of Boethius known as *The Metres of Boethius*, recently analysed in Donoghue (1987a). He notes numerous correspondences where the differences between the prose and the poetic versions fall out naturally from Kuhn's laws, and verb-second sentences appear as verb-first sentences in verse, as here:

Prose version:
    ac se anwealda hæfð ealle his gesceafta swa
    'but the creator has all his creatures thus'

    mid his bridle befangene
    'with his bridle controlled'
    (49.2. Donoghue 171)

Verse version:
    Hæfð se alwealda ealle gesceafta
    'has the creator all creatures'

    Gebæt mid his bridle
    'ordered with his bridle'
    (xi. 22-3a, Donoghue 171).

However, a sentence such as *gewurdon þas wundor* can perfectly well be an instance of VS, not '*inverted* SV'—*both* interpretations are equally compatible with Kuhn's laws. The verb-initial declarative sentences of Old English do not in general require explanation by way of Kuhn's law interference. They occur (though not commonly) in OHG (Maurer 1926), and they are common in North Germanic; they must be presumed to have been a clause type in Common Germanic. Thus the rare verb-first declarative clauses in early Old English prose may either be imitations of a poetic pattern, as Campbell suggests, or instances of syntactic options generally available in the spoken language.

3.2 Ambiguity of clausal status after initial adverbs

In verse the distinction between the so-called 'demonstrative order' (i.e. [X].VS) and the order SV collapses under certain conditions. The crucial condition for this collapse is that the clause begins with an adverb that can also be a subordinator — *þa, þonne, þær, ær, nu,* etc. — in which case, as Campbell says, 'all unaccented adverbs and pronouns, and the verb if it be unaccented, are drawn into that dip [at the beginning of the clause]' (1970:95). In other words, the subject-verb order in subordinate clauses undergoes 'inversion', and thereby fails to discriminate between subordinate and main clauses in a reliable way.[9] Unfortunately Campbell cites no really persuasive examples with full NP subjects. He claims that *ær þa scipu cuomon* 'conflicts with the law of sentence particles' (96), which entails that the preferred order should then be *ær cuomon ða scipu* (but he cites no example of this type). His closest-to-persuasive example is Matt. viii, 18 *ða geseah se Hælend* (undoubtedly subordinate, he claims, because of the Latin original).[10] Campbell suggests that examples like Or. 14, 26 *Nu hæbbe we scortlice gesæd* , and Bede 166, 28-9 *ða com he ærest upp* (both of which are subordinate clauses with main clause word order) are due to analogical extension from the types just cited.

The ambiguity of VS order in *verse* is not to be doubted, of course. Campbell cites the following example:

ða wæs morgenleoht
'when/then was morning-light'

scofen ond scynded. Eode scealc monig
'shoved and hastened. Went warrior many'

Swiðhicgcende to sele þam hean
'strong-minded to hall the high-one'
(Beo. 917)

He asks 'Do we translate: "Then the morning light..." or "when the morning-light..."?' This problem has long been a crux in Old English studies. It has led different editors to punctuate identical passages differently.

The metrical requirement that particles must be drawn into the first dip would, as we interpret Campbell's view, provide a basis for ambiguous examples like *þa ne mehte seo firz hie na hindan offaran* 'when/then the army could never overtake them from behind'. (AS *Chronicle* 893.93-4) under the influence of subordinate verse clauses of the type *þa com se cyning*.[1,1] One might even argue that 'verb-raising' (see Koopman 1989) owes a debt to this rhythmic source.

Perhaps we should interpret Campbell's examples as the verb-fronting rule applying in subordinate clauses by analogy with main-clause order. Such examples would signal the beginning of the end of the critical verb-second vs. verb-final distinction in main vs. subordinate clauses, and if motivated by Kuhnian considerations, as Campbell thought, they can be argued to constitute a genuine 'confusion' introduced into the prose through poetic influence.

3.2.1 Difficulties with Campbell's ambiguity hypothesis

Having set Campbell's hypothesis in this favourable light, we have to acknowledge, nevertheless, that in prose the extent of actual ambiguity in respect to clausal status is minimal. If there were verse influence, it should be the case that prose had a percentage of CONJ V S (i.e. XVS) order in subordinate clauses which is not substantially different from the percentage found in the poetry. But, according to Pintzuk (1987:2), 33% of the subordinate clauses of Beowulf have the auxiliary verb in second position, given that proclitics do not count as occupying a position: e.g. *þæs ðe ic moste minum leodum...swylc gestrynan* 'because I might acquire such a thing for my people' (Beo. 2797-98). This order is very rare in the prose.[1,2]

Indeed, it appears again that if Kuhn's laws were the source of any 'obscuration', it was only in the verse, not in the prose. Metrical constraints can seriously impair the distinction between principal and subordinate, and that is an obscurity.[1,3] The prose largely sorted out the distinction by — among other things — rejecting the order *þa com se cyning*, and indeed any manifestation of VS, in subordinate clauses, with rare exceptions. If prose allowed *any* ambiguity after *þa, þonne, nu, ær*, etc., it is best accounted for by analogical extension of verb-second order from main down into subordinate clauses *and* the existence of contextual and intonational clues in speech.

3.3 Failure of the verb-second constraint to become well-established in Old English main clauses.

Old English and other Germanic languages typically obeyed a verb-second rule in main clauses.[1,4] For it to be seen as highly regular in Old English, we must accept Kemenade's analysis of personal pronouns as syntactic clitics. With orientational adverbs such as *þa*, verb-second is almost totally regular and cannot be included among examples which 'obscure' the regularity of Old English word order in comparison with other Germanic languages. It can be argued — but Campbell does not do so, at least not more than implicitly — that Kuhn's laws would strongly encourage verb-second order after unstressed initial adverbs like *ða*, since the first dip is established by the adverb and the dip must, by Kuhn, then attract any other unstressed particles, among them crucially the finite verb. And because a clause-initial noun (a single noun, not a full NP) must, by Kuhn, be immediately followed by a dip containing the particles, the verb-second order would be even more strongly encouraged.

However, Campbell claimed that this *metrically optimal* development did not take place, or was at least heavily obscured. This position withdraws to some extent from his criticism of Bacquet 1962. Bacquet failed to see the regularity of verb-second structures such as *Æfter þæm þe Romeburg getimbred wæs iiii hunde wintrum ond xxvi, feng Alexander to Mæcedonia rice* (Orosius, ed. Sweet, p. 122). Campbell wrote that 'Such inversion [subject-verb inversion after an initial adverb] is part of the general tendency to invert subject and verb in principal clauses if the subject has not the first place, so that the verb remains in the second place. This mechanical process gives no special emphasis' (1964:192). It is, *pace* Mitchell,[1,5] much more than a tendency in the prose of Alfred's time and later.[1,6] In the light of Kemenade's clitic analysis of personal pronouns, it appears reasonable to assume that the verb-second constraint in fact had become so nearly categorical in the grammar of Old English by about 890 that exceptions in the prose have to be viewed with a jaundiced eye.

Campbell does not view them with a jaundiced eye. While he recognises that the constraint was very regular after *þa, þonne, þær* (which he says was 'no doubt' due to avoidance of ambiguity[1,7] between principal and subordinate clause status), he believed the language *failed* to generalise it categorically, with consistent verb-second in main clauses. His words are: 'It is best established after *þa, þonne, and þær*, but it is very inconsistent after all other adverbs and after adverbial phrases. Thus the types *Be ðam cwæð Crist* and *Be ðam Crist cwæð* are equally common, and so are both orders after the *her* of the annals...' (1970:96).

3.3.1 The regularity of verb-second in prose main clauses

A survey of well-known statistical studies of word order in Old English prose throws considerable doubt on Campbell's assertion.

Sprockel (1973: 235) points out that 'if we exclude *her*, which is not really a "head", monosyllabic heads [where "head" means a word, phrase, or clause preceding subject and/or verb—DM and RS] are followed by VS word-order in 91%, polysyllabic heads in 64% and compound heads in 72% of cases'—and nearly all of the examples that reduce the percentages below 100 are in hand A, the hand of the scribe who assembled earlier chronicle fragments.

Bean (1983: 66ff) has a diagram (4.1) which shows a dramatic decrease in occurrence of X'SV (the *be þam Crist cwæþ* type) between the early entries of the *Chronicle* (up to 865) and the entries for the mid-ninth century and subsequently.[1][8] Her table summarising main clause order in Ohthere (Table 6.9, p. 131) shows 80% VS order (verb-first + verb-second, mostly the latter) against a trivial 8% V-3 (X'SV + OSV). Her figures for Wulfstan are just as dramatic. VS order (verb-first + verb-second including SVO) is 82%, against 2% X'SV and 4% OSV. The status of pronouns in these counts is not clear, since although Bean comments on the positioning of pronouns discursively, she does not separate them in her totals. Her figures for Aelfric's *Preface to Genesis* are similar to the Wulfstan figures: 79% against 10%.

Denison's study (1986: 281) of the *Chronicle* 892-8 shows VS order (encompassing, as in Bean, VSX, X'VS, OVS, SVX) in no less than 94% of the relevant clauses (main clauses not introduced by *and, ac, or ne*). Of these 73 main clauses not introduced by conjunctions, only five are X'SV (7%), and only seven are V-1 (about 10%). The rest are unarguably V-2, and only the five X'SV clauses are incompatible with the standard verb-fronting analysis.

Kohonen's otherwise extremely useful study (1978) unfortunately does not allow us to extract corresponding figures: his categories, chosen on the basis of typological distinctions and functional explanations, simply do not discriminate V-2 clauses, nor does any combination of his categories (as Bean's and Denison's do) allow one to retrieve information about 'second position', even though he *does* discriminate pronominals from full NPs.

Mitchell (1964:124) observes that 'In simple sentences and principal clauses beginning with an adverb other than *ne*...or with an adverb phrase, the word-order V.S is the norm in Old English prose'. He then discusses several counterexamples 'which cannot be removed unless one assumes the role of a prescriptive grammarian for Old English' (125). But if one eliminates the *her* examples (early *Chronicle*, as noted above) and the examples that fall away under Kemenade's clitic analysis, only one real counterexample remains (*Cura Pastoralis* 405/35 *þa he þis eal dyde, þa he stod æfter us gewend*...). Within his explicit statistics for Continuation I of the *Chronicle* (Table 3 and Table 6, pp. 126 and 129), there are four 'sequences of S.V after an adverb or adverbial phrase' (1130/17, 1127/22, 1124/49, 1131/37) out of 96 adverb-initial main clauses. These are taken by him to be counterexamples. But since three of the four have pronominal subjects and

1124/49 has *mon* as the subject, all but the *mon* are regular within the clitic analysis. His counterexamples from Aelfric's *Stephen* are even less compelling. Of the eight that he cites, six (50/21, 50/25, 52/3-4, 54/7, 56/5 and 56/34) are of the form ADV PRONOUN V-finite—i.e. all with clitic subjects. One (56/30) is a genuine verb-final fossil, irrelevant to the present issue. Only one, 52/3 *Efne nu Paulus blissaþ mid Stephane on heofenan rice*, is a problem. If understood with *nu* modifying *blissaþ*, as Thorpe's translation suggests—'Behold, Paul now rejoices with Stephen in the kingdom of heaven'—then it is a valid counterexample. Possibly, however, *nu* can be taken with *efne*, 'Behold now, Paul rejoices...'.

So far as we know, there are no counts in the literature which unambiguously retrieve that percentage of the main clauses to which the grammar would assign the status of 'verb-second' in accord with Kemenade's analysis in every detail. The studies we are familiar with which supply information about the relevant category sequences do not discriminate the subsets in which pronouns occupy the S and O slots. It is nonetheless clear that the sentences which require special explanation, on the grounds that they do not conform to the regular word-order rules of Old English, are precisely those of the type *Be þæm Crist cwæþ*. In the first 210 clauses of Alfric's *St. Edmund*, considering only main clauses that do not begin with a conjunction *ond, ac, or ne*, there are 38 V-2 against only 8 V-3, of which four are X'SV and four are SX'V. Of the first four, three are suspect; they are of the form *Hwæt þa* S V and should probably be counted as V-2, since *hwæt þa* can be reasonably taken as an exclamation, an opening formula of the *her* type. Of the four SX'V, the X' is consistently *þa* and should probably be viewed as unstressed in that position (in contrast with post-verbal position) and therefore cliticised. These four nonetheless present a problematic case for which we do not at present have a motivated explanation.

While this cursory survey certainly has not by any means discounted all instances of the type that prompted Campbell's retreat from his original position, it has, we believe, made it clear that the instances of X'SV (where S is a full NP) are the ones to be focused on in search of an explanation of irregularities of verb fronting in prose. These are statistically the odd ones, and we believe they are also grammatically the odd ones, contrary to the view that they are unproblematic because they resemble later English. More to the point, they are also the very examples that go unexplained under Campbell's hypothesis: they cannot be instances where verse conventions have muddied the waters of prose style—only the verb-early types can be instances of that influence, to the extent that it can be demonstrated to exist at all.

4 Conclusion

As the prose matures, the underlying syntactic system is increasingly *less* obscure, a fact for which the Kuhn's law aspects of the poetry should quite possibly be given credit, since the laws reinforced the position of proclitics and finite verbs in the dip after the first stressed word (if we can speak of 'dips' in prose), thus encouraging a surface verb-second output. This is the reverse of Campbell's suggestion. Old English main clauses become *more* like Dutch and German, in the prose. It is only much later that English changes into an atypical West Germanic language—specifically, (a) when the language loses most of the structures from which a language learner might infer that heads are to the right (Old English) rather than to the left (MnE) of their dependent elements (i.e. the syntactic base order changes from verb-final to verb-medial, around 1200); and (b) when it loses the verb-second constraint in favour of subject-verb syntax (starting, in some dialects, in the 14th century).

NOTES

1. The research reported here is part of a larger project aimed at developing a better grasp of the history of English word order. We are grateful to Daniel Donoghue and Susan Pintzuk for comments on an earlier draft of this paper, though of course they are not to be blamed for our errors of fact or interpretation.
2. Daunt 1946 represents a position distinct from any of those with respect of the issue of relations between verse and prose *rhythm,* but she does not discuss differences of a syntactic nature.
3. For details see Kemenade 1987 and Koopman 1989.
4. There are two types of commonly unstressed categories: (a) items that everyone would agree are unstressed, like prepositions, adjectival pronouns, light adverbs, deictics, and prefixes; and (b) theta-role pronouns (those that can be subjects or objects), heavier adverbs, finite verbs, occasionally non-finite verbal forms. The members of category (b) are the sentence particles, which are variable with respect to stress. These items may alliterate, and when they are not in the first dip they are normally stressed. So Kuhn's basic categorisation is this:

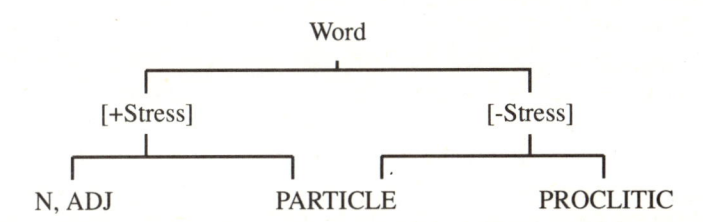

```
                            Word
              ┌──────────────┴──────────────┐
           [+Stress]                     [-Stress]
         ┌─────┴─────┐                      │
       N, ADJ    PARTICLE               PROCLITIC
```

To state what the diagram is intended to dramatise, particles can be stressed or not; the question of *whether* they are stressed in any given instance in older Germanic verse is what Kuhn's laws are intended to determine. What is *absolutely disallowed* by Kuhn's laws is a clause beginning with any unstressed item except for a sentence particle.

Kuhn distinguishes sentence particles from 'sentence-part particles'. The distinction is between sentence-level constituents ('sentence elements' in Mitchell's terminology) and phrase-level constituents.
5. Kuhn himself did not argue that they are specific to verse. He saw his generalisations as pertaining to the interrelation between the prosody and syntax of speech (for Common Germanic), and he found support for them in the individual poetic traditions of the various

daughter languages.

6. Hereafter we refer to this combination as a 'full NP'. In later poetry, such as *Maldon*, such sequences occur (e.g. 72a *Se flod ut gewat* , noted in this connection in Bliss 1958:104).

7. We would say 'fossils' except for the static connotations of that word. We want to express a continuing sense of rule-governed options. Fossilisation entails that rule-governed options are no longer open (e.g. the plural form of *ox* in MnE is a fossil; we can no longer freely create *-en* plural(s)).

8. As Campbell puts it (p. 95), 'the verb is drawn into the position before the first stress': that is, there is an inversion of subject and verb.

9. Donoghue 1987a:186 has an insightful discussion of this issue.

10. *Videns autem Iesus turbas multus*—the possibility of Latin influence exists here, at least in that the subject follows the verb.

11. These are 'unambiguously subordinate', according to Andrew 1940:18. But this judgment is simply mistaken. Mitchell 1963:318 asserts flatly that 'Andrew's arguments from word-order are invalid (for word-order in the poetry cannot tell us whether a clause is principal or subordinate)'. Even in the sophisticated prose of Ælfric, word order is sometimes quite helpless to resolve this problem: e.g. *ða geseah Hinguar, se arlease flotman, ðæt se æðela cyning nolde Criste wiðsacan ac mid anrædum geleafan hine æfre clypode, het hine ða beheafdian*...'then/when Hinguar, the wicked pirate, saw that the noble king did not want to forsake Christ, but always called out to him with steadfast faith, [he] commanded then that he should be beheaded' (*St. Edmund* 102-4).

12. While the subordinate order XVS is rare in the Anglo-Saxon Chronicle, according to Bean's (1983:104) figures, SVO is as common as SOV in all subordinate clauses except relative clauses (where verb-final predominates). SVO sentences count as SV 'common order' in Campbell's syntactic typology, which confusingly assigns what should be seen as a unified syntactic phenomenon (verb-second) to two distinct categories (X)VS and SV. SV order in subordinate clauses, in those instances where the subject is pronominal, nevertheless appears to provide a valid example of the phenomenon he is explicating. For example, in *þæt hie ne mehton þa scipu ut brengan* 'that they might not bring out the ships' [AS Chronicle 895:10], the Kuhnian particles all appear in what would be the first dip if it were poetry.

13. Zimmermann 1983 argues that such ambiguity was minimal even in Beowulf.

14. See in particular Koopman 1984 and Kemenade 1987.

15. Mitchell 1985:§3929, commenting on Campbell's use of the word 'tendency' in the passage just quoted, claims that 'it is obviously no more than a tendency'. We have discussed Mitchell's list of counter-examples in Stockwell and Minkova (forthcoming) and shown that only one of them is valid if pronoun cliticisation is taken into account. It does not appear to us that even one of Mitchell's putative counter-examples cited in this connection from the Peterborough Chronicle (1964:125) is valid.

16. The Anglo-Saxon Chronicle up to 892 contains many exceptions to the rule; later exceptions are trivially few, mostly with *her* as a formulaic introduction to the Chronicle entry. We discuss the question in more detail below.

17. This idea has been elaborated substantially in Vennemann 1984. He takes it to be fundamental to the ultimate change to SVO order in Middle English and later.

18. X' in Bean's notation stands for orientational adverbs like *her, þa, þonne,* and adverbial phrases.

REFERENCES

Andrew, S. O. 1940. *Syntax and style in Old English.* Cambridge: C.U.P.

Bacquet, Paul. 1962. *La structure de la phrase verbal à l'epoque Alfrédienne.* (Publications de la faculté des lettres de l'université de Stasbourg 145). Paris.

Bean, Marian C. 1983. *The development of word order patterns in Old English.* London and Totowa, N.J: Croom-Helm.

Bliss, A. J 1958. *The metre of Beowulf.* Oxford: Blackwell.

Campbell, Alistair. 1964. Review of Paul Bacquet, *La structure de la phrase verbal à l'époque Alfrédienne. Review of English Studies* 58:190-3.

Campbell, Alistair. 1970. Verse influences in Old English prose. *Philological essays: Studies in Old and Middle English language and literature in honour of Herbert Dean Merritt*, ed. James I. Rosier. Janua Linguarum, series major 37. The Hague: Mouton. 93-8.

Daunt, Marjorie, 1946. Old English verse and English speech rhythm. *Transactions of the philological society* 56-72.

Denison, David, 1986. On Word Order in Old English. *Dutch quarterly review of Anglo-American letters* **16**. 277-95.

Donoghue, Daniel. 1987a. Word order and poetic style: auxiliary and verbal in *The metres of Boethius, Anglo-Saxon England* **15**:167-96.

Donoghue, Daniel. 1987b. *Style in Old English Poetry.* New Haven: Yale University Press.

Hock, Hans Henrich. 1985. Pronoun fronting and the notion Verb-Second position in Beowulf. *Germanic languistics*, ed. J. R. Faarlund. Bloomington, Ind: IULC, 70-86.

Kemenade, Ans van. 1984. Verb second and clitics in Old English. *Linguistics in the Netherlands* 1984, ed. H. Beenis and W.U.S van Lessen Kloeke. Dordrecht: Foris, 101-10.

Kemenade, Ans van. 1987. *Syntactic case and morphological case in the history of English.* Dordrecht: Foris.

Kohonen, Viljo. 1978. *On the development of English word order in religious prose around 1000 and 1200 A.D.* Abo Akademi Foundation.

Koopman, Willem, 1984. Some thoughts on Old English word order. *Current research in Dutch and Belgian universities on Old English, Middle English, and Historical Linguistics.* Ed. by Erik Kooper, Utrecht, 3-20.

Koopman, Willem, 1989. Old English constructions with three verbs. *Folia historica linguistica* **9**.1.

Kuhn, Hans. 1933. Zur Wortstellung und -betonung im Altgermanischen. *Belträge zur Geschichte der deutschen Sprache und Literatur* **57**:1-109.

Maurer, F. 1926. *Untersuchungen über die deutsche Verbstellung in ihrer geschictlichen Entwicklung.* Heidelberg: Winter.

Mitchell, Bruce. 1963. Adjective clauses in Old English poetry. *Anglia* **81**.298-322.

Mitchell, Bruce. 1964. Syntax and word-order in *The Peterborough Chronicle* 1122-1154. *Neuphilologische Mitteilungen* **65**.113-44.

Mitchell, Bruce, 1985. *Old English syntax.* Oxford: Clarendon.

Pintzuk, Susan. Forthcoming a. Old English as a verb-second language: evidence from Beowulf. University of Pennsylvania dissertation in progress. Presented orally at LSA 1987.

Pintzuk, Susan. Forthcoming b. Verb movement in Old English. Presented orally at LSA 1988.

Sprockel, C.S 1973. *The language of the Parker Chronicle.* The Hague; Martinus

Nijhoff.

Stockwell, Robert P. and Donka Minkova. Forthcoming. Subordination and word order change in the history of English. *Studies in memory of Leon Kellner*, ed. by D. Kastovsky. Amsterdam: Mouton de Gruyter. Presented orally at CHES, Vienna September 1988.

Todt, August. 1894. Die Wortstellung im Beowulf. *Anglia* 16:226-60.

Thorpe, Benjamin, ed. 1844. *The Homilies of the Anglo-Saxon church.* Part I. London.

Vennemann, Theo. 1984. Verb-second, verb late, and the brace construction in Germanic: A discussion. *Historical syntax.*, ed. Jacek Fisiak. The Hague: Mouton 627:36.

Zimmermann, Rüdiger. 1983. Parataxis and hypotaxis in Old English. *Languages in function.* Ed. by Sandor Rot. Budapest, 347-52.

7

COMPUTERS ARE USEFUL - FOR *AUGHT* I KNOW

Matti Rissanen

1 Introductory

The purpose of this paper is to point out the new possibilities provided by computerized corpora for handling the evidence offered by Old English texts, and to introduce briefly the Old English section of the *Helsinki Corpus of English Texts*. An example of the use of this section, taken from the domain of indefinite pronouns, is given at the end of the chapter.

This chapter contains very little 'interpretation of available data within a theoretical framework' that the Editor, Dr Fran Colman, calls for in her letter to the contributors. But I hope it will, in a small way, contribute to answering the question of 'how much linguistic information about Old English can we reconstruct?' asked by Dr Colman in the same letter.

At first sight, the thought of using a computer in Old English studies may seem suspicious, if not outright blasphemous. But on closer analysis the computer offers a particularly useful tool in this area of research. The entire Old English corpus of texts is not only 'closed', it is also relatively small. For this reason, the demand has often been expressed that studies of the Old English language should be based on all extant textual evidence, although few studies can, in practice, claim absolute representativeness in this respect. A computerized corpus not only makes the fulfilment of this demand possible; it also speeds up the searching and organisation of the data enormously. In practice, this means that many problems of Old English which have earlier remained untouched simply because the search for evidence would have demanded an excessive amount of time and work can now be tackled. In particular, computerized corpora are useful in studies based on the distribution of variant forms and on the quantitative analysis of textual evidence.

The most important computerized collection of Old English texts is, of course, the *Toronto Corpus of Old English* (henceforth, the *Toronto Corpus*), prepared by the *Dictionary of Old English* project. This data-base exists on computer tape and as a microfiche concordance, and its usefulness for research has been amply evidenced by a number of recent studies. The *Toronto Corpus* consists of all extant Old English texts, all in all more than three million words.[1]

The first large corpus of Old English texts especially constructed for structural and lexical studies forms part of the *Helsinki Corpus of English Texts: Diachronic and Dialectal*.[2] The Old English section of the *Helsinki Corpus* (henceforth the *Helsinki Sub-corpus*) consists of about 500,000 words of continuous text sampled from prose and poetry. The texts are edited from the Toronto computer tape.[3]

The number of text files is 70 (some files contain several documents, letters, etc.) and the average size of the extracts from longer texts is from 5,000 to 10,000 words. Every sample of text has been provided with parameter code markings which give basic information on the background of the text.

The advantages of a smaller, structured selection of text samples (about one-seventh of the *Toronto Corpus*) are obvious when high-frequency items, words or constructions, are under investigation. In a study of the Old English indefinite pronouns (Rissanen 1987), I was faced by 8,368 instances of *man,* used either as a noun or as a pronoun, and by about 9,000 instances of the forms of *hwa/hwæt* and *hwilc,* used either as interrogatives or as indefinites, in the *Toronto Corpus.* The *Helsinki Sub-corpus* reduces the number of the occurrences of *man* to about 1,150 and that of the *hw-* forms to about 1,700; in this way the collecting of the relevant instances becomes decisively easier and less time-consuming. If the selection of the texts of the Sub-corpus has been successful, we can assume that the representativeness of the results remains adequate. After the general trends of usage have become apparent from the Sub-corpus, the checking and sharpening of the results from the massive *Toronto Corpus,* particularly in regard to low-frequency forms, can be done easily.

The textual coding of the *Helsinki Sub-corpus* is intended to help the rapid and easy automatic classification of examples. When decisions were made concerning the inclusion of texts in the Sub-corpus, particular attention was paid to representativeness in relation to the following four factors:[4]

1. Chronological coverage of the Old English period
2. Coverage of Old English dialects
3. Coverage of most important text types
4. Major authors of the period.

Each text sample has been coded in regard to these four parameters : date, dialect, type of text and author (if known). In addition, the relationship of the text to a possible Latin original was noted. The majority of the texts represent prose writing, but a fairly extensive selection of verse has also been included. In Sections 2-5 I will briefly comment on the selection criteria, along with some problems connected with determining the parameter code values for the text samples.[5]

2 Chronological Coverage

To make the study of diachronic developments within Old English easier, the period is divided into four sub-periods:

OE1 pre-850
OE2 850-950
OE3 950-1050
OE4 1050-1150

While there is little difficulty in finding texts representing OE2 and OE3, OE1 and OE4 necessarily remain under-represented. We have included practically all extant pre-850 texts: *Cædmon's Hymn*, *Bede's Death Song*, *Leiden Riddle*, *Ruthwell Cross* and the earliest documents (Birch 451, Harmer 1-3 and 5, Robertson 3), but the size of this part of our corpus is nevertheless only about 3,000 words. The only texts whose original versions seem to represent the latest sub-period are chronicle entries, the *Vision of Leofric*, and a few documents (William's Laws, Robertson, Appendix 1, 3, 4). There are, however, a number of texts whose manuscripts date from this period, although the originals were probably written before 1050. If these texts are included, the size of the OE4 section is about 75,000 words.

It is only natural that, when selecting the samples for the *Helsinki Sub-corpus*, we have tried to avoid texts which pose overwhelming problems of dating. Yet we must admit our insufficient knowledge and feeling of uncertainty in regard to the dating of many of our corpus texts. Among other things, we found it advisable to include a sizeable selection of Old English verse. In order to avoid taking a stand in the dispute concerning the dating of the poems, we have consistently coded their date of composition as X (='unknown'), if external evidence does not suggest a reliable dating.

Another problem in giving the texts a sub-period coding (OE1-4) is the discrepancy between the date of the composition of the original text and that of the extant manuscript included in the corpus. We have solved this problem by giving the text a combined date coding, indicating both the period of composition and the period of the writing of the extant manuscript when the two are different. Thus, e.g., the extracts from the *Blickling Homilies* are coded OE2/3, *Life of St. Chad* OE2/4, and *Beowulf, Christ, Andreas*, etc. OEX/3. Texts with late extant manuscripts also give more substance to our latest Old English sub-period (OE4): *Life of St. Chad, Adrian and Ritheus, Dicts of Cato*, the C MS of Gregory's *Dialogues*, some of Ælfric's letters and Wulfstan's homilies, etc., are extant in post-1050 manuscripts.

3 Dialectal coverage

The dialectal distribution of Old English texts is as uneven as the chronological one. We have made an attempt to include samples of most non-West-Saxon texts: *Vespasian Psalter, Rushworth I, Lindisfarne Gospels, Durham Ritual*, and the early Northumbrian poems mentioned in the preceding section. We have also included the Kentish and Mercian documents (Harmer 1, 2, 3, 5, 12; Robertson 1, 3, 6, 10, 16, 32; Whitelock 14, 15: *Codex Aureus*).

In giving the dialect codes to our samples, we have followed a traditional and conservative line, trusting that the users of our corpus are well aware of the hazards of defining the dialects of Old English texts, and that they will be able to decide how reliable the definition of the dialect of each individual text can possibly be.[6] A simple code value (WS, AM [=Mercian], AN [=Northumbrian], K) has been given to those texts which are traditionally mentioned as specimens of the dialect in question. As representatives of West-Saxon we have coded, e.g., the early annals of the *Anglo-Saxon Chronicle*, Alfred's *Laws*, *Cura Pastoralis*, *Orosius*, *Boethius*, most of Ælfric's and Wulfstan's writings and the *WS Gospels*. The non-West-Saxon texts mentioned in the preceding paragraph have been coded as representatives of their respective dialects.

In the case of the majority of the texts a coding indicating mixed dialect is, however, necessary. *Old English Bede*, Gregory's *Dialogues*, *Martyrology*, *Alexander's Letter*, *Wonders of the East*, and some medical texts have been coded as WS/A or WS/AM. In many cases, the coding added to the dialect definition is /X, which indicates that the secondary dialectal influences have not been specified. The special language form of the main body of Old English poetry is marked as WS/X; the two Kentish poems are marked as K/X. The developing West-Saxon-based standard evidenced by 11th-century documents and other non-literary writings (excluding Ælfric's and Wulfstan's text), is coded as WS/X.

4 Type of Text

From the point of view of the representativeness of the Sub-corpus, the coverage of as many types of writing as possible is, of course, of primary importance. The following code words are used to specify our Old English text types (a summary of the most important texts representing each type is given in brackets):

LAW (Alfred, Ine, Cnut, Æthelred, Northumbrian priests, William the Conqueror)
DOCUMENTS (from Harmer, Whitelock, Robinson, Birch, etc)
HANDBOOK ASTRONOMY (Prognostications)
HANDBOOK MEDICINE (Læceboc, Lacnunga, Med. Quadrupedibus)
SCIENCE ASTRONOMY (De Temp. Anni, Byrhtferth's Manual)
PHILOSOPHY (Boethius, Dicts of Cato)
HOMILY (Ælfric, Wulfstan, Blickling Hom.)
RULE (Bened. Rule, Durham Ritual, Institutes of Polity)
RELIGIOUS TREATISE (Cura Pastoralis, Ælfric's Letters, Adrian and Ritheus, Solomon and Saturn, Vision of Leofric)
PREFACE/EPIL. (Alfred's and Ælfric's prefaces)
HISTORY (A-S Chronicle, Bede, Orosius)
GEOGRAPHY (Wonders of the East)
BIOGRAPHY LIFE SAINT (Martyrology, Gregory's Dialogues, Ælfric's Lives, St. Chad, St. Margaret)
TRAVELOGUE (Alexander's Letter)
FICTION (Apollonius of Tyre)
BIBLE (Vespasian and Paris Psalters, Heptateuch, West-Saxon, Lindisfarne, Rushworth Gospels)

As the code words are intended to be descriptive of the texts of the entire *Helsinki Corpus*, some of them (Pref./Epil., Biogr., Fiction, etc.), do not specify the Old English text types in an ideal way. It is also evident that the groupings are somewhat arbitrary, and there is bound to be heterogeneity and internal variation within the individual texts grouped under one and the same text type. On the other hand, the application of a uniform text-type classification throughout the millenium of our texts may prove helpful in diachronic studies based on the *Helsinki Corpus*. Furthermore, the text-type division should give the user a fair idea of what kind of writing he can expect to find in the corpus, and, even more importantly, what types of text are not included.

Verse texts are not divided by text type because the classification indicated above seemed arbitrary and inappropriate for Old English poetry. In addition to the poems mentioned above, the following are included in our Sub-corpus: *Genesis, Exodus, Elene, Fates of Apostles, Dream of the Rood, Juliana, Riddles, Phoenix, Battle of Brunanburh, Metrical Psalms, Meters of Boethius*, and a number of the shorter poems of the *Exeter Book*.

5 Other Aspects of Selection and Coding

In selecting the samples of the Sub-corpus, an attempt has been made to include a fair amount of text from the major known authors of the Old English period: Alfred, Wærferth (*Dial. Greg.* and documents), Ælfric, and Wulfstan (Homilies, *Institutes of Polity*). All Cynewulf's signed verse has also been included.

It has also been considered important to code the relationship of the text to a possible Latin original. This parameter is problematic, as Latin influence is to some extent present in the majority of Old English texts, both in prose and in poetry. For this reason, we have adopted a very strict line in attributing a text the code value TRANSLATION: for this coding, the Latin original must be available to allow a comparison between the original and the translation. The Mercian and Northumbrian Bible translations and *Durham Ritual* are coded as glosses.

6 Computer Programs and Availability of the Corpus

At the moment, the Oxford Concordance Program (OCP) and the WordCruncher (developed at Brigham Young University), are used for searching and sorting the data of the *Helsinki Corpus*. The OCP classifies the samples according to the parameters described: the appropriate code values are given at the head of each sample in angular brackets—in the so-called COCOA format (see Hockey and Martin 1988). The main advantages of the WordCruncher are its user-friendliness and the interactivity between the word index, list of concordanced examples and text samples (see *WordCruncher* 1987). Both programs can search words and their parts, and combinations of these elements.[7] Furthermore, a concordance program particularly designed for use with the *Helsinki Corpus* is under preparation at the University of Helsinki. It is hoped that this program will combine some of the advantages typical of the OCP and WordCruncher.

The Helsinki Corpus, in all its parts, can be ordered for scholarly use through the Oxford Text Archive (one-file format, main frame tape only) or the Norwegian Centre for the Humanities in Bergen (various formats).

7 *Awiht/a(u)ht* in Old English

As an example of the possibilities offered to Old English research by the *Helsinki Sub-corpus* and the *Toronto Corpus*. I will present a brief survey of the occurrences of the pronoun *awiht/a(u)ht* in Old English. This pronoun is one member of the rich set of the Old English indefinites indicating, roughly, 'some' or 'any'. This pronominal paradigm comprises more than a dozen nearly synonymous forms, some of them very frequent (*sum, ænig, man*), some occurring only once or twice in Old English texts (for a list of the forms and their frequencies, see Rissanen 1987: 411-412).

Awiht/a(u)ht is roughly synonymous to *ænig*, but it is always used independently (i.e. not in determiner function), and its referent is always inanimate 'anything'. It offers a rewarding topic of study because of its diachronic interest: it is one of the few forms of the Old English 'some/any' indefinites which did not become obsolete with the generalization of the two prototypical forms, *some* and *any*, in the course of the Middle English period.[9] Furthermore, its early occurrences give an opportunity for phonological, syntactic and semantic observations. Finally, its frequency is sufficiently low to make comparisons between the two corpora easy and illustrative.

Table 1 shows the forms of *awiht/a(u)ht* in the *Toronto Corpus* and the *Helsinki Corpus*. Only those forms are included in which the form is used with the meaning 'some/any'.[10]

TABLE 1

The forms of the indefinite *awiht/a(u)ht* in the *Toronto Corpus* and the *Helsinki Sub-corpus*

	Torronto Corpus	Helsinki Sub-Corpus
aht	96	9
ahte	2	2
auht	32	7
auhte	1	-
awiht	55	9
awihte	1	-
awuht	13	4
awyht	5	1
æwiht	1	-
oht	18	5
ohtes	2	2
owiht	48	10
owihte	7	4
owihtes	1	-
Total	282	51

As the total number of words in the *Toronto Corpus* is about three million and in the *Helsinki Sub-corpus* about half a million, the ratio of the occurrences of *awiht/a(u)ht* in the two corpora, 6:1, is almost exactly the expected one. Practically all the relevant forms of the *Toronto Corpus* can be found in the *Helsinki Sub-corpus*. The missing forms, *auhte, awihte, æwiht* and *owihtes* each occur only once in the *Toronto Corpus*, and they are of minor importance in the study of this pronoun.

If the distribution of the individual forms in the two corpora is compared, it can be easily seen that some forms, notably *auht, awuht,* and *oht, owiht(e)* are proportionally over-represented and some, notably *aht,* under-represented in the *Helsinki Sub-corpus*. The reasons for this phenomenon will be discussed at the end of this chapter.

There are two interesting details of orthographic variation which, in all probability, also have bearing on pronunciation: the initial vowel is either ‹a› or ‹o›, and the vowel preceding ‹h› shows variation between ‹i› and ‹u› (*awiht/owiht* vs. *awuht*), or between ‹u› and zero (*auht* vs. *aht/oht*).

The present discussion concentrates mainly on prose usage. In Table 2, the thirty prose instances found in the *Helsinki Sub-corpus* are arranged according to the two major parameters in our coding system, time and dialect. The grouping of the occurrences by the sub-period is based on the date of the extant manuscript.

TABLE 2

The forms of *awiht/a(u)ht* in the prose samples of the *Helsinki Sub-corpus*: distribution by time and dialect

	WS	WS/X	WS/A(M)	AM/X	AM
-850					owiht(e)(1)
850-950	awuht(2)		aht(1)		
	auht(4)		owiht(1)		
	owiht(1)		oht(es)(1)		
950-1050	aht(1)	aht(1)	awiht(2)	oht(1)	owiht(1)
			owiht(3)		
1050-1150	aht(1)	awiht(1)	aht(2)		
		auht(1)	oht(es)(2)		
		aht(1)			
		oht(2)			

The figures yielded by the *Helsinki Sub-corpus* are, of course, too low for definite conclusions, but certain trends are fairly obvious; these trends can easily be verified by distribution figures derived from the *Toronto Corpus*. In the texts representing the 'pure' WS dialect, there is only one instance showing the initial ‹o›:

(1) Gif hio leng libbe ðonne se ðe hie utlædde, nage hio his ierfes *owiht*.
    (Alfred Laws 54)

In the two instances taken from Alfred's Introduction to his laws, the form *awuht* is used:

(2) Gif hwa gewerde oðres monnes wingeard oððe his æcras oððe his landes *awuht*, gebete swa hit mon geeahtige (Alfred Laws, Introd. 36).

(3) Forðam ic ne dorste geðristlæcan þara minra *awuht* fela on gewrit settan, forðam me wæs uncuð, hwæt þæs ðam lician wolde ðe æfter us wæren. (Id. 46).

Thus *owiht*, which shows both the non-WS initial ‹o› and the non-Alfredian ‹i› before the ‹h› (see below), might imply that the law texts proper go back to earlier sources and do not represent Alfred's own language form in the same way as the Introduction. Unfortunately there are no other instances of the *wiht/wuht* variation in Alfred's *Laws* or the Introduction; in Ine's *Laws*, there are two instances of *wiht* (*fulwihte* 90; *nane wiht* 116) and one of *wuht* (*nan wuht* 116).

In the two Mercian instances, the initial vowel is ‹o› and the vowel preceding the ‹h› is ‹i›:

(4) gif aenig monn ðas ure gewitnisse incerre on *owihte*, ðaet he aebbe ðaes aelmaehtgan Godes unhlisse (Doc. Harmer No. 3, p. 6).

(5) ne forþon ondredaþ eow hiae þe nis forþon *owiht* bewrigenes þæt ne sie vnwrigan & degles þæt ne sie witen. (Rushw. Gosp. 10.26).

The initial vowel is ‹o› in the one instance in Harmer No. 12 (*þæt he...oht þæs abrecan wylle*, p. 21), which represents the Mercian dialect in a less 'pure' form (cf. Harmer 1914: 131). Furthermore, both ‹o› and ‹a› can be found in other texts which show Anglian characteristics (Læceboc 330 *aht*; Blickl. Hom. 111, Med. Quadr. 3 *awiht*; Alexander's Letter 3, 30, 37 *owiht*; Wærferth GD C 38, 73 *aht*; 35 *oht*. Chad 174 *ohtes*).

The *Toronto Corpus* confirms this dialectal variation; the forms with initial ‹o› can be regarded as non-WS. Of the 74 prose instances of *oht/owiht*, none occurs in typically WS texts (with the exception of the passage given as example 1 above); on the other hand, there are 15 instances in *Bede*, three in *Lind. Gosp.*, etc).[1][1]

The development of the contracted forms *a(u)ht/oht* from the longer ones is apparent from Table 2. The longer forms mainly occur in texts which originate from the pre-950 period (*Doc. Harmer*, Alfred's *Laws*, *Bede*), although in some instances (*Med. Quadr.*, *Blickl. Hom.*, *Alexander's Letter*), the extant MS is later and the text is consequently classified under the period 950-1050.

The development of *auht* is obviously a feature typical of early West-Saxon. There are four prose instances in the *Helsinki Sub-corpus* in Alfredian writings (*Boethius* 2; CP 2). The only later instance is in the *Dicts of Cato*:

(6) Ne wen þu na þæt se yfla *auht* godes gestryne mid his yfle, (Dicts of Cato 8)

There is little doubt that *auht* developed from *awuht* which is also an exclusively West-Saxon form. With one exception (*Genesis* 496) all the thirteen *awuht* forms in the *Toronto Corpus* go back to Alfredian West-Saxon texts (*Meters of Boethius* 5 instances, CP 4. *Solil.* 1, Introd. Alfred's *Laws* 2). The prose occurrences of *auht* come from *Boethius* (19 instances) and CP (5). Campbell does not seem to have noticed the West-Saxon character of *awuht/auht* as he derives *(n)auht* from *(n)awiht* by the loss of the unaccented vowel (1959: #393; cf. #338, n. 3).

On the whole, the usage in Old English poetry confirms the picture presented above. It is noteworthy that the frequency of occurrence of *awiht/a(u)ht* in poetry is remarkably high; 21 occurrences out of the total of 51 in the *Helsinki Sub-corpus*, while the proportion of verse is only about one-fifth of the Sub-corpus. As can be expected, the longer forms prevail: there are 16 instances of these forms as against 5 of *a(u)ht/oht*. The occurrence of the shorter forms in *Beowulf* 2314 and *Christ* 238 may imply that the contraction had taken place early in Old English (cf., however, Amos 1980: 64-69).

(7)   No ðær *aht* cwices
    lað lyftfloga læfan wolde. (Beowulf 2314-15)

(8) Sylfa sette þæt þu sunu wære
    efendeardigende mid þinne engan frean
    ærþon *oht* þisses æfre gewurde. (Christ 236-238).

Forms with an initial <o> are proportionally more common in poetry than in prose : 9 out of 21 in the *Helsinki Sub-corpus*. This is probably due to the Anglian undercurrent in the Old English poetic language, particularly as eleven out of the twelve instances with the initial <a> came from *Paris Psalter* or *Meters of Boethius*. The twelfth occurs in *Beowulf* (example 7, above), but the form is *owihte* in *Beowulf* 1822 and 2432.

Additional evidence of the significance of the chronological and dialectal distribution of the forms discussed above can be found in the distribution of the negative forms *nawiht/na(u)ht* illustrated in Table 3.

TABLE 3
The forms of *na(n)wiht/na(u)ht* in the prose samples of the *Helsinki Sub-corpus*: distribution by time and dialect

	WS(/X)	WS/A(M)	AM(/X)	AN
-850				
850-950	nawuht(3)	nowiht(1)	nowiht(4)	
	nanwuht(14)	nanwuht(1)	noht(2)	
	nowiht(1)	noht(6)		
	nawht(1)	naht(4)		
	nauht(23)			
	naht(4)			
	noht(4)			
950-1050	nawuht(2)	nowiht(1)	noht(2)	noht(7)
	nauht(1)	noht(10)		
	naht(16)	naht(6)		
1050-1150	nanwyht(1)	noht(2)		
	naht(13)	naht(5)		
	noht(2)			

The figures in Table 3 need little comment: the similarity of distribution between the affirmative and negative forms in prose texts is obvious.

The infrequency of the negative forms in Old English poetry is worth noting (7 instances out of the total of 136 in the *Helsinki Sub-corpus*)—the negative structure probably developed so late that it never became an integral part of the poetic language.

What, then, accounts for the continuous use of *awiht/a(u)ht* (>*aught/ought/owt*) in Middle and Modern English, while most of the other Old English variants of 'some/any' indefinites became obsolete? It seems that both syntactic and semantic characteristics of this pronoun contribute to its survival. Although *ænig* was the prototypical pronoun for indefinite non-specific reference (cf. Rissanen 1987: 414-418), its use had certain constraints revealed by the figures of distribution in Old English texts. While *ænig* can be used both independently and dependently (i.e. in pronoun and determiner functions), it occurs independently in only 63 out of the total of 329 prose instances in the *Helsinki Sub-corpus*.[1] [2] In most of these instances (49), its referent is animate;

this is the case particularly when it does not govern a genitive (31 out of 36 instances).

It seems that the syntactic and semantic constraints of *awiht/a(u)ht* support its use in exactly the kinds of context in which the use of *ænig* is avoided though not impossible. Besides *hwa/hwæt*, *awiht/a(u)ht* is the only 'some/any' pronoun that is always used independently. Its referent is always inanimate, 'anything'. It is, by origin, probably emphatic in the same way as *ænig*; this is indicated by the high frequency of both these pronouns in negative contexts (cf. Rissanen 1987: 418-419). Furthermore, *awiht/a(u)ht* is not ambiguous like *hwæt*, which is also always used independently with an inanimate referent. These characteristics seem to have made *awiht/a(u)ht* a useful supplementary member in the variant field of 'some/any' pronouns, not only in Old English but also in Middle English. Its obsolescence in early Modern English is probably caused by the establishment of the set of compound pronouns including *anything*.[1] [3]

There is little doubt that the high frequency of the negative form, which lies behind both *not* and *nought*, supported the survival of *aught*. In the *Helsinki Subcorpus* the occurrence of the negative form is distinctly higher than that of the affirmative form (136 as against 51) while the proportion with, e.g., *nænig/ænig* (125/477) and *nan/an* (c. 750/1300) is clearly in favour of the affirmative forms.

7 Final Remarks

As can be seen from the above discussion, the combined use of the *Helsinki Subcorpus* and the *Toronto Corpus* provides a fairly efficient tool for the study of Old English structures or lexical items. The implications based on the distribution of forms in the smaller, structured and coded corpus can, where necessary, be confirmed with a more detailed — although more laborious and time-consuming — study of the corpus containing all Old English writings.

A survey of the forms of *awiht/a(u)ht* also shows that our corpus gives a somewhat skewed picture of the distributions of the *Toronto Corpus* in at least two respects: the form *auht* and the forms with an initial ‹o› are over-represented (cf. Table 1 above). *Auht* is a typically Alfredian West-Saxon form, prevailing notably in CP and *Boethius*. As Alfredian texts form the main bulk of extant pre-950 prose, over-representation is unavoidable if a fair amount of text dating from this early period is to be included. In the 850-950 section of the *Helsinki Subcorpus*, Alfred's texts do not seem to be over-represented, and thus the skewing effect is not very serious.

The high proportion of forms with an initial ‹o› in the *Helsinki Sub-corpus* is due to our wish to include as much non-West-Saxon material in our corpus as possible. It can be argued that the predominance of West-Saxon in the total corpus of extant Old English texts is accidental, and that the emphasis given to the Anglian element in a structured corpus rectifies a skewedness rather than creates one. Furthermore, from the point of view of the later development of English, the non-WS strata are of prime importance.

It is essential, of course, that the users of the *Helsinki Corpus*, as of all computerized corpora, are aware of the inbuilt restrictions of the contents of the corpora. Even at best, any collection of written text samples can only give an incomplete and unreliable picture of the reality of the language. Generalizations based on these samples can only gain value and validity by the student's intuitive mastery of the language form he is studying and by his capacity to analyse his material and draw conclusions on the basis of his analyses (cf. Rissanen 1989). But a sensible use of computerized corpora certainly enables the student to diminish the time spent on monotonous drudgery and to focus his energy on more creative aspects of research.

NOTES

1. For an introduction to this corpus, see Venezky & Healey (1980): Venezky and Butler (1985); Healey (1985); Holland (1986), etc.
2. The texts and text extracts in the *Helsinki Corpus* cover a millennium, from the eighth century to the beginning of the eighteenth. The size of the Corpus is c. 1.5 million words. For a description of the Corpus, see, e.g. Ihalainen, Kytö and Rissanen (1987), Kytö and Rissanen (1988), Kytö (1989), Kytö (1991).
3. For permission to use the Toronto texts, I am most indebted to the editors of the *Dictionary of Old English*, Antonette diPaolo Healey and the late Ashley Crandell Amos.
4. The compilation of the *Helsinki Corpus* has been mainly the work of three groups of pre- and post-doctoral scholars at the English Department of the University of Helsinki. The Old English group consists of Dr Leena Kahlas-Tarkka, Dr Matti Kilpiö, Mr Ilkka Mönkkönen and Mrs Aune Österman. Miss Merja Kytö and the present writer participated in the work of all groups, including the Old English one.
5. The compilers of the *Helsinki Corpus* are well aware of the fact that the parameter codings describing the individual texts may be inaccurate, either owing to insufficient knowledge of the history of Old English writings or to our oversights in incorporating the results of manuscript research. We will be most grateful to the readers of this paper and to future users of our Corpus for all corrections and other comments concerning our texts and their codings.
6. See Hogg (1988) for a recent emphatic caveat against too straightforward a treatment of the Old English dialects.
7. In this context, it is worth mentioning the program called KAYE, created by Dr Geoffrey Kaye of IBM. This program, still under development, has been experimented with on searches covering the entire corpus of Ælfric's writings.
8. *Aught/owt* exists even today in dialectal and colloquial usage and in the archaic expression *for aught I know*. See, e.g. OED, Supplement (1982), s.v. *owt*.
9. The few instances in which the word means 'anything worth', 'worthy', as in *þe aht(es) wære/wæron* (Chron. 992E. (1086), are omitted as the simple pronominal meaning of *aht* is here questionable. In a few instances, the use of *awiht/a(u)ht* seems to approach that of an adverb (cf. Wülfing 1894: 459: Ingersoll 1978: 198-200). As the distinction is hard to make, these instances have been included in the present discussion.
10. Campbell does not seem to recognise the dialectal significance of this variation in the initial vowel (cf. 1959: #132 note).
11. This tendency later resulted in the development of the compound forms *anyone, anybody, anything*.
12. In Middle English, the pronoun *o(ug)ht/aught* is at least as common as in Old English. In the (somewhat more extensive) ME section of the *Helsinki Corpus*, there are 77

instances of this pronoun. The longer form *(e)awiht* can be found in the earliest Middle English SW and SWM texts (*Bodley Homilies* 1 example, *Lambeth Homilies* 3, *Ancrene Wisse* 1, *Hali Maidh.* 1).

In the 16th and 17th century samples of the *Helsinki Corpus* there are 17 instances of *aught/ought* . Towards the end of the early Modern English period, the use of *aught* in the written standard seems to be stereotyped: out of the six *Helsinki Corpus* instances dating from 1640-1700, five are of the type *for aught I know* .

REFERENCES

Amos, Ashley Crandell 1980. *Linguistic means of determining the dates of Old English literary texts.* Cambridge, Mass.: The Medieval Academy of America.

Campbell, Alistair, 1959. *Old English grammar.* Oxford: Clarendon.

Einenkel, Eugen 1904. Das englische Indefinitum. *Anglia* **27** (15). 1-204.

Harmer, F. E. ed. 1914. *Select English historical documents of the ninth and tenth centuries.* Cambridge: C.U.P.

Healey, Antonette diPaolo 1985. The Dictionary of Old English and the final design of its computer system. *Computers and the Humanities.* **19**. 245-49.

Hockey, Susan and Jeremy Martin 1988. *Oxford Concordance Program: User's manual, Version 2* . Oxford: Oxford University Computing Service.

Hogg, Richard 1988. On the impossibility of Old English dialectology. In Dieter Kastovsky and Gero Bauer (eds.). *Luick Revisited,* 183-203. Tubingen : Gunter Narr.

Holland, Joan 1986. *The Microfiche Concordance*: a lexicographer's tool. *American Notes and Queries* **24**. 120-23.

Ihalainen, Ossi, Merja Kytö and Matti Rissanen 1987. *The Helsinki Corpus of English texts: Diachronic and Dialectal*—report on work in progress. In Willem Meijs (ed.) *Corpus linguistics and beyond: proceedings of the Seventh International Conference on English Language Research on Computerized Corpora* . 21-32. Amsterdam: Rodopi.

Ingersoll, Sheila Most 1978. *Intensive and restrictive modification in Old English.* Heildelberg: Carl Winter.

Kytö, Merja 1989. Progress report on the diachronic part of the Helsinki Corpus. *ICAME Journal* **13**. 12-15.

Kytö, Merja forthcoming. *Manual to the diachronic part of the Helsinki Corpus of English texts:* coding conventions and list of source texts.

Kytö, Merja and Matti Rissanen 1988. *The Helsinki Corpus of English texts:* classifying and coding the diachronic part. In Merja Kytö, Ossi Ihalainen and Matti Rissanen (eds.). *Corpus linguistics, hard and soft: Proceedings of the Eighth International Conference on English Language Research on Computerized Corpora,* 169-179.

Mitchell, Bruce 1985. *Old English Syntax* . I-II Oxford: O.U.P.

Rissanen, Matti 1987. Old English indefinite pronouns meaning 'some' and 'any', with special reference to *hw-* forms. In Kahlas-Tarkka, Leena (ed.). *Neophilologica Fennica.* 411-428.

Rissanen, Matti 1989. Three problems connected with the use of diachronic corpora . *ICAME Journal* . **13**. 16-19.

Venezky, Richard L. and Antonette diPaolo Healey 1980. *A Microfiche Concordance to Old English.* Newark DE and Toronto.

Venezky, Richard L. and Sharon Butler 1985. *A Microfiche Concordance to Old English: the high frequency words* . Newark DE and Toronto.

WordCruncher 1987. *Text indexing and retrieval software. Version 4.1.* Provo, Utah:

Brigham Young University and Electronic Text Corporation.

Wülfing, J. Ernst 1894. *Die Syntax in den Werken Alfreds des Grossen*, I. Bonn: P Hanstein.

8

DIE-CUTTING AND DIATOPIC VARIATION: THE VARIANT ‹LIOF-› ON LATE ANGLO-SAXON COINS

Veronica Smart

The starting-point of this chapter is the paragraph in the Bibliography of Campbell (1959: 358) which introduces numismatic material.

> A very large number of OE coins inscribed with the names of kings and moneyers survive. On these, however, abnormal and bad spelling is so frequent that only recurrent forms are of any linguistic value. Forms abound which diverge from the dialect which might be expected in the relevant kingdom, e.g. on Anglian coins *Ealræd Beagstan* and many names in *heah*, on WS coins *Biorn-*, *Liof-* beside *Beorn-*, *Leof-* ...

This is all too illustrative of the suspicion in which coin-legends are held by many language scholars, in spite of the strides which have been made in numismatic research over the last forty years. There have of course been honourable exceptions; the onomast von Feilitzen used numismatic material with careful discrimination, and Colman (1984) has made an excellent review of the interpretation of coin-legends in OE phonology. Nevertheless, the bibliography in which the above statement occurs is probably the introduction to the Anglo-Saxon coinage which most language students receive.

The latest entry relating to coins there is 1915, so perhaps it is not surprising that no notice is taken of the work that has distinguished Viking imitations from the official coinage at several periods, thus taking out many corrupt forms in the legends. It would also appear that, at any rate in the late Anglo-Saxon coinage, there are few orthographic features that are not paralleled in documentary sources, although this may involve some reassessment of native development and Anglo-Norman influence. Since the renaissance in Anglo-Saxon numismatics begun by Dolley in the 1950s coin-evidence deserves better than to be pushed off-stage because its face doesn't fit. It needs, however, to be interpreted in the light of numismatic concepts, and the results of this may not always coincide with its face-value.

Throughout the early history of the Anglo-Saxon coinage mint-names do appear on some issues, but it is not until the reform of Edgar towards the end of his reign (973?) that the coins are invariably mint-signed. This feature locates the named moneyer geographically, but another factor in determining the form in which the moneyer's name may appear was first suggested by Dolley (1958) in a study of the considerable variation in styles of portrait and lettering which occurs within Æthelred II's *Small Cross* types. He concluded that in these issues the dies for the coins could not have been cut in all of the individual boroughs which minted coins, but rather in die-cutting centres in the major towns which supplied a number of other mints. This concept has been followed up in other types, until the current view of the late Anglo-Saxon coinage is one in which there was at first after Edgar's reform a fluctuating policy towards die-provision; at times the coinage appears to be organised around local centres whilst at others there is a tendency towards centralisation with some tolerance of local dies. This latter position seems to be the norm after the early 1020s, probably working towards the situation described in Domesday Book for the end of Edward the Confessor's reign where, when the coin-type was changed, the moneyers obtained their dies from London.

I have shown elsewhere (Smart 1983) how dramatically the form of moneyer's name can be affected by a shifting of die-provision from local to national, in the sharp dichotomy of ‹ÆÐEL-› and ‹ÆGEL-› forms from one type to the next in Cnut's coinage. This, I suggested, was not in itself a diatopic variation in phonology, although the presence of early ‹ÆGEL-› forms strengthens the evidence for weakening and loss of [ð] in this element (Ekwall 1947: 197; Colman 1981). Rather, in Cnut's second issue a 'national' centre (probably London or Winchester) adopted a new orthographic convention to represent an already existing pronunciation whilst some Northern local centres clung to the traditional spelling.

In this chapter I intend to show how a dialect feature in an element of certain moneyers', names may be given a false distribution if this is based solely on the mint-names with which it occurs. I have taken the ‹LIOF-› variant as being diagnostic of a Kentish feature which is spread beyond its usually accepted sphere of influence in its occurrence on the coinage.

Mint	Moneyer	Identification No.		Die-centre and Comments
		Æthelred II		
		Type B 1 First Small Cross (c. 979-85)		
London	LIOFRIC	BEH	2791	London or S.E. (Dolley and Talvio 1977)
		Type D Long Cross (c. 997-1003)		
(Lincoln	BEH LIOFRIC but misread; BEH 1809)			(Van der Meer 1961:174)
Stamford	LIOFNEA	BEH	3533	Barbarous
		Type E Helmet (c.1003-1009)		
London	LEOFSTAN	BEH	2799	Most dies for this type from London or Winchester: type not yet fully analysed (Blackburn and Lyon 1986: 224)
	LIOFÞINE	BEH	2802	
	LIOF OLD	BEH	2810-11	

Diatopic Variation

Mint	Moneyer	Identification No.		Die-centre and Comments
		Type A Last Small Cross (c.1009-1016)		
Canterbury	LIOFNOÐ	BEH	237	Southeastern
	LIOFSTΛN	BEH	238	'Eastern' = London
			239	Southeastern
			240	Southeastern
Dover	LIOFRIC	BEH	421	London
Lewes	LIOFSTAN	BEH	1455	London
	LIOFÞINE	BEH	1456	London
			1457	Southern A i.e. Winchester but London reverse
			1458	'Eastern' = London
			1459	'Eastern' = London
		Cop	463	London
London	LIOFRED	BEH	2790	London
	LIOERI	BEH	2801	London
			2789	London
		Cop	898	London
	LIOFSTAN	BEH	2792	London
			2793	London
			2794	London
		Cop	899	London
London	LIOFSTAN	BEH	2795	London
			2796	London
			2797	London
			2798	London
		RPM	1033	London
	LIOEÞI	BEH	2800	London
		Cop	900	London
	LIOFÞNE	BEH	2803	London
		RPM	1034	London
	LIOFÞOLD	BEH	2804	London
			2805	London
			2806	London
			2807	London
			2808	London
		Cop	901	London
			902	London
Romney	LIOFSTAN	BEH	3317	London
Lincoln	LIOFRIC	BEH	1808	London
Stamford	LIOFÞINE	BEH	3534	London

Mint	Moneyer	Identification No.		Die-centre and Comments
		Cnut		
		Type E Quatrefoil (c. 1017-23)		
Canterbury	LIOFNOÐ	BEH	165	London A l(ate)
		Cop	170	London A l
			171	London C m(id)
	LIOFSTAN	BEH	166	London A m
Dover	LIOFǷINE	Cop	394	London C m
London	LIOFRED	BEH	2632	'anomalous'
	LIOFRIC	BEH	2636	London B
			2637	London B
			2638	London B
			2639	London C e(arly)
			2640	London B
			2641	London C m
			2642	London B
			2643	London B
		Cop	2862	London B
			2865	London B
			2866	London B
	LIOFRIIC	Cop	2870	London C m
	LIOFSI	BEH	2644	Lewes
		Cop	2871	London A m
	LIOFSTAN	BEH	2651	London C m
			2652	London C m
			2653	London C m
		Cop	2876	London C l
			2877	London C l
	LIOFǷI	BEH	2655	London A l
	LIOFǷIN	BEH	2656	London C l
	LIOFǷINE	BEH	2657	London C m
			2658	London C m
			2659	London C e
		Cop	2880	London C l
			2881	London A l
	LIOFǷINIC	Cop	2882	London A l
	LIOFǷNE	BEH	2661	London C m
			2662	London C m
			2663	'Thetford C' atypical, perhaps London
		Cop	2883	London C m
	LIOFǷOLD	BEH	2664	London C m
			2665	London C l
			2666	London C l

Diatopic Variation

Mint	Moneyer	Identification No.		Die-centre and Comments
			2667	London C m
			2668	London C m
			2669	London C l
		Cop	2884	London C m
			2885	London C m
Southwark	LIOFRIC	BEH	3414	London B
Chichester	LIOFRIC	BEH	209	Chichester
			210	Chichester
		Cop	240	Chichester
			241	Chichester
Winchester	LIOFÞOLD	BEH	3798	Winchester
Bedford	LIOFN	BEH	63	'anomalous' London imitative
	LIOFSI	BEH	1286	same obverse die as next -attrib. BEH Lewes
			64	'anomalous' London imitative
	LIOFÞINE	BEH	65	London C l
Thetford ?	LIOFÞINE	BEH	3517	Stamford A but London reverse. The mint may be Bedford.
Cambridge	LIOFSI	BEH	1052	Thetford C but London reverse
			1053	London C m, same reverse as last
	LIOFSIG	BEH	1054	London C l
			1055	London C m
			1056	London A l
		Cop	1094	London A l
	LIOFSII	BEH	1057	London C m
			1058	London C m
			1059	London C l
			1060	London C m
		Cop	1095	London C l
Ipswich	LIOFRIC	BEH	954	London A l
Northampton	LIOFÞINE	Cop	1203	London C l
		Cop	1204	London C l
		Cop	1205	London C m
		Cop	1206	London C l
	LIOFÞOLD	BEH	1147	London C m
Lincoln	LIOFÞINE	BEH	1646	'anomalous' London copying *Last Small Cross* London style.

The above tables give a very clear indication that the great majority of coins showing the LIOF-variant were struck from dies cut at a centre established as London by Dolley (1958) and by Blackburn and Lyon (1986) in a long-awaited study of Cnut's first issue *Quatrefoil* which has made this analysis possible.

In some early unpublished attempts at the *Quatrefoil* classification, the styles which Blackburn and Lyon ascribe to mid- and late- London A groupings were designated Southeastern, probably pursuing the idea of a major successor to Dolley's prolific Canterbury centre in Æthelred's *Last Small Cross* issue. The two authors of the present *Quatrefoil* paper are convinced of a London locus for all these groups, since although London A has a slightly more southerly bias in distribution than London B, all three styles are heavily centred on London; out of 633 coins from the London mint which they classified 615 are of stylistic groups London A, B and C. Only the earliest London A group is unrepresented amongst the ‹LIOF-› coins, and the most obvious and minimal deduction from the tables above must be that London has to be included in any area in which **Liof-** was regarded as an acceptable spelling for this element.

It must be stated at the outset that even at those mints which exhibit ‹LIOF-› reflexes the predominant form is ‹LEOF-›. At the London mint in *Quatrefoil*, where the ‹LIOF-› form is most heavily represented, more than twice as many of the coins listed in BEH have ‹LEOF-› as have ‹LIOF-› (90:39). Other forms such as ‹LEF-› ‹LYOF› ‹LIF› also occur which will not be treated here.

We will look first at the mints within the south-eastern area where it would appear natural for the ‹LIOF-› variant to occur. In Æthelred's last issue *Last Small Cross* all the London-minted coins that have this variant are struck from London-cut dies, as is the case with earlier instances in the reign as far as it may be ascertained. In *Quatrefoil* one coin (of ‹LIOFRED›, BEH 2632) is classified as 'anomalous' in Blackburn and Lyon, but it has similarities to the mid-period coins of London A, and Lyon considers that the lettering points to a London workshop. BEH 2644 ‹LIOFSI› is from dies of the style associated with Lewes, a point of origin not impossible to be included in the fringe of a Kentish dialect-region, but perhaps to be considered with the output of the Chichester and Winchester workshops discussed below. BEH 2663 ‹LIOFÞINE› is classified as Thetford C, and it is interesting that Blackburn and Lyon annotate this workshop as often imitating the London style. Stewart Lyon has informed me in correspondence that this coin is indeed one of those which imitates London C and agrees that it could well be from non-standard dies of a London workshop.

In a similar way, whilst most of Æthelred's *Last Small Cross* ‹LIOF-› coins from the Canterbury mint are struck with southeastern dies, one, BEH 238 ‹LIOFSTAN› is given by Dolley as Eastern. However, Dolley's description of the Eastern style included a caveat that 'it is likely that in time a number of Eastern coins will be transferred to a new class of London B' and although this suggestion has not been followed up in print Lyon informs me that BEH 238 would fall into the category of dies from a second London workshop. This reclassification also applies to BEH 1458 and 1459, coins of the Lewes mint which Dolley gave to the Eastern die category.

Another Lewes coin BEH 1457 was assigned by Dolley to the Southern A workshop which he placed in Winchester. The most marked stylistic feature in both *Last Small Cross* and *Quatrefoil* is of course the portrait, and Dolley's classification of this coin depends on the obverse die which is indeed a Winchester product, but all the ‹LIOFÞINE› coins of the Lewes mint share a common reverse die of London style, probably originally issued with one of the London obverses and subsequently mis-paired.

Turning next to the incidence of ‹LIOF-› at those mints outside the acceptable southeastern dialect region, in Æthelred's reign the pattern is significant. Two coins purport to bear a Lincoln mint-signature but one is mis-transcribed in BEH; it is a die-duplicate of BEH 209 ‹LEOFRIC ON CEN›. The other, of *Last Small Cross* type BEH 1808 is noted by Hildebrand as being smaller and lighter than normal, and is omitted by Mossop (1970) who probably regarded this as an indication of inauthenticity, but Lyon accepts the dies as of a late London style.

Of two coins with the Stamford mint-signature and ‹LIOF-› legends one of *Long Cross* type reading ‹LIOFNEA› (for **Liofheah** ?) is barbarous in style and the legend is retrograde, indicators of Scandinavian imitation. The one remaining coin with a ‹LIOF-› legend issued outside the southeastern mints in Æthelred's reign is BEH 3534 ‹LIOFÞINE›, of the *Last Small Cross* type. Of seventy-one coins in BEH from the Stamford mint in this type examined by Dolley, sixty-nine were from dies cut in the northern workshops he attributed to York, but which further refinements divide between York and Lincoln. The remaining two used London-cut dies and it is on one of these that the ‹LIOFÞINE› legend appears. There are also two Stamford coins of this type which render the name ‹LEOFÞINE›, using Lincoln style dies.

In Cnut's *Quatrefoil* type there are two groups of ‹LIOF-› legends from mints outside the south-east. Several moneyers in the Hampshire Basin area appear with ‹LIOF-› forms in their names: ‹LIOFRIC›, ‹LIORÞINE› at Chichester and ‹LIOFÞOLD›, at Winchester, to which must be added ‹LIOFÞINE›, and ‹LIOFSTAN› from Mrs Harvey's as yet unpublished corpus of the Winchester mint. The two Chichester moneyers use dies of local origin employed for all but one of known Chichester coins in this type. The Winchester ‹LIOFÞOLD› coin in BEH is of the distinctive Winchester style.

In the southern Danelaw the pattern is quite different, and as with Lincoln and Stamford under Æthelred, very interesting. The majority of instances of ‹LIOF-› forms at these mints are consequent on the introduction of London-cut dies.

Under Bedford, Lyon classifies the two coins BEH 63-4 as 'anomalous'. I had previously noted them as 'London' and Lyon concedes that they have similarities with the London style but suggests only imitation. He regards the lack of a double inverted V at the front of the drapery on the bust as crucial, and suggests further that the blundering of the reverse legends ‹LIOFN ON BEDFN› or ‹ON REDFN› and ‹LIOFSI ON BEDFFI› argues against the dies having been cut in London. He associates with this group BEH 1286 which BEH attributes to Lewes. The obverse die for this coin is the same as that used in BEH 64, the moneyer's name is the same and the mint-signature, recorded by BEH as LÆÞEEI, is irregular for

Lewes and somewhat similar to that of BEH 64. One could argue for some kind of unofficial work copying a London prototype; at any rate this group has no affinities with northern or eastern die-cutting styles. BEH 65 is of regular London style.

Cambridge seems to have drawn its dies from several sources; the London workshops provided just over half of those analysed by Blackburn and Lyon and centres in East Anglia most of the rest. Of eleven coins with ‹LIOF-› forms in the name **Leofsige** ten are from London-cut dies. The other, BEH 1052, has an obverse from the Thetford centre, but the reverse is the same as that used for BEH 1053 and thus here too the ‹LIOF-› legend emanates from the London workshops. The sole ‹LIOF-› coin of the Ipswich mint in this type is also from London dies.

A coin attributed by BEH to Thetford but possibly from Bedford, BEH 3517 ‹LIOFÞINE ON DEFO› or perhaps ‹BDEFO› is classified by Blackburn and Lyon as being from Stamford dies, but again the style and lettering of the reverse is not compatible with the obverse and Lyon considers it might well be a London die.

The provision of dies to Northampton in *Quatrefoil* is extraordinarily widespread, from Lincoln south and west through Winchester to Gloucester. The ‹LEOF-› forms of the moneyers' names reflect this diversity, but ‹LIOF-› only occurs on dies from London.

To sum up: The study covers the incidence of ‹LIOF-› on late Anglo-Saxon coins where the pattern of regional die-distribution can be established, up to about 1023 when the provisions of dies to the mints seems to have undergone a major shift in favour of centralisation. Between Edgar's reform, about 973 and 1009 the ‹LIOF› variant rarely appears and its significance is difficult to assess but in Æthelred's *Last Small Cross* and Cnut's *Quatrefoil* types where the die-distribution patterns have been extensively analysed, this reflex is closely correlated with the products of the London workshops. The extension of the ‹LIOF-› variant northwards, from London, ostensibly apparent from several mint-signatures of the southern Danelaw, is dependent on dies made in and supplied from the London area. It would appear, however, that in Cnut's first type workshops in Chichester, Lewes and Winchester also produced a few dies with this variant, suggesting that as far west as Winchester **Liof** represented an acceptable spelling of this element.

The incidence of Winchester as well as London means that unfortunately it is not possible to use this particular criterion to solve the problem of the location of 'national' centres in the later more centralised issues.

These conclusions may further suggest that numismatic causes should be sought to explain other apparent discrepancies between the evidence of the coin legends on the one hand, and orthodox dialect-boundaries on the other.

NOTE

1. I wish to acknowledge the help of Stewart Lyon with whom I discussed some ideas on this subject at an early stage, and who on reading a draft of this paper was able to confirm some of my suggestions from his comprehensive collection of photographs from the Royal Coin Cabinet, Stockholm. References to Lyon without formal citation therefore indicate private correspondence.

REFERENCES

BEH: See Hildebrand

Blackburn, Mark and Stewart Lyon 1986. Regional die-production in Cnut's Quatrefoil issue. In M.A.S Blackburn (ed.) *Anglo-Saxon monetary history. Essays in memory of Michael Dolley*. 223-72. Leicester: University of Leicester Press.

Campbell, A. 1959. Old English Grammar. Oxford: Clarendon Press.

Colman, Fran, 1981. 'The name-element Æthel- and related problems'. *Notes and Queries* 28 no. 4. 295-301.

Colman, Fran 1984. Anglo-Saxon pennies and Old English phonology. *Folia Linguistica Historica* 5. 91-143.

Cop 1964, 1966, 1970, 1972: see Galster

Dolley, R.H.M 1958. Some reflections on Hildebrand type A of Æthelred II'. *Antikvarist Arkiv* 9.

Dolley, R.H.M and Tuuka Talvio. 1977. The regional pattern of die-cutting exhibited in the *First Hand* pennies of Æthelred II preserved in the British Museum. *British Numismatic Journal* 47. 53-65.

Ekwall, Eilert. 1947. *Early London Personal Names* = Skrifter Kungl. Humanistika Vetenskapssamfundet i Lund 43.

Galster, G. ed. *Sylloge of Coins of the British Isles. Nationalmuseum, Copenhagen.* Volumes 4, 7, 13-15, 18. London: Oxford University Press and Spink and Son.

Hilderbrand, Bror Emil. 1881. *Anglosachsiska Mynt funna i Sverige jord, ny tillökt upplaga 1881*. Stockholm

van der Meer, G. 1961. Some correction to and comments on B.E. Hildebrand's catalogue of Anglo-Saxon coins in the Swedish Royal Coin Cabinet. In R.H.M. Dolley (ed.) *Anglo-Saxon Coins.* 169-87. London: Methuen.

Mossop, H.R. 1970. *The Lincoln Mint.* Newcastle: Corbett and Hunter.

Smart, Veronica 1983. Variations between Æthel- and Ægel- as a name-element on coins. *Nomina* 7. 91-4.

9

ELLIPTICAL AND IMPERSONAL CONSTRUCTIONS: EVIDENCE FOR AUXILIARIES IN OLD ENGLISH?*

Anthony R Warner

1 Introduction

What kind of grammatical status did the ancestors of our modern auxiliaries have in Old English? On one view 'pre-modals' (and presumably other 'pre-auxiliaries' too) were simply verbs, cf. Allen (1975), Lightfoot (1979). But there is some evidence to suggest that they were already beginning to develop distinctive properties in Old English, cf. Plank (1984), Goossens (1987) among others. At ICEHL 5 I claimed that some of these verbs showed a grouping of characteristic properties in Old English, further suggesting that their pattern of distribution in elliptical and impersonal constructions might provide 'potentially important evidence' for a syntactically distinct classification (Warner, 1990: 547-8). Here I want firstly to examine the data which underlay this claim in an attempt to characterize these two distributional properties, secondly to try to interpret and assess it as evidence for a formal distinction, thirdly to make some comments about the nature of this distinction and note some more general implications. This will involve me in a series of arguments from Old English data to the reconstruction of Old English syntax which I will try to make explicit in line with the theme of this volume.

The argument of this chapter will be based on the following general theoretical position. I shall assume firstly that a word class approach will be appropriate and illuminating, and I shall not assume that syntax necessarily prescribes a special configuration for auxiliaries distinct from that introducing verbs. The arguments for a node AUX directly dominated by S for Present-day English seem unconvincing (cf. especially the critiques of Pullum and Wilson 1977 and Gazdar *et al.* 1982), those for INFL are theory particular and of uncertain relevance. Moreover, even within such analyses, the notion 'word class' is clearly important. Secondly, I shall make a series of interlinked assumptions about the word class structure of a language (including its subclasses). I take this to be established by correlations of properties, so that the group of properties typical of one class stands in opposition to the group typical of another. A class need not be homogeneous or indeed show sharply definable boundaries, but normally has a 'nuclear' or 'prototypical' set of members alongside other less fully characterized members (and items of less firmly assignable status). Formal properties, which in practice are largely syntactic and morphological, are of particular importance for word class structure. At a cross-linguistic level, however, the identity of a class is semantically based. Here it depends on the notional characterization of its prototypical membership, perhaps also on the set of grammatical properties associated with it. To exemplify, at this level the noun is the class whose prototypical members denote continuing entities and which may be associated with categories of number, definiteness and inherent gender. This is essentially the position of Lyons (1966) or Huddleston (1984); cf. also Anderson (in press b).

Like any broad framework this leaves us with most of the questions to answer, and allows for substantial disagreement between analysts. At our present level of understanding it tolerates the difference between those who interpret the modern auxiliaries as a distinguished subcategory of verbs, and those who see them as more radically opposed to the class of verbs, or even as not constituting a notionally coherent class (Huddleston 1984) or a class at all (Emonds 1985). But it clarifies the questions we can put to our Old English data to illuminate the status of a potential group of auxiliaries (or of modals) within such a framework. If we take as uncontroversial the assumption that in Old English the items concerned do indeed belong to a more general class including verbs, we can ask :

(i) Do these words have formal properties which distinguish them from other verbs?

(ii) If so, do such formal properties typically co-occur with each other, or with other properties which are uncommon in the general class of verbs, so that there is a measure of predictability between properties which might characterize a distinct group?

(iii) If (i) and (ii) are given positive answers, then, is there an appropriate notional characterization of nuclear members or of the associated grammatical properties which might enable us to identify the group cross-linguistically?

In this chapter I will put these questions to a potential group of auxiliary (and modal) verbs in Old English in respect of their occurrence in elliptical and impersonal constructions, because these constructions look *prima facie* candidates for evidence of formally distinct properties. The verbs which will turn out to be involved in some way are (to generalize) Mitchell's ' "modal" auxiliaries' (without *agan* , but with the addition of *uton*), *beon/wesan*, *weorðan*, pro-verbal *don*, and *onginnan* (cf. Brinton 1988). Note that many of the verbs here are ancestors of the modern auxiliaries as defined by the 'NICE' properties (for which see e.g. Palmer 1987: 14ff.): The conclusion I will be led to as most plausible for Old English is that there was already a formal subcategorial distinction within the class of verbs, and that (given an important caveat about the force of the term) the grouping was probably worth the notional label 'auxiliary'. (This is far from the claim that auxiliaries were a 'word class' in Old English, or that they were in a full sense of the word notional 'auxiliaries'. Either claim would be too brutal a simplification). Thus I attempt here to clarify some of the formal arguments for the position I put forward in Warner (1990: 547), that Old English already had a 'grouping of "less verbal" verbs' or uses of verbs and that 'it may even be necessary to recognize a category "auxiliary" with some strictly syntactic properties'. That paper was essentially concerned with historical developments and with the semantics of the central members of the Old English 'modal' group. Here I amplify, and make more precise, the major syntactic considerations involved.

In this chapter the three questions posed above are taken in due order. To start with, the possibility of distinctive formal properties is considered, first in elliptical constructions (in §2), then in construction with impersonals (in §3).[1] In §4 there follows a discussion of the possibility of a distinctive correlation of properties (question (ii) above) and of a notional basis for the grouping which emerges (question (iii)). Some final reflections follow in §5.

2 Elliptical Constructions

2.1 In today's English elliptical constructions like those given below provide one of the standard criteria for auxiliary status. Since it is a preceding auxiliary and not a missing verb phrase which characterizes this construction, it is better to avoid the common term 'Verb Phrase Deletion' and call it 'post-auxiliary ellipsis' (Warner 1985: 55). Instances of this construction require a linguistic antecedent (using 'antecedent' in the familiar recent sense which subsumes cataphoric as well as anaphoric reference) in the discourse, and may occur in a range of structures. Infinitive *to* may also precede an ellipsis site, and I here accept the position argued in Pullum (1982) that this *to* is itself an auxiliary, so that examples like (1.f) show post-auxiliary ellipsis after *to*.

(1. a) - Will Paul bring Mary?
  - Well, Tom says he thinks he won't.
  b) - Paul will bring Mary because he should.
  c) Is Paul bringing Mary?
  - If he isn't, I'll tell him he should.
  d) - Is Paul bringing Mary?
  - If he doesn't, I'll tell him he should.
  e) Paul and Mary are very happy. At least, I think they are.
  f) - Will Paul bring Mary?
  - Well, Tom says he wants to.

There is also another construction in which an auxiliary precedes a partial ellipsis. Here some of the complementation of the missing head is retained.

(2. a) Probably drives him crazy to have her call him all the time. It would me.
  b) If you don't believe me, you will the weatherman!
  c) John will eat the bananas, even if he won't the apples.
  d) - I just hope it will make you happy.
  - Hasn't it you?
  e) I processed everyone's [cheque], but I must not've yours.
  f) Mary gave money to the orphanage partly because she hadn't to the church.
  g) I'm going to call him back on Monday, as I am several other people.
  h) - That carpet reminds me of the kind of thing you see in waiting rooms.
  - It doesn't me.

This construction is discussed by Levin (1978, 1980) who calls it 'pseudogapping'. The examples of (2) are attested utterances cited from Levin (1980: 76-77) except for (c) and (f). But despite an overt similarity to gapping structures like (3.a), pseudogapping looks more like post-auxiliary ellipsis than it does like gapping. Indeed, where an auxiliary precedes a gap but is followed by adverbial modification, the difference between these structures can be neutralized. Both ellipses share the auxiliary context (which is *do* in default of another form), and the freedom to occur within a range of structures as illustrated above. Gapped constructions, by contrast, lack their highest auxiliary, and are virtually restricted to coordinate structures in Present-day English, cf. (3) and Quirk *et al.* (1985: §13.92).[2]

(3. a)   Paul will drink tea, and his wife, coffee.
    b)   *If Paul will drink tea, (then) his wife, coffee.
    c)   *Paul will drink tea, partly because his wife, coffee.

Granted the substantial overlap between post-auxiliary ellipsis and pseudogapping, it seems clear that these two constructions should be generalized as different aspects of essentially the same phenomenon. This conclusion is reinforced by the occurrence of parallel constructions with pro-verbal (or 'substitute') *do* in British English. It may 'stand for' an entire preceding verb phrase, in parallel to post-auxiliary ellipsis, or it may take (in whole or in part) the construction of another verb which is its antecedent, in parallel to pseudogapping, cf. (4). It seems to be the non-auxiliary verb which has these otherwise auxiliary properties. But the point is that they go together and that this implies that there is a generalization across these constructions. So in Present-day English we have two constructions which are at some level essentially identical, and which together characterize the set of auxiliaries and pro-verbal *do* (but cf. note 2 for *to*). The occurrence of *do* here raises in an acute form the question whether these constructions with *do* and with auxiliaries should be analysed as fundamentally elliptical or as containing a verb proform (or 'substitute' verb), as suggested (for example) by Napoli (1985). I want to remain neutral with respect to this question. Both here and below in discussing Old English I will for convenience continue to use the term 'ellipsis' without prejudice to this point of analysis.

(4. a)   I rely on friends, just as you have always done.
    b)   I would like to rely on friends, and I wish I could do.
    c)   I rely on my friends, as you can surely do on yours.
    d)   Probably drives him crazy to have her call him up all the time. It would do me.

Now, in brief, it looks as if there is a very similar situation in Old English (and Middle English). It must therefore seem at least possible that the availability of elliptical constructions, and more especially the occurrence of pseudogapping, gives us a criterion to isolate and perhaps to characterize 'auxiliaries'.

2.2   Arguing for ellipsis in Old English.
Old English (and Middle English) contain a construction apparently parallel to

today's post-auxiliary ellipsis in which the infinitive complement of a verb is absent, but may be retrieved from linguistic context. Apparent ellipses after *beon/wesan* are also found. Here are some examples.³

(5. a) forðy is betere þæt feoh þætte næfre losian ne mæg ðonne þætte mæg 7 sceal.
'therefore better is the property which can never perish [lit: never perish not can] than that which can and will.'
Bo. 11.25.24.

b) Wenst ðu þæt se godcunda anweald ne mihte afyrran þone anweald þam unrihtwisan kasere,...gif he wolde? Gise, la, gese; ic wat þæt he mihte, gif he wolde.
'Thinkest thou that the heavenly Power could not (lit: not could) take-away the empire (from) that unrighteous Caesar,...if he would? Yes, O yes, I know that he could, if he would!'
Fox's translation (corrected)
Bo 16.39.30

c) 7 cwædon þæt hie þa burg werian wolden, gif þa wæpnedmen ne dorsten.
'and said that they (= the women) would defend the city [lit: the city defend would (subj.)], if the men (did) not dare.'
Or 194.12

d) hi...gearowe wæron ehtnysse to ðoligenne. and deaðe sweltan gif hi ðorfton
'they...were prepared to undergo persecution and to suffer death [lit: ready were persecution to suffer and death (dat.) die] if they needed.'
Ælfric, Catholic Homilies second series (ed. Godden 1979, EETS SS5) 78.212

e) wa þam, þe godcunde heorde underfehð and naþær gehealdan ne can ne hine syfne ne þa heorde, þe he healdan scolde to godes handa; and wyrst þam, þe can and nele.
'woe to-him who undertakes spiritual custody [lit: spiritual custody undertakes] and knows how to preserve [lit: neither to-preserve not knows] neither him self nor the flock which he ought to guard on God's behalf [lit: to God's hand] and worst to him, who knows (how to) and will-not.'
Wulfstan, Homilien (ed. A. Napier 1883) 276.14

f) deofol us wile ofslean gif he mot.
'(the) devil will kill us if he can...' ÆCHom i. 270.10

(6a.) *est*? is hit swa? *est* hit is; *non*? nis hit swa? *non* hit nis.
'*est*? is it so? *est* it is; *non*? isn't it so? *non* it isn't.'
Ælfric, Grammar (ed. Zupitza 1880) 227.8

b) and gehwa wende þæt he þæs cyldes fæder wære. ac he næs
'and everyone thought that he was [= *wære*] that child's father, but he wasn't;...'
ÆCHom i.196.12

c) Ys þæs of þinum geferum? Gea, he ys.
'Is this (one) of your companions?' – 'Yes, he is.'
Est iste ex tuis sociis? Etiam est.
Ælfric, Colloquy (ed. G. Garmonsway 1947) 49

d) Wære þu todæg beswuncgen ? Ic næs
'Were you beaten today ?' – 'I wasn't ...'
Fuisti hodie uerberatus ? Non fui,...
Ælfric, Colloquy (ed. G. Garmonsway 1947) 280

e) *amabar* ic wæs gelufod, *amabaris* ðu wære, *amabatur* he wæs
'*amabar* I was loved, *amabaris* you (sg.) were, *amabatur* he was; ...'
Ælfric, Grammar (ed. Zupitza 1880) 140.2

I will argue that at least in some cases such examples involve distinct elliptical (or pro-verbal) constructions in Old English which I will call 'post-verbal ellipsis'. Here it is necessary to distinguish cases where a verb of motion or 'be' is to be supplied in translation as part of the meaning of the verb together with its construction. There is no need to suppose any syntactic ellipsis in such instances, which can be accounted for in terms of the semantics of the combination verb + adverbial/prepositional phrase or predicate (see Mitchell 1985: §1007 for the first of these). We must also distinguish cases where an apparent gap may be related to some specific aspect of the construction, as, for example, in some instances of coordination or comparative clauses.[4] Given these distinctions we may go on to ask whether the apparent ellipses of (5) and (6) involve special constructions, or whether these might simply show intransitive uses of the verb in question (cf. Mitchell 1985: §§ 1000 ff.) Consider the modern sentences below. These might seem at first sight to be elliptical, in that the sense of *eating* or *to climb the wall* is to be supplied in the second conjunct.

(7. a) Paul is eating, but Tom hasn't started.
b) Tom climbed the wall, but Paul didn't even try.

But these are unlike cases of post-auxiliary ellipsis in that *start* and *try* are not restricted to contexts with a linguistic antecedent. Both may occur without a complement where the sense is obvious from the nonlinguistic situation, as in (8).

Notice that *start to* and *try to*, which would involve post-auxiliary ellipsis after *to*, are not possible without a linguistic antecedent.

(8. a) You may start (*start to).
   (Spoken instruction at beginning of an examination)

   b) I don't see why you even try (*try to).
   (Lecturer commenting to student on fail-grade essay)

So we must distinguish cases of ellipsis which require a linguistic antecedent from examples where the sense can be made more complete by information derived from the general situation. This may indeed involve reference to a piece of preceding text, but it may equally be nonlinguistic in origin. *Start* and *try* fall into this second broad category.[5]

There are several verbs which seem from BT(S) and OED to lack a more general intransitive or absolute use of appropriate sense of which apparently elliptical uses might be taken as a special case. *Dearr, mot* and *sceal* in particular occur here, as does *beon/wesan*. These seem (in the relevant senses) to occur either with a complement, or without one in a context of apparent ellipsis where there is a potential linguistic 'antecedent'.[6] So there are apparently 'grammatically "defective", constructions which exhibit a 'structural "gap" ', in the terminology of Quirk *et al.* (1985: §12.34).[7] We may contrast *cann* and *mæg* which do have relevant intransitive or absolute uses, so that apparently parallel examples need not involve ellipsis, (though there may be semantic reasons for supposing that ellipsis is involved).

There are also instances which seem to parallel the modern 'pseudogapping'. Here the verb occurs with some or all of the complements of the infinitive which is to be contextually supplied, see (9). There is also a more doubtful example involving a participle after *beon/wesan*, see (10).[8]

(9. a) We magon monnum bemiðan urne geðonc 7 urne willan,
   ac we ne magon Gode.
   'We can hide from men [lit: from-men hide] our thoughts and our desires,
   but we cannot [lit: not can] from-God.'
   CP 39.12

   b) se ðe wille godcundne wisdom secan ne mæg he hine wiþ ofermetta.
   'he who will seek heavenly wisdom [lit: heavenly wisdom seek] may not
   [lit: not may he] (seek) it with arrogance...'
   Bo 12.26.22

   c) Be ðæm is awriten ðæt Dryhten besawe to Abele 7 to his lacum,
   7 nolde to Caine ne to his lacum.
   'Concerning this (it) is written that (the) Lord had-regard for Abel
   and for his gifts, and would-not for Cain nor for his gifts.'
   CP 234.5

d) þu wilnodest to us þæs godes ðe ðu to him sceoldes.
'you desired from us the good that you should (have desired) from him.'
Bo 7.19.13

(10) ac hit nis nanum anum men getiohhod, ac is eallum monnum.
'But it is offered to no one man [lit: no one man (dat.) offered],
but (it) is to all men.'
Fox's translation.
Bo 37.112.27

The sentences of (9) are clearly in some sense 'elliptical', for the constructional peculiarity of pseudogapping depends on the properties of an item which is not there. Thus the dative *Gode* in (9.a) has the case of a complement of *bemiðan*, not *magon*, though *bemiðan* is not present in the final conjunct. Moreover, all the examples I know of have a linguistic antecedent. So it seems reasonable to conclude that distinct elliptical constructions are probably represented in these sentences in Old English. They apparently exhibit a structural 'gap', and the missing material is recovered from the neighbouring text and not from the wider context of situation. These are two of the five criteria for elliptical constructions given by Quirk *et al.* (1985: §§12.32ff.)[9].

2.3 The distribution of these constructions in Old English

Referring back to the first question above, I have argued that Old English had two construction types, post-verbal ellipsis and pseudogapping. We must now ask what their distribution was.

A. Wülfing gives instances of pseudogapping for Alfredian Old English with *mæg*, *sceal*, and *wile*, and both he and Antipova supply apparent examples of post-verbal ellipsis for these three verbs and for *dearr*, *mot*, and *þearf* (Wülfing 1894-: 1901: §§389-97, Antipova 1963) ('apparent' because the possibility of an intransitive construction without real ellipsis cannot be ruled out for all items as noted above). Apparent post-verbal ellipsis is found elsewhere with *cann* (cf. (5.e) above.'[10] To these verbs we may add *uton* 'let's'. A search through the Venezky and Healey concordance (1980) yielded a few clear instances of pseudogapping, but only the example cited below as (11.b), and a couple of glosses where a Latin subjunctive has been rendered merely by *uton*, to provide relatively weak or indirect evidence for post-verbal ellipsis.

(11. a) He us gegearwað galnesse; uton we ongean clænnesse.
'He prepares wantonness for us; let us in-return purity'
HomS 34 (PetersonVercHom 19) 86

b) He winnð mid ofermodnesse; uton we ongean mid eaðmodnesse.
'He fights using [lit: with] pride: let us in-return using [lit: with] humility.'
HomS 34 (PetersonVercHom 19) 85

c) caraxemus (glossed) utan
    'Let us write' 'let's
    AldV 7.3 (Meritt) 179
    There is no form of *caraxare* in the preceding context.

B. *Beon/wesan* occur with ellipsis of a range of predicates (as exemplified in (6), possibly also with partial ellipsis as in (10)). Since the construction is clearly elliptical and depends on linguistic context, and since the range of predicates includes verbal predicates, it seems plain that this is at least closely related to post-verbal ellipsis with the verbs of A. I do not, however, know of examples with *weorðan*, and neither Antipova's survey (1963) nor Brown's (1970) explicit report of *Cura Pastoralis* give any.[11]

C. I do not know of examples with 'perfect' *habban* until Middle English.[12] Examples of 'possessive' *have* with a contextually supplied object occur in Old English, but there is a more general possibility of object-ellipsis, so that this is not necessarily to be classified with the other 'auxiliary' instances (Mitchell 1985: §1570ff. and refs., Visser 1963-1973: §§612ff.). *Onginnan* and *aginnan* 'begin', which behave like auxiliaries in impersonal constructions, both have an intransitive sense 'undertake an action, proceed to an action' which occurs in potential ellipsis contexts and elsewhere, so that no distinct construction need be involved in potential ellipsis contexts. In neither case have I noted examples with pseudogapping which might support the case for ellipsis. But I have not searched systematically in Venezky and Healey (1980).

D. A parallel construction is also found from Old English with pro-verbal *don*. This may 'stand for' a verb phrase which is retrieved from linguistic context, as today. *Don* may also occur with the complements of its verbal antecedent, so that the pseudogapping construction is paralleled. This strongly suggests that these constructions with *don* are to be identified at some level with those given above in (5) and (9), so that we should add *don* to our list of verbs for OE. But 'supportive' *don* is not found in recorded Old English (van Ostade's (1988) recent defence is not convincing), so that 'empty' *don* does not precede an infinitival verb phrase. So a straightforward ellipsis is not involved here, and an account involving proforms may have to be given for *don* and perhaps also for the other verbs cf. A and B above.[13]

(12. a) Eower lareow, ne gylt he gafol? Þa cwæð he: Gyse, he deð.
    'Your master, doesn't he pay tribute [lit: not pays he tribute] ?
    Then he said: Yes, he does.'
    Magister vester non solvit didrachma? Ait: Etiam
    Matt (WS) 17.24.

b) ne cepð nan hungrig man næfre his gereordes na swyðor, þonne þa sceoccan doð þære sawle.
    'No hungry man ever desires his food more strongly [lit: not desires no hungry man never his food (gen.) not more-strongly], than the devils do the soul (gen.)'
    Wulfstan, Homilien (ed. A. Napier 1883) 249.1

c) gif þe licode his dysig 7 his unrihtwisnes swa wel swa his dysegum deorlingum dyde.
'if his folly and his injustice had pleased thee [lit: if thee (dat.) pleased his folly and his injustice] as well as it did his foolish favourites [lit: as well as his foolish favourites (dat.) did].'
Fox's translation.
Bo 27.62.12

d) Hwi nolde god him forgyldan his bearn be twyfealdum. swa swa he dyde his æhta?
'Why would-not God compensate him (for) his children twice over, just as he did (for) his possessions?'
Ælfric, Catholic Homilies second series (ed. Godden 1979, EETS SS5) 267.210.

2.4 Characterizing the distribution of these constructions

It is striking that the verbs of A and B above are selected from those that investigators have typically classified as auxiliaries, and which might well be seen as a potential auxiliary group. From this perspective it is worth remarking the presence of *uton*, 'let's', which is qualified to belong in such a group both by sense and by morphology, since it is clearly to be interpreted synchronically as a preterite-present (cf. Mitchell 1985: §916a for its status as a verb). The apparent absence of *weorðan* and 'perfect' *habban* and the presence of pro-verbal *don* (classified as an auxiliary by Wülfing 1894-1901) are also noteworthy. It is also worth remarking that these ellipses are not restricted to reduced 'auxiliary' senses of Mitchell's (1985) '"modal" auxiliaries' and that post-verbal ellipsis is not restricted to 'periphrastic' constructions with *beon/wesan* (cf. (5.c), (5.e), (6. a-c), (9.c) above and other examples given by Wülfing 1894-1901 and Antipova 1963).

But given that examples of these types of ellipsis are found with verbs which could be interpreted as a potential auxiliary group, is such ellipsis restricted to this group? We await detailed descriptions and analyses of ellipsis in Old English, as of the possibilities for co-ordination and exbraciation which are very relevant to such accounts. Clearly, one interim view might be as follows. The post-verbal ellipsis of an infinitive was relatively widely available in Old English. And the gapping of verbs seems to have been less restricted than today since there is evidence of occurrence in subordinate as well as co-ordinate structures, see (13), so that one of the arguments for distinguishing gapping and pseudogapping in Present-day English does not hold for Old English.[14] Thus examples resembling the modern post-auxiliary ellipsis and pseudogapping might be accounted for under these generalizations, and the apparently restricted distribution of these constructions ('only after members of a potential auxiliary group') might be attributed to the greater frequency of these verbs and (perhaps) their saliency to investigators, and the willingness of investigators to observe and classify in terms of notional or anachronistic groupings.

(13. a)   Forðæm þa goodan næfre ne beoð bedælde þara edleana hiora goodes, ne ða yflan næfre þara wita ðe hi geearnigað.
'For the good are never destitute (of) the rewards (of) their good, nor the wicked ever (of) the punishments which they deserve.'
Fox's translation.
Bo 37.112.16

b)   for þæm he riht 7 ræt eallum gesceaftum, swa swa good stiora anum scipe.
'for he directs and rules all creatures as a good pilot (steers) a ship.'
Fox's translation.
Bo 35.97.10

c)   Diligamus deum quia ipse prior dilexit nos. Ðet is luuian we ure drihten. for þon he luuede us er we hine.
'that is, Let us love our Lord, for he loved us before we (loved) him.'
Morris's translation. Old English Homilies vol i 123.34
(ed. Morris 1867, 1868; EETS 29, 34).

But this view raises a question over the systematic status of apparent ellipsis of a subordinate verb and its complements after verbs in Old English. Real ellipsis may, indeed, be less general than might at first appear, given the distinctions drawn above for Present-day English. It is clear that throughout English other expressions (nouns, adjectives and participles as well as verbs) have been able to occur in contexts where the sense of a verbal complement is to be supplied. But some of the expressions concerned have absolute or intransitive uses, which may imply that this sense need not be retrieved from linguistic context. So, for example, beside (14.a) with retrieval from preceding text, we find the absolute instances of (14.b). The implication is that the pragmatic principles which supply the meaning required in the second case may also cope with the former, and that no linguistically supplied ellipsis need be involved.

(14. a)   Clypa, ne ablin ðu, ac ahefe up þine stefne swa beme
'Cry-out, do not cease [lit: not cease thou] but raise up your voice like (a) trumpet...'
HomS 13 (Ass 11) 9

b)   Þa cwæþ he to Petre, 'To hwan ablinnest þu, Petrus?'
'Then said he to Peter, "Why ceasest thou, Peter? "...'
Morris's translation.
BlHom 189.2

Peter has previously been told to pray to God for help against the sorcerer. This is apparently the sense which is to be supplied here. But it is mentioned nineteen lines (and several events) earlier in the text, so direct linguistic retrieval seems unlikely to be in question.

Or take the case of *lætan*. BT (*lætan*) says 'The ellipsis of a verb in the infinitive, the meaning of which may be inferred from the context, not unfrequently takes place after *lætan*...'. But in at least the great majority of relevant citations the required sense is one of (abstract) position, motion or possession, and there is an object or predicate: these seem to be better interpreted straightforwardly in terms of the semantics of the combination of *lætan* with its complements rather than as elliptical uses (cf. the parallel suggestion for verbs of group A in § 2.2 above).

Moreover, if there are expressions without relevant absolute uses, this need only mean that the situation was akin to that in Present-day English. Today some expressions which are not auxiliaries may have the sense of a VP complement supplied from the linguistic context, though it cannot be retrieved from non-linguistic context, e.g. *able* as in *I will come if I am able*, or *want* in *You may go if you want*. (For other instances see Jespersen 1909-1949: V.20.5 on the 'latent infinitive', Quirk *et al.* 1985§ 12.65.) Thus post-auxiliary ellipsis is distinctive today because of its regularity with auxiliaries, and its relationship to pseudogapping, not because similar ellipses are absent elsewhere.

There is, however, an alternative view, in which the elliptical constructions exemplified above are interrelated, and their occurrence is a distinctive grammatical property of specific lexemes: a potential auxiliary group, including *don*. This is equally an interim view, but several considerations hold in its favour.

(i) It is consistent with the data for the combination of post-verbal ellipsis and pseudogapping in so far as it is reported in the major relevant sources. Antipova surveys a substantial range of texts (434 printed pages) and concludes that 'The composition of the group of substitute-verbs in OE does not differ much from that in Modern English' (1963: 136). Brown (1970) is explicit about the restriction of such constructions in *Cura Pastoralis*. And there is nothing to contradict this in the sections on ellipsis in Mitchell (1985), Visser (1963-1973) and Wülfing (1894-1901).[15] Here the apparently restricted distribution of pseudogapping is particularly important.

(ii) The fact that *don* occurs with these constructions, and does not appear in their non-elliptical congeners has two important implications. First, it supports the generalization of pseudogapping with post-verbal ellipsis, as does the overlap between the range of verbs with which pseudogapping is reported and those found with apparent post-verbal ellipsis. Second, it implies that it is the introducing verb which should be characterized as permitting these constructions. In the case of *don* this follows because it is clear that no general process of ellipsis can be involved, but that it is rather the presence of *don* itself which licenses the construction.[16] For the other verbs it follows because it is difficult to avoid the conclusion that the constructions found with *don* and with the verbs of A above are to be identified at some level in Old English, and it is hard to resist the generalization to *beon/wesan*. But even without going this far, it at least provides the parallel which makes lexical dependence a real possibility. And on the assumption that post-verbal ellipsis and pseudogapping are restricted as suggested, it is difficult to see how this could be appropriately stated otherwise. Note that the context of ellipsis cannot be given in semantic terms, since the range of senses involved in the examples cited above shows no sign of restriction (for example to prototypically 'modal' senses in the verbs of A). Nor can pseudogapping be stated as a purely semantic property, since both the semantic and rectional characteristics of the elliptical verb are involved. And any unrestricted syntactic statement will overgeneralize.[17] It is clear then that what is involved is well interpreted as a grammatical property of a lexeme.

(iii) The existence of a parallel situation in Present-day English, where there are two interrelated constructions involving the ellipsis of all or part of a verbal complement, and where the occurrence of these constructions is licensed by (and therefore a property of) the introducing verb, shows that linguistic theory must permit this particular constellation of properties. Other things being equal, this account of Old English is therefore a linguistically natural one.

(iv) The fact that there is continuity of these two construction types with *do* and a group of potential auxiliary verbs throughout English (Middle English apparently adding *ouen* and 'perfect' *hauen* among others) is consistent with the account offered above. Continuity of phenomena does not, of course, imply continuity of analysis. There is not here, then, a point in support so much as the absence of the point against which a (major) discontinuity would have implied.

(v) An account of these constructions as a property of their introducing verb is restrictive and empirical. It gives us a narrower and more interesting characterization. As a hypothesis it is 'dangerous' (therefore interesting) in that it makes clear predictions. In particular, pseudogapping should not be distributed independently of post-verbal ellipsis, and if it is characteristic of an auxiliary group it should not be found with other verbs. It is therefore easy to see what would constitute a refutation of the hypothesis, so that it is an empirical one and is worthy of adopting as verisimilitudinous in the Popperian sense.

The methodology which underpins this second account is merely that of general linguistics adapted to serve a topic in Old English with its partially recorded and partially investigated data. We interpret partially established distributional facts in the light of universal grammar (here in the guise of a parallel with Present-day English) and history (though support here is weak) to arrive at a plausible hypothesis. This is supported in so far as it is empirical (both in the sense of fitting a sufficient range of data and in the more theoretical sense of stating clearly what would refute it), and it is to be evaluated against other contenders. The greater reliance on 'external' considerations here is risky but necessary for the resurrection of a dead language.

Given these considerations it seems to me that the second account clearly wins on points. There is no knock-out; it is verisimilitudinous rather than true. Without a more detailed account of ellipsis and coordination (underpinned by a better general understanding of these construction types than general linguistics gives us at the moment) it is at best plausible, an interim hypothesis which is preferable to another. Its status must not be forgotten, though statements of any abstractness about the grammar of Old English will surely always be preferred hypotheses. Strictly, then, what we can say at the moment (from the major sources surveyed) is that the view that some Old English verbs (a potential auxiliary group, including pro-verbal *don*) shared a formal property distinguishing them from other verbs is a plausible one. This obviously leads on to questions about the status of these items. But this discussion will be postponed until the possibility of a further formal property shown in impersonal constructions has been examined.

3 Transparency to Impersonal Constructions

3.1 In Old (and Middle) English there occur impersonal constructions which have oblique arguments, but which lack a nominative subject. The verb if finite is third person singular.

(15. a) and hi wæron ða nacode, and him ðæs sceamode.
'and they were then naked, and they were ashamed of that [lit: them (dat.) of-that (gen.) shamed].'
ÆCHom i.18.11

b) gif us ne lyst ðæra ærrena yfela ðe we ær worhton
'if we do not desire [lit: us (acc./dat.) not pleases (3 sg.)] the former evils (gen.) we did [lit: that we previously did]...'
Sweet's translation.
CP 445.29.

A striking characteristic of some of Mitchell's "modal" auxiliaries' and *beon/wesan* together with a couple of other verbs at these periods is that they occur within such constructions, so that they too lack a nominative subject by virtue of their colligation with the non-finite impersonal verb. Thus the impersonal retains its rectional characteristics despite occurring in construction with another verb, and this other verb is apparently in some sense independent of or transparent to the construction with which it co-occurs.

(16. a) þonne mæg heora wiðerwinnan sceamian, þonne hi hi geseoð mid sigores wuldre to heofonum astigan.
'then may (sg.) their enemies (acc. pl.) shame, when they see them [lit: them see] rise up to heaven with the glory of victory [lit: with victory's glory to heavens rise].'
Wulfstan, Homilien (ed. A. Napier 1883) 199.12

b) hine sceal on domes dæg gesceamian beforan gode
'he [lit: him (acc.)] shall at Doomsday be-ashamed before God...'
Wulfstan, Homilien (ed. A. Napier 1883) 238.12

c) Forþon ne þearf þæs nanne man tweogean, þæt seo forlætene cyrice ne hycgge ymb þa þe on hire neawiste lifgeaþ.
'Because no man need have any doubt of this [lit: because not need of-it no man (acc.). doubt], that the forsaken church (will) not take-care for those that live in her neighbourhood [lit: in her neighbourhood live],...'
Morris's translation.
BlHom 41.36

d) þonne ic wat þætte wile weoruldmen tweogan
'[if you now, Lord, are not willing to govern fate] then I know that human beings will doubt [lit: will (3 sg.) human-beings (acc.pl.) doubt] ...'
Meters of Boethius(ed. Krapp 1932, Anglo Saxon Poetic Records vol 5: 152 ff.) 4.51

Returning to the first question of my introductory section, ('Do these verbs have formal properties which distinguish them from other verbs?') we may ask:

(i.a) Should the occurrence of a verb in the 'transparent' position in this construction be accounted for by a formal property? Or, more specifically, how should we characterize the construction, and what does that characterization imply for the status of these verbs?

(i.b) What is the range of verbs found in the 'transparent' position within this construction, and, more particularly, does occurrence here distinguish a potential auxiliary group from other catenatives?

Here both the logic of the argument and the dictates of suspense require me to begin with the second question. In attempting to answer it I draw on a corpus of instances collected from entries for the major impersonal verbs in BT(S); from Elmer (1981), Mitchell (1985), van der Gaaf (1904), Visser (1963-1973); and from a search through the Old English microfiche concordance (Venezky and Healey 1980) under the infinitives of the major impersonal verbs (sometimes also their participles).[18]

3.2 The range of verbs transparent to impersonal constructions

Not all instances of a potential 'auxiliary' plus 'impersonal' verb give equally convincing evidence of the type of transparency which is in question here. Examples like (16.a-c) above, where the only arguments are clearly oblique, are centrally relevant. But 'impersonal' verbs may appear in neutralized constructions, and some also have personal uses. When one of the arguments is a following clause or infinitive, or is a noun phrase whose case is not distinctively oblique, the distinction between personal and impersonal rection may be neutralized. In such instances, the 'impersonal' verb has a potential overt subject, though the parallels available for a particular verb may lead us to prefer an 'impersonal' interpretation of the construction (as, for example, they do for Old English *tweogan, tweonian* 'doubt' in (16.d) where *þætte* might be seen as a candidate for subject).[19] The relevance of constructions with 'weather' *hit* (as in *hit rinþ* 'it is raining') is also not beyond doubt in earlier English. The problem for the present argument is that we cannot be confident that *hit* here is chosen for essentially syntactic reasons. If it alternated only with zero that might have seemed plausible. But days dawn, and hail and milk may rain in Old English. We cannot, then, rule out the possibility that *hit* was a referential pronoun of broad sense, as Bolinger (1973, 1977) has claimed for *it* in parallel constructions today. This would imply that *rinþ* 'rains', etc., selected a 'cognate subject', so that the restriction *rinþ* imposed on its subject, *hit*, was semantic rather than syntactic. The occurrence of an intervening verb in an impersonal construction would therefore reliably show only a semantic rather than a semantic and syntactic transparency as in the cases of (16) above. There is a similar difficulty for constructions where an 'expletive' subject *hit* 'stands for' a following clause or infinitive, since here one might envisage an analysis with a referential *hit* of very general sense (cf. Bolinger 1973: 1977) in apposition to the following element.

Analysts will differ in their assessment of the relevance of the categories just outlined to the question of the syntactic transparency of an intervening superordinate verb. In what follows I have concentrated in the first instance on the central impersonal constructions of (16), and my statements will be based on examples of this type unless otherwise indicated. But reference will sometimes be made to less central instances. Verbs found in the type of (16) are :

A. The following members of Mitchell's '"modal" auxiliaries': *mæg*, (*mot*), *sceal, þearf, wile* .

In my Old English data *mæg* and *sceal* are well attested, followed by *þearf*, see (16). There are a couple of instances with *wile*, see (16.d), but none with *mot*.[20] But both of these verbs also occur in related types of example, as here.

(17. a)   Me mæig...gif hit mot gewiderian, mederan settan
          'One can .. if it may be-fair-weather, plant madder, ...'
          Law Ger 12

     b)   oðþæt hit wolde dagian.
          'until it was-about to-dawn...'
          Ælfric, Lives of Saints vol I (ed. Skeat, EETS OS 76, 82) xxi. 123

I have not found examples with *cann, dearr* or *uton*. This could be due to the fact that the infinitive following *uton* 'let's' regularly represents an action as under the control of its subject, and this is at least predominantly true also of *cann* and *dearr*.[21] But this does not square with the type of semantics generally assumed for impersonal constructions (cf. e.g. McCawley 1976, Fischer and van der Leek 1985). Moreover, these three verbs presumably select their subjects (but cf. n.21), so they cannot be transparent to the semantics of the construction that they enter. I have also not found examples with Old English *agan* .

B. In Old English (and early Middle English) verbs which lack a direct (accusative) NP object but which have a non-predicative NP or PP complement form an impersonal passive with *beon/wesan* or with *weorðan*. This construction parallels the one discussed above in that it is the participle which dictates the absence of a nominative subject and the case or preposition associated with the construction's NP arguments. *Beon/wesan* or *weorðan* are transparent to these syntactic interrelationships. Two examples are given in (18) below. For others, see Visser (1963-1973: §§1933, 1959), Mitchell (1985: §§849 ff.). There are also colligations of *beon/wesan* and *weorðan* with the second participle of impersonal verbs which are at least open to interpretation as perfects as in (19), (cf. Denison 1990 a; Mitchell 1985 : §734).

(18. a) forlæt þine anwylnysse. þæt ðinum life beo geborgen.
'Forsake thy self-will, that thy life (dat.) may-be saved.'
Skeat's translation.
Ælfric, Lives of Saints vol I (ed. Skeat, EETS OS 76, 82) viii.114

   b) Swa wyrð eac gestiered ðæm gitsere ðæs reaflaces
'So also the avaricious man can be cured of extortion,...'
[lit: So becomes also restrained (to) the miser (of) the plundering].
Sweet's translation.
CP 341.11

(19. a) he...ongan...þus cweðan: 'wel is þe gelumpen, þu earma,...'
'he began to speak as follows: "It has turned out well for you [lit: well is you (dat.) happened], you miserable (being),..."
GDPref 3 (c) 4.185.7

   b) ac me todæg swa wundorlice is gelumpen.
'But to-day it has befallen me so wonderfully...'
[lit: me (dat.) today so wonderfully is befallen.]
Skeat's translation.
Ælfric, Lives of Saints vol I (ed. Skeat, EETS OS 76, 82) xxiii. 742.

C. Examples with *onginnan* are plentiful, and Denison (in press) notes an instance with *aginnan*. I have not noticed 'perfect' *hauen* until Middle English. Its relatively late appearance is not unexpected given that we would expect the perfects of impersonals to be formed initially with *beon/wesan* (as exemplified above) since they are distinct from the transitive prototype of the *have-* perfect, from which it traditionally spreads (cf. Mitchell 1985: §§724-733).

(20. a) þa ongan hine eft langian on his cyþþe
'Then he later began to long [lit: began him (acc.) later to-long] for his native-land,...'
BlHom 113.14

b) Hwæt, þe ongan lystan ure, nales us þin
'Indeed, you (acc./dat.) began to-desire us (gen.), not we (acc./dat.) you (gen.);...'
Bo 7.19.13

3.3 Characterizing the 'verb with impersonal' construction

3.3.1 For convenience I will call the verbs which 'intervene' in impersonal constructions 'I-verbs'. The group clearly overlaps substantially with those found with post-verbal ellipsis and pseudogapping, as with those we might think of as belonging to a potential auxiliary group for other reasons. But the topic of such correlations will follow. The questions for now are whether and how I-verbs are distinct from other 'catenatives' (or verbs taking a nonfinite complement).[22] It seems clear that there is no direct relationship of semantic selection between an I-verb and an NP to which oblique case has been assigned. In GB terms, the I-verb does not assign a θ-role to such NPs (or at least does not do so independently). Thus the I-verb seems to show a semantic as well as a syntactic transparency to the construction. Moreover, when they have a nominative subject, these verbs show evidence of semantic transparency in their occurrence with passives (cf. Warner 1990) and in the wide range of subjects they permit. This is a property found with Present-day 'subject-raising' verbs like *seem*, as with auxiliaries. We should, then, broaden the enquiry to distinguish in principle between three types of construction: the 'verb with impersonal' construction, a possible subject-raising construction, and catenative constructions with subject selection.

Now, given the finding that occurrence in the 'verb with impersonal' construction was restricted to a small number of verbs in my survey, a reasonable hypothesis would be that semantic transparency was a property of this construction, but that the majority of catenative verbs were 'Equi' verbs having a relationship of selection with their (nominative) subjects and therefore not able to occur in it.[23] This hypothesis seems rather plausible. It provides a good fit with the data. It is economical in ascribing to catenatives (like *gieman* 'care') properties which are probably required for an appropriate semantics. And it is consistent with what otherwise seems to be a valid generalization about the mapping relationship between syntax and semantics: that an NP to which a verb assigns case is a semantic argument of that verb, or the subject of one of its clausal arguments, but not also an argument of a superordinate verb. Moreover, the adoption of this hypothesis is defensible in the present context since it increases the work done by a semantic distinction and thereby reduces the importance of any formal distinctions required. So it is inimical to the assignment of a separate status to an auxiliary group. Since it is reasonably plausible, it should therefore be adopted in the course of any argument tending to show such a status. Thus it is reasonable to conclude that the distinction between the 'verb with impersonal' construction and catenative constructions with other verbs was probably a matter of semantics, whether or not a formal distinction was also involved.

Given this, can we distinguish between the grammar of the 'verb with impersonal' construction and 'subject-raising' type constructions for Old English? Or is the 'verb with impersonal' construction simply what results when a 'subject-raising' verb is married with an impersonal? Two kinds of approach to this question are useful: distributional and theoretical. As we shall see, neither gives good grounds for such a distinction.

3.3.2. The immediately relevant question about distribution here is whether the set of verbs which 'intervene' in 'verb with impersonal' and 'subject-raising' type constructions are the same or different. If the 'verb with impersonal' construction is essentially just impersonal + 'subject-raising' the two set of verbs should be the same. But if there is a further constructional difference, we might expect the sets of verbs not to be identical. There is, however, a problem in the low incidence of 'subject-raising' type constructions in Old English outside the verbs listed above. One clear potential group is that of aspectuals, and we might wonder whether *onginnan*, *aginnan* are alone in appearing in impersonal constructions with the infinitive. But the apparent lack of examples needs to be interpreted in the light of two facts. One is the generally low incidence of such catenatives, apart from *onginnan*, which is clear from Venezky and Healey (1980), or from Callaway (1913). Thus Callaway's survey of Old English infinitives lists over a thousand examples with *onginnan* and *aginnan*, but gives only some 85 for *beginnan*, 40 for *(ge)wunian*, and less than 50 altogether with all the other 'aspectualizers' Brinton lists for Old English (Brinton 1988: 110; Callaway 1913: 67-68, Appendix A.II). The other is the fact that some of these verbs are derived historically from senses in which they presumably selected their subjects. One may question to what extent individual verbs (such as *fon* and its compounds, or *gewunian*) had completed the transition to transparent 'aspectualizer' (or 'raising' type verb), despite Brinton (1988: ch.3). Perhaps then, the apparent absence of the 'verb with impersonal' construction with other aspectuals is simply an accident of the record, due to low frequency.

In the case of other verbs, an inspection of Callaway (1913) shows a handful of undoubted examples of 'subject-raising' type catenative constructions with infinitives (including 'second passives') in glosses and close translation (*Bede* and Wærferð's *Gregory*) (esp. 1913: 59-60, 72, 82). But there seem to be few serious possibilities elsewhere.[24] The apparent absence of the 'verb with impersonal' construction with these verbs, then, is even less remarkable. So it does not seem to be possible to discriminate on distributional grounds between a more general group of 'raising' verbs and a group of verbs which occur in the 'verb with impersonal' construction.

3.3.3. Other types of evidence can be brought to bear on this question. Regrettably, the historical evidence here is not helpful. 'Subject-raising' type constructions become more general only in the second half of the Middle English period, at a time when distinctively impersonal constructions were on the decline. Moreover *semen* 'seem', perhaps the commonest relevant verb, is itself found 'impersonal' (in constructions such as *him seemes werye* 'he seems weary', *him semed to be a kynges ayre* 'he seemed to be a king's heir') so that potential evidence would be neutralized. The occurrences of a parallel construction in Icelandic, however, is suggestive. Here epistemic modals (including *kunna* 'may', *ætla* 'will'), aspectual verbs (including the perfect *hafa* 'have' and verbs for 'begin', 'stop') and *virðast* 'seem' may all occur in 'verb with impersonal' constructions, besides showing other evidence of transparency (Thráinsson 1979: §6.3; 1986: esp. 239, 248-58). Thráinsson analyses them all as one broad class, though he discriminates subclasses. To Thráinsson its members are 'AUX-like' in taking a VP complement and not assigning a θ-role to their subject (1986: 258), though he refers to other work which analyses the class as 'subject-raising'. The importance of the parallel is the existence in a related language of a similar (indeed wider) class of verbs in which the absence of a θ-role assignment to a subject corresponds to occurrence in a 'verb with impersonal' construction, without there being any further opposition to a class of 'subject-raising' verbs which lack the property.

3.3.4. More purely theoretical considerations are also relevant, and I will briefly consider these constructions from the point of view of Head-driven Phrase Structure Grammar and Government Binding Theory.

In Head-driven Phrase Structure Grammar (or HPSG) it is straightforward to characterize a set of 'subject-raising' type verbs which have the properties of syntactic and semantic transparency noted for 'verb with impersonal' constructions. (My account is based on Pollard 1985; see also Pollard and Sag 1987 for revisions which do not affect the essential point made here.) Lexical entries in this theory contain complexes of syntactic information in the form of features with their values (which may be complex) along with associated phonological and semantic information. A complex syntagm is derived from the signs which comprise it by the 'unification' of the information composing the constituent signs. This process is specified in the general theory, and typically preserves information. Verbs are subcategorized for their subjects and other complements by a multi-valued feature SUBCAT, and any semantically interpreted NP carries an index. The SUBCAT feature in some present-day lexical entries will be:

(21. a)   *sing*   SUBCAT ⟨NP: 16⟩
    b)   *love*   SUBCAT ⟨NP: 17, NP: 18⟩
    c)   *seem*   SUBCAT ⟨VP[+TO], NP: ⟩
    d)   *may*   SUBCAT ⟨VP[+BSE], NP: ⟩

The associated entry for *may sing* will be :

(22)   *may sing*   SUBCAT ⟨NP: 16⟩

Here *seem* and *may* are entered with a syntactic specification for their subject, but no index. Thus the subject has no status as an argument of these verbs. The fact that *may* combines with a VP *sing* satisfies the first part of its SUBCAT specification, and the second part is unified with the indexed value for *sing*'s subject to give SUBCAT ‹NP: 16›. Nominative case will be assigned to pronominal subjects by a general convention. Now in Old English what is different is that verbs may assign oblique cases to their subjects (in this theory the subject is the last NP a verb combines with), overriding the general convention assigning nominative. To exemplify from combinations with *hingrian* 'be hungry' when it occurs with the accusative of the person affected, SUBCAT features will be as follows:

(23. a) *hingrian*   SUBCAT ‹NP[ACC]: 24›
    b)   *mæg*   SUBCAT ‹VP[+ BSE], NP: ›
    c)   *mæg hingrian*   SUBCAT ‹NP[ACC]: 24›

This will ensure that *mæg hingrian* combines with an NP marked for appropriate case. So, within this theoretical approach there is no reason for characterizing *mæg*, etc., differently from other 'subject-raising' type verbs, or as 'monoclausal' in any distinctive sense. Essentially one analysis is given for all 'subject-raising' type verbs, whether or not they are members of the auxiliary group, and all may equally be expected to occur transparently in 'verb with impersonal' constructions.

In GB the situation is less clear. Given the various universals postulated in this theory, we might anticipate some substantive characterization of 'auxiliary', perhaps involving INFL or SpecV, in answer to the question whether the 'verb with impersonal' construction is formally distinct from a 'subject-raising' type of construction, or more generally whether it has formal properties beyond those motivated by its semantics. Unfortunately the published analyses of finite impersonal constructions that I know do not give much discussion to the syntactic mechanisms which account for the positioning of case-marked NPs in such constructions. Fischer and van der Leek (1983) argued that impersonal verbs optionally assigned lexical (inherent) oblique case to NPs in their complement. When no case was assigned, NP-movement to subject position resulted in nominative case and a personal construction. They remained neutral on the question whether a subject position was obligatory in Old English as universal grammar might require (1983 : 357, cf. Chomsky 1981: 40, 1986: 4). But on the presumption that it was obligatory, they again appealed to NP-movement, which they assumed could move a case-marked NP into subject position (leaving a trace unmarked for case). This view would apparently permit an analysis of the 'verb with impersonal' construction in the same terms as a 'subject-raising' construction. In either case the superordinate verb would be characterized as failing to assign a θ-role to its subject, and as having S-bar-deletion, (or perhaps a VP complement as suggested by Thráinsson). So, if NP-movement may move a case-marked NP, then the 'verb with impersonal' construction does not of itself supply evidence for 'auxiliary' status within GB. To establish this we need arguments based on further data (like those Thráinsson attempts to develop for Icelandic).

In their later account Fischer and van der Leek (1985) discuss the assignment of oblique case in impersonals, but not the possible ordering (and reordering) of the oblique NPs. And on the assumption that subject position was not obligatory, their 1983 discussion was similarly focused. On the face of it this leaves a range of possibilities to investigate in accounting for occurrence in 'subject-like' positions, and no immediate basis for assuming any special characterization of I-verbs, though this question might clearly repay further investigation.

My discussion has been restricted to the basic characteristics of the 'verbs with impersonal' construction, and is therefore strictly limited. So far as it goes, in GB the verdict is for the moment a neutral one. On some assumptions the construction could essentially parallel 'subject-raising'. But the possibility of developing arguments here for distinctive 'auxiliary' status and properties remains open.

3.3.5. The methodology which underpins this account is again that of general linguistics adapted to the data needs of Old English. As before we interpret partially established distributional facts in the light of general linguistic considerations (including parallel situations and theoretical statements) and history (though, as before, support here is weak). In conclusion, we lack both distributional and theoretical reasons for distinguishing the 'verb with impersonal' construction from a 'subject-raising' construction. This means that the most straightforward account (on the basis of the limited investigation made here) will be to treat the 'verb with impersonal' construction as parallel to 'subject-raising'. In the theories examined here formal properties will be involved. In HPSG verbs will have a non-indexed 'subject' NP in SUBCAT. In GB they will have S-bar deletion. But this may be to some extent a theory particular matter, for though these properties are formal they are in a sense motivated by, or restatements of, the verb's lack of a semantic relationship with an NP argument. In HPSG the lack of an index corresponds to the lack of an argument in the semantics; in GB S-bar-deletion is required if the structure is to surface. So the formal property is interinvolved with the semantic property, and this weakens its value to any argument for a sub-category. Thus it seems likely that constructions of the type of (16) show at best a formal peculiarity which is semantically underpinned, rather than a more independent formal property.

4 Significance

4.1. Let us turn now to the second of my initial questions, and ask whether there is a sufficient correlation of properties to characterize some kind of distinct grouping for 'auxiliary' verbs in Old English. This depends on the view that word classes are defined by the correlation (or mutual predictability) of properties which stand in opposition to similar correlations for other classes, and that formal properties are of especial importance in such correlations. Thus the fact that a verb may 'intervene' in an impersonal construction is by itself a poor argument for its auxiliaryhood: it may simply identify a 'raising verb' (cf. Anderson in press a). We need a set of interrelated properties, some of which are formal. Three points may be made about the possibility of such a correlation in the present case.

(a) There is a considerable overlap in membership of 'ellipsis'-group verbs and I-verbs, see Table 1.

TABLE 1

	Occurrence of verbs		
	in post-verbal ellipsis	in pseudo gapping	'intervening' in impersonal constructions
cann	(+)		*
dearr	+		*
mæg	(+)	+	+
mot	+		(?)+
sceal	+	+	+
þearf	(+)		+
uton		+	*
wile	(+)	+	+
beon/wesan	+	?+	+
weorðan			+
on-/aginnan	**		+
don	+	+	?*

+ attested in the construction
(+) instances which might be intransitive
* reasonably regarded as absent for semantic reasons
** neutralized with use as intransitive verb

The degree of apparent mismatch is reduced if we accept that only verbs which fail to select a subject may be I-verbs, so the absence of *cann, dearr, uton,* and perhaps *don* follows independently, though this, of course, weakens the contrast with other verbs not in the Table. And some readers may feel that the fact that pseudogapping has not been noted with the less frequent verbs might perhaps be a consequence of the relative infrequency of the construction. But *onginnan* and *weorðan* are striking as members of one class not yet reported for the other: note that Antipova (1963) and Brown (1970) do not report them with ellipsis.

(b) Most of the verbs in the Table also belong to wider groups defined by these two other properties:

- Possession of preterite present morphology. Note the existence of several forms which should be analysed synchronically as 'preterite present': *eart, earon, sindon; uton;* and *wilt.* The anomalous third person indicative singular *wile* also helps to distinguish this from regular weak verbs.

- For those with the infinitive, regularity of occurrence with the plain infinitive, rather than the *to*-infinitive. Note that *onginnan* preponderantly takes the plain infinitive; Callaway found only 37 instances of the inflected infinitive in over a thousand examples (1913: 67).

Moreover, the verbs listed in the Table are (to a varying extent in different uses) distant from the verbal prototype of reported event or action, that is, they all share the property that they are notionally rather bad exemplars of the category 'verb' (cf. Hopper and Thompson 1984).

(c) One of the properties investigated here is clearly formal, the other seems to be partly or more weakly so. They are open to treatment as syntactic idiosyncrasies which are lexically specified. 'Ellipsis'-group verbs might be treated as proforms or as subcategorized for an elliptical construction; I-verbs may be lexically specified as raising verbs, say by having a non-indexed 'subject' NP in HPSG, or as having S-bar-deletion and no subject θ-role assignment in GB. Here the property of permitting ellipsis is especially interesting since it does not seem to correlate directly with any semantic or other property. The property of occurring with impersonals, however, is less impressive as a criterion for classification since it seems likely to be the formal reflex of a semantic property.

In order to interpret the significance of these points we clearly need a formal and substantive theory of word classes. This we do not have. So no final answer is possible. But it seems likely that any theory of word classes will reflect general aspects of human categorization, and Rosch and her associates have developed what is intended as a general theory of cognitive classification (though experimentally it is based on noun categories, and there may be problems over its more general application), cf. Rosch (1977, 1978 and refs.). Within this theory, classes are defined in terms of clusters of associated properties which oppose one another. For us, however, the most significant point is that the clustering is 'cleanest' and clearest at a central level (in the sense that boundaries are there best defined, and indeterminate memberships are least numerous), while at subordinate levels of categorization classes are less clearly defined. They also have fewer distinctive properties, and share more properties with the subclasses they oppose. It is such subordinate levels which would be in question here. If these properties of Rosch's model survive into a theory of word classes, and reflection on the difficulties of subclassification in today's English shows that this is not an unreasonable position, then the unfocused nature of the groupings discussed above can be interpreted as merely what one would expect of a subordinate level of classification. The intersection of a series of sets (defined by the properties in (a) and (b) above) provides the core of a subclass whose boundaries and precise membership are poorly defined because that is the nature of subclasses, but in which *beon/wesan* and those uses of Mitchell's ' "modal" auxiliaries' which lack subject selection are presumably prototypical. So despite the fact that each of the criteria above defines a different group of verbs (or uses of verbs), it seems clear that there is a clustering in Old English which would be a candidate for a weakly defined subordinate-level category in Rosch's sense. Moreover, some of the criteria involve formal properties, and there is a correlation between criteria from different linguistic levels. Both of these points are particularly characteristic of word classes. So to readers who are willing to accept the assumptions made here and in the course of this chapter (and its limitations) it must, then, seem likely that we should interpret Old English as having had such a linguistically significant subordinate-level category.

4.2 Notional correspondences

Applied to the present case, the third of my initial questions becomes: 'Is there a notional correspondence between this subordinate-level category and the cross linguistic "auxiliary verb"?' The question of the appropriate notional characteristics for a class of auxiliaries is open to much interpretation. One view might be to take the characteristics claimed for the syntactic node AUX by Steele *et al.* (1981) (and cf. her 1978) and regard at least some of them as potential class properties of 'auxiliary verb'. Tense and modality are central. Aspect is listed among the 'limited and specifiable set of notional categories which may be marked there [*sc.* in AUX]' (1981: 146). Modality is implicated in both 'ellipsis'-group verbs and I-verbs. *Mæg, mot, sceal* and *þearf* may apparently involve deontic (as well as dynamic) modality in Old English. *Sceolde* may be evidential. And there is some evidence that particular uses of *mæg* and *sceolde* in particular were developing an effective equivalence to the subjunctive (Mitchell 1985: index, 'verbs, "modal" auxiliary, with infinitives as periphrases for simple subjunctive'; and cf. Anderson in press a). Elsewhere I have argued that some of these words were developing the subjective epistemic and subjective deontic uses which I take to be most characteristic of modality (Warner 1990; for the possibility of epistemics see also Goossens 1982 and Kytö 1987.). *Uton* also clearly expresses subjective deontic modality.

Turning to tense and aspect, *wile* may arguably already convey a 'pure' future sense in Old English (Warner 1990), non-past forms of *beon/wesan* show a contrast which is both temporal and aspectual, while *onginnan* and *weorðan* may carry aspectual senses (cf. Brinton 1988). On this view, then, 'ellipsis'-group verbs and I-verbs consist very largely of verbs which have at least some developing senses appropriate to a universal 'auxiliary verb', though not the paradigmatic systematicity we might look for. The clustering of these properties is clearly not accidental.

There is also the further point that the semantic transparency of I-verbs is notionally appropriate to auxiliaries, which, as a group, are clause modifiers (cf. Huddleston 1974, Lyons 1977: ch. 17, and the recent discussion of 'aspectualizers' in Brinton 1988). Recollect that 'raising' structures in Old English are poorly attested outside the verbs considered here (perhaps adding other aspectuals on the evidence of their occurrence with 'weather' *hit*), being only found otherwise in a handful of cases where Latin is apparently being rather literally rendered. If an extended 'auxiliary' group of verbs may virtually be identified with the class of 'raising' verbs in Old English except where it is heavily influenced by Latin, this is suggestive for their characterization.

There is also a stricter and more traditional account of auxiliaries as 'helping' verbs, used to form the tenses, moods and aspects of other verbs (cf. OED 'auxiliary', Huddleston 1984). This implies membership of a small set of paradigmatic contrasts, cf. Anderson's (in press b) identification of 'the formation of "syntactic paradigms"' as an essential characteristic of auxiliarization. This is presumably present in Old English for *uton*, and perhaps for some uses of *mæg* and *sceolde*, cf. Anderson's discussion of the 'paradigmatisation' of *sceolde* (in press a, and see also in press b). Pro-verbal *don* may also belong here.[25] But if we relax the strict requirement in order to catch preceding stages of development, and focus on the semantic areas involved, there is clearly some overlap between the 'modality' discussed above and the use of subjunctive inflections, and a more direct correspondence in the case of tense and aspect with *wile, is* versus *bið* and *onginnan*. The semantics of this area is at least interestingly 'pre-auxiliary', and some account of this must be given.

Both of the positions discussed above point to some level of development of notionally auxiliary semantics, though the first does so more clearly. Such semantics is less central to the group than it becomes later in several ways. For one thing, it is for most items found alongside other usages to a greater extent. For another, the semantics of deontic and epistemic modality is less developed. But it may also be less central in a more abstract sense. I suppose that a class is focused and identified internally by its coherency and correspondence to the notional characteristics of the class, and externally by the fact that its prototypical properties are in opposition to the prototypical characteristics of other classes. Both internal and external factors will always be involved, but I see no reason why the balance between them should always be the same. I suspect that in Old English the developing identification of the auxiliary group and congeners may at a notional level have depended relatively more heavily on the fact that they were in opposition to prototypical verbs than it did on their possession of distinctively auxiliary notional properties. If this is so, then pigeonholing this group under the notional label 'auxiliary verb' would be an oversimplification. I prefer to conclude that the following view is plausible, where the term 'subordinate-level category' is used in Rosch's sense of a relatively poorly defined, less distinct level of categorization: Old English had a linguistically significant 'subordinate-level category' of verbs with some of the semantic characteristics of the notional class 'auxiliary verb'.

5 Final Reflections
5.1 If the interpretation of post-verbal ellipsis and pseudogapping given above is correct, then the developing auxiliary group corresponded well with a formal property (or properties) from the earliest period for which we have evidence. This implies the early importance of formal properties, and suggests that later semantic and other developments may have depended as much on syntactic distinctness as vice-versa. Contrast the priority given to semantic developments in Brinton's (1988) history of English aspectual verbs.

5.2 But although these ellipses are syntactic properties of lexemes, and apparently arbitrary from the point of view of formal grammar, their early appearance raises the question of motivation. The fact that 'proform' is a general grammatical category, and that ellipsis is associated with particular grammatical forms (e.g. *as*, *than*) also makes one suspect that the proform (or pre-elliptical form) here may be associated with grammatical subclass status, and itself be a motivated property of auxiliaries. If this turns out to be the case, the argument of this chapter can, of course, be revised and strengthened.

Thus Old English as interpreted here poses a question for general linguistics.

5.3 Lightfoot (1979) isolated the history of modals. But the formal properties considered here imply that from Old English it is a wider auxiliary group which should be the focus of our attention (a point also made partly for other reasons in Warner 1990).

5.4. Interpretations of the history of periphrastic *do* have recently focused on causative or 'full verb' (with 'anticipative') *do* as sources (e.g. Ellegård 1953; Visser 1963-1973; §1413ff; Denison 1985), though Hausmann's (1974) analysis integrates pro-verbal *do* as a separate category, not simply because of its relation to 'anticipative' *do*. The fact that pro-verbal *do* is formally closely associated with the auxiliary group in Old English implies that we may need to rethink its significance. Note that it does not seem to 'stand for' Mitchell's' "modal" auxiliaries' (despite Visser 1963-73: §187), so that it may be a source of periphrastic *do*'s general restriction to association with non-auxiliary verbs.

5.5 If the 'verb with impersonal' construction discussed above and the 'subject-raising' type construction are indeed closely related in that the same set of verbs may 'intervene' in each case, we have an *a priori* distributional argument (which may not survive in all frameworks) that one of the case-marked NPs with an impersonal is its 'subject'. This would provide evidence to support Anderson's (1988) argument that impersonals have (cyclic) subjects because the 'verb with impersonal' construction must involve 'subject raising'. See his paper for a review of the 'modicum of evidence (1988: 22) Old English supplies for the occurrence of a (cyclic) subject with impersonals and some typological considerations; also Warner (1983) for criticisms of Lightfoot's arguments for subjecthood (1979: 232-235).

NOTES

* I wish to thank John Anderson and Fran Colman for their helpful comments on this paper and David Rix for helping me make sense of the Russian text of Antipova (1963). But I hereby absolve them from all blame.

1. There may clearly be other formal properties besides the two suggested here. Two *a priori* likely areas to find a distinction between a potential auxiliary group and other verbs are word order patterning and 'clitic climbing' possibilities in pronouns. I have investigated these without, however, finding any clear evidence of a formal distinction.

2. Including asyndetic coordinations, as in (3.a) without *and.* But gapping may also make some restricted contribution to ellipsis in comparatives. Levin (1978) identified post-auxiliary ellipsis and pseudogapping, but in 1980 she distinguished them. Her reasons, however, all involve particular restrictions on pseudogapping which are absent on post-auxiliary ellipsis. This type of argument merely shows that pseudogapping is a subcase of

post-auxiliary ellipsis with a more limited distribution. And many of the restrictions she cites are ready understandable as limitations on a more marked construction containing a contrastive element, cf. her perceptually-based account of the 'like-subject condition' on pseudogapping, or the absence of pseudogapping after *to*, which may merely show a lexically-based restriction on this item.

3. I have sometimes used abbreviations in references to texts: for major prose texts those of Mitchell (1985 vol. i: xxx ff., vol. ii: xl ff.); for minor texts those of Healey and Venezky (1980). For the reader's convenience here is a short expansion of abbreviations for the major texts: see Mitchell for editions, etc. ÆCHom = Ælfric's Catholic Homilies, ÆLS = Ælfric's Lives of the Saints, Bede = Bede's Ecclesiastical History, BlHom = Blickling Homilies, Bo = Boethius, Chron = Anglo-Saxon Chronicle, CP = Cura Pastoralis, GD = Gregory's Dialogues, Matt(WS) = Matthew (etc.) West Saxon Gospels, Or = Orosius.

4. To exemplify rejected types of example :
(i) þæt hie of his rice uuoldon
     'that they were-willing (to go) out-of his kingdom...'
     ChronA 76.14 (878)
(ii) Hige sceal þe heardra
     'Resolution must be the tougher,...'
     The Battle of Maldon (ed. Gordon 1937) 312
     (See in particular BT(S), Mitchell 1985: §3863, and Visser 1963-1973: §§234, 1895 for further examples of (ii)).
(iii) Eft ne mot nan mann ne ne sceal secgan
      'Neither again may any man (say), nor ought he to say,...'
      Skeat's translation.
      ÆLS 12.177
(iv) þonne beo we urum Hælende fylgende, swa se blinda wæs
     'then are we following our Saviour, as the blind man was,...'
     BlHom 23.11

5. Further distinctions are of course required, cf. Quirk *et al.* (1985: §§12.31ff.). Hankamer and Sag (1976) would presumably interpret *try* as showing 'Null Complement Anaphora', *start* as an intransitive verb of rather open sense (1976: 412 note 21).

6. In the types of (i) and (ii) in note 4 the meaning of the infinitive which is supplied in translation corresponds to (and is predictable from) an aspect of the complementation of the verb. This is a distinct category from a more general intransitive or absolute use which would be appropriate to post-verbal ellipsis contexts. Besides these types BT(S) *durran* and [*motan*] I(b) 'with ellipsis of infinitive' only have instances like (5) or (9) with retrieval from linguistic context. As well as all of these types, [*sculan*] III 'without an infinite' has instances meaning 'be necessary', 'be appropriate', 'avail'. But these do not give suitable sense in post-verbal ellipsis contexts. (It may be that *don* can also be supplied, but I prefer to take the apparent ellipses at *Riddle* 83.8 (BT [*motan*]) and ÆLS 5.370 (OED Shall, 28) to be different constructions : post-verbal ellipsis with following antecedent in the first case, type (ii) above in the second, cf. BT *ymb, prep.* I(3)(d) *Beon/wesan ymb.*) A similar line of argument might hold for BT(S) *willan*, but there seem to be absolute examples elsewhere.

7. The 'construction' might be accounted for in semantic terms, as requiring the sense of a verb and its complements to be retrieved from linguistic context. The point would however remain that a distinct statement must be made to characterize such uses. But the generalization of post-verbal ellipsis and pseudogapping will be argued for below. Since pseudogapping exhibits the rectional characteristics of the retrieved verb, a purely semantic

account will not be possible, granted that 'Case/θ-role correlations in OE are not entirely systematic' Anderson (1986: 173).

8. Although Antipova (1963: 131) takes this example to be elliptical (and cf. Fox's translation), it is conceivable that it is not, but shows *wesan* + dative 'to belong to, for a person to have something,' (BT *wesan* I(8)(a)): 'but it belongs to all men.' The parallels given in BT, however, retain the full sense of their gloss, which is not really appropriate here: the crown is offered to all men, but is only achieved by the virtuous. On the whole a pseudogapping interpretation seems preferable, but a contextually weakened sense of *wesan* + dative cannot be ruled out with confidence. The example given by Visser (1963-1973 : §1745) I take to be post-verbal ellipsis in type, not pseudogapping.

9. It is possible that two more of their criteria also held: that the missing expression should be precisely recoverable, and that its insertion should result in a grammatical sentence with the same meaning as the elliptical sentence. These four criteria are those met by today's post-auxiliary ellipsis and pseudogapping to which the Old English constructions are on the face of it straightforwardly parallel.

10. Besides Antipova and Wülfing, see esp. BT(S), Brown (1970), and, for all periods, Visser (1963-1973: §§ 309, 573, 1743 ff.). Wülfing (§388) cites an instance with *cann* (Bo 24.55.15), as does Antipova (p. 127, ChronE 251.32 (1123)), but I think them less satisfactory than (5.e) as potential ellipses (though (5.e) is itself not certain). Visser is wrong to imply that pseudogapping occurs only from late Old English: Wülfing gives plentiful examples from early Old English.

11. Visser (1963-1973: §1756) gives a supposed instance with *weorðan* from early Middle English, but it is inadequate.

12. Note that the putative Old English example of ellipsis after 'perfect' *habban*, which Visser (1963-1973: §1753) takes from BT, is not a good one, cf. Mitchell (1985: §1004).

13. For further instances see in particular Visser (1963-1973: §§181ff., 580 ff.), OED *do*, v. 24a, c.

14. There is a very restricted parallel to gapping in modern comparatives, and (13.c) is early Middle English (though in a text which partly derives from Old English material). So Old English gapping may be more like modern gapping than I have assumed.

15. Or in Kohonen's remarks on ellipsis (1978: §5.6), or the other (brief) accounts of ellipsis involving verbs that I know in the monograph literature. The possibility of a parallel to pseudogapping with infinitive-taking verbs more generally is not raised in Mitchell's survey of elliptical patterns (§§3858 ff.) or sections on nonexpression of the infinitive (see index), or in Visser's discussions of gapping and pseudogapping (§§186, 586, 595; 573).

16. Here I assume a lexicalist syntax. Suppose alternatively that pro-verbal *don* realises the tense which survives the ellipsis of V and some or all of its complements, perhaps implying some version of *do*-support here in Old English (cf. Hausmann 1974). The generalization of post-verbal ellipsis and pseudogapping is still supported. The contexts in which they occur are (i) in construction with tense, and (ii) in construction with certain verbs. Pressure to adopt a generalization of these contexts is less strong than in a theoretical position where they are already more similar because both are characterized by lexemes. But a generalization across tense and specific verbs would nonetheless contribute a direct line of argument for auxiliary status, itself a lexical property. Thus a different theoretical position implies different arguments and different intermediate conclusions, but points to a similar ultimate conclusion.

17. For example the statement 'any plain infinitive governed by a verb may undergo ellipsis' would predict a very wide distribution for these ellipses.

18. This gives me a collection of nearly 50 examples of 'central' impersonal constructions

(as in (16)) in the infinitive. Denison (in press) provides a detailed and independent survey of the data, and has a discussion of its significance for the category status of the verbs involved.

19. For the status of *þætte* in (16.d) see comments on (2.g) in Warner (1990). The potential subjecthood of a following clause or infinitive in earlier English has been much debated, cf. Mitchell (1985: §1507) for a brief comment.

20. Possible: *Elene* 915, *JDayI* 80. Denison (in press) says there are two probable examples of his type (i) (which includes my 'central' impersonals, but allows nonargument *hit* subject), but only cites the ambiguous *HomS* 25 412 (which I prefer to take as his type (ii), with nominative subject).

21. But note the transparent 'passive' with *dearr* at *GD* 232.7 cited by Callaway (1913: 83).

22. Denison (in press) did not find any relevant impersonal constructions with the first (or present) participle, nor have I noted any, so the questions here involve constructions with subordinate infinitives.

23. In a particular theory this might involve a syntactic mechanism (e.g. case conflict); I don't wish to imply a necessarily semantic anomaly.

24. Note that the construction of *Hy...wyrðe þinceaþ* 'They seem worthy ...' *Beowulf* 368 is not under consideration here since it is not catenative.

25. I suppose that *beon/wesan* and *weorðan* are verbs taking predicates which may be participle phrases (which after all have an independent distribution) rather than formatives specific to the perfect, passive or progressive. But some might wish to regard them as grammatical formatives in the first two cases.

REFERENCES

Allen, Cynthia. 1975. Old English modals. In Jane B. Grimshaw (ed.) *Papers in the history and structure of English.* 89-100. University of Massachusetts Occasional Papers in Linguistics, no.1.

Anderson, John M. 1986. A note on Old English impersonals. *Journal of Linguistics* 22. 167-177.

Anderson, John M. 1988. The type of Old English impersonals. In John M. Anderson and Norman Macleod (eds.) *Edinburgh studies in the English language.* 1-32. Edinburgh: John Donald.

Anderson, John M. In press a. Should. In Dieter Kastovsky (ed.) *Proceedings of the Conference on Historical English Syntax,* Vienna, September 1988. Berlin: Mouton de Gruyter.

Anderson, John M. In press b. Grammaticalisation and the English modals. In P. Kakietek (ed.) *Modality in English and other languages.*

Antipova, Ye Ya. 1963. Glagol'noe zameščenie v drevneangliiskom yazyke. *Vestnik Leningradskogo Gosudarstvennogo Universiteta. Series: Literature, History, Language.* Vol 8 part 2: 125-136.

Bolinger, Dwight. 1973. Ambient 'it' is meaningful too. *Journal of Linguistics* 9. 261-270.

Bolinger, Dwight 1977. *Meaning and form.* London and New York: Longman.

Brinton, Laurel J. 1988. *The development of English aspectual systems.* Cambridge: Cambridge University Press.

Brown W.H., Jr. 1970. *A syntax of King Ælfred's "Pastoral Care".* The Hague: Mouton.

BT = *An Anglo-Saxon dictionary based on the manuscript collections of the late Joseph*

Bosworth, ed. and enlarged by T. Northcote Toller. London: Oxford University Press. 1898.

BTS = *An Anglo-Saxon dictionary based on the manuscript collections of the late Joseph Bosworth. Supplement* ed. by T. Northcote Toller. London: Oxford University Press. 1921, and *Enlarged addenda and corrigenda to the Supplement*, ed. by A. Campbell, Oxford: Clarendon Press. 1972.

Callaway, Morgan, Jr. 1913. *The infinitive in Anglo-Saxon*. Washington: Carnegie Institution of Washington.

Chomsky, Noam. 1981. *Lectures on government and binding*. Dordrecht: Foris.

Chomsky, Noam. 1986. *Barriers*. Cambridge, Mass: MIT Press.

Denison, David. 1985. The origin of periphrastic 'do': Ellegård and Visser reconsidered. In Roger Eaton *et al.* (eds.) *Papers from the Fourth International Conference on English Historical Linguistics*. 45-60. Amsterdam: John Benjamins.

Denison, David. 1990. The Old English impersonals revived. In Sylvia Adamson *et al.* (eds.) *Papers* from the *Fifth International Conference on English Historical Linguistics, Cambridge 6-9 April 1987*, 111-140, Amsterdam: John Benjamins.

Denison, David. In press. Auxiliary + impersonal in Old English. *Folia Linguistica Historica*.

Ellegård, A. 1953. *The auxiliary 'do': the establishment and regulation of its use in English*. Stockholm: Almqvist & Wiksell.

Elmer, W. 1981. *Diachronic grammar: the history of Old and Middle English subjectless constructions*. Tübingen: Niemeyer.

Emonds, Joseph E. 1985. *A unified theory of syntactic categories*. Dordrecht: Foris.

Fischer, Olga C. M. and Frederike C. van der Leek. 1983. The demise of the Old English impersonal construction. *Journal of Linguistics* 19. 337-368.

Fischer, Olga C. M. and Frederike C. van der Leek. 1985. A 'case' for the Old English impersonal. In Willem Koopman *et al.* (eds.) *Explanation and linguistic change*. Current Issues in Linguistic Theory 45. 79-120. Amsterdam and Philadelphia: John Benjamins.

van der Gaaf, W. 1904. *The transition from the impersonal to the personal construction in Middle English*. Anglistische Forschungen 14. Heidelberg: Carl Winter.

Gazdar, Gerald; Geoffrey K. Pullum; and Ivan A. Sag. 1982. Auxiliaries and related phenomena in a restrictive theory of grammar. *Language* 58. 591-638.

Goossens, Louis. 1982. On the development of the modals and of the epistemic function in English. In A. Ahlqvist (ed.) *Papers from the fifth International Conference on historical Linguistics*. 74-84. Amsterdam: John Benjamins.

Goossens, Louis. 1987. The auxiliarization of the English modals: a functional grammar view. In Martin Harris & Paolo Ramat (eds.) *Historical development of auxiliaries*. 111-143. Berlin: Mouton de Gruyter.

Hankamer, Jorge and Ivan A. Sag. 1976. Deep and surface anaphora. *Linguistic Inquiry* 7 391-428.

Hausmann, Robert B. 1974. The origin and development of Modern English periphrastic 'do'. In John M. Anderson and Charles Jones (eds.) *Historical Linguistics: Proceedings of the First International Conference on Historical Linguistics*. Vol I. 159-189. Amsterdam: North-Holland.

Healey, Antonette diPaolo and Richard L. Venezky. 1980. *A microfiche concordance to Old English: The list of texts and index of editions*. (= Parts I and II of Venezky and Healey 1980) Toronto: Pontifical Institute of Mediaeval Studies.

Hopper, P.J. and S.A. Thompson. 1984. The discourse basis for lexical categories in universal grammar. *Language* 60. 703-752.

Huddleston, Rodney D. 1974. Further remarks on the analysis of auxilaries as main verbs. *Foundations of Language.* 11. 215-29.

Huddleston, Rodney D. 1984. *Introduction to the grammar of English.* Cambridge: Cambridge University Press.

Jespersen, Otto. 1909-49. *A Modern English grammar on historical principles.* 7 parts. Published and reprinted in London: George Allen and Unwin.

Kohonen, Viljo. 1978. On the development of English word order in religious prose around 1000 and 1200 A.D.: a quantitative study of word order in context. Åbo: Research Institute of the Åbo Akademi Foundation.

Kytö, Merja. 1987. *Can (could)* vs. *may (might)* in Old and Middle English: testing a diachronic corpus. In Leena Kahlas-Tarkka (ed.) *Neophilologica Fennica (Modern Language Society 100 years).* 205-240. Mémoires de la Société Néophilologique de Helsinki vol. XLV.

Levin, Nancy S. 1978. Some identity-of-sense deletions puzzle me. Do they you? In Donka Farkas *et al.* (eds.) *Papers from the Fourteenth Regional Meeting Chicago Linguistic Society.* 229-240. Chicago: Chicago Linguistic Society.

Levin, Nancy S. 1980. Main-verb ellipsis in spoken English. *Ohio State University Working Papers in Linguistics* 24. 65-165.

Lightfoot, David W. 1979. *Principles of diachronic syntax.* Cambridge: Cambridge University Press.

Lyons, John. 1966. Towards a 'notional' theory of the 'parts of speech'. *Journal of Linguistics* 2. 209-236.

Lyons, John, 1977. *Semantics.* 2 vols. Cambridge: Cambridge University Press.

McCawley, Norico. 1976. From OE/ME 'impersonal' to 'personal' constructions: What is a 'subject-less' S? In Sanford Steever *et al.* (eds.) *Papers from the parasession on diachronic syntax.* 192-204. Chicago: Chicago Linguistic society.

Mitchell, Bruce. 1985. *Old English syntax.* 2 vols. Oxford: Clarendon Press.

Napoli, Donna Jo. 1985. Verb phrase deletion in English: a base-generated analysis. *Journal of Linguistics* 21. 281-319.

OED = *The Oxford English dictionary,* ed. by J.A.H. Murray, H. Bradley, W.A. Craigie, and C. T., Onions. Oxford: Clarendon Press. 1933.

van Ostade, Ingrid Tieken-Boon. 1988. The origin and development of periphrastic auxiliary 'do': a case of destigmatisation. *Dutch Working Papers in English Language and Linguistics* 3. Leiden: University of Leiden.

Palmer, F.R. 1987. *The English verb.* 2nd edition. London: Longman.

Plank, Frans. 1984. The modals story retold. *Studies in Language* 8. 305-364

Pollard, Carl. 1985. *Lectures on HPSG.* Unpublished mimeo. Stanford: Center for the Study of Language and Information.

Pollard, Carl and Ivan A. Sag. 1987. *Information-based syntax and semantics, vol I: Fundamentals.* Stanford: Center for the Study of Language and Information.

Pullum, Geoffrey K. 1982. Syncategorematicity and English infinitival *to. Glossa* 16. 181-215.

Pullum, Geoffrey K, and Deirdre Wilson. 1977. Autonomous syntax and the analysis of auxiliaries. *Language* 53. 741-88.

Quirk, Randoph; Sidney Greenbaum; Geoffrey Leech; and Jan Svartvik. 1985. *A comprehensive grammar of the English language.* London and New York: Longman.

Rosch, Eleanor. 1977. Human categorization. In N. Warren (ed.) *Studies in cross-cultural psychology.* 1-49. London: Academic Press.

Rosch, Eleanor. 1978. Principles of categorization. In Eleanor Rosch and Barbara B. Lloyd (eds.) *Cognition and categorization.* 27-48. Hillsdale NJ: Erlbaum.

Steele, Susan. 1978. The category AUX as a language universal. In Joseph H. Greenberg (ed.) *Universals of human language, Vol 3: Word structure.* 7-45. Stanford: Stanford University Press.

Steele, Susan, *et al.* 1981. *An encyclopedia of AUX: a study in cross-linguistic equivalence.* (Linguistic Inquiry Monographs, 5.) Cambridge Mass: MIT Press.

Thráinsson, Höskuldur. 1979. *On complementation in Icelandic.* New York: Garland.

Thráinsson, Höskuldur. 1986. On auxiliaries, AUX and VPs in Iceland. In Lars Hellan and Kirsti Koch Christensen (eds.) *Topics in Scandinavian syntax.* 235-265. Dordrecht, etc.: Reidel.

Venezky, Richard L. and Antonette diPaolo Healey. 1980. *A microfiche concordance to Old English.* Newark, Del. and Toronto: Pontifical Institute of Mediaeval Studies.

Visser, F. Th. 1963-73. *An historical syntax of the English language.* 3 parts. Leiden: Brill.

Warner, Anthony R. 1983. Review of Lightfoot (1979). *Journal of Linguistics* 19. 187-209.

Warner, Anthony R. 1985. *The structuring of English auxiliaries: a phrase structure grammar.* Bloomington: IULC.

Warner, Anthony R. 1990. Reworking the history of English auxilaries. In Sylvia Adamson *et al.* (eds.) Papers from *Fifth International Conference on English Historical Linguistics. Cambridge 6-9 April 1987,* 537-558. Amsterdam: John Benjamins.

Wülfing, J.E. 1894-1901. *Die Syntax in den Werken Alfreds des Grossen.* 2 vols. Bonn: Hanstein.

10

ANOTHER OLD ENGLISH IMPERSONAL : SOME DATA*

W. van der Wurff

1 Introduction and Preliminaries

In recent years there has been a fair amount of interest in what are called the 'impersonal' verbs of Old English. Questions that have been posed and investigated mainly have to do with the proper analysis of these verbs in Old English, and with their further development in Middle English and into the modern period. From recent contributions such as Anderson (1988) and Denison (1990), it is clear that the debate about the theoretical aspects of these questions is by no means settled yet; I refer to these studies for details and references.

Perhaps more surprising is the fact that, even now, much of the debate is still concerned with empirical aspects of these questions, such as the distribution of the various verbs across construction-types, the type-token frequency of different constructions and the changes in the various types through time. With the publication of Ogura (1986), which makes available a solid base of data for at least the Old English period, it is to be expected that it will be possible for future investigations to make further headway in solving the more theoretical problems associated with impersonals.[1]

Having brought up some wide issues which will serve as background to this chapter, let me now narrow down the field of inquiry. The subject of this paper will be the combination of adjective plus infinitive in Old English. Since this combination shares certain properties with impersonal verbs, it is sometimes referred to as an impersonal predicate; but little actual work on the construction has been done, and although Callaway (1913) provides a lot of data, his collection is by no means complete, and it leaves a lot of questions about the distribution of specific features and subtypes unanswered. It is my purpose here to give a description and classification of the data, based on a fresh corpus study, and also to use these data to investigate the restrictions to which certain subtypes seem to have been subject in Old English.

To see the similarity between impersonal verbs and the combination adjective plus infinitive in Old English, first consider the following three sentences.

(1)   hit gedafenað Drihtne to gehyrsumienne swiðor þonne mannum
      it befits the Lord to obey more than men (ÆHom 9 178).[2]
      (=it is fitting to obey the Lord rather than men)

(2)   us gedafenað swyðor mid geswince to campigenne for þam
      us befits rather with effort to fight for the
      undeadlicum cynincge

immortal king (ÆLS (Forty Soldiers) 26)
(=it is more fitting for us to fight with much effort for the immortal king)

(3) þær ðe bið gesæd hwæt þe gedafenað to donne
there to-you is said what you befits to do (ÆCHom 1.8.124.22)
(=there you will be told what is fitting for you to do)

In (1), the Old English impersonal verb *gedafenian* is used with *hit* as a dummy subject, and an infinitival clause as complement. In (2), there is no overt subject, but there is an infinitival complement just like in (1). In both (1) and (2) the infinitive has no overt subject; if there is a dative NP in the matrix clause, as in (2), this NP can be interpreted as subject of the infinitive. In (3), the impersonal verb takes a lexical NP (*hwæt*) as subject, and this NP can also be interpreted as object of the infinitival complement. As in (2), the dative NP (*þe*) can be interpreted as subject of the infinitive.

These three sentences illustrate three constructions in which Old English impersonal verbs are used; with dummy *hit* as subject, without any overt subject, and with a full lexical NP as subject. The second type has often been called the 'true' impersonal, and its use has received extensive commentary, while the alternation with the third type has also attracted a great deal of attention; the first type (which, it is true, is not very frequent) has perhaps been neglected a little, especially in more theoretical work. I should add that the presence of an infinitival complement, as in all of (1) – (3), is by no means obligatory for impersonal verbs. Depending on the verb in question, finite clause complements, NP complements and absence of complementation can all be found. The choice of examples with an infinitive, though, allows us to observe particularly clearly the close parallel between certain impersonal verbs and the combination of adjective with infinitive, as in (4) – (6):

(4) hit is unieðe to gesecgenne hu monige gewin wæron
it is hard to say how many fights were (Or 1 12.52.8)
(=it is not easy to say how many fights there were)

(5) þam broþrum wæs symble swyðe gewinnful & uneaðe
to the brothers was always very troublesome and hard
niþer to astigenne to þam wæterseaðe
down to go to the water-well (GD 2(C) 5.112.15)
(=it was always very troublesome and difficult for the
brothers to go down to the well)

(6) se deada byð uneaþe ælcon men on neaweste
the dead is difficult for every man in neighbourhood
to hæbbenne (HomS 17 (BlHom 5) 78)
to have
(=the dead man is difficult for everyone to have close by)

Where (1) – (3) have a form of *gedafenian* (4) – (6) have a form of *beon/wesan* followed by the adjective *uneaðe* but the same remarks apply concerning the nature of the matrix subject and the interpretation of the non-overt subject and, in (6), object of the infinitival complement. This parallelism has been recognised for a long time now for the cases in (2) and (5); see Van der Gaaf (1904) and references to earlier work given there. However, discussions of Old English impersonals have not so far taken into account the full set of correspondences. Whether the correspondence is as close as I am suggesting by the choice of sentences with an infinitival complement in (1) – (3) might be open to some dispute.[3] There is no doubt, however, that the combination of adjective and infinitive shares with impersonal verbs their main characteristic, i.e. the possibility of having an empty subject, in some cases alternating with dummy *hit* or a lexical NP.

In the following sections I will set forth the results of my corpus study of the constructions seen in (4) – (6) in Old English. That is, I will present the empirical data on the combination of adjective and infinitive in Old English, paying attention to such factors as frequency of the different construction types, further subdivisions in the three types, the order of constituents, the range of adjectives found in the different constructions, distribution across texts, and so forth. On the basis of these findings, I will also try to establish for the different attested subtypes whether they were completely grammatical in Old English, and/or whether there were restrictions on their use.

This corpus study can provide the data for more theoretically oriented work, either in approaches integrating the combination of adjective plus infinitive with the data for other impersonal predicates in Old English, or in an approach more specifically concerned with the combination adjective plus infinitive itself. There has, in fact, already been some work along the latter lines; see Allen (1980), Van Kemenade (1987), Van der Wurff (1987; 1990) and Fischer (1988). It is to be hoped that the availability of fuller data will stimulate further work.

On the empirical side, this corpus study can be regarded as a step towards a descriptive history of the constructions in (4) - (6) in English. For such a history, the greater part remains to be filled in. The construction in (6), for example, of course also exists in present-day English, and under the name of Tough-movement, a great deal has been written about it — yet there is only one paper, Mair (1987), which is specifically directed at corpus work for this construction. It could be argued that several of the theoretical accounts of this construction in present-day English are flawed by this virtual lack of empirical validation, especially since there is some disagreement about the grammaticality of certain types of sentences with Tough-movement; compare Iwakura (1980 : 76), Joseph (1980: 36ff) and Nanni (1980 : 57ff). Apart from their place in the history of English, the present data can also be used for comparative purposes. With data from the earliest stages of the other Germanic languages, it should be possible to attempt reconstruction of the patterns available for adjective plus infinitive in Proto-Germanic.

Before I present the data, let me explain the method I have adopted to locate all the relevant sentences, and also some details of what I considered 'relevant'. The corpus I have investigated is the microfiche concordance of Old English, i.e Healey and Venezky (1980) and Venezky and Butler (1983). The clue for the search was the adjectival candidate, which means any adjective (in all possible variant spellings) known or suspected to form combinations with an infinitive. Prior information on this point was available on a systematic basis in Callaway (1913; 1918) and Ogura (1986); in other secondary sources, such as Wulfing (1987 : § 488f), Van der Gaaf (1904; 1928), Visser (1963-1973: §§898 ff, 1388, 1921) and Mitchell (1985: §§928 ff, 1539 ff), such information could be deduced from the examples given. For every adjective established in this way, the related forms were also treated as candidates. For example, in addition to *toweard*, given by Callaway (1913), *toweardlic*, not given by any of the secondary sources, was also considered a candidate, and rightly so as it turned out. Several other candidates were established by extrapolation from present-day English: *behefe* is one example.

Not surprisingly, the search also yielded examples in which it was difficult to decide whether the adjective and the infinitive really formed a combination, or of what kind. Especially for the Old English glosses, a comparison with the Latin original is often necessary to understand what the glossator was trying to convey. In other cases, I have tried to take a decision on the basis of the context and through comparison with other examples. The number of these more or less doubtful cases, however, is not very high in proportion to the total number of examples found. I will discuss several cases as we go along.

As a general rule, I have counted sequences with two adjectives and an infinitive, as in (5), only once, under the adjective closest to the infinitive. So (5) only counts as an example for *uneaðe*, not for *gewinful*. For sentences like (5) or (4), another procedure would certainly be defensible, but for sentences like (6) but with two adjectives, the infinitive need only depend on the second adjective. An example is (7).

(7)   þeah þe heo si us unwyrðelice & unrihtlic to sprecane
      although it is us unworthy and not-right to say. (GDPref 3(C) 15.209.16)
      (=although it is unworthy and not fit for us to utter)

Here the infinitive *to sprecane* certainly depends on *unrihtlic*, but whether it also depends on *unwyrðelice* is not certain. Therefore it seems best only to count the second adjective. To avoid complications in tabulating the results of the counting, I have applied this method throughout.

In sentences with two infinitives, however, I have taken the view that the second infinitive depends on the adjective just as much as the first one. An example is (8).

(8)   and me þis is lang to secganne and to writanne
      and me this is long to say and to write. (HomU 35.1 (Nap 43) 198)
      (=and this takes a long time for me to say and write)

So (8) gives us two examples, both for *lang*. These decisions concerning adj_1 + adj_2 + inf and adj + inf_1+inf_2 should be kept in mind when interpreting the data given in the following sections, since they affect the counting.

Another decision I had to take involved examples having adj+NP+inf, as in (9).

(9) ic hæbbe me lange tid on to plegenne
I have me long time on to play. (HomM 8 (Murfin) 13)
(=I have a long time on which to play)

Since it is well-established that Old English allowed infinitival relative clauses, we can interpret the infinitival clause in (9) as depending on the noun *tid*, with the presence of *lange* as an accidental feature. For this reason, I have left all such examples out of consideration.[4]

Bearing in mind these decisions, the following data can be regarded as a record of the combination adjective plus infinitive in Old English, which should supersede the incomplete collection in Chapters 1, 11 and 12 of Callaway (1913). It should, however, be realised that some further relevant adjectives may exist, which are not given in any of the secondary sources, and which I did not think of as candidates. It is also possible that some tokens of particular adjectives in the corpus may have slipped my attention.[5] However, rechecking my results against the secondary sources did not bring to light more than a handful of errors, and in view of the large number of examples found, any remaining oversights cannot substantially affect the frequencies of distribution or the classification adopted.

2 Linguistic Classification: The Syntactic Types[6]

A basic division of all the examples is one according to the nature of the subject, as I showed by means of (4) – (6). I give another example of the type with dummy *hit* in (10)—I will from now on refer to this construction as type A. The subjectless construction I will call type B—(11) is one more example.

(10) hit is god godne to herianne & yfelne to leanne
it is good good one to praise and bad one to blame. (BedePref 2.10)
(= it is good to praise the good man and reproach the bad man)

(11) hwilum bið god wærlice to miðanne his
sometimes is good cautiously to hide one's
hieremonna scylda & to licetanne suelce he hit
subjects' sins and to pretend as if one it
nyte hwilum eft to secganne
knows not sometimes again to say (CP 21.151.8)
(= sometimes it is good cautiously to hide one's
subjects' sins, and to pretend as if one does not
know it, sometimes again it is good to say it)[7]

Type C is the construction in which there is a lexical NP subject modified by the adjective, as in (6). For this type, a further subdivision has to be made. In some cases, the matrix subject is to be interpreted also as the subject of the infinitival clause; in other cases, it functions as the direct object of the infinitive; in still other cases it must be taken as object of a preposition, and in some sentences even as part of an unrealised prepositional phrase in the infinitival clause. I will call these types (C(S), C(DO), C(PO) and C(PP). (12) – (15) are examples for each of these types.

(12)   ...þæt þu swiðe geornfull wære hit to gehyranne
       that you very eager were it to hear. (Bo 22.51.6)
       (= that you were very eager to hear it)

(13)   sio bið god to etanne
       that is good to eat (Lch II (1) 14.1.1)
       (= that is good to eat)

(14)   þa stanas sint ealle swiðe gode of to drincanne
       the stones are all very good from to drink. (Lch II (2) 64.3.2)
       (= the stones are all very good to drink from)

(15)   se x niht mona he is god to standanne mid
       the 10th night's moon it is good to stand with
       æðelum monnum & to sprecanne hymb heora weorc
       noble men and to speak about their work
       (Prog 6.9 (Foerst) 10)
       (= the 10th day after the new moon, that time is good
       to stand with noble men and talk about their work)

The classification of (12) – (14) can be considered relatively straightforward. That (15) is indeed best interpreted as C(PP) is clear from the existence of some examples which show alternation between type C(PO) and type C(PP). In fact, (15) itself is one of these examples; it continues as follows:

(16)   & eac byscop an to cesane & ealdormen & cyningas
       and also bishop on to choose and ealdormen and kings
       (= and also to choose a bishop, ealdormen and kings on)

In all, I have found 1091 examples of the combination adjective plus infinitive in the corpus. Of these, 392 occur in glosses, 699 in non-glossic, or as I shall call them, original Old English texts. The frequencies of the different types are given in Table 1.

TABLE 1

Total numbers for adjective plus infinitive, according to syntactic type and textual cateory.

	A	B	C(S)	C(DO)	C(PO)	C(PP)
Original texts	54	196	143	251	37	18
Glosses	10	269	62	21		30
Total	64	465	205	272	37	48

Type A, it will be obvious, is not frequent. Included in the count are five examples like the following, in which the word *þæt* is found instead of *hit*:

(17) þæt is witodlice idel to wuldrigenne
 that is truly idle to feel glorius.
 (HomS 38 (Szarmach VercHom 20) 122.v)
 (=it is indeed idle to feel glorious)

It is striking that the other four examples all feature the adjective *idellic*. If these examples are counted differently, the total number of examples for type A would be further reduced. On the other hand, the frequency of type A would increase if we included examples like (18) in this type

(18) ac þæt is lang and wundorlic to secganne, hu þa
 but that is long and miraculous to say how they
 wurdon generede
 were saved (HomU 35.1 (Nap 43) 49)
 (=but that is a long story and miraculous to say, how
 they were saved)

While no other interpretation for (17) seems plausible, (18) can be regarded as an example of type C(DO), with the *hu*-clause in apposition to *þæt*, and that is what I have done with such sentences (compare also Mitchell 1985: §1487 f). This way of looking at (18), I may add, should not be regarded as an inescapable fact, but as a practical decision which may or may not have to be adjusted on the basis of further study.

Of the 59 examples of type A with the word *hit*, 37 are of the type seen in both (4) and (10), i.e. they have *hit*, adjective and infinitival clause (with an inflected infinitive), in that order. None of these examples is a gloss. There are seven further examples of type A (again all in original texts) in which there is an additional dative NP, as in (19).

(19) hit is earmlic and sorhlic eallum cristenum mannum
 it is pitiful and sorrowful for all Christian men
 to gehyranne and to geseonne eall, þæt man us foresægð
 to hear and to see all that people us foretell (HomU 37 (Nap 46) 252)

(= it is pitiful and distressing for all Christians to hear and
to see what people foretell us).

In six of these seven cases, the dative comes between adjective and infinitive, as in (19);[8] one example has the dative between *hit* and the adjective.

There are five examples (all in original texts) with the order adjective+*hit*+inflected infinitive, as in (20).

(20)   laðlic is hit forðy on helle to bionne
       terrible is it therefore in hell to be
       (HomS 4 (Foerst VercHom 9) 202)
       (=therefore it is terrible to be in hell)

None of these examples has an accompanying dative NP.

Nine sentences (all of them glosses) have type A with an uninflected infinitive, in the order: adjective, *hit*, infinitive. None of them has a dative, so they are all like (21).

(21)   wyrðlicor hit ys teonan swigende forfleon þænne
       more honourable it is harm silent flee than
       andswarigende oferswyþan
       answering overcome (LibSc 2.29)
       (= it is more honourable to flee from harm silently
       than to speak out and overcome it)

One of these nine sentences has a passive infinitive:

(22)   selust hit soðlice ys mid gyfe beon gestaþelud heortan
       best it truly is with grace be settled heart
       (LibSc 47.4)
       (= it is truly best for the heart to be settled with grace)

Probably, this feature is a direct transposition from the Latin original, which reads:

(23)   optimum enim est gratia stabilari cor
       best indeed is with grace be settled heart

Finally, there is the following example (a gloss) of type A, with an (uninflected) passive infinitive and the order: infinitive, *hit*, adjective.

(24)   mid þam eallum þa ane eadignesse beon gewilnude hit is swutul
       with those all all the one happiness be wanted it is clear
       (BoGl (Hale) P.2.52)
       (= through all of which it is clear that only happiness was longed for)

In this example too, the use of the passive infinitive, if not the whole construction, must probably be ascribed to direct influence of the Latin original:

(25) quibus omnibus solam beatitudinem desiderari liquet
      through which all only happiness be wanted is clear

We may conclude that type A with a bare infinitive was not a native pattern in Old English : it is only used in glosses (10 times), where it always corresponds to a Latin infinitive, while the 54 original examples of type A all have an inflected infinitive. That the latter pattern was fully grammatical cannot be doubted, but for the former pattern the conclusion must remain somewhat tentative. This can be seen from the fact that none of the glossic examples of type A has an inflected infinitive—this would be entirely understandable if type A with a bare infinitive was possible also in native Old English; there would then not be any need to diverge from the Latin form (a bare infinitive) in glossing. In that case, the absence of type A with bare infinitive from original Old English texts would have to be put down to chance, or to some stylistic, pragmatic or even social restriction on the use of the construction which could be relaxed under pressure of the need to provide formal equivalents, i.e. in glossing. However, it is probably simpler to say that a bare infinitive in type A was not possible, and that the absence of an inflected infinitive from the glossic examples is due to a combination of chance and glossing techniques.[9]

Of course, Latin does not have any form corresponding to Old English *hit*, in this type of sentence. In most cases, indeed, such Latin sentences are glossed without the use of *hit*, so as a type B sentence. Table 1 shows that this is actually more than 25 times as frequent as the use of type A. Nevertheless, 10 examples do have *hit* in the Old English gloss, so the use of type A was probably a well-established possibility in Old English.

The over-all evidence for type A, then, shows that it was a fully grammatical pattern in Old English. However, type A can hardly go back to PIE, and perhaps not even Proto-Germanic. If we want to get a little closer to its origins, the heavy concentration of type A in sentences with *hit* +adj+infl inf (75% of all original examples) could be used as a clue. Assuming that syntactic innovations typically affect one linguistic environment before encompassing further environments, *hit* +adj+infl inf must have been the initial or canonical form for the construction. In the corpus, it is well-established there, but the scatter over other sentence-types is very limited : even the presence of a dative NP, as in (19), seems to act as a heavy constraint (only 16% of all original examples; for type B, this is 59%). Fronting of the adjective, as in (20), is only found in 9% of all original examples, and several other logical possibilities (such as sentences with a dative NP and fronted adjective, or with a dative following the infinitive) fail to occur at all.

All this does not show that type A was a recent innovation in the corpus. We might also hypothesize that, after its initial introduction in the canonical pattern, the construction remained largely stationary in terms of linguistic environments. In the following sections, I will have more to say about the constraints operating on the use of type A.

For type B, the scatter over the various subtypes is much greater. Table 2 shows the frequency of occurrence in the corpus for all the various possibilities. Glosses are again counted separately.

TABLE 2

Frequency of type B, according to nature of the infinitive, presence of dative NP, order of constituents, and textual category.

		Original	Gloss
Adj+infl inf	no dative	87	18
(N=221)	dat+adj	71	4
	adj+dat	22	16
	infl inf+dat	3	
adj+bare inf	no dative	1	159
(N=215)	dat+adj	7	6
	adj+dat	5	37
	bare inf+dat		
infl inf+adj	no dative		3
(N=4)	dat+infl inf		1
	infl inf+dat		
	adj+dat		
bare inf+adj	no dative		5
(N=25)	dat+inf		19
	inf+dat		
	adj+dat		1

If the frequencies for type A were put in a table like this, 27 of the 32 cells would be empty (disregarding the further permutations involving the position of *hit*). Table 2 has 14 empty cells. Much of this difference can probably be accounted for by the difference in overall frequency for types A and B, yet there is probably also some effect of a difference in integration of the two types in the grammar of Old English.

Table 2 tells us that type B was in all likelihood only possible with the adjective followed by the infinitive, rather than the other way round. The 29 examples with infinitive first are all from glosses, and preserve the Latin word order.[10] See for example (26), a gloss on (27).

(26) ða oðera ða to talanne longsum is
the others whom to enumerate long is
(LibScProl MtLi (Skeat) 1)
(= the others, whom it will take a long time to enumerate)

(27) ac reliquorum quos enumerare longissimum est
but others whom enumerate longest is

Example (26), incidentally, illustrates a property of type B which it may be useful to explain here, since it distinguishes types B and C(DO) in several seemingly ambiguous cases. The point is that the relative marker *ða* in (26), obviously a plural, cannot be interpreted as the subject of the relative clause (which would make the sentence into an example of type C), since it does not agree with the verb *is*. Rather, *ða* must be interpreted as object of the infinitive, and *is* has no subject, so the sentence belongs to type B. The same reasoning applies to several other examples which at first sight seem to be indeterminate between types B and C.

Even so, some truly indeterminate examples remain, i.e. those with a relative marker that is singular but not unambiguously nominative or accusative. Such examples (there are not more than a handful) I have consistently included under type C(DO), for the simple reason that this type is more frequent among the original examples in the corpus than type B (see Table 1). An example of such an indeterminate construction is (28).

(28)   æghwæt godes, þe wæs yðe to donne
       something good that was easy to do
       (HomU 9 (VerchHom 4) 150)
       (=something good that (it) was easy to do)

Returning to Table 2 now, we can see that there are many examples of type B with a bare infinitive in the glosses, and 13 examples from original texts. The question is whether a bare infinitive in type B (or in certain subtypes of B) was fully grammatical in Old English. The use of a bare infinitive in the glosses is of course of little value in answering this question, since direct Latin influence is at work here. The very large number of such examples is simply a consequence of the large number of such sentences in glossed Latin works. More significant may be the fact, already pointed out in n. 9, that in 42 sentences with type B in glosses, the Latin infinitive has been turned into an inflected infinitive in Old English. For that Latin in (29), for example, the gloss given in (30) follows the more usual strategy of rendering a Latin infinitive by an Old English bare infinitive, but the gloss in (31) has an Old English inflected infinitive, a strategy found in 16% of all type B glosses.

(29)   bonum est confidere in domino quam confidere in hominem
       good is trust in Lord than trust in man
       (= it is better to trust in the Lord than to trust in men)

(30)   god is getrywan on drihtne þanne getrywan on mann
       good is trust in Lord than trust in man
       (PsGlC (Wildhagen) 117.8)

(31)   god is to getriwenne on drihten þeæhþe to getriwenne on mæn
       good is to trust in Lord than to trust in man
       (PsGIE (Harsley) 117.8)

The existence of glosses like (31) is certainly compatible with the assumption that the construction in (30) is of doubtful grammaticality, although, to be sure, it does not exactly disconfirm other possible assumptions.

As far as the 13 original examples of type B with a bare infinitive are concerned, all of these have several elements intervening between the adjective and the infinitive, a factor whose significance was already pointed out by Callaway (1913: 21, 158). A typical example is (32).

(32) selre us is to sweltenne and soðlice andbidian þæs ecan æristes
      better us is to die and indeed wait for the eternal resurrection
      (ÆLS (Maccabees) 142)
      (= it is better for us to die and indeed to wait for the eternal resurrection)

Note that Callaway's principle only specifies where a bare infinitive might occur; it is not violated by examples like (33), where the second infinitive is at a greater distance from the adjective than in (32).

(33) betere is to heorcnienne þæs hælendes willan þonne him
      better is to listen to the Saviour's will than him
      to offrienne ænig oðre lac
      to offer any other gift (ÆHom 31 18)
      (=it is better to obey the Saviour's will than to offer him any other gift).

In the 13 examples of type B that do have an uninflected infinitive, the number of intervening elements, and their length, varies. (34) has the shortest distance between adjective and the (first) infinitive.

(34) selre þe bið anegede faran to heofonan rice þonne
      better you is one-eyed go to heaven's kingdom than
      mid twam eagum beon aworpen on ecere susle
      with two eyes be cast into eternal torment
      (ÆCHom 1.34 510.25)
      (= it is better for you to go to heaven one-eyed than
      with two eyes to be thrown into eternal torment)

In this case, however, the sentence is really a direct translation of the Latin in Matthew 18:9, so, (34) does not qualify as a firm counter-example to Callaway's principle. We conclude that the principle, if interpreted correctly, i.e. as a statement of a numerically weak tendency, is valid for type B in original examples.

In 12 examples of type B with a bare infinitive, the infinitive has the passive form. Ten of the examples are glosses, and all of these reproduce a Latin passive form, as in (35), where the Latin has *flagellari* 'be beaten'.

(35) leofre ys us beon beswungen for lare þænne hit ne cunnan
      dearer is us be beaten for teaching than it not know (ÆColl 9)
      (=we'd rather be beaten for our studies than not know things)

Of the two original examples of type B with a passive infinitive, one can be seen in the second part of (34). But as I pointed out, that example shows direct Latin influence. This only leaves (36) as an original example with a passive infinitive.

(36) rihtlic is me swa besmitenre fram þinre clænan
right is me so defiled from your pure
ungewemmednysse beon ascirod and from aworpen
spotlessness be removed and from it thrown
(LS 23 (Mary of Egypt) 2.436).
(= it is right for me to be separated and cast out from
your pure spotlessness, since I am so defiled)

If, in this case, Latin influence does not play a part, it is still only one example. Moreover, there is some additional evidence, which shows that a passive infinitive in type B was sometimes actively avoided. It is found in examples like (37), where a Latin passive infinitive (*mitti* 'be sent') is rendered by an active form in Old English, in spite of the presumably resultant unintelligiblity of this part of the sentence.

(37) god is ðe halt to gonganne in life ece ðonne
good is you lame to go to life eternal than
twoge fæt hæbbe sende in tintergu fyres unadrysendlic
two feet having send into torment of fire unquenchable
(MkGl (Ru) 9.45)
(= it is better for you to go to eternal life lame, than, having
two feet, to be sent into the torment of the unquenchable fire)

There are five other examples like this in the corpus (all from the gospels, translating the same Latin sentence as either (34) or (37)); they seem to show that in each case the glossator was unwilling to use a passive infinitive in a type B construction. This reluctance may also explain why in a few other examples, a verb meaning ' to go' is substituted for the Latin 'to be sent / thrown'. In yet other cases, the same Latin type B construction is changed into one with a finite clause in the Old English gloss. None of these shifts and changes would make much sense if a passive infinitive in type B was fully grammatical in Old English, so, in spite of (36), this pattern was probably not available in Old English.

Just as in type A, the pattern with an inflected infinitive following the adjective seems to have been the norm in type B.[11] It is used in 93% of all original examples. Table 2 shows that there are many such (original) examples with a dative NP, with dative + adjective being some three times as frequent as the reverse order. Contrary to what we might expect, none of the three examples with the dative following the infinitive has an especially heavy dative NP. (38) is one of the examples, and the other two are very much like it as far as heaviness of the final NP is concerned.

(38) þær bið yfel to wunigenne ænigum wisan men
      there is bad to live for any wise man
      (ÆAbusMor 275)
      (= it is bad there for any wise man to live)

Type C as a whole is more frequent than types A and B taken together. Table 1 shows that, compared to type B, type C is not strikingly frequent in glosses, so even on that count it would be difficult to claim that type C is a Latin-inspired construction.

The norm for type C seems to be to have the adjective followed by the infinitive. Table 3 gives the figures for the two different infinitives.

TABLE 3

Frequency of type C, according to nature of the infinitive, order of constituents, and textual category.

	Original	Gloss
adj+infl inf	436	51
adj+bare inf	11	34
infl inf+adj	2	10
bare inf+adj		18

The 28 examples in glosses with infinitive (bare or inflected) followed by the adjective all preserve the Latin word order. One example is (39), which is also special in having a passive infinitive; the Latin is given in (40).

(39) þæt innledisce hergeate þæt cyningum beon geseald gewun ys
      the native equipment that to kings be given usual is
      (RegCG1 14.5)
      (=the native equipment which is customary to be given to kings)

(40) indigenio heria qui regibus dari solet
      native equipment which to kings be given is usual

The two original examples having the (inflected) infinitive followed by the adjective are (41) and (42).

(41) ælces cynnes treow, fæger on gesyhðe & to brucenne wynsum
      of every kind tree beautiful in sight and to eat pleasant
      (Gen 2.9)
      (=every kind of tree, beautiful to see and pleasant to eat)

(42) his lac...þæt he on gehendnysse to bicgenne gearu hæfde
      his gift that he in nearness to buy ready should have
      (ÆCHom 1,28 406.18)
      (= his gift...that he should have it at hand ready to buy)

For (41), direct Latin influence is of course very likely, compare Mitchell (1985: §928). In the case of (42), either the use of the verb *habban* may be responsible for the special word order, or it might be said that the infinitive does not really depend on the adjective here; it might then be an example of a final infinitive. In the absence of native judgements, this is difficult to decide (but compare (56)). We can at any rate safely say that type C with infl inf+adj only accounts for (at most) 0.0045% of all original type C sentences in the corpus.

The 34 glosses with adjective plus bare infinitive all reproduce a Latin infinitive. One example is (43).

(43) ne ðe ðon gidyrstig wæs ænig of ðæm dæge hine forðor gefregna
      not so audacious was any from that day him further question
      (MtGl (Li) 22.46).
      (=after that day, no one was so audacious as to question him any further).

Of the 11 original examples with adj+bare inf, five have the adjective followed by two infinitival clauses, the first of which has an inflected infinitive, as in (44).

(44) ic eom gearo to gecyrenne to munuclicre drohtnunge,
      I am ready to turn to monastic life
      and woruldice ðeawas ealle forlætan
      and wordly customs all leave
      (ÆCHom 1,35 534.32)
      (=I am ready to turn to a monastic life, and give up
      all worldly customs)

Three examples have the infinitive separated from the adjective by at least two constituents, as in (45).

(45) þæt hy gearwe beon ealle endemes heora nihtsang
      that they ready are all together their evensong
      ætgædere singan
      together sing (RegC 1 (Zup) 177)
      (=that they are ready to sing their evensong all together)

As a whole, these eight examples fit in well with Callaway's principle, which was discussed in connection with type B.

There remain three examples of type C with a bare infinitive. *Guth* A, B 1077, a fairly unclear sentence, has two instances of the bare infinitive, one of which closely follows the adjective, but both infinitives may be in apposition to a noun rather than being dependent on an adjective. Finally, there is the following example:

(46) we ðe næron wurðe beon his wealas gecidge
      we who were not worth be his slaves called

(ÆCHom II,21 181.49)
(=we who were not worthy to be called his slaves)

For the use of a passive infinitive in this example, Bock (1931: 202 fn.2) cites Latin influence; compare also n. 11. It may also be significant that the sentence preceding (46) in the text also has a passive with *geciged* (though a finite one). Perhaps some form of parallelism was being aimed at, although that of course does not mean that an unacceptable construction would become acceptable. In Section 3, I will discuss an additional explanation that has been proposed for the use of the passive in (46).

Let me also add here the third instance, besides (39) and (46), of a passive infinitive in type C that I have found. It is (47), a gloss with *beon gedon* for Latin *agi* 'be held'.

(47)   embegang...se þe gewun ys on claustre beon gedon
       procession which usual is on cloister be done
       (RegCGl 5.65)
       (=a procession, which it is customary to hold in the cloister)

It is noteworthy that all the 11 original examples of type C with a bare infinitive belong to type C(S). Type C(DO) is nearly twice as frequent in original Old English as type C(S), yet it never takes a bare infinitive. It would be nice to have analyses for types C(S) and C(DO) (which must be based on the core pattern for both types, i.e. adj+infl inf), that would predict this surprising fact without further stipulation. Some sort of differentiation of the inflected infinitives in the two types would seem necessary for that. But this is obviously not the place to pursue such more theoretical matters. Nonetheless, it seems appropriate to raise them, if only to indicate that certain, in a sense marginal, data thrown up by this corpus study can provide a means to ascertain the wider validity of analyses of the core cases of type C.

Let me briefly summarise the conclusions we have drawn from the figures in Table 3. In original Old English, type C with adj+infl inf is fully grammatical; adj+bare inf is possible in just a few cases, as determined by Callaway's principle, and perhaps never in type C(DO); all other combinations were not grammatical. These statements hold for sentences in which the adjective modifies the subject of the relevant clause. When the adjective modifies the object, as in (42), a pre-adjectival inflected infinitive might be possible. Table 3 does not include information about the presence of a dative NP in type C, but it may be worth pointing out that such a dative only occurs in the patter adj+infl inf, both in glosses and original examples, but not in any of the other patterns.

In examining the more marginal patterns of type C, I have for the most part ignored the distinction between the types C(S), C(DO), C(PO), and C(PP), since the totals for these patterns are small. It is more rewarding to look at the subdivisions in the core pattern of type C; I present this information in Table 4, where NP stands for the matrix subject (or, more precisely, the NP modified by the adjective; more on this later).

TABLE 4

Frequency of type C with adj+infl inf, according to syntactic subtype, order of constituents, and textual category.

		C(S)		C(DO)		C(PO)	C(PP)
		or	gl	or	gl	or	or
NP+adj+inf	no dat	129	22	140	12	35	14
	dat+NP			5			
	NP+dat	2		60	2	1	
	dat+inf			25	5		4
	inf+dat			4			
adj+NP+inf	no dat	1	9	8		1	
	dat+adj			3			
adj+inf+NP	no dat			3	1		
	dat+adj			1			
	total	132	31	249	20	37	18

It is clear from Table 4 that type C(S) is overwhelmingly of the sort seen in (48).

(48) hie beoð bealdran ða godan to swenceanne
      they are bolder the good to trouble (CP 47.361.10)
      (=they are bolder to trouble good people)

The two examples of type C(S) which have a dative NP are both found in the following sentence :

(49) wæs he...ealre his þeode leof heora rice to habbanne & to healdenne
      was he all his people dear their kingdom to have and to hold
      (Bede 5 17.450.2)
      (=he was dear to all his people to have and rule the kingdom).

In all other cases of types A, B and C with a dative depending on the adjective, this dative can be interpreted as subject of the infinitive. This, of course, is not possible in type C(S), so we would not expect a dative in this type. (49) is the only example of its kind. This may mean that it should not be included in the present data, or, as seems more likely, that the adjective *leof* has some special semantic/syntactic property which makes *leof*+dat+adj+inf in type C(S) available.

The one original Old English example of C(S) with the adjective in front-position is (50).

(50) toþæs mihtig he þonne wæs ælce untrumnesse to hælenne
      so mighty he then was each infirmity to heal
      (LS 17.1 (MartinMor) 221).
      (= so powerful he then was to heal every infirmity)

One example is not much, but this sentence seems reliable enough and, given also the occurrence of this order in 15 examples of type C(DO), it is likely that (50) represents a fully grammatical pattern.[12] Its very low frequency may be attributable to some special function it carries in structuring the information content of the sentence.

Table 4 shows that a dative NP depending on the adjective is quite common in type C(DO). As in type B (compare Table 2), the dative is in the great majority of cases close to the adjective, strongly suggesting that there is some syntactic connection between the two, with the proportion of dat+adj to adj+dat roughly the same for both types (2 or 3 to 1). The figure of four for post-infinitival datives in type C(DO) given in Table 4 is slightly inflated. Owing to the method of counting explained in Section 1 (see also n. 7), (51) contains two of the four examples.

(51) swa swa nu eorðe is & wæter sint swiðe earfoðe to
just as now earth is and water are very hard to
geseonne oððe to ongitonne dysgum monnum on fyre
see or to perceive for foolish men on fire
(Bo 33.81.2).
(= just as now earth and water are very hard for
foolish people to see or perceive in fire)

Here the dative NP is not particularly heavy; compare my remarks about example (38). However, if we accept that the dative depends on the adjective and also that *on fyre* is part of the infinitival clause, the word order in (51) is peculiar anyway, so it may be best not to base any conclusions on it. In the two other examples of type C(DO) with a dative following the infinitive, the dative NP can be considered heavy. Both (52) and the other example have a relative clause as part of the final NP.

(52) hit bið swyðe gedwolsum to rædenne ðæm ðe ðæs
it is very misleading to read for him who of the
Ledenes wise ne can
Latin manner not knows (ÆGenPref 93)
(= it is very misleading to read for anyone who does
not know the Latin idiom)

The four examples with dat+NP+adj+infl inf do not have long or complex dative NPs. Example (53) has the longest one, but a single dative pronoun also occurs.

(53) forðæm þæm unandgytfullum þæt gastlice
therefore for the uninsightful the spiritual
angyt is earfoþe to understandenne
meaning is hard to understand (BenR 42.6)
(=therefore the spiritual meaning is hard to
understand for those lacking in insight)

The 15 examples of type C(DO) with the adjective first shown in Table 4 fall into two categories. The first (five examples) seems syntactically determined, in that in each case the adjective is premodified by *hu*, and the adjective phrase as a whole must then be clause-initial. An example is (54).

(54)   scrutniað nu þa mid hu waclicum wurþe godes rice
       consider now then with how weak price God's kingdom
       bið geboht and hu deorwurðe hit is to geagenne
       is bought and how precious it is to own
       (ÆCHom 1,38 582.25)
       (= consider now then at what a small price God's
       kingdom can be bought, and how precious it is to have)

In the remaining ten examples, the word order probably has to do with discourse factors; thus (55) seems to give some special prominence to *eaðelic*.

(55)   þæt him wære eaðelic se wifhired to healdanne & to rihtanne
       that him was easy the nunnery to hold and to rule
       (GD 1(C) 4.27.4)
       (=that the nunnery was easy for him to lead and rule)

However, some of these examples, including (55), look slightly suspect, in that we may wonder whether a nominative (in (55), *se wifhired*) is really intended. But whenever the NP is unambiguously marked for nominative, I have counted the example under type C(DO). Among the 10 examples, there is also the following :

(56)   þæt hi...habban æfre gearo to teonne forð þone
       that they have always ready to draw forth the
       wisdom and þa lare
       wisdom and the teaching (ÆCHom 1,12 190.5)
       (=that they always have wisdom and doctrine ready to draw forth)

As in the case of (42), there are various ways of looking at this example. Note that the fact that the same adjective features in both sentences could be used to argue that there is indeed a connection between the adjective and the infinitive, as I am assuming for counting purposes.

Before we leave type C(DO), let me point out that the total number of original examples for it in the corpus is quite high. It is higher than for types B and C(S), and it is several times that of type A. These proportions are quite different in Present-day English. Thus, Mair (1987) reports that Tough-movement (which includes type C(DO) as well as type C(PO)) in the Survey of English Usage Corpus is relatively infrequent. My own study of the (American) Brown Corpus indicates (among other things) that types A and C(S) are much more frequent now than type C(DO), a result which can no doubt be matched for British English. Whatever the reasons for these developments, it is hard to agree with Lightfoot

(1979 : 298 fn.2), who says, concerning the history of sentences like 'John is easy to please' : 'Jespersen ... cites several examples from Chaucer, but there seem to be few cases prior to that'.

From Table 4 it can easily be seen that type C(PO) is not at all frequent in the corpus. In the glosses, there are no examples at all; no doubt this is due to the absence of this construction in Latin. All the examples are included in Table 4, so type C(PO) only occurs in the core pattern of type C, with adjective followed by an inflected infinitive. Moreover, even within this core pattern, type C(PO) does not have a wide scatter, as the uneven distribution in Table 4 shows. But it would be dangerous to assume on the basis of these facts that type C(PO) was an incipient one in Old English. Referring to Mair (1987) again for a Present-day English corpus study, from the information given there it can be deduced that C(PO) is quite rare in modern (British) English — yet the Old English data show that the construction has been around for at least one thousand years now.

For the Old English data, a possible explanation for the low frequency of type C(PO) may be sought in the lower overall frequency of prepositions in Old English compared with later stages of the language. In particular, the use of various prefixes to turn intransitive verbs into transitives would at the same time turn potential C(PO) examples into C(DO) examples. However, with all the other changes that have taken place in the lexicon, it is not easy to observe the effects of the loss of this type of derivation by simply comparing an Old English example of type C(DO) with its present-day equivalent. Nevertheless, further investigation in this area, with more sophisticated procedures, might be worthwhile.

In all 37 examples of C(PO), the preposition immediately precedes the inflected infinitive. The preposition *on* is far and away most frequent: it occurs 27 times. In seven sentences, it combines with an infinitive meaning 'to be/to stay', as in (57); and also in seven examples with *on* the infinitive denotes 'seeing/looking at', as in (58).

(57)　heo is gesundful and myrige on to wunienne
　　　it is healthy and pleasant on to live
　　　(ÆCHom I, 12 182.33)
　　　(=it is healthy and pleasant to live on)

(58)　heo wæs swiþe fæger an to locianne
　　　it was very beautiful at to look
　　　(Or 2 4.74.11)
　　　(=it was very beautiful to look at)

The other prepositions occurring in type C(PO) are *mid* (3 times), *in*, *of* *ymb* (twice each) and *to* (once).

Ten examples have a matrix subject expressing a point or period of time, as in (59).

(59)　twegen dagas, þe syndon swyðe derigendlice ænigne
　　　two days that are very harmful any
　　　drenc on to ðicgenne, oððe blod on to lætenne

drink on to drink, or blood on to let
(Days 6 (Henel) 1.1)
(=two days that are very harmful to drink any drink on,
or to let blood on)

All of these examples have *on* as the stranded preposition.

The one example in the corpus of type C(PO) with the adjective in front-position (HomU 32 (Nap 40) 121) has the sequence *hu*+adj, just like several of such examples in type C(DO), compare (54).

Finally, Table 4 shows that type C(PP) is even less frequent than type C(PO) in the core pattern of type C. It should be realised, however, that there are 30 more tokens for C(PP), but these are all glosses. They all reproduce the construction of the original, as (60), a gloss on (61).

(60) mona se nigoþa on eallum intingum to dondum god ys,
 moon the ninth on all things to do good is
 wyrtun don
 garden do (ProgG1 2.1 (Foerst) 9.1)
 (=the ninth moon is good to do all things, to work in the garden)

(61) luna ix omnibus causis agendis bona est, hortum facere
 moon nine all things doing good is garden do

In seven of these glosses, there is an inflected infinitive; (60) shows one. But none of the glosses with C(PP) occurs in the core pattern for type C. i.e. with adj+infl inf, while all the original examples do. This peculiar distribution indicates that the construction is not likely to be due to Latin influence, even though a superficial look at the total numbers for C(PP) in original texts and glosses (as given in Table 1) might seem to suggest this.

All of the 18 original examples of type C(PP), and in fact also all 30 examples in glosses, have a subject expressing a period or point of time. I gave one example in (15).

In (15)-(16), we saw alternation between types C(PO) and C(PP), which indicates the parallel that I am taking as the basis for classification. There is one more example with this alternation in coordinate clauses in the same sentence.

(62) he is god hordern on to scæwiene & minster to
 it is good storeroom on to watch and monastery to
 gereranne & to sættenne
 build and to establish (Prog 6.9 (Foerst) 16)
 (=it is good to inspect the storeroom on and to build
 and establish a monastery)

Of course this type of variation in Old English can also be found in sentences with an expression of time followed by a relative clause. This parallel might be adduced as further support for an analysis of types C(PO) and C(PP) in terms of a relative clause strategy, as proposed in Van Kemenade (1987).

In this section, we have so far been concerned with the numbers of examples for the various subtypes of the combination adjective plus infinitive. The classification adopted was based on such features as nature of the matrix subject, nature of the infinitive, presence of a dative NP and constituent order. With the help of information concerning textual category of the examples (glossic or original), we have also tried to establish in how far the different subtypes were grammatical in native Old English.

To complete this part of the linguistic classification, it is necessary to address one further point : the nature of the matrix verb. In 92% of all 1091 examples in the corpus, the matrix verb is a form of *beon/wesan*, as in nearly all examples presented so far.

There is one sentence with type A which has the verb *ðyncan:*

(63) hit þuncþ monige monnum wunderlic to herenne & eac
      it seems many men miraculous to hear and also
      uneaðelic to lyfene, hu deofel æfre þa durstinesse
      difficult to believe how devil ever the audacity
      hæfde
      had (HomU1 (Belf 10) 81)
      (= to many people it seems miraculous to hear and also
      difficult to believe how the devil ever had the audacity).[13]

Type B has *ðyncan* as matrix verb 11 times (all in original examples), and in 15 sentences (11 of these are glosses) there is no matrix verb. (64) and (65) are examples of both types.

(64) sumum menn wile þincan syllic þis to gehyrenne
      some man will seem strange this to hear
      (ÆLS (Maccabees) 564)
      (= it will seem strange to some people to hear this)

(65) he bið þam godum glædmod on gesihþe...lufsum ond
      he is to the good pleasant in sight lovable and
      liðe leofum monnum to sceawianne þone scynan wlite
      pleasing to dear men to see the beautiful appearance
      (Christ A, B, C 910)
      (= he will be to good people pleasant to see, lovable, and it is pleasant
      for dear men to see the beautiful appearance)

While (64) and the ten other sentences like it seem unproblematic, (65) and the three other original examples with type B lacking a matrix verb are somewhat suspect. All of them seem to change construction in mid-sentence, from type

C(DO) to type B. For that reason these (few) examples do not fit well in the classification adopted here.

Type C shows the widest range of matrix verbs, although there too *beon/wesan* is used in about 90% of all cases. In Table 5 I give the other verbs that occur, and their frequencies in original texts and glosses.

TABLE 5

Frequency of matrix verbs in type C, according to textual category.

	Original	Gloss
no verb	14	20
ðyncan	13	
weorðan	2	
beon tohabbanne		1
beon hæfde		1
beon gesewen	1	
habban	3	
gedon	2	
macian	1	
ongietan	1	

Unlike for type B, most verbless examples of type C seem convincing enough.[14] One example is (66), where a form of 'to be' may be provided for the interpretation.

(66) and þær wæs micel gærs on ðære stowe myrige on to sittenne
      and there was much grass in that place pleasant on to sit
      (ÆCHom I, 12 182.11)
      (=and there was a lot of grass in that place, pleasant to sit on)

Similarly, the examples with *ðyncan* and *weorðan* in type C are quite straightforward. (67) is an example with *ðyncan*.

(67) gif hit ne ðuhte æðryt to awritenne
      if it not seemed tedious to write (ÆTemp 10.22)
      (=if it did not seem tedious to write)

When one of the verbs *habban*, *gedon*, *macian* or *ongietan* is used, the construction is slightly different from the description I have used so far. In these cases, the adjective modifies not the subject of the clause but the direct object. A clear case is (68).

(68) se ælmihtiga god stilde þana strangan sæ...and
      the almighty God made quiet the strong sea and
      gemacode hine swiðe wynsum on to wunigenne
      made it very pleasant on to live (LS 9 (Giles) 59)

(=the almighty God made the rough sea quiet,
and made it very pleasant to live on)

Although there are only seven of these direct object sentences, they show that the notion 'subject' is not essential to a definition of type C. I have given two of the three examples with *habban* in (42) and (56); the third one (Bede 5 12.418.27) also has the adjective *gearo*, which strengthens the case for my interpretation of these sentences.

Although this third example with *habban* and also (68), so two out of seven examples, are of type C(PO), this may be a coincidence. Type C(PP) does not occur here, but we have seen that it is very infrequent as a whole. Examples (42) and (56) have type C(DO) and (69) illustrates type C(S) with the adjective modifying a direct object.

(69) he gedyde hi sona mihtige and strange to
he made them at once mighty and strong to
wiðstandenne heora feondum
withstand their enemies (ÆHomM 15 (Ass9)125)
(=he made them at once powerful and strong to
withstand their enemies)

Types A and B do not occur at all in constructions like (68) - (69). For type B, in fact, it requires some thought even to imagine what such a sentence would look like. Using modern English sentences for ease of exposition, type B in its normal form has the structure of (70), while a type B sentence modelled on the pattern of (68) – (69) will be as in (71).

(70) *is easy to understand his words

(71) *this made easy to understand his words

Since type B is frequent enough in Old English, the absence of structures like (71) is probably not due to chance but to grammatical factors.
A sentence of this kind with type A would have the structure of (72).

(72) this made it easy to understand his words

The absence of such sentences in the corpus is not terribly surprising, since type A itself is not very frequent. It might be suggested, however, that the absence of these structures also has to do with the way type A was still spreading through the grammar of Old English. Somewhat extending the suggestions I made earlier in this section, we might assume that clauses with *hit* +adj+infl inf, and a finite form of *beon/wesan*, formed the canonical pattern for type A, in which it was well-established. Structures like (72) represent a generalisation of the type to a syntactic environment with dummy object *hit*, and it is possible that this extension had not taken place in Old English yet.

3 Linguistic Classification: The Adjectives

The little research that has been done on the combination adjective plus infinitive in Old English has already yielded several hypotheses about syntactic properties of adjectives in Old English (and also later stages of the language). Thus the 'impersonal' nature of various adjectives was already recognised in the last century; see Van der Gaaf (1904) and references. Among more recent work, there is Van der Wurff (1987), who casts this traditional view into a modern theoretical framework, which leads to an 'ergative' analysis; Van Kemenade (1987), who suggests that certain adjectives in Old English can mediate in an antecedent-relative relation; and Fischer (1988), who observes that syntactic properties of certain adjectives in Old English and Middle English may have been responsible for the rise of the passive infinitive in type C.

In this section, therefore, I will investigate the range of adjectives used in the different types, again with the aim of providing the data on which more theoretical work (like that mentioned above) can draw to arrive at a more complete understanding of this type of impersonal in Old English.

In all, 207 adjectives are used in types A, B and C together (counting comparatives and superlatives separately). Many of these are represented in only one or two examples, but there are some which are quite frequent. In Table 6 I give the full figures for all adjectives with more than 15 tokens in the data, specifying for each the construction types in which it is used, and also distinguishing original examples from those found in glosses. To establish whether a particular adjective fulfilled the quota of 15, I have added up all the tokens for absolutive, comparative, superlative and also negated form of the adjective. For example, *eaðe*, which has only 11 tokens, is included because *eaðor* and *uneaðe* fill up the quota. I will refer to the set of absolutive, comparative, superlative and negated form as the 'headword'; when I want to single out one of the four (insofar as they are all four used with an infinitive), I will refer to it as an 'adjective' or 'form'. Although inclusion in Table 6 depends on the total frequency of all forms in the headword, the information given is arranged according to form.

TABLE 6

Headwords with frequency f>15, according to form, syntactic subtype, and textual category:

column I = original texts
column II = glosses

	A I	A II	B I	B II	C(S) I	C(S) II	C(DO) I	C(DO) II	C(PO) I	C(PP) I	C(PP) II
god	3	2	20	87			13	1	10	10	17
betere	1	2	6	48			6				
betst			2				5				
selre			12	8			2				
selost	1	1	2				11				
alyfed	2		38	16			10	2			
gearo					40	5	2		1		
ungearo							1				
eaðe			5				6				
eaðor			8	7			6	2			
uneaðe	4		1		2		4				
leof			1		4		1				
leofra			15	4			2				
leofost			1				5				
wyrðe				1	10	15	6				
wyrðost					1						
rihtlic			2	22			1			4	
rihtlicra							1				
rihtlicost							1				
unrihtlic							1				
earfoð	4		5				14				
earfoðre	1		1								
earfoðest							1				
lang	4		10				11				
hræd					3	9					
hræddra						2					
hrædost							10				
gelefed				21				3			
riht	1		3	3			3	4			
rihtor							3	1			
unriht							1	1			
langsum	5		7	1			6				
wynsum		1		9			3		3		
wynsumre							2				
unwynsum									1		
nytlic				2							13
nytlicor				2							
nytlicost							2				
toweard					8	8					

Several observations can be made concerning Table 6, some of which also apply to less frequently used headwords. To begin with, it will be obvious that the role of the headword *god* is disproportionate: of the total of 1091 examples, 25% feature this headword. The adjective *god* is also the form most widely distributed across the construction-types; it is found with types A, B C(DO), C(PO) and C(PP), all in original examples.

Especially the co-occurrence of *god* in types C(PO) and A/B is remarkable. There are only four adjectives in the corpus that also show this pattern. They are:

egeslic (A and B), *licwierðe* (one example of B, but in a gloss) *wynsum* (once type A, nine times type B, but all in glosses) and *wundorlic* (type A). Just as for the Present-day English data of this type (where many more adjectives show this co-occurrence), the analysis of these constructions poses severe problems for any theory trying to make predictions about empty subjects, the occurrence of dummy *(h)it* and preposition stranding; see Chomsky (1981 : 308 ff.) for the problem and an attempt at solution, and Jones (1983) for some criticism. The fact that the number of relevant adjectives in the Old English corpus is so small (especially if we only consider original examples) may make it possible to circumvent these problems by some sort of dual subcategorisation, a possibility somewhat grudgingly left open in Van der Wurff (1987), where the theoretical considerations are set forth as they apply to Old English.

The second most frequent headword in Table 6 is *alyfed*. This form may of course also be a past participle, and its inclusion in the present study might well be objected to. However, the negative *unalyfed* is well-attested, suggesting that *alyfed* itself could also be used as an adjective. Also the fact that the form participates in the constructions described here, and that quite frequently, could be used to argue that it has adjectival status in these cases. There are only four other forms like this in the data : *gelefed* (see Table 6; only used in glosses), *lefed* (only used once, in a gloss), *gelicod* (five times, all in glosses), and *gelæred* (once). If these forms are excluded because they occur either too infrequently or only in glosses, then the question arises why *alyfed* is the only passive form used in original examples with all of types A, B and C. Saying that it can function as an adjective may only be part of the answer, but I think it is a necessary part.

Table 6 shows that *alyfed* occurs in types A, B and C(DO). The data for all the adjectives indicate that this distribution is probably part of a unidirectional implication saying that an adjective occurring in type B will also occur in type C(DO).[15] At first sight, this is not so clear, since there are 43 adjectives in the corpus which support this implication, as against 35 which do not. However, of the 35 not evidencing the implication, 18 have only one token in the data, 11 occur only twice, five are used three times, and one, *gelicod*, five times (but only in glosses, all in type B). If we leave out of account the first two groups, because they cannot be significant in deciding on the validity of the implication, and also *gelicod*, because it may not be acceptable in original examples at all, we arrive at a ratio of 43 to 5 for the significant cases. If it is held that the implication is important from a theoretical point of view, as argued in Van der Wurff (1987), we can say that the data from the corpus give the correlation between types B and C(DO) some empirical support. All the relevant headwords in Table 6 also show the effect of the implication.

The third most frequent headword in Table 6 is *gearo*. It shows heavy concentration in type C (S). There are in all 53 adjectives occurring in type C(S) : 43 of them are restricted to that type. 24 of these occur only once, but even allowing for this, the data do not suggest that there is a strong correlation between the occurrence of an adjective in type C(S) and some other type. If anything, the opposite is more likely to be true, as indeed the semantic differences between type

C(S) and each of the other types would suggest.

That the headword (and also the adjective) *gearo* does show co-occurrence in C(S) and C(DO) is therefore probably an idiosyncrasy. There are only six other forms that occur in both of these types in original examples. They are *uneaðe*, *leof*, *lustbære*, *wyrðe*, *gewuna*, and *wundorlic*. In Fischer (1988) the interesting suggestion is put forward that the use of a passive infinitive in example (46), the only original example of type C with such a passive, may be due to the fact that *wyrðe* is 'double-handled'.

(46) we ðe næron wurðe beon his wealas gecigde
 we who were not worth be his slaves called
 (ÆCHom II, 21 181.49)
 (=we who were not worthy to be called his slaves)

If an active infinitive were used in this example, it might be unclear whether type C(S) or type C(D) was intended, which would make the meaning of the sentence ambiguous; this was solved by using the passive infinitive, perhaps in imitation of Latin. Fischer (1988 : 93f.) also suggests that the introduction of more of these 'double-handled' adjectives in Middle English, through borrowing from French and Latin, was one of the reasons why the passive infinitive in type C came to be used more widely in that period. Referring to Bock (1931), Fischer (1988 : 77 f) also points at the development of the passive infinitive with *to* in Middle English as a factor making the use of the passive infinitive in type C more acceptable. See also n. 11, where I apply Bock's ideas to type B.

If this explanation for (46) is correct, we might ask why the six[16] other adjectives in the corpus that are 'double-handled' are not attested with a passive infinitive. Since the number of examples involved is small (except for *gearo* in type C(S), see Table 6), this may well be a matter of chance. Probably the obligatory use of the bare infinitive in the passive in Old English also played a role here; see above.

If we also say that an adjective is 'double-handled', if it only occurs in type C(S) or type C(DO), but has a related form which supplies the missing type, as Fischer (1988 : 68 f.) in a way does by giving examples with *wyrðe* and *wyrðelic*, and also *gearo* and *ungearo*, there will be 14 more 'double-handled' adjectives than the ones I have mentioned so far.

However, grammatically speaking, it may be better to keep such related forms strictly separate as far as their use in different constructions is concerned. This point can easily be demonstrated by reference to some Present-day English examples. Thus, *easy* and *uneasy* show quite different syntactic properties—this is probably because there are two forms *easy*, only one of which has a negative; compare Nanni (1978). Similarly, while (73) is fine, (74), although it can be found, is odd.

(73) this man is impossible to work with

(74) ?*this man is not possible to work with

This contrast probably has a semantic basis; see Riviere (1983). Finally, the difference between *worth* and *worthy* may also be useful to cite in this connection.

Returning to Table 6 now, we come to the headword *eaðe*. It, and also *earfoð*, are representative of what Nanni (1978; 1980) calls the *easy*-class of adjectives, i.e. adjectives meaning 'easy', 'difficult', etc., and occurring in the Tough-movement construction. Of course, it is not only words meaning 'easy' or its opposite than can occur in Tough-movement — see for example the list in Lasnik & Fiengo (1974 : 568). In Old English, if we take co-occurrence in types B and C(DO) as the criterion, the group of adjectives will have 43 members in the corpus, only some of which are of the *easy*-type (that is, *earfoð*, *eaðe*, *leoht* and related forms, all together 12 adjectives).

Allen (1980: 383 fn. 25) was the first to point out that *easy*-type adjectives do not seem to occur in type C(PO) in Old English. Table 6 shows that this is true for *eaðe* and *earfoð* ; it is also true for related forms that are found in the data. There is only one example, with *leohtre*, which might raise some doubt about the claim. It is found in the following sentence:[17].

(75)   for þam þe leohtre is þam bearnum maga
       because lighter is for the children kinsmen's
       swingcela to geþolianne þonne Godes yrre on to
       lashes to suffer than God's anger on to
       beyrnanne
       run (ThCap 2 (Sauer) 33.369.8)
       (=because it is lighter for children to suffer the
       lashes of kinsmen, than ? ? ?)

The first part of this sentence is clearly an example of type B. But what exactly is the role of *on* in the second infinitival clause? If it is a stranded preposition, it might turn the clause into an example of type C(PO). However, I think we should reject such an interpretation for (75). The reason is that there are Old English examples like the following:

(76)   leahter we onbeyrnað
       reproach we incur. (LibSc 37.11)
       (=we incur reproach)

Here *onbeyrnan* functions as a transitive verb taking a direct object. As far as I have been able to establish, it only occurs in glosses. For (76), the Latin reads:

(77)   crimen incurrimus
       reproach we incur

The other examples of *onbeyrnan* also correspond to Latin *incurrere*. Apparently, to gloss this Latin verb, *onbeyrnan* was formed from the existing verb *beyrnan* and the prefix *on-*. Example (75) shows, I think, exactly the same use of *onbeyrnan* as a transitive verb. Although *ThCap 2* is not a gloss, it is a translation and according to Sauer (1979: 119) it differs from *ThCap 1* in being 'eine ziemlich wörtliche, oft beinahe mechanische Übersetzung'. Not surprisingly, the Latin sentence to which (75) corresponds has the verb *incurrere* :

(78) quia leuius est filliis parentum flagella
      because lighter is for children parents' lashes
      suscipere, quam dei iram incurrere
      undergo than God's anger incur

Unlike the other attested examples with *onbeyrnan* in Old English, (75) has the inflected infinitive of the verb, which may make it somewhat difficult to recognise, but this type of formation can be paralleled in Old English. For example, (79) and (80) are different versions of the same sentence, with *on to gebringenne* in (80) clearly corresponding to the undoubtedly transitive verb *to donne* in (79), and therefore best interpreted as the inflected infinitive of the existing (transitive) verb *ongebringan*.

(79) se þe naht unstrang nis wræce to donne
      he who not at all weak is not vengeance to do
      (GD 1 (C) 9.63.13)
      (=he who is not at all weak to take vengeance)

(80) se þe nis na unstrang wrake on to gebringenne
      he who is not weak vengeance on to bring (GD 1 (H) 26.63.13)
      (=he who is not weak to bring about vengeance)

We may conclude that the second infinitival clause in (75) is also a type B clause, which exactly parallels the first one, and means 'to incur God's anger'. This interpretation accounts satisfactorily for both the form and the meaning of the sentence. With (75) taken care of in this way, the data I have gathered from the corpus do not contain an *easy*-class adjective in type C(PO).

The next headword in Table 6, *leof*, makes clear why I decided at an early stage to keep the different degrees of the adjective separate. The form *leofra* is much more frequent than the absolutive and superlative forms, and it occurs in type B at least 15 times as often as either of the other forms. All the examples with *leofra* have an accompanying dative NP, and it may be appropriate to regard adjective+dative as an idiom in this case.

The headwords *rihtlic*, *gelefed*, *wynsum*, *nytlic* and *toweard* show that the quantitative contribution of glossic examples in the data can equal or exceed that of original examples. In general, this means that hypotheses heavily dependent on glossic examples will need to be inspected carefully, and it is certainly advisable to keep the two categories apart in frequency counts as far as possible. The total number of adjectives used in glosses among the data is 63. Of these, 32 are used in a particular construction type in a gloss and also in an original example, and 31 are used in a particular type in a gloss only. In the latter case, of course, we cannot tell whether the adjective really occurred in that type in original Old English.

However, the score of roughly 50% for 'validated' glossic examples is not bad at all, and makes clear that, as far as the choice of the adjective was concerned, there was at least some attempt to produce grammatical Old English in these sentences. In Table 6, in which the most frequently used adjectives are given, no more than 10% of the cells contain glossic examples only.

Since types A, C(PO) and C(PP) are not frequent, Table 6 contains little that is remarkable for these types. I give the full data for type A in Table 7.

TABLE 7

Frequency of adjectives in type A, according to textual category.

Adjective (N=34)	Original	Gloss
langsum	5	
lang, idellic, uneaðe, earfoð	4	
god	3	2
alyfed, earmlic, wundorlic, nyttre, sarlic, sorhlic	2	
betere	1	2
selost	1	1
wyrðlicor		2
strang, unaræfnedlic, biterlic, swetlic, earfoðre, uneaðelic, egeslic, halwende, idel, lað, laðlic, ungeliefedlic, lustbærre, riht, scandlic, toweardlic	1	
sweotol, dysig, wynsum		1

We have seen in Section 2 that type A overwhelmingly occurs in the pattern adj+infl inf in original Old English, and that the presence of a dative strongly inhibits the use of type A. In the latter case, the use of type B is much more frequent. If we believe that change is implemented through a shift in the constraints operating on the use of constructions, we would like to find out what other constraints operated in Old English to determine the choice between types A and B, and how they have shifted in the course of the centuries to produce the Present-day English situation, in which B is absent and A has probably also overtaken type C(DO) in frequency of use. With the limited evidence available for Old English, our understanding of the determining factors in that period must probably remain sketchy. We may guess that the constraint involving the presence of a dative NP was gradually relaxed; study of Middle English materials should show this. The continued strength of the constraint involving the nature of the infinitive (inflected or bare) suggests that there is, in Old English but also later, some basic grammatical distinction between the two infinitives; compare also the remarks just below example (47).

The data in Table 7 allows us to identify specific adjectives as linguistic factors favouring the use of type A: *lang(sum)*, *idellic*, *uneaðe* and *earfoð* are the most important ones in the corpus. No doubt Middle English data will show a significant increase in the number of these adjectives and/or a change in the weight of the constraint (in Old English, even for these most favourable adjectives, the proportion of type A to type B is less than 50%). On the other hand, the sheer number of adjectives in Table 7 supports the conclusion we arrived at in Section 2: type A must have been well-established in the grammar of Old English.

In Table 8, I give the full figures for all adjectives found in type C(PO).

TABLE 8

Frequency of adjectives in type C(PO)

adjective (N=21)	original
god	10
myrige, wynsum	3
ana, derigendlic	2
gecoplic, eatolic, egeful, egeslic, fæger, gearu, glæd, glæshluttor, grim, hal, licwierðe, lustfullic, lustsumlic, lyðre, onderslic, unwynsum, wundorlic	1

The predominance of *god* in this type is noticeable; it is a bit greater than we might expect on the basis of the total frequencies in original examples (compare Table 6). Of the other adjectives, about half denote some degree of (un)pleasantness. The adjective *myrige* stands out because type C(PO) accounts for 100% of all of its examples in the data — though even for this adjective the small total number of examples may well mean that this fact is due to chance. This, I presume, is certainly the case for *gecoplic*, *eatolic*, *fæger*, *glæd*, *glæshluttor*, *grim*, *lustfullic*, *lyðre*, *onderslic* and *unwynsum*, all of which only occur once, in type C(PO). Just as for type A, the scatter of type C(PO) over so many different adjectives indicates that the construction was a well-established one in the grammar of Old English, a conclusion which the facts of distribution discussed in Section 2 did not really allow us to draw for type C(PO).

Type C(PP), finally, is heavily concentrated in just a few adjectives, as Table 9 shows.

TABLE 9

Frequency of adjectives in type C(PP), according to textual category.

Adjective (N=4)	Original	Gloss
god	10	17
nytlic		13
derigendlic	4	
rihtlic	4	

This heavy concentration of type C(PP) in just a few adjectives could be used to argue that the construction was a fairly recent introduction in the grammar of Old English. As we have seen in Section 2, the original examples of type C(PP) are limited in other (linguistic) respects too : they do not occur with a fronted adjective, or a bare infinitive (although there are several examples where Callaway's principle would allow one), the adjective always modifies the subject of the clause (so there are no examples like (68) – (69) with type C(PP)), and this subject always expresses (a period of) time.

4 Distribution Across Texts

As is to be expected, the number of instances of adjective plus infinitive in the different texts varies widely. In Table 10, I give the numbers for all texts featuring 25 or more tokens.

TABLE 10

Frequency of adjective plus infinitive in (collections of) texts with f ≥ 25, according to syntactic subtype.

	A	B	C(S)	C(DO)	C(PO)	C(PP)	Total
ÆCHom I		14	8	11	5		38
ÆCHom II		10	7	10			27
ÆLS	4	7	13	4			28
Bede	2	7	9	9	3		30
Bo	2	3	5	21	3		34
CP	6	13	18	18			55
GD		11	6	10	2		27
HomS	11	5	14	18			48
HomU	9	13	6	20	2		50
LS	5	3	15	7	3		33
Or	4	6	3	10	2		25
Prog	1	9			8	10	28
Poetry		21	12	17	1		51
Li		68	8	8			84
Ru		30	7	5			42
LibSc	6	55	11	4			76
ProgGl						30	30
PsGl	1	97	13				111

The main Alfredian texts are there, and also Ælfric's major works. *HomU*, *HomS* and *LS* of course stand for collections of texts that are in some ways quite diverse; as it would be little use giving the details for each of the homilies or saints' lives separately here, I am using the cover terms. The high numbers in Table 10 for *CP*, *HomS* and *HomU* are noticeable. Among the glosses, the high number for *PsGl* is due to the existence of so many versions, yielding many glosses for one example in the Latin. Together, *PsGl* and *LibSc* are responsible for most of the 87 glossic examples having the form *god* in type B (see Table 6). Under *Poetry*, I have taken together all poetic texts, none of which has more than six tokens by itself.

Type A is completely absent from the poetry, and there is no text only featuring type A but not the others (by way of comparison: of the total of 91 texts I have distinguished, 23 had only one token, of which there were five for type B, nine for C(S) and nine for C(DO)). In all of Ælfric's works taken together, the proportion of type A to type B is about 1 to 10. All the Alfredian texts in Table 10 in the aggregate have a ratio of about 5 to 10, so this very simple measure shows that the general belief that dummy *hit* became more frequent in the course of the Old English period needs to be modified somewhat. Further study, taking into account factors of dialect/style/genre/source text etc., will undoubtedly bring to light a more complex development, but the lack of controlled data would make this a difficult enterprise. The further development in Middle English might show up possible effects of such differentiation more clearly.

In Table 10 types B, C(S) and C(DO) are fairly evenly distributed over the texts included, with Ælfric having a somewhat higher ratio of type B to the total number of examples for all types than the other texts. Since Table 10 contains the texts with most tokens, virtually all cells for types B, C(S) and C(DO) are filled. The data for all 74 original texts show that type B occurs in 49 of them, type C(S) in 37 and type C(DO) in 52. A comparison with the total frequencies for these types in original texts (as given in Table 1) does not immediately bring out any tendency in any of these three types to cluster in specific texts.

There are 13 original texts which have type B but not type C(DO), while there are 36 which have both types. As with the distribution of types over the individual adjectives, there is a tendency for type B to entail type C(DO) in individual texts, with no major difference in frequency.

Type C(PO) only occurs in 15 texts (as I pointed out in Section 2, these are all original ones). Again, there is no evidence of clustering in specific texts, or, I might add, in either later or earlier texts. An exception is *Prog*, which has 8 tokens of C(PO), all with a temporal noun as the matrix subject; (15) - (16) is an example.

A quite noticeable clustering of instances is found for type C(PP), as the data in Table 10 already suggest. I give the full data for the distribution of its 48 tokens in Table 11.

TABLE 11

Frequency of type C (PP) in texts	
Days	4
Mart	4
Prog	10
Prog Gl	30

Days and *Prog (Gl)* of course abound in temporal matrix NPs, which we saw is a constant feature of type C(PP). The four examples in *Mart* show that the occurrence of this type is not due to some idiosyncrasy on the part of especially the *Prog(Gl)* scribe or author.

This discussion of the relation between construction type and text has necessarily been quite general. I have not, for example, addressed such questions as: is type C(PO) with the preposition *on* and an infinitive denoting 'to see/to watch' restricted to some specific text(s)? does type C with the adjective modifying a direct object only occur in later texts? in what texts does type B with a bare infinitive occur? One reason for not considering such questions here is the practical one that there are simply too many questions like this to include them all in a broad survey of the type I am giving here. If it is thought worthwhile to investigate such points in studies focusing on specific areas of the material presented here, this chapter will actually have fulfilled one of its purposes.

A second reason for the general nature of this section is that, as the questions become more detailed, the number of examples involved becomes smaller, and not much may be gained by establishing the places of occurrence of the feature in question. An exception should be made for the basic division between glosses and original examples, but this parameter was of course taken into consideration in Sections 2 and 3.

5 Concluding Remarks

The presentation of the data in Sections 2-4 has taken into account such factors as type of infinitive, type of matrix verb, presence of a dative NP, syntactic relations between the various constituents, order of constituents, groupings among the adjectives, and distribution across texts. On the basis of the data, we have also tried to draw conclusions about the constraints operating on the use of the various subtypes. A number of more theoretical studies of the data could be profitably pursued. A very general approach was pointed out in the introduction, where I suggested that the combination of adjective and infinitive represents a body of data that should be studied along with other Old English impersonals. In Sections 2-4, I have only here and there drawn attention to certain theoretical aspects of the data discussed in this article, but one can readily identify further questions and areas for more detailed study.

Both for such theoretical work and in its own right, an empirical investigation of (selected portions of) texts from later periods would be well worth having.

NOTES

*I wish to thank Willem Koopman and an anonymous referee for comments on an earlier version.

1. Among these are also questions of language typology, since impersonals seem to be widespread cross-linguistically. See, for example, Keenan (1985: 227 ff.) on impersonal passives, and Sridhar (1979) and Klaiman (1981) on impersonal verbs in several Indian languages. Anderson (1988) investigates certain properties of OE impersonal verbs from

this wider perspective.

2. For indentification of all OE texts and examples, I use the system of reference of Healey and Venezky (1980).

3. Ogura's (1986) data show that structures like (1) and (2) are not very frequent, although there are enough reliable examples. Example (3) is more problematic, since the pattern is very rare and it is open to a different interpretation (with *hwæt* in (3) taken as an accusative): compare *ÆHom* 3 104.

4. Jones (1983) shows that the sequence adj+NP +inf in present-day English is rather different from adj+inf. The data in OE do not easily allow a difference to be established, but it does seem safest to treat the two as separate categories. Example (9) provides some support for the distinction: in terms of the subdivision to be introduced in Section 2, (9) would be an instance of type C (PO), whereas *lang,* which has 25 tokens in my data, does not otherwise occur in that subtype.

5. Anyone who has ever tried to go through the entries for *god* 'good' in the microfiche concordance will understand how this could have happened.

6. Also included here is information on whether the examples are from glosses or not; as might be expected, this parameter correlates significantly with the occurrence of particular syntactic types. More complete information on distribution across texts is given in Section 4.

7. Because of the decisions explained in Section 1, (10) counts as two examples for *god,* and (11) as three examples for *god.* My interpretation of the third infinitival clause in (11) follows from the idea that there is parallelism with the first two — I have applied this idea to all such examples, unless there is a clear indication to the contrary.

8. Example (19) counts as two occurrences of the pattern *hit*+adj+dative+inflected infinitive, since there are two infinitives. Again, I assume parallelism between the two combinations of adjective infinitive, compare n.7.

9. In glosses with type B, the bare infinitive is used 227 times and the inflected infinitive 42 times. Assuming that this rate reflects glossing techniques and should be the same in type A, we would expect one or two inflected infinitives in type A glosses. The factor of chance would then be responsible for the absence of these one or two examples. I see no problem here.

10. All 240 glosses of type B with adjective followed by the infinitive similarly imitate the word order of the Latin original.

11. This fact may actually be the reason why a passive infinitive in type B was apparently impossible; following ideas of Bock (1931: 202) we can say that, since no inflected passive infinitive is attested in OE (Mitchell 1985:§922), there would be two contradictory requirements for type B sentences with a passive infinitive. Bock (1931: 202) also discusses how inflected passive infinitives were avoided in some other constructions. Where Callaway's principle would make a bare infinitive possible, the explanation just given would not hold. It is striking that in both (43) and (36), Callaway's principle could apply quite apart from the effect of Latin influence in these sentences.

12. The nine instances in glosses do not tell use much, as they reproduce the Latin order. Seven of the nine are actually all glosses on one Latin original, *Ps* 13.3.

13. This is not the one example with *hit*+dat+adj referred to below example (19) . The reason is that whenever an example has *ðyncan* and a dative NP, I have taken the dative as depending on the verb *ðyncan* and not on the adjective. Apart from (63) for type A, there are nine examples like this in type B, and 12 in type C. There are no examples with two datives, one with the adjective and one with the verb.

14. I have also included here the examples of the phrase *hrædest to secganne,* which occurs three times. There are five examples in which the verb *is* is used, and two with both an

overt subject and *is*. The latter cases provide the rationale for the classification adopted here.
15. Type A is not frequent enough in the corpus to permit its inclusion in this implication.
16. Fischer (1988), basing herself on the data given in Callaway (1913), only mentions *gearo* as a second adjective possibly allowing both C(S) and C(DO).
17. I would like to thank David Denison for drawing my attention to the possible implications of this example.

REFERENCES

Adamson, S., V. Law, N. Vincent and S. Wright, eds. (1990). *Papers from the 5th International Conference on English Historical Linguistics*. Amsterdam: John Benjamins.

Allen, C. (1980). Movement and deletion in Old English. *Linguistic Inquiry* **11**. 261-323.

Anderson, J. (1988) The type of Old English impersonals. In J. M. Anderson and N. Macleod, eds. *Edinburgh Studies in the English Language*. 1-32. Edinburgh: John Donald.

Bock, H. (1931). Studien zum präpositionalen Infinitiv und Akkusativ mit dem *To*-Infinitiv. *Anglia* **55**. 114-249.

Callaway, M. Jr. (1913). *The Infinitive in Anglo-Saxon*. Washington: The Carnegie Institution.

Callaway, M. Jr. (1918). *Studies in the Syntax of the Lindisfarne Gospels*. Baltimore: The Johns Hopkins Press.

Chomsky, N. (1981). *Lectures on government and binding*. Dordrecht: Foris Publications.

Denison, D. (1990). The Old English impersonals revived. In: Adamson *et al.*, 111-140.

Fischer, O. C. M. (1988). The rise of the passive infinitive in English. *Amsterdam Papers in English* 1,2. 54-107.

Gaaf, W. van der (1904). *The Transition from the Impersonal to the Personal Construction in Middle English*. (=Anglistische Forschungen 14). Heidelberg: Carl Winter's Universitätsbuchhandlung.

Gaaf, W. van der (1928). The post-adjectival passive infinitive. *English Studies* **10**. 129-138.

Healey, A. di Paolo and R. L. Venezky (1980). *A Microfiche Concordance to Old English*. Toronto: Center for Medieval Studies, University of Toronto.

Iwakura, K. (1980). On *wh*-movement and constraints on rules. *Linguistic Analysis* **6**. 53-95.

Jones, M. A. (1983). Getting 'tough' with *Wh*-movement. *Journal of Linguistics* **19**. 129-159.

Joseph, B. (1980). Linguistic universals and syntactic change. *Language* **56**. 345-370.

Keenan, E. L. (1985). Passive in the world's languages. In: T. Shopen, ed. *Language typology and syntactic description, vol. I: Clause structure*. 243-281. Cambridge: Cambridge University Press.

Kemenade, A. van (1987). *Syntactic Case and Morphological Case in the History of English*. Dordrecht: Foris Publications.

Klaiman, M. H. (1981). *Volitionality and Subject in Bengali: A Study of Semantic Parameters in Grammatical Processes*. Indiana University Linguistics Club.

Lasnik, H. and R. Fiengo (1974). Complement object deletion. *Linguistic Inquiry* **5**. 535-571.

Lightfoot, D. W. (1979). *Principles of diachronic syntax*. Cambridge: Cambridge University Press.

Mair, Ch. (1987). Tough-movement in present-day British English — A corpus-based study. *Studia Linguistica* **41**. 59-71.

Mitchell, B. (1985). *Old English Syntax*. 2 vols. Oxford: Clarendon Press.

Nanni, D. L. (1978). *The 'easy' class of adjectives in English*. Indiana University Linguistics Club.

Nanni, D. L. (1980). On the surface syntax of constructions with *easy*-type adjectives. *Language* **56**. 568-581.

Ogura, M. (1986). *Old English 'Impersonal' Verbs and Expressions*. (=Anglistica 24). Copenhagen: Rosenkilde and Bagger.

Riviere, C. (1983). Modal adjectives: Transformations, synonymy, and complementation. *Lingua* **59**. 1-45.

Sauer, H., ed. (1978). *Theodulphi Capitula in England: Die altenglischen Übersetzungen, zusammen mit dem lateinischen Text*. München: Wilhelm Fink Verlag.

Sridhar, S. N. (1979). Dative subjects and the notion of subject. *Lingua* **49**. 99-125.

Venezky, R. L. and S. Butler (1983). *A Microfiche Concordance to Old English: The High-Frequency Words*. University of Delaware.

Visser, F. (1963-1973). *An historical syntax of the English language*. Vols I-IIIb. Leiden: E. J. Brill.

Wülfing, J. (1897). *Die Syntax in den Werken Alfreds des Grossen*. Vol 2. Bonn: P. Hanstein's Verlag.

Wurff, W. van der (1987). Adjective plus infinitive in Old English. In F. Beukema and P. Coopmans, eds. *Linguistics in the Netherlands 1987*. 233-242. Dordrecht: Foris Publications.

Wurff, W. van der (1990). The easy-to-please construction in Old and Middle English. In: Adamson *et al.*, 519-536.